# HOW
# TO LIVE
# WITH
# LIFE

*Introductions by Arthur Gordon*

THE READER'S DIGEST ASSOCIATION,
PLEASANTVILLE, NEW YORK
THE READER'S DIGEST ASSOCIATION LTD.,
MONTREAL, CANADA

# THE CHALLENGE OF EXISTENCE

Every human being on this earth faces a constant problem: how to make the most of life. There is no simple solution; the art of living is the most difficult of all the arts. But, fortunately for all of us, experience can be shared. Insights can be learned. Wisdom can be taught. In this book are presented the experience, insights and wisdom of men and women who have lived deeply, thought profoundly and cared enormously about sharing with others what they have learned. Statesmen and scientists, businessmen and housewives, novelists and astronauts, clergymen and psychiatrists — each has found some fragment of truth that cushions the harsh impact of reality or brightens the marvelous tapestry of living. Here, then, are their answers to the most fundamental of all questions: how to live with life.

# I

*"I never met a man I didn't like," said Will Rogers.*
*A remarkable statement from a remarkable individual.*
*And there is a matching statement that might well go with*
*it: No one ever met a man who didn't like Will Rogers.*
*The ability to get along with people is the secret of*
*success in everything from matrimony to moneymaking.*
*If you can care about people (and have them care about*
*you), if you can reach people (and let them reach you),*
*if you can bind yourself into the fabric of society with*
*a network of relationships that grows stronger and more*
*harmonious with the passing years—then your life*
*will have richness and meaning to the end. The basic rule,*
*as everyone knows, is the Golden Rule. But behind*
*that majestic utterance stand many lesser laws and*
*insights, each with its own value and its own validity.*
*Here you will find some of these laws and insights as*
*discovered and used by the people who tell about them.*

# HOW
# TO LIVE
# WITH
# PEOPLE

## Chapter 1/Reaching Out

*A closed hand, so the old saying goes, can't receive.
Neither can a closed mind or a closed heart. To get
through to people, to win their affection or their loyalty,
a person must be willing to risk rejection and
consequent hurt. He must be willing to abandon the
armor of indifference that so many of us wear.
But when the risk is taken, when one person reaches
out across the silence to touch another person, the
rewards—for both of them—can be very great.*

## Have You Made Any New Friends Lately?
**VANCE PACKARD**

The other night I became homesick while watching—of all things—a movie about life in a Samoan village. Now I've never been in Samoa. But the joyous fun that all the people of this village, from toddlers to elderly sages, were having together at a moonlit fiesta filled me with longing. I kept thinking of the wonderful "socials" I attended as a farm boy in Bradford County, Pennsylvania.

I'm glad that I was raised before baby-sitters came into vogue, because my family took us to everything: Grange socials, church suppers, band concerts and picnics. After the adults' talks and the singing, we who were boys Indian-wrestled, chased the girls and gorged ourselves on scalloped oysters. Everyone in that part of the country, regardless of age or economic status, went to these socials: the blacksmith, the storekeeper, the farmers, the farmhands and children.

Perhaps the reason all these wonderful festivities remain so vivid in my mind is that they represent a way of life that is becoming hard to find in the 1960's. Today we tend to confine our pleasurable moments to people pretty much like ourselves in age, income, occupation and education. Children are sent upstairs or out to a movie when the adults have a party. And grandparents usually are expected to stay discreetly out of sight.

In the course of gathering material for a book, I found that people all over the country are more and more inclined to stick to their own "niche" in choosing friends. Sociologist Bevode McCall, for example, made a study of friendship patterns among people in a small town in the American South, using five principal class groupings. Several thousand persons were asked to name their three best friends. In only 3 percent of the friendships reported was there a mutual crossing of a social class line.

Today, if a husband works for a large company,· he and his wife often find there is an unwritten rule dictating whom they can properly entertain. The families of professors in university towns frequently find that they, too, have a local pecking order to observe in their party-giving. And many students seem to be absorbing the examples of their elders. The campus leader at a Midwestern university said, in explaining the secrets of his success, "You have to be careful not to associate with the wrong crowd here—or you won't be accepted by the others." I suspect that the great growth of mass-produced suburban communities has much to do with this narrowing of our social lives. Builders find they can operate most profitably if they lay out several hundred houses that cost approximately the same amount. And they can sell them faster if they exploit our "birds of a feather" tendencies. Said one builder, "People don't seem interested in new associations with people different from themselves."

Some people contend that we are happiest when we stick to "our own kind" in developing friendships. The person who wears blinders of this sort will never experience the enthrallment of having as companions such colorful and often vividly articulate individuals as clam diggers, house detectives, lumberjacks, seamen or antique refinishers. He'll never know the exhilaration that comes from the discovery of someone exciting in a seemingly unlikely place.

I confess that when I first left college I took a similar attitude toward people outside my tiny world. As a "hardened" young newspaperman in New York City I was rather proud that I didn't know a single person in the apartment house where my bride and I lived. One day my father and mother came to visit the Big City. The very first morning I found Dad chatting animatedly with the doorman. As I hurried Dad away, he said, "You know, he's from Bellefonte. He thinks he played football against you."

Later that morning I took Dad and Mother on a sightseeing tour to Staten Island. On the boat trip Mother sat down beside a dark-complexioned girl and soon was chatting excitedly with her. Again I was mortified. Afterward Mother told me that the girl was a medical student from Kenya and had been explaining to her some of Kenya's hair-raising problems in coping with yaws, sleeping sickness and leprosy. Tactfully I tried to suggest to my parents that in New York one does not chat with people one does not know. Dad asked, "Why not?" My mouth opened, but no good answer would come out. Only then did it dawn on me that I, like many other people, had harnessed myself with blinders.

Since then I have had the good fortune, partly because of my work, to be thrown with a great variety of people: high-altitude window washers, zoo keepers, heads of state, junk dealers, divorce lawyers, gold miners, movie stars, lonely multimillionaires, Vermont carpenters. Their differentness, I've found, gives them an infinite capacity to fascinate—and to broaden one's personal horizon. It is more often shyness than snobbery, I believe, that keeps people apart.

Once I hired a local handyman to clear a patch of my land. When he finished, I invited him to join a small party that had begun on our porch. The conversation took a literary turn, which I feared might bore him. Instead, he was soon enchanting us all. He mentioned that his family still had in its possession an ancient Persian edition of the *Rubaiyat* of Omar Khayyam. I knew almost nothing about Omar Khayyam until this handyman began enlightening us. Omar, it seemed, was a mathematician (whose book on algebra was used as a text in his time), an astronomer (who did a more precise job of reforming the solar calendar than was accomplished by the later Gregorian reform), as well as a poet who could make words sing or cry. The stimulation of this talk sent us all to his book. I had discovered a new and exhilarating interest in an unexpected place.

Another reward that comes from broadening your friendships is the new insight you can gain from people who have a different perspective. One day I had a long ride in a Boston taxicab with a jovial elderly driver. We had chatted on a variety of subjects when he suddenly exclaimed: "You know, I have achieved the supreme happiness: I'm glad I'm doing what I'm doing. I've learned not to fight my background. I'm glad I'm who I am." Subsequently I read an **erudite dissertation** by a psychiatrist on the problem of achieving peace of mind, and, stripped of jargon, the doctor's recommendations coincided exactly with the elderly cabby's observation about acceptance of oneself.

The point can also be made, I think, that you will improve your chances of having good luck if you broaden your range of friendships. One spring day I found my wife chatting with the man who had come to repair our ailing stove. This man, it turned out, was not only a repairman but also a part-time artist and occasional short-story writer who for many years had been a world traveler. Since we were about to visit Western Europe, I sought his thoughts on what we should see. A few nights later, at our urging, he and his wife showed us color slides of places they felt would be particularly appealing to us, and he gave us addresses of some of his many European friends. His guidance helped make our trip an illuminating and unforgettable experience.

Some social stratification is probably inevitable in any complex society. But we miss much of life's richness if we fail to take affirmative action to counteract the pressures that throw us only with "our own kind." Each of us can do a number of things to broaden his personal world. Here are a few:

*Revamp that one-layer guest list.* In a Connecticut town that has been publicized as being overwhelmingly exclusive I know a couple whose greatest fun is in the diversity of their guests. In their home I have recently met exchange students from six European and Asian countries, a Negro couple, two schoolteachers from an underprivileged section of New York City and a commercial fisherman.

*Change worlds once a year.* You can do this by taking a vacation in an out-of-the-way place where you'll be among people very different from yourself. I know one New York executive who "goes native" with his family in a fishing village on the New England coast every summer. He and his sons serve as hands on a commercial swordfishing boat.

*Join projects that cut across status lines.* The simplest approach, perhaps, is to become active in town politics, or in the solution of school problems, or in community fund-raising projects, for these tend to be of concern to everyone. I know of many wives who have become part-time hospital volunteers and social workers in order to broaden their personal horizons.

*Revive the old-fashioned family parties.* I'm for fewer cocktail parties and for more parties that bring together young and old for singing and festivities. Some time ago my wife and I invited two couples to our home and specified—to their surprise—that they bring their children. Altogether there were sixteen of us. After supper we played charades, a game I hadn't played in ten years. It was great fun. And do you know what impressed us adults the most? We were amazed to discover how grown-up, bright and downright lovable our children became when we gave them a chance to mix with us on a family basis for an evening of fun.

❖

### AS EASY AS THAT

"*T*here you sit," Harry Lauder, the Scottish singer and comedian, used to taunt his audiences merrily, "—been side by side for two hours, and not one of you spoke to the fellow in the next seat!" And few there were who, under that warmhearted influence, did not turn and speak to the stranger beside them. It's as easy as that. A word, a smile, and the stranger at your elbow may become an interesting friend. All through life we deny ourselves stimulating fellowship because we are too proud or too afraid to unbend.                    —*Donald Culross Peattie*

# The High Art of Flattery

PHYLLIS MC GINLEY

Some people collect old Meissen or music boxes or original Picassos or blue-chip stocks. I collect compliments, and they are far more rare. The authentic masterpieces which I keep for display in the private showcase of my mind are few enough to count on the fingers of a pair of hands. For a compliment is not flattery or even praise. Praise is warming and desirable, and it is what the human race lives on like bread. But praise is an earned thing. It has to be deserved, like a hug from a child. A compliment is manna, a free gift.

Flattery, too, has its great uses, oiling as it does the wheels of conversation or good fellowship. Whether honest or not, a word of commendation can turn a bleak morning into June, or nourish the spirit and the body as efficiently as prayer or vitamins. But flattery differs from a compliment, often because it is studied. A compliment, the kind I cherish, is never artful. It must never sound planned or contrived—and it has to be completely unexpected.

Let me see if I can give examples. If my husband and I come home from a party and he mumbles to me while he unclasps his cuff links, "No, honey, you didn't talk a bit too much tonight. You were perfectly fine," that is praise. If at some neighborhood soiree an aging cavalier singles me out three times running to swing me about the floor and then exclaims, panting, "Good Lord, woman! Compared to those young things you can certainly dance!" that is flattery.

But not long ago I was flung a nosegay which held for me the true complimentary bouquet. At a meeting on behalf of a worthy cause, I sat across from a man as celebrated for his blunt and moody conversation as for his witty books. I do not know him well and have always been a little in awe of him. In the middle of the meeting I looked up to find him glaring at me, or at least looking at me with what I believed was a glare. I moved my hat more nearly to the center of my head and straightened my spine. Then he spoke. The tone was accusing, but the words rolled out like music. "Tell me," he said, "are your daughters pretty, too?"

I have dusted off that compliment a dozen times by now, and it sits at the moment in the front of the display case. To a graying housewife whom, even at her best, no artist has ever longed to immortalize in deathless oils, it was like being made a present of the Comstock Lode.

The best-known compliment of the era is the often-cited remark made by Charles MacArthur to Helen Hayes when they first met: he offered her a bag of salted peanuts, regretting that they weren't emeralds. That owns all the essential ingredients. It has spontaneity, uniqueness and wit. But on an occasion long ago, my husband (then merely a young man whose piano playing I enjoyed) said something similar to me and something very nearly as masterful.

It was the day he rescued me from a wild beast. The wild beast was nothing more savage than a wasp, but I have always feared wasps with the terror other people reserve for mice or sharks or snarling dogs. Alerted by my girlish screams of terror, he captured the ravening insect in a handkerchief and dropped it out the window. When I turned to him with murmurs of gratitude, he managed to gild the moment. "Think nothing of it," he said. "I wish it had been a dragon." It's no wonder we were married three months later.

Still, a compliment need not be merely gallant. I keep that small jewel well polished in my memory, but mounted next to it on its own cushion is something he said to me not long afterward when we were happily starving together. It was during the Depression, at a period when our savings account was nonexistent and a riotous night on the town meant for us the dollar dinner at Joe's and a foreign film. Yet he came home from the office bemusedly one evening, threw his arms around me and announced, "I've been thinking. I love you so much that I'm going to leave you all my money." And so honest was the outburst that for some time neither of us began to laugh.

For the genuine, fortuitous jewel, however, one must depend on children. Children have had no time to learn flattery, and praise is not native to them. When they speak, they speak from naturally hard hearts, unnaturally touched. "Dear Mommy," wrote my younger daughter when she was six or seven and visiting my husband's people in the Middle West. "I am having fun. But I am sad because you are so far away. I miss you with my arms and my legs and my whole stomach." The letter is tied up somewhere in a drawer marked "Special Correspondence," but I never need to bring it out. I learned it forever on first reading.

There are some people, like this daughter, who have a natural turn for compliments as other people are born with perfect pitch or long eyelashes. I think it is a talent which should be cultivated the way we train a good soprano voice. The loving-hearted are too infrequent in the world not to embrace. We were discussing with her recently a certain delightful couple that our whole family dotes on. "The Harrisons?" she cried. "They're wonderful! They're so wonderful I'm going to"—and she paused—"why, I guess when I get married I'll invite them to be guests of honor at my wedding!" I hope the Harrisons are connoisseurs. I plan to present that to them like a plaque.

Compliment inventors are often compliment receivers, too. When this girl was very little, one came to her from Sarah, a housekeeper of ours, born in Alabama and endowed with a picturesque idiom. This daughter was her darling. One day when she came downstairs in a new party frock, stepping proudly in patent-leather pumps, Sarah gave her a glance, raised her arms skyward and erupted into speech. "My, my!" she clucked. "Look at my baby! Know what my baby is? She's the President of the Bright Morning Star."

Among my souvenirs are a few oblique pieces of adulation. As the stamp fancier cherishes his errata—the issues printed upside down, the blurred specimens quickly withdrawn from circulation—so I value the flawed compliment. In fact, I consider it the cream. Very dear indeed is the comment of an old friend, offered to me a number of years ago. She was a good deal older than I, so I leaned on her as one would on a kindly aunt, knowing that she believed me, however wrongheadedly, to be comely, clever and destined for high places. The one thing of which she could not convince me was that I owned a brilliant and bewitching smile. I knew only too well that, having been brought up on the Colorado prairies, where orthodontists did not exist, I would never qualify in a contest for Miss Ipana. But, "Phyllis," she told me dreamily one day, "you have *fascinating* teeth. They're so individual—no two alike." That friend has gone on to more flowery places, where she is no doubt consoling some angel whose harp has come untuned, with the assurance that dissonances are always interesting.

But treasure lies all about us. I have another crony living down the street in our village whom I revere. It is she who, when we were on a shopping expedition together, warned me away from a sale of sports blouses. "Not the round collars, dear," she cautioned me. "You know what round collars do—they call attention to the face." Her literary judgments are equally striking. "I think it's wonderful the way you write," she said once. "It's *beyond* me how you can go on and on about nothing the way you do."

The most cherished object in my whole display case, however, came from not a friend but a stranger. And it was strictly professional. I once found myself the speaker of the day at a convention of very distinguished booksellers, publishers and some of the informed general public. I was unprepared for the well-wishers and autograph seekers who thronged around me after the luncheon with graceful words and pleasant flatteries. I felt for once like a small lioness and was just on the verge of emitting a roar or two from sheer high spirits.

Then suddenly, out of the press, rushed a woman in a flowered hat and a mink stole who seized my hand ardently, leaned close and said to me in a breathless voice, "Oh, Miss McGinley, I *am* so happy to meet you. I keep your book right on my bedside table. And someday I mean to read it." That jewel is too precious to be put with the others. I plan to keep it, as the lady did my book, beside my bed, where it will warm me better than a stove.

Never accept flattery as though it were a compliment, and never treat a compliment as though it were merely flattery.

—*Russell Lynes*

# The Glory of a Gift

JOHN C. CORNELIUS

Horace Mann was dedicating a recreational home for boys that he had planned for years. "If all the money and energy you have expended result in the salvation of only one boy," he told the assembly which had helped make his dream come true, "they will not have been in vain."

Later, one of the contributors remarked, "My dear Mr. Mann, weren't you exaggerating a bit when you said all our expenditure would be worthwhile if we saved just *one* boy?" Mann's reply came instantly: "Not if it were my boy." Not if it were my boy or your boy. My neighbor or your neighbor. That is what the great philanthropist was saying, and it seems to me that his attitude epitomizes the true essence of giving.

We hear that man is a selfish creature, that his basic impulses concern only his personal welfare. But this is deceptive; for man has a dual nature. He is at once selfish and selfless. Like all other creatures, he must be concerned with his personal welfare. Yet he also preserves the welfare of his group, and, if necessary, will even die for that group.

Does this talk of our impulse to preserve and protect our fellow man seem a long way from the subject of charity? It isn't, really. For there is hardly a legitimate charity in existence that is not dedicated to that one goal: the preservation and protection of our fellow man. We feel joy when we give, because, basically, we are satisfying a deep desire.

In this sense, giving of ourselves for the betterment of the less fortunate is the cheapest and most effective mental therapy available today. To deny ourselves the joy of giving is to deny our basic needs. People want to give. People want to serve their fellow men. And if we deny that desire, we risk emotional death, just as a man who denies his hunger risks physical death.

Yet, amid the complexities and distractions of life, how often we lose touch with that simple truth. The daily world presses in upon us. Rightly, we think of our mortgages. Rightly, we think of our children's education. Rightly, we think of our obligations to ourselves. But, wrongly, we tend to overlook the fact that the act of giving is also an act of self-fulfillment. Yet there are people, perhaps many, to whom the idea that giving can be joyous seems remote and unreal. I have met these people on numerous occasions when raising funds for various charities. For them the opportunity to contribute is no privilege. Feeling hounded and harassed, they give—but grudgingly, complainingly.

The feelings of such people, in the matter of giving, cannot be ignored. We may feel sorry for them, but we cannot change them. I can, however, point out to them that if they obtain no joy from giving for selfless reasons, they might obtain a real measure of satisfaction for the most selfish and practical reasons. For it is a fact that a few dollars contributed to an effective and well-run charity can frequently save thousands of dollars for the taxpayer.

The care of a mental or physical cripple involves huge expense. If only a few mental cripples are rehabilitated, be they criminally inclined or emotionally disturbed, donations to organizations that help such people are paid back many times over. Listen to some of the mathematics of giving, and then let me know where you can get a better return on your money.

In my state of Minnesota during one year, it cost the taxpayers $1639 to keep one prisoner at Stillwater penitentiary —almost $50,000 for thirty years. The Boys' Club of my city, on the other hand, spends $60 a year for each boy in the club. If that $60 later prevents one boy from spending one year in jail, the taxpayers save $27 on every dollar they donate to his club. If that $60 prevents one man from spending thirty years in jail, the saving to the taxpayer is nearly $820 for each dollar donated. And this doesn't count the hundreds of thousands of dollars involved in the loss of that person's services to society and of his tax dollars, the expense of keeping his family on relief and the many other costs society incurs whenever a man goes to prison.

An insurance executive pointed out to me that an unrehabilitated paraplegic may accumulate medical expenses of $100,000 over fifty years. But a paraplegic who goes through a three- or four-month training program (cost: about $4000) would have medical expenses of about $15,000 over the same period. Most important, of course, is that the paraplegic is happier and has something to live for. But the cold-blooded mathematics of giving shows that each dollar contributed to the rehabilitation of paraplegics saves at least $21 in taxes. For those who find no joy in giving, let there be joy in this arithmetic!

But what of the people who complain of being hounded by more and more and newer and newer charities year after year? "Every time you turn around," they say, "there's some outfit you never heard of asking for money." True. But there is a good reason for it. We have more charities today because we can do more to help the luckless members of our society.

I, for one, don't believe that we have more problems. But in the old days we had to accept life's tragedies. Now we have more technical knowledge and more people dedicated to solving those problems. This is something all of us can be thankful for. "But there are limits to how much I can give," people say. Also true. But the answer is simple. Give what you can. Choose your favorite charities and, if necessary, restrict your giving to them. The joy of giving is still yours. Remember, when you help a fellow up a steep hill, you get nearer the top yourself.

### TIME FOR OTHERS

Why do we so frequently feel: "What I do doesn't really make a difference"? We fall into a familiar error, using the wrong yardstick with which to measure goodness. We think that good actions are really important only in time of crisis, only when an extraordinary demand calls for extraordinary effort. Yet the time of crisis is but a small part of the opportunity given each of us to contribute to other people's lives.

—*Rabbi Bernard Mandelbaum and Victor M. Ratner*

### THE THREE KICKS

When William Allen White gave Emporia, Kansas, a 50-acre wooded plot for a park and agreed to beautify it for five years, he said: "This is the last kick I'm getting out of these dollars— but it's the biggest. I have always felt that there are three kicks in every dollar: one when you make it—and how I do love to make a dollar; one when you have it—and I have the Yankee lust for saving; and the third when you give it away. The last kick is the biggest one of all. —*Edmond M. Kerlin*

# Love Is Healing
HOWARD WHITMAN

Science in recent years has discovered love. Psychiatrists have concluded that the great taproot of mental ills is *lovelessness*. Child psychologists, wrangling over scheduled versus demand feeding, spanking versus nonspanking, have found that none of it makes much difference *so long as the child is loved*. The sociologists have found love the answer to delinquency, the criminologists have found it the answer to crime.

Love might be called the soil in which the loved one grows. It enriches him without limiting or restricting him. Love is basically a "giving" operation, though we often think of it as "taking."

"The love of a person," says Dr. Harry A. Overstreet, "does not imply the possession of that person. It means granting him, gladly, the full right to his unique humanhood. One does not truly love yet seek to enslave by bonds of dependence or possessiveness." Dr. Erich Fromm puts it this way: "To love a person implies caring for and feeling responsible for his life, for the growth and development of all his human powers."

In institutions which deal in human relations, love is being used more and more as a medicine. At the Menninger Clinic in Topeka, Kansas, I found that in the treatment of mental illness one of the standard prescriptions used by the physicians was " 'love' unsolicited." Patients whose illness was rooted in lovelessness were shown a special attitude of love whether they earned it or not. For example, Mr. C. had been an unwanted child. He had grown up into a "lone wolf" unable to make warm, human attachments with anyone. He lived in a world without love. He came to the clinic at thirty-five, diagnosed "schizophrenic." He had simply withdrawn from the real world into a delusional one of his own. At the clinic he refused to budge out of his room and sat without making any effort to communicate.

The doctors prescribed " 'love' unsolicited" for him. Doctors and nurses treated him with warmth and affection. They played checkers with him. They said, "How well you look, Mr. C.," and "It certainly is a pleasure to visit with you." One morning Mr. C. walked out into the garden. The love of those around him had made the real world seem not quite so horrible after all. He began to recover.

At the Hawthorne–Cedar Knolls School, an institution for problem children near New York, I saw love used as medicine in another way. A new boy, Charlie, aged fifteen, arrived at the school with advance billing by the Children's Court as "incorrigible." He had stolen money from his parents, his language was foul, his behavior like a wildcat's. "Coach" Robert Exton, then housefather at the cottage where Charlie was assigned, did not agree that this boy—or any boy—was "incorrigible." He took Charlie for a stroll. The boy began swearing. "Some people may like dirty language, Charlie," said the coach quietly, "but I don't seem to go for it, somehow. Would you do me a favor—?"

Charlie, surprised at the friendliness of Exton's tone, flushed a little and went silent. Then Charlie tried another tack. "I brought some riding boots down here and I'm going to wear them to dinner, see?"

"Sure," said the coach. "That's okay with me." "Okay with

you, yeah!" Charlie rasped. "Except that you're going to lock my boots up!"

"Oh, no, we don't think it necessary to lock anything up at our cottage."

"Nothing? Boy, are you dopey!" "Perhaps," the coach said. "By the way, here are my car keys. I wonder if you'd hold on to them for me. I've a hole in my pocket." When they turned back to the cottage, Exton said, "Come in any time you want to, Charlie." Six months later I checked back on the "incorrigible" boy. He had received a good deal of love by then. On his chest was a medal he had won—for good citizenship.

Even in the treatment of sexual promiscuity I found love used as a medicine. Doctors at the San Francisco Public Health Clinic discovered that promiscuous girls often had been emotionally crippled by lack of love. They were incapable of a mature love relationship, and neither gave nor received love in their sex behavior. But they had, nevertheless, "an excessive need for love based upon unfulfilled needs of their childhood." In restoring them to emotional health, the clinic gave them the love they had been in need of all their lives—the affirmation of themselves as people, the self-respect, the strength to grow.

"People believe that nothing is easier than to love," says Dr. Fromm. "But on the contrary, while every human being has a capacity for love, its realization is one of the most difficult achievements."

A man may think he loves his wife because she is beautiful, talented, competent. This is not love. It is approval. Love depends not upon the attributes of the love object, but upon the individual's ability to love. This ability must be cultivated. It does not always "come naturally" as so many of us believe. Dr. William C. Menninger said to me, "I think that the best thing parents can do for their children is to teach them how to love."

The only way to teach love is by example. By cultivating our own capacity to love, we teach those around us to love. Children must receive love in order, later, to give it. We do not love our children simply because we protect and provide for them. The animal does that for its young. The test is: To what extent do we affirm our children as people? How much do we respect their individuality? How much do we help them grow independently—instead of smothering and possessing them?

Overindulgence of children is a dangerous form of pseudo-love. At the Children's Village, Dobbs Ferry, New York, three hundred young boys are being retrained for good citizenship. Many of these youngsters have known only indulgent pseudo-love—a guilt-ridden attitude which "buys off" a child rather than strengthening his growth and responsibility. "Every day," stated Harold F. Strong, former director, "we are undoing the damage done by parents who have confused the word 'love' with 'appeasement.'"

The discovery of love has also shown that self-love is good —that we must love ourselves if we expect to be able to love others. The late Joshua Loth Liebman pointed out that the Biblical injunction "Thou shalt love thy neighbor as thyself" presupposed that we would love ourselves. To the degree that we hate ourselves or others we are emotionally ill; our ability to love has become thwarted.

"Case after case shows a lack of self-love at the root of mental illness," reports Dr. Alexander Reid Martin, formerly of the Payne Whitney Psychiatric Clinic in New York. "If people had a healthy love of themselves instead of carrying hidden burdens of self-contempt, our psychiatric case load would be cut in half."

I asked Dr. Robert H. Felix, when he was director of the National Institute of Mental Health in Washington, D.C., for a definition of self-love. Dr. Felix replied, "One has a feeling of dignity, of belonging, of worthwhileness, a feeling of adequacy—yet a healthy sense of humility."

A mature, healthy personality, with a strong ability to love, does not "love" just his wife or a few special friends. He loves—period. Says Dr. Overstreet, "If what we call love in relation to one person or to a few people creates in us no added capacity for goodwill toward many, then we may doubt that we have actually experienced love."

Dr. G. Brock Chisholm, the famous director-general of the World Health Organization of the United Nations, has recognized that our global future depends upon the number of mature individuals we can produce, people capable of love, capable of approaching the problems of our changing world as "love people," not "hate people."

### THE PURIFIER

Love of beauty and of all lovely and wonderful things is indispensable for our growth. It brings reverence and a sense of transcendence into personal love, and indeed into all of life. . . . In the words of a poet who was also a man of science—Robert Bridges: "Love is a fire in whose devouring flames all earthly ills are consumed."     —*Julian Huxley*

In chalk lettering inside a chalk heart on the wall of a New York City library was the delightful scrawl: "Billy Maher Loves Everybody."     —*Meyer Berger*

# Can You Listen?

*Based on the book: "Are You Listening?"*

DR. RALPH G. NICHOLS AND LEONARD A. STEVENS

In this age of telephone, radio and television, most of us spend more and more time listening to the spoken word. Paul T. Rankin, of the Detroit Public Schools, once made a two-months' study of the personal communications of sixty-eight people in different occupations. He found that, on the average, 75 percent of his subjects' waking day was spent in verbal communication—30 percent in talking, 45 percent in listening.

Yet most of us don't know how to listen. For several years at the University of Minnesota, we have examined and measured the listening ability of thousands of students and, more recently, that of scores of business and professional people. The person tested listens to short talks and then is examined for his grasp of the content. Our general conclusion is that the average person is a "half-listener"; he retains only about 50 percent of what he hears right after he hears it.

"This is a big difficulty with inexperienced salesclerks," John J. McGrath, manager of training for a large New York department store, told me. "A customer will say: 'I want to see that blouse on display. I'd like size 14 with short sleeves.' The clerk rushes away and brings back a size 14, with *long* sleeves. The customer repeats: 'Short sleeves.' Back goes the clerk while the customer waits. There is unnecessary handling of merchandise and an irritated customer. That is why in our training we stress, 'Listen before you act.'"

Behind the widespread inability to listen lies a major over-sight in our system of classroom instruction. The skill has been neglected. Until recently, training for listening has con-sisted mainly in the command heard by students from the first grade through college: "Pay attention!" Yet listening is a mental skill that can be developed through training and prac-tice. We now give listening courses at the University of Min-nesota, and every group we have ever trained has averaged better than a 25 percent gain in proficiency.

The act of listening requires that you do more than simply let sound waves into your ears, just as the act of reading requires that you do more than look at print. Good listening demands active participation. But there are several stumbling blocks in the way. One problem is that we think much faster than we talk. The rate of speech for most Americans is about 125 words a minute, but we think four times that fast. This means that in each minute a person talks to us we normally have about 400 words of thinking time to spare.

If we are poor listeners, we soon become impatient; our thoughts turn to something else for a moment, then dart back to the speaker. These brief side excursions continue until our mind tarries too long on some other subject. Then, when our thoughts return to the person talking, we find he's far ahead of us. Now it's harder to follow him and increas-ingly easy to take off on side excursions. Finally we give up; the person is still talking, but our mind is in another world.

The good listener uses his thought speed to advantage; he constantly applies his spare thinking time to what is being said. Are the speaker's facts accurate? Do they come from an unprejudiced source? Am I getting the full picture or is he telling me only what will prove his point?

All studies in listening point to the importance of *interest*.

Bad listeners seldom give a subject or a speaker a chance; they declare a subject dry after a few sentences and sign off, giving only passive attention. Good listeners, on the other hand, try to find something interesting in what is being said, something that can be put to use: "What is he saying that I need to know? Is that a really practical idea? Is he reporting anything new?" Such questions keep us on the track and help to sharpen our listening skill.

A speaker can seldom talk for long without touching on some pet bias or conviction of the listener. The bad listener mentally starts to plan a rebuttal, formulate a question designed to embarrass the speaker, or perhaps he simply turns to thoughts that support his own feelings. The good listener learns to keep listening. He tries not to get too excited about a speaker's point until he is certain he has heard it through and understands it.

People who have developed their listening skill have learned to focus their attention on central ideas. They are not led astray by trying mentally to record each fact as it is presented. Facts are useful chiefly for bolstering the theme under discussion. Concentrate on the theme and you will find that this will help you to remember the facts cited.

Concentration is more than half the battle. Poor listeners tend to be too easily distracted. A good listener, on the other hand, instinctively *fights* distraction. He will close a door, shut off the radio, and he will interrupt only when it is necessary to clear up one point before proceeding to another.

One of the reasons for paying close attention to what is being said is simply that it is courteous to do so. But there is a selfish reason too. Our students soon discover that the way you listen has a great deal of control over the way people talk to you. Intelligent listening on your part helps the speaker to express what he has in mind and thus makes him more able to give you information that you may need. How you listen therefore has a direct bearing on what you learn.

When you have mastered the skill of listening you will discover an extra dividend: the fact that you have learned how to heed the spoken word will mean—automatically—that you will have become a more interesting speaker yourself. Just as you will get more fun and reward from listening, so others will get more out of what you have to say.

### ELOQUENCE

*T*wo of us sat together on the terrace of a summer hotel. "See that young woman over there?" said my friend. "A chap is talking to her—talking rapidly, eagerly. Now watch her. She is meagerly endowed—no lure that you can see; and yet there isn't a beauty in this hotel that attracts men as she does."

"Is she an heiress?" I asked.

"No. It isn't money. See the way she listens to that chap, her interested expression? She knows a great secret."

"What's the secret?"

"She knows that there is no more gratifying tribute one can give to another than absolute, undivided and sympathetic *attention*. Every man that talks to her finds that he is interesting to her. He just *knows* it, and he likes her for letting him know it. The oil of encouragement fairly pours from her eyes and lubricates a man's ideas."

"You grow eloquent!"

"Why not? Remember what Saint-Beuve said of exquisite Madame Récamier: 'She listens with seduction.' Her inspired attention invited and drew confidence. That was her great charm, her genius for listening."                    —*The Mentor*

# Joy in Doing Good on the Sly

GORDON POWELL

All of us have experienced, at times, the warm glow that comes from performing a good deed and getting credit for it. But there is a *special* kind of satisfaction that comes from doing good and keeping it secret. Those who practice this higher altruism are connoisseurs of inner joy at its loftiest refinement.

Recently I read of a man in Boston who went to an understaffed orphanage every Wednesday afternoon to spend an hour or two entertaining the youngsters—doing card tricks, telling stories, giving the harassed matron and her staff a period of rest and freedom. When the curious tried to discover his identity, the stranger would only say, "That's not important." Cut from the same cloth was an elderly stranger who appeared one day at a hospital in Peterborough, New Hampshire, saying, "I know you must have many odd jobs that need doing. Let me help." For four months he performed countless menial tasks: sweeping the parking lot, building ramps, removing lint from the laundry. Once asked his name, he smiled and shook his head. "If you knew who I am," he said, "you'd feel obliged to feel obligated. That would spoil it." Only after he had moved away did the hospital learn that he was a former vice-president of the Pennsylvania Railroad. Recently retired and widowed, he had filled months of forced inactivity and grief with cheerful service, rehabilitating his own spirit as well as spreading cheer all around him.

The art of secret altruism does not come naturally. It must be cultivated, for it goes against the natural grain of our ego. We want others to recognize any act of ours that we consider especially noble or unselfish. When such notice is not forthcoming, we're tempted subtly to call attention to it. In so doing, however, we often discover that the deed has been devalued by suspicion that its performance was prompted, at least partly, by some credit we crave. Also, in our eagerness to help, we sometimes fail to realize how embarrassing our gift may be to the sensitive, or how heavy upon the recipient may seem the obligation of gratitude.

Doing good anonymously avoids these pitfalls. A fairly prosperous family I once knew yearned to help an aged aunt. She was living on a pittance, but abhorred anything resembling charity. When the family heard from their lawyer that the poor but proud aunt had received a small inheritance from a distant cousin—only a small amount of money, which would soon be spent—they quietly arranged with the lawyer to add secretly a considerable capital sum to the bequest. The aunt, provided with an adequate income, lived out her life without ever suspecting that there had been a kindly duplicity.

Jesus was the supreme preacher and practitioner of doing good secretly. He decried ostentatious charity, warned His followers to "Take heed that ye do not your alms before men, to be seen by them." After healing the leper, He sternly told him, "See that thou tell no man," and left the scene immediately.

It is often within our own circle that we find our finest opportunities for hidden helpfulness. Years ago the sculptor Sir Hubert von Herkomer found a delightful solution to a distressing family problem. His father, who lived with him, had in his own day won fame for his wood carving. And though the old man still worked at it, he repeatedly went to bed heartbroken because age had dulled his skill. Worried over his father's unhappiness, Sir Hubert hit upon the idea of stealing downstairs at night to touch up his father's work. A few deft strokes made all the difference. The old man would come down in the morning, look at the work and exclaim, "It's not bad, not bad at all. I'll make something of this yet!"

As a minister, I am constantly coming upon people who, unknown to others, are devoting themselves to little deeds of secret kindness. Invariably they are happy, serene people. Our church in New South Wales, Australia, has a maternity hospital with a special wing for unmarried mothers. Each time a baby is born to one of these unhappy girls, a large bouquet of flowers arrives from an anonymous giver. With it comes only the message, "From someone who understands." During the years hundreds of girls, feeling abandoned and desperately lonely, have found the way to new life from this thoughtful action. But, knowing the giver—a woman who herself has suffered much sorrow—I know her own rewards to be great.

Secret giving need not be costly in either time or money. It calls only for a keen eye and an understanding heart. I can think of a doctor who, knowing that one of his patients needed a certain expensive medicine he could ill afford, arranged with a wholesale drug firm to send the required drug with a "sample" label pasted on it. I think, too, of a teacher who, sensing that a bright but uninterested pupil had hidden talents that needed sparking, subscribed to a science magazine to be delivered regularly to the boy's home. The magazine turned the trick and, while the boy never learned who his benefactor was, he went on to become a brilliant scientist.

I think, also, of a friend who makes a hobby of writing unsigned but encouraging letters to men in public life who, in his estimate, are performing with integrity despite stinging criticism. His theory: For the most part, politicians get letters of appreciation only from people who want something in return. They get anonymous letters only from cranks who want to blow off steam when angry. "Why not," he asks, "blow off a little appreciation as well—and with no strings attached?"

Those who do good quietly and without thought of reward are the ones who understand what Wordsworth meant when he wrote of "that best portion of a good man's life: his little, nameless, unremembered acts of kindness and of love." It's amazing how much good can be done in this world if one does not care who gets the credit—and how it can set one's life aglow!

※◆※

### THE GREAT COMFORTER

Composer Johannes Brahms' father refused steadfastly to take any money from his son, and it required all of Brahms' tact and delicacy to support him. Once, when the two parted, Johannes said, "Believe me, Father, music in every situation is the greatest comforter. Whenever you are discouraged and feel you need something to lift you up, just take my old score of Handel's *Saul* and read it over. I'm sure you'll find there whatever you need."

Sometime later the old man had occasion to remember Johannes' words and looked through the old score. What he found was indeed the one thing he needed: his son had carefully put a bank note between each page.                           —*Bernard Grun*

## Chapter 2/ The Mating Instinct

*Boy meets girl . . . the oldest and perhaps the most
exciting story in the world. But it can be a perplexing
one, too. The old, sedate days of lengthy courtship
and long engagements seem to be over. Are moral
standards changing? Is going steady a good idea?
Does marrying young make sense? What makes us fall
in love with a certain person anyway?
Here a professor of psychology, a physician and other
students of human nature offer provocative answers.*

## The True Nature of Love
Condensed from the book: Love and Marriage
F. ALEXANDER MAGOUN

hat is love? In spite of all
that science and religion have told us, people do not want to
understand the true nature of the most potent force in the
world. They believe in the Hollywood myth—physical
beauty and poetic passion, two hearts in stardust beating as
one; the chase, the capture and the surrender. All that may
well be a thrilling part of attraction and courtship; but it is
not and never can be love. Love and a physical embrace
become almost synonymous in young minds; both create ecstasy. But few young people are taught the possibilities
of and need for growth beyond that beautiful excitement.

There will be less disillusion and heartache in marriage
when we begin to understand that from the illusions of ro-

mance a deep and abiding love may emerge. *Love is the passionate and abiding desire on the part of two or more people to produce together conditions under which each can be, and spontaneously express, his real self; to produce together an intellectual soil and an emotional climate in which each can flourish, far superior to what either could achieve alone.* In a true marriage, man and woman think more *of the partnership* than they do of themselves. It is an interweaving of interests and a facing of sacrifice together for the sake of both. Its feeling of security and contentment comes from mutual efforts. In marriage, as in dancing, the happiness does not stem from the way the individual moves, but in the togetherness of the behavior.

*The more completely one can express his real self to another person the more deeply he can love.* This means that a man can speak honestly to his wife, letting her know what is actually in his mind, without fear of misunderstanding or any form of reprisal. If a man can say, without trepidation: "My dear, I can forgive your mother, but I can never forget how she stood in the doorway saying those awful things to me"—he may be spontaneously expressing himself. He may decide not to say anything of the kind, in order to spare his wife unhappiness. But if he refrains because he is afraid that she will misunderstand him and take revenge, these two people are not producing together the intellectual and emotional climate in which each can be his real self.

There are many false emotions that may lead us into unhappy marriages. For instance: sexual desire aroused by physical beauty or perhaps sheer energy. That is why we need to know the difference between physical attraction and deep affection. Another false emotion is the need of living life vicariously through another person because of inability to be one's self. It may be that the wife was the daughter of a poorly paid minister; hence, she goads her husband on to make more money and so to be like the man she wanted her father to be. Other misleading emotions include the compulsive desire to feel needed; a man's wish for a woman to mother him; a woman's determination not to be an old maid.

We may think we are in love because of the way another person makes us feel, but love is not delight in ME, love is self-realization together in us. Two mutually infatuated people can want each other desperately, without love, and without sensing the emotional insincerity which consumes them. Neither perceives he is experiencing little more than a cheap reassurance. What seems to be love is but blind delight in being treated as if one were perfection itself.

Self-realization together includes the right of each partner to pursue individual interests. It often takes five years for a young couple to discover that "we do everything together" is sentimentality and not love. Among such couples, if the man likes fishing and the woman does not, they give up fishing. If she likes concerts and he does not, they give up music. Their activities are confined to what both enjoy; in a constricted life "they do everything together" because they fear that individual activity may cause them to drift apart. By yielding to this fear they narrow their lives, invite boredom and may soon be drifting apart—doing even that "together."

Sooner or later the reassurance of complete agreement is gone. Troubled faces confront each other across the breakfast table. By dinnertime they may be angry faces, divided as only emotional distance can divide. Quiet desperation is followed by panic. But two people really in love are not too concerned over disagreement, knowing that mere differences of opinion are not the same thing as loss of emotional unity.

True love is not so blind! It sees faults as well as virtues, unhesitatingly accepting the fact that no one is perfect. Love says, and with honest feeling, "I know that I shall be irked by your inability ever to be on time. I know that you will be irritated by my smoking. I know that differences in our energy and tempo will annoy both of us until we learn how to work them out together. But, despite these difficulties, we see so much of value in each other that we surely can create together a life far superior to what either of us could achieve alone. What matters is that we each sense and like the kind of person the other is, and want to cherish him for what he really is."

No two human beings can possibly live together in the most intimate emotional relationship known without sometimes frustrating each other. Understanding is needed because where love is blocked it turns to anger and hate. To think that there are no things to be given up *for* each other is to suppose that love costs nothing. Love is self-discovery and self-fulfillment through healthy growth with and for the other person.

Real love will grow as the years go by. *The very experience of loving will lead to the discovery of how to love better.* The only thing in the world as strong as love is truth, and there are reasons for believing that as far as marriage is concerned they are different aspects of the same thing. A deep and abiding love is the emotional response to an intellectual recognition of the truth about another person. Love's development, like that of a tree, is not a steady process but an irregular one. The art of love is patience till the spring returns. But what we have really loved can never be lost. Its influence on our personality is always with us, and perhaps even death does not take it away.

# Matrimony Is Not for Children

LESTER DAVID

**I**t was a beautiful wedding. True, the bride was only sixteen and the groom just nineteen, but they looked grown-up as they stood there, she so radiant, he so tall and protecting. No one could foretell that less than a year later this fine young man would say to this lovely girl, "I wish you were dead, because then I'd be free." Or that, later the same day, she would slash her wrists.

Yet that is what happened to Clarissa and Ralph, two New York City youngsters whose case is in the files of the Family Service Association of America. Clarissa did not die, but she and Ralph are as close to heartbreak as two human beings can be. Their plight is tragic enough. But perhaps even more shocking is the reason behind it. *Clarissa and thousands of other high-school-age youngsters are actually propelled into these pitiable situations by their own parents, who don't realize what they are doing.*

Clarissa's story is typical of the results of such pressure. At thirteen she was already beautiful, tall and well formed. Her mother began to take her to grown-up parties, theaters and restaurants, saying, "Other mothers may be jealous of their pretty daughters, but I'm not. I want everybody to see her." It was a mistake. Clarissa came to enjoy the grown-up company and loved the attention. Soon she found the world of thirteen-year-olds dull and childish compared to the new, exciting experiences. There was no turning back; she skipped adolescence after barely entering it.

In high school she met Ralph and married him. He had planned to continue college after marriage, but soon a baby was on the way. He was forced to leave school and forget his dream of a medical career; at seventeen, she was facing motherhood in a bleak single room. The couple, engulfed in self-pity, too immature to handle their plight, lashed out at each other.

Disastrous premature marriages such as this are now one of America's great social problems. According to the U.S. Bureau of Vital Statistics, more and more girls are marrying early. There are other problems, too. A University of Nebraska survey reveals that 31 percent of girls who married between fourteen and eighteen were pregnant at the time. The U.S. Children's Bureau reports that more than 500,000 babies are born each year to girls still in their teens.

Let us look more closely at girls such as Clarissa who teeter to the altar on high heels they have barely learned to wear. What makes them rush so? By far the most significant factor is the encouragement of "Little League" romance, or dating in the pre-teen years. Dr. Winston Ehrmann, of Colorado State University, recently concluded an extensive study of the dating habits of young people in this country. Depth interviews with 1157 teen-agers revealed that one out of every four girls began regular dating before she was thirteen. According to studies, dancing, even kissing and petting, are commonplace among eleven- and twelve-year-olds.

In many cases, the initial push comes from the parents. It is Mother who suggests dancing classes and evening dances, who buys her young daughter a wardrobe for every occasion, arranges boy-girl parties for her. Mothers defend their attitudes by claiming that "times have changed." One suburban mother declared, "Today, with jet planes and so on, everything is swift and modern. Our children are growing up faster, too. Early socializing is here to stay, so we had better accept it." Other women argue that pre-teen dancing improves social poise; boys and girls "get used" to each other, so that by the time dating begins in earnest, there will be a minimum of awkwardness.

Educators and psychologists puncture these arguments. What happens, they ask, when dancing and kissing become kid stuff? Will newer thrills be sought at appallingly tender ages? And how much harm is done to a child's sense of personal worth when he is plunged into a social and sexual whirl when he is least sure he can handle himself in it?

The truth is that many mothers encourage early dating for reasons they may be quite unaware of. Among the most revealing, as reported by psychiatrists and sociologists:

Parents seek social status for themselves through their children's popularity. It is a mark of prestige to have a daughter who is much in demand.

They want their children to have "all the fun and advantages" they themselves missed. Often a mother who felt herself less popular than others in her own youth is desperately afraid that her child will have the same painful experience.

They want to relive the carefree days of youth through their daughters' experiences. Many women, unwilling to face the harsh reality that their own youth is behind them, look for fun once again in dates—this time their daughters'. The young girl, knowing she has her mother's approval, will ask her how to attract boys, and receive advice far too sophisticated for an adolescent.

Another major factor emerging from the studies and observations of behavior experts is this: mothers are making young girls conscious of the trappings of femininity years before they should be concerned with them. There is nothing wrong with dressing a little girl to look pretty and feminine, or with teaching her the *basic* principles of fashion, which are good taste and appropriateness. But more and more mothers are moving beyond this, and the potential harm can be far more serious than they suspect. The clothes-and-beauty habit is hard to stop. By the sixth grade, impatient for the maturity that is still years away, the young girl clamors for a brassiere and nylons. By junior high, she wants low-cut, slinky dresses and high heels. Cosmetics departments report brisk sales of makeup kits for the under-thirteens.

This accent on sexuality is widespread even in the fun we are providing for our young girls. In one U.S. Midwestern city, at a pre-teen beauty contest sponsored by a mothers' club, eight- to twelve-year-olds pirouetted in bathing suits before an audience of adults. In Los Angeles, two hundred young girls entered a Brigitte Bardot look-alike contest, wearing towels and bikinis in imitation of the famous French "sex kitten."

What can parents—particularly mothers—do to prevent their daughters from marrying while still in high school? They can take these steps while the girls are growing up:

*Understand that early dating is dangerous* even if "everyone is doing it," and have the courage to take a firm stand against it.

*Neither permit nor encourage a hectic social life* for the eleven- to fourteen-year-old. Remember that the best "advantage" you can give a young girl is the ability to be self-reliant. And she can learn this only by having time to be alone and at peace, just with and by herself.

*De-emphasize things too sophisticated* for a young girl.

*When girls get together with boys, discourage the imitation of adults* and encourage activities appropriate to their ages. Refuse to permit parties where the boys bring their own girls.

*Make your daughter feel it's great to be just what she is.* A child who is unhappy in her age group looks forward to the next one, where things may be better. As she grows, express your deep interest in what she is doing. Praise efforts and accomplishments warmly and often.

*Make her home an attractive, inviting, happy place.* Many young girls marry early to escape from an unhappy home.

There are no easy answers to the problems created by too-early marriage. But it is clearly necessary to face the blunt truth that young lives may well be wrecked unless brakes are applied to the steady march of child-women toward the altar.

### EAST VS. WEST

**T**o Americans, the arranged marriage has a bad name. We weep for all the poor girls forced into marriage against their will. Yet Dr. David Mace, executive director of the American Association of Marriage Counselors, notes in his *Marriage East and West* that many of these victims of the arranged marriage have not seemed to mind it at all. Indeed, young women from the Far East, observing Western courtship customs for the first time, often feel sorry for American girls. The idea of being forced to go out alone into the open market, and to preen and flirt in the hope of attracting a husband, strikes them as undignified and demanding. The daughter of a traditional Chinese family knew that finding her a husband was her parents' sacred duty, and she grew up confident that it would be wisely and capably fulfilled.

—*Ernest Havemann*

# There Are No Shortcuts to Marriage

MARY STEICHEN CALDERONE, M.D.

hy is it that an increasing number of young people are having early sex experiences? Is it because we adults have not realized the importance of making young people understand *what sex is for?* Many of us taught our children the "facts of life," thinking that we had done a complete job when we talked about the reproductive role of sex. It never occurred to most of us that this is just a small part of sex education. The major part has to do with understanding the role of sex in our fundamental polarity, or orientation, or drive, toward the basic man-woman relationship. Without this polarity a person becomes confused and chaotic, and finds it hard to establish firm, straight roots in life.

There is a developmental scale in human relationships, beginning with child to parent, and progressing to friend to friend, lover to lover, man to woman, and finally, full cycle, parent to child. Note that I distinguish between the lover-to-lover and the man-to-woman relationships: the former is by its very nature transitory, though it may be and often is transmuted into the permanent man-woman relationship that should transcend all others.

The meaning and significance of the man-woman relationship has been and always will be sought by each human soul. This meaning is like quicksilver; we think we have it, then it may elude us for a time. The search continues as long as we live, for this most fundamental of human relationships can never be considered a finished product. In recent times the search for this basic relationship has been profoundly modified by the superimposition on it of another process that used to precede it. Formerly, a young girl had time, between twelve and eighteen, to learn, to feel, to experience, to observe, to meditate, to experiment in the meaning of being an adult. And from eighteen to twenty-one she had time to test her abilities to carry on adult responsibilities and also her ability to form friendships with both men and women, before reaching a final decision on marriage.

Now "growing up" starts earlier, and is considered to have been completed by sixteen or seventeen at the latest. But it simply is not possible, no matter how you rush it, for a person of seventeen to be able to develop the judgment and maturity that a slower pace would have ensured by twenty-one. Indeed, the speeding up of the process may produce such dislocations that what the person *might* have become at twenty-one may now be impossible to achieve.

Lester Kirkendall, author of *Premarital Intercourse and Interpersonal Relationships,* points out that any relationship between two people is bound to be dynamic; for a short or a long period of time it grows, matures, changes, becomes transmuted into another kind of relationship, perhaps more positive, perhaps negative. Nor can its conclusion be foreseen in its earliest days. This should lead one to question the concept of "love [that is, enduring love] at first sight."

Kirkendall suggests some of the elements essential to any longtime relationship—confidentiality, for instance. Surely a person with whom you are going to live over a period of time must be one in whom you have confidence and to whom you can give confidence. When someone you hardly know tells you all the intimate facts of his or her family and love life, do you not recoil from this overconfidentiality? Confidentiality by its nature must be a step-wise, time-wise process.

Another major element of a relationship is empathy—the ability to feel *with* another person. Empathy must be a two-way process, and the infinite variety of cues and clues about each other's feelings and convictions is impossible to learn except over a period of time. The most delicate and critical element of a deep relationship is trust, and there is absolutely no way of arriving at trust overnight. And so it is obvious that there are no shortcuts. That is why thoughtful adults, who have watched sadly and helplessly while young people try these shortcuts, conclude that sex experience *before* confidentiality, empathy and trust have been established can hinder, and may actually destroy, the possibility of a solid, permanent relationship.

Sexual acts between a man and a woman probably do not remain meaningful for any appreciable length of time outside marriage. It is the intent behind the legal ceremony of marriage that provides continuity to the sexual relationship, gives it meaning and validity, turns it into something to develop, to deepen, to protect and to sacrifice for. In the repeated sexual act within marriage, a man and a woman are saying to each other, "I chose you once above all others, and I now choose you again. I'll choose you tomorrow and next year and the year after that and when we're forty or fifty or sixty and neither of us is any longer so attractive."

For herein lies the key: Marriage is not something *imposed* by society and religion—far from it. Marriage is a state freely and consciously and joyfully *sought* by men and women. It is an elective state. What is the secret of the highly constant polarity of most human beings toward this relationship? The answer is that only within the self-sought marriage bond can two people create for themselves the security of peace and solitude and time—lifetime—by which they can accomplish that which is pivotal and central to all else, namely, total communion.

The report of the Committee on the Family of the Lambeth Conference of the Anglican Church put it this way: "The need of man and woman for each other, to complement and fulfill each other and to establish a durable partnership against the loneliness and rigor of life. . . ." Time—time to laugh, to cry, to fight, to work, to hope, to fear, to know each other in the Biblical sense, to procreate—for all these shared experiences the state of marriage is essential, not only as symbol but as protector.

Most people who have had a stable marriage will tell you that the waiting was well worth while—rewarded by the golden moments of true communication, both sexual and nonsexual. "A durable partnership against the loneliness and rigor of life." Only time can assure this—first, time to grow up into the person you were meant to be; then time to identify and to get to know the person you want to relate to; and, at long last, time to commune with that person within the permanence of a marriage relationship.

### RECIPE FOR DATING

*A* father put off telling his motherless daughter the facts of life as long as possible. But when she fell in love for the first time at sixteen, he realized that he had to talk to her. I overheard his concluding remark—"Jean, the best advice I can give you is written on the top of a mayonnaise jar." That night, when I mixed the salad for dinner, these words on the mayonnaise jar leaped up at me: KEEP COOL BUT DON'T FREEZE.    —*Mrs. J.A.W.*

# Whatever Became of Romance?

HARRIET VAN HORNE

**W**hatever happened to the romantic tradition in America? In an age in which sadism holds the edge over sentiment in popular entertainment, and a well-adjusted sex life is a goal in itself, romance lies a-bleeding—and women are infinitely the poorer for it.

Our channels of mass communication are overloaded with sex symbols. The marriage manual has replaced the slim volume of verse on the engaged girl's reading list. The hero in our fiction and drama has given way to a scruffy character you might call the antihero. The dream goddess of the hour is an erotic hoyden in gingham rompers. Love, the post-Freudian generation may tell you, is what happens in Victorian novels and old movies on television. Love is for the squares. Yet we all know, in the secret hearts we so casually deny, that love, for young and old, is the ultimate salvation. All who have loved and been loved recognize the great enduring truths in classic love poetry. Love *does* add a precious seeing to the eye. Love *does* soften brutes and add grace to virtue. And love *does* bear it out—"even to the edge of doom."

The romantic tradition could be defined as an un-self-conscious respect for an emotional arrangement between a man and a woman, with each side happy to express the best of its own characteristics. Within the framework of this tradition there is room, on one hand, for gallantry, for the courtly gesture; on the other, for feminine reserve and demureness and calculated pretty ways. Far from being the antithesis of sex, it heightens and underscores sex by dramatizing the differences between masculine and feminine, rather than obliterating them, as does today's cult of casual involvement.

Too often, the woman in our society is obliged to put down her natural feminine instincts. She is shaped by the times—and the shape is no longer gentle and womanly. To be sure, the instinct to make a nest and mother the young is too powerful to be snuffed out altogether. But what of every woman's instinct for flirtation, for the intrigue and ceremonies of courtship? Why must the romantic temper be proclaimed unstylish, not to say unsporting?

It's difficult to ascribe to a single moment the demise of the romantic tradition in our society. But somewhere between the solemn sex studies of Sigmund Freud and the wanton posturings of Brigitte Bardot, romance breathed its last. Romance is absolutely antecedent to love. Its death diminished each of us, and society suffers. Indeed, we see the suffering all around us today, in manners and morals and, saddest of all, in the minds and hearts of its young.

A few summers ago I was witness to a pathetic little scene on a country terrace. On this sweet June evening, the younger members of the family, all in their teens, had foregathered for a nonalcoholic cocktail before going on to a dance. They were nice, conventional youngsters, tanned and scrubbed and terribly "adjusted." They talked of swimming and tennis and who had the fastest sports car. Suddenly, far across the lawn, her white skirts almost ghostly in the gathering dusk, a lovely young girl appeared. Everything about her—eyes, hair, skin—seemed to glow. We older guests watched her progress with tender, if envious, eyes.

Clearly dazzled, a young boy rose to greet this vision floating our way. " 'She walks in beauty, like the night . . .' " he quoted. Around him, like the shattering of fine, rare glass, there was a burst of laughter. The boy blushed a dark red under his tan. "Or something corny like that," he mumbled. It was a painful moment for lovers of love and all its tender ways. What sociologists are pleased to call "the peer group" had, on this night of starry skies, set this boy firmly on the road away from romance.

How wonderful if boys like this could, on such a night, talk with some old lover's ghost! All, or very nearly all, the great men and women whose names belong to the ages *loved*—mind, heart, body and soul. And they carried their love proudly, as an army carries its banners.

Even the men one would imagine incapable of a sensitive or delicate passion nevertheless loved. Jonathan Swift, sometimes called "the hangman of humanity," put down his cruel pen and wrote to his beloved Stella in baby talk. Among Swift's personal effects, found after his death, was a lock of hair, wrapped in a small scrap of paper on which he had scribbled "Only a woman's hair." Dr. Samuel Johnson was so devoted to his wife, Tetty (an unattractive lady many years his senior), that long after her death he kept her wedding ring near him. Keats, dying of tuberculosis, desperately lonely, still could write, as the end neared: "I am certain of nothing but of the holiness of the heart's affections, and the truth of imagination."

The heart, as another poet has said, is never given out of the bosom in vain. Of all unrequited loves, one of the most touching was that of William Hazlitt, the eighteenth-century essayist, for a common lodging-house girl called Sarah. Though she accepted Hazlitt's gifts, Sarah mocked and deceived. When finally she left him for another, his wound was deep and bitter. Still, not long afterward, he could write to a friend, "When I am dead, who will love her as I have done? When she is old, who will look in her face and bless her?" Heartbreak comes, wisdom lingers. Listen again to Hazlitt, this man who loved not wisely but well. "Perfect love has this advantage," he wrote. "It leaves the possessor of it nothing further to desire."

In a world that fails to honor the romantic tradition, that takes a let's-be-practical approach to courtship and marriage, it is woman who is most cruelly cut down. Without romance, a glory passes from her life. And there may steal into her room at night a terrible uneasiness. Is this all it means, being a woman?

### THE LITTLE STARS

*T*here's a bumper crop of plain sex in the new books—well, maybe "plain" is not quite the word; "explicit" would be nearer. Sex, of course, is as old and as prevalent as weather; they both will go right along, and it's pretty tiresome to talk such a lot about either of them—a bit of advice that I should like to see taken by many of our newer writers. Certainly, nobody wants to complain about sex itself; but I think we all have a legitimate grievance in the fact that, as it is shown in present-day novels, its practitioners are so unmercifully articulate about it. There is no more cruel destroyer of excitement than painstaking detail. He who reads these play-by-play reports of passion responds with much the same thrill he would experience in looking over the blueprints for some stranger's garage.

Can you remember the days when there used to be rows of asterisks? How those little stars twinkled and gleamed, and how warmly they shone upon the imagination!      —*Dorothy Parker*

# Why We Choose the Mate We Do

MORTON M. HUNT

To poets and philosophers, the idea that someone might try to unlock the riddles of love with calculating machines and mathematical equations might seem absurd. Love, like faith in God, is supposed to lie above the reach of scientific study. Or at least it was, until the American sociologist Robert F. Winch of Northwestern University came along. Athletic, genial Professor Winch has used the insights of psychology, the data of sociology and the rigorous proofs of statistical analysis in arriving at his "complementary" theory of love. According to his evidence, obtained in an eight-year study of twenty-five young couples, *the love of man for woman and woman for man is basically self-serving: its primary purpose is to benefit the lover, not the beloved.*

Each of us, he says, tends to fall in love with someone whose personality is the complement of our own and through whom we can therefore relieve our own frustrations and vicariously live out our impossible wishes. A tough, brusque, hard-driving man may long in secret to be a cared-for child again. He cannot be this, so he falls in love with a frail girl he can enjoy sheltering—and through whom, by proxy, he enjoys that would-be other self. She, meanwhile, has always yearned to be more aggressive, and because she identifies her life with his, she indirectly achieves her wish. Each benefits and fulfills the other—and so love, though selfish in its origin, succeeds in being a mutual blessing.

Professor Winch conceives this dovetailing of psychological needs to be the essential reason for love and a far stronger force than sexual desire, beauty, similarity of tastes, etc. Indeed, this theory answers the often-asked question, "What does he see in *her?*" A sharp tongue in a woman will look like shrewishness to one man, delightful vivacity to another; a preoccupation with homemaking may seem wonderfully feminine to one man, merely insipid to another.

The need theory also explains why many men and women fall in love with the very opposite of what they thought they were looking for. Herb always thought of his ideal girl as "blonde and sweet and quiet"—and married Harriet, who is dark, bouncy and talkative. Jonathan always expected to fall in love with a girl who was intelligent, ambitious, energetic —and chose Jean, a languorous, well-groomed birdbrain.

This is no mystery to Winch. Since it is true, he says, that married people tend to resemble their mates in religious affiliation, ethnic background, social class, level of education and other social characteristics, it may be thought that a person tends to fall in love with someone like himself on the level of emotional needs. But such a mate would duplicate, rather than complete, his personality. Hence, even if a man finds such a girl, either he fails to fall in love, or the love fails to prosper. When the psychological opposite of oneself comes along, although she contradicts the ideal image, a mightier and more satisfying love springs up.

But mark this paradox: It sometimes happens that the man who falls in love with the opposite of what he thought he wanted soon sets about trying to remake her into the original image; and if he succeeds, she will no longer be the person he fell in love with. The man who tries to make his childish wife more competent, the woman who tries to make her easygoing husband more ambitious, may succeed only in creating a partner who will no longer satisfy his or her emotional needs. Happily, says Winch, the reformer usually picks a partner who cannot really change so radically. He thus can play reformer year after year without loss, since his beloved never becomes what he *thinks* he wants, but remains what he *truly* wants.

Winch's findings help make sense out of the crushes of the bobby-soxer. Because the adolescent lacks a feeling of importance as a person, his need for recognition and identity is overwhelming. The easiest way to meet it is to fall in love with someone famous, such as a movie star, thus gaining a vicarious sense of fame. As boys and girls finish high school and go to work or to college, their needs change. More sure of their personal value, they gradually cease to ascribe marvelous properties to mere physical attributes, and begin to respond to deep-lying traits of character. This is the kind of love that produces marriage.

Something akin to the theory of complementary needs had been advanced by some psychiatrists in recent years to explain many aspects of dating, courtship and marriage. Yet it lacked what Winch calls "hard" evidence: detailed data, careful surveys, precise statistical analysis. Hoping to put the theory on a scientific basis, Winch obtained grants from Northwestern University and the National Institute of Mental Health. Then, with a small staff of sociologists and graduate students, he compiled a list of all married students at Northwestern, struck off those who belonged to minority groups (to eliminate confusing side issues) and picked twenty-five couples at random for study.

Over a five-month period these fifty young husbands and wives came in voluntarily for individual interviews. They were a varied assortment: tall men and short; pretty girls and homely ones; country- and city-bred types; working wives, teaching wives, housewives. All were childless; all had been married less than two years and therefore could still remember vividly their meeting, courtship and first months of marital adjustment. Each spoke for a total of about five hours, and also took two psychological tests.

The interviewing and testing were designed to ferret out clues to the general traits and psychological needs of each subject. These include the need to dominate, the need for achievement, the need to be deferent (to admire someone else), to express hostility, to abase oneself (or take blame for things), to take care of or be taken care of by someone, and so on. The result was a dossier on each person of up to two hundred pages. For the next two years Winch and his staff worked on detailed analyses of the fifty individuals. Assigning each a set of numerical values (a "1" in achievement meant, for example, that the individual had a very low need to be successful or to create something; a "5" in achievement meant the extreme opposite), the staff was able to consider the men and women as so much statistical information. By the use of equations they could then test whether the husbands' scores were really correlated with their wives' in complementary traits.

When his staff had completed the psychological analyses of all fifty subjects, Winch—who had not met or interviewed any of the subjects personally—read a summary of each case history and tried matching the men to the women on the basis of the theory of complementary needs. Of the twenty-five marriages, he guessed twenty correctly. Statistically, there is less than a one-in-ten-million chance of getting such a score by pure luck; the reasonable conclusion, therefore, would be that Winch was indebted to a valid theory.

In the great preponderance of cases, the correlations revealed that individuals who liked to dominate, teach or direct—whether male or female—had fallen in love with persons of the opposite sex who liked to be steered, to have decisions made for them or to be instructed and criticized. They showed, too, that a strong need for recognition in one spouse was frequently linked with a small need for recognition in the other; that an easygoing attitude was often mated with a flashing temper. However, some computations showed certain complementary linkages to exist only weakly, if at all. Sociability in one spouse, for instance, seemed not to be tied up at all with reserve in the other.

The ultimate test consisted of taking a sample of correlations and measuring what proportion of them favored the theory and what proportion went against it. Winch's group used statistical methods on a total of 388 pairs of traits, found that 256 of them showed correlations favoring the theory. This was something less than a perfect score, but, tested by the formulas of probability, it proves to be a result that would occur by accident only once in a thousand times.

Naturally Winch hopes that the need theory will yield practical applications. American divorce, for example, has been studied from many angles: the part played by money, women's careers, differences in education and so on. Perhaps most broken marriages may prove to be more the result of the failure by one or both partners to recognize their own important needs. And perhaps understanding of the need theory could lead to elimination of a number of elements of friction. Young people especially may gain self-knowledge early enough to help them avoid impulsive marriages. Since the need patterns of the young adult are radically different from those of the adolescent, it follows that juvenile love is a hopelessly inadequate basis on which to choose a lifelong partner. The proof is that girls who marry under the age of twenty have, statistically, three times as great a chance of winding up in divorce court as those who marry between the ages of twenty-two and twenty-four. The data for boys tell the same story.

What implications does the need theory have for married people? Professor Winch maintains that it can give both husband and wife a clearer way of thinking about each other, about what each of them wants in marriage, and about ways in which they can satisfy each other and themselves at the same time.

Marriages which are in serious difficulties may benefit from the new tools that the need theory puts into the hands of professional counselors. Winch's wife, Martha, is executive director of the Family Service of Highland Park, Illinois, where she has counseled troubled couples for many years. She feels that the need theory gives a marriage counselor a positive approach to problems. Not only does the counselor assess the sources of frustration which loom so large to the couple in conflict; he (or she) is now enabled to look for and point out those complementary and cohesive factors which originally produced love and which can be strengthened to restore the original balance.

In sum, the need theory seems likely to help all who love by bringing them a keener understanding of what produces and sustains that most marvelous and desired of all emotions.

⇒ ◆ ⇐

Success in marriage is much more than finding the right person: it is a matter of being the right person.    —*Rabbi B. R. Brickner*

## Chapter 3/*Marriage Is What You Make It*

*Tennyson believed that marriages are made in heaven.*
*Cervantes said that marriage is a noose. Sidney Smith*
*observed that "marriage resembles a pair of shears,*
*so joined that they cannot be separated; often moving*
*in opposite directions, yet always punishing anyone who*
*comes between them." Ibsen wrote that "marriage*
*is something you've got to give your whole mind to."*
*Clearly, the most difficult, demanding, maddening,*
*rewarding and blissful of all human relationships . . .*
*is the wonderful, unpredictable state of matrimony.*

## Sense and Nonsense About Honeymoons
JEROME AND JULIA RAINER

The honeymoon should be a lark, a picnic, a holiday from reality for two, an escape from accountability to anyone but each other. It should be a retreat to a limbo of directionless joy where the deepest intimacy between bride and groom may be experienced. But according to some of the most respected marital advisers, the honeymoon and the nuptial night appear to be a kind of soul-testing trial, the outcome of which can make or mar the entire marriage. This is an unfortunate impression to convey.

We do not wish to downgrade the necessity for frank and honest sexual information. The marriage manuals have rendered a valuable service in dispelling a sense of shame and in increasing knowledge of the physiology of sex. However, when they utter doleful prophecies that "the least false step by the bridegroom will make a wound in her heart that will never heal," or that "the course of marriage is determined by the wedding night," we wish to take vigorous exception. An initial misstep will have no such dire effect. Life is full of second chances.

The fact is that many of the manuals reflect the sexual customs of the Victorian era, when shame, inhibition and prurience were common. Today, American sex customs are frank, intense and unrepressed, and the picture of a shy and fearful bride, which may have been accurate five decades ago, is highly unrealistic. It is as though the bride and groom had never danced or played riotously on beaches, never talked earnestly of plans for their life together—as if they were physical and emotional strangers to one another.

What do these modern couples need to know? First, they need to know that sexual experience on the nuptial night and the honeymoon has no bearing on the emotional health, the physical well-being or the social relationship of the partners, even if physical culmination is less than perfect. The intimacies of the honeymoon are events in themselves, insulated by the special climate that is natural to the honeymoon holiday. To many, the joys of simple physical embrace and nearness to each other, without fear of intrusion, are in themselves a culmination.

There are months, years, a lifetime ahead for the cultivation of sexual technique. This is one thing that can be counted on to improve with time and deepening love. One of our medical consultants has pointed out what he calls "the tyranny of the *should*," which has caused trouble to many married couples. Relying heavily on standardized advice, they accuse their mates, verbally or mentally, of falling short of expectation. Unreal expectations can lead to tension, friction, quarreling. Why should these couples be troubled with such hazards? They are in love. They have no need for promises of celestial delight, for "exploding fireworks" and "blazing pinwheels." They can enjoy love in reality without such embellishing words.

The kind of guidance that is most needed by modern honeymoon couples is some preparation for the transition from "being in love" to the more advanced state of a loving relationship—what the psychiatrists call "relatedness." Being in love casts a memorable glow and is essential for mating, but it is not serviceable for a long-lasting marriage. The loving relationship is the mortar that keeps the marriage solid and lasting, and every couple should recognize that their rhapsodic condition will inevitably spend itself and be replaced by a more enduring emotional state. Relatedness is no short and simple process; it requires a widening awareness and understanding of the other's personality—the admirable as well as the unadmirable facets.

So let us keep the honeymoon what it is meant to be, a holiday from responsibility, a waltz in the moonlight. It is an institution. Its carefree refreshment is something to return to time and again throughout a marriage, when the newlyweds, by then wise "oldlyweds," deposit the children with Grandma and Grandpa and go away to enjoy each other again in a new setting.

*T*he great secret of a successful honeymoon is to treat all disasters as incidents and none of the incidents as disasters.

—*Harold Nicolson*

# How to Get Along with a Man

PHYLLIS MC GINLEY

The world is brimful of reci-
pes telling girls how to please gentlemen and ensnare
spouses. But I sometimes think the pundits have got hold of
the wrong end of the stick. Capturing male fancy isn't all
that difficult. Nine tenths of the girl babies born into the
world have the gift perfected by the time they are drinking
out of a cup. I recall a demonstration of native talent by a
member of my own household when she was four and out
with me for a Sunday call. We must have dropped in at cocktail time, for there were present a large number of grownups.
When the moment came to go, she detached her hand from
mine, walked over to the tallest and likeliest male stranger
and murmured meltingly, "Will you tie my bonnet for me?"

If all girls do not play the music thus by ear, they've
usually learned, by eighteen, at least to carry the tune. Moreover, they have studied how to take an intelligent interest in
whatever interests their prey—if need be, they can ski down
terrible mountains, reef a sail or listen interminably to the
sound of locomotives on hi-fi. Yet this getting along with
*men* isn't what's truly important. The vital knowledge is
how to get along with a man, one man. Concerning that I
think our mothers and grandmothers knew more than we.

For one thing, they recognized their luck. They never
stopped preening themselves on having the good fortune to
be married women. For every right-thinking woman knows
the profit in matrimony is by all odds hers. Simone de Beau-

voir, the French writer, insists that men invented marriage to keep women in their place as the second sex. But why would a man deliberately go out of his way to dream up an institution so hampering to his liberty, so chafing to the wild male spirit and above all so expensive? No, marriage was all a woman's idea, and for man's acceptance of the pretty joke it becomes us to be grateful. If ever I were intrepid enough to instruct my daughters on the care and taming of husbands, I should put gratitude first on my list. For its sake a man will endure a great deal—extravagance, too much marjoram in casseroles or a tendency to sinus trouble.

Faults there are bound to be, marked like towels—His and Hers. But the woman who gets along with a man knows how to get along also with his defects: she adopts them. The most successfully married couples I know have, perhaps unconsciously, worked this out. Is the lord of the manor unpunctual about letters or meeting one at the station? Does he drink too much coffee, clutter ashtrays, turn on all the lights and leave them burning? Is he a pantry raider, an ice-tray emptier? Let it not exacerbate the soul. Be unpunctual together. Let the lights burn and the ice melt in the sink. Faults shared are comfortable as bedroom slippers and as easy to slip into.

Next to gratitude, and ornamenting it, I should put appreciation. Particularly appreciation of his wit. A husband expects a certain amount of disillusionment. He knows that a helpmate before breakfast is bound to be less picturesque than the *soignée* creature with whom he danced at the assemblies. He has braced himself for hairnets and flannel bathrobes. What he hasn't counted on is a wife who interrupts his newest jape with, "Better call the carpenters, honey, about that window," or greets its point with a chill stare.

67

Let's see—that's three items on the list, and it seems skimpy advice for a woman to have accumulated after more than twenty years. What about the hot meal at night and the good breakfast? And is there to be no sound counsel on staying slimly seductive, on asking intelligent business questions, on getting one's way without a fuss? I'll have to admit I am a poor oracle. I've seen marriages fly apart at the seams and I've seen them firmly welded as a battleship, and there was never a rule of thumb to go by. Good housekeepers may come to grief and bad ones may prosper. I have known happy women who understood more about business than their husbands, and equally happy ones who thought a Dow-Jones average had something to do with golf.

As for glamour, even that is moot. One friend of mine, although she can scarcely make out the name on a restaurant marquee, leaves her glasses at home because her husband thinks they are unbecoming, and *she's* happy. I also know a witty woman novelist who buttons her sweaters unevenly and forgets her lipstick, and *her* husband hasn't spoken a cross word to her in years. And when it came to the final question, I'd have no answer at all. In a successful marriage, there is no such thing as *one's* way. There is only the path of both, the bumpy, difficult but always mutual path. Pressed, I might add a trifle so old-fashioned as to seem fresh. It concerns the selection of a proper family tree. Nothing helps so much in getting along with a man as seeing to it that he stems from a long line of monogamous ancestors.

And there the list would have to end: gratitude, a sharing of faults, an attentive ear and a stout conviction that marriages were meant to last. They might seem poor weapons in a woman's arsenal. But who wants weapons when she has —and is aware that she has—all the luck?

68

# What Women Want in the Men They Marry

DAVID R. MACE, PH.D.

A well-known Belgian family organization has been trying to find out just what women are looking for in the men they marry. An Italian magazine has reprinted the Belgian list of husbandly virtues with the comment that Italian wives are in complete agreement. Many of the qualities listed, moreover, agree closely with those that American and Canadian women, when asked for their opinions, considered desirable. So we may take it that they represent the aspirations of the Western wife. Let us look at these seven virtues, arranged in the order of importance to which the women assigned them.

*Tenderness.* There can be little doubt that this is the quality women most appreciate in the men they love. And it is equally certain that it is a quality that is short among Western men—perhaps in men the world over. "If only my husband could whisper, 'I love you,' just once in a while!" sighed one wife. The trouble is that our society trains its men to keep their emotions under strict control. Seemingly this doesn't go well with the kind of outflowing warmth that our women need. Yet they want their men to be strong, too. Indeed, their idol seems to be the man who is vigorous and self-assertive as he faces the world in general, but becomes gentle and sweet in his relationship with the woman he loves. Are our women asking too much?

*Courtesy.* Women often complain that their men, once courtship is over, lapse into boorish indifference. "If he would only show me as much consideration as he does complete strangers!" one woman said. "When we are alone, he forgets all his manners." Bad manners in a husband's behavior toward his wife are inexcusable. But again, there is an interesting cultural conflict. In our time, women have asserted their independence and denounced the traditional concept of the female as the weaker sex. Is it possible that, in sighing for the gallantry of an earlier age, women want the advantages of both their new and their former roles?

*Sociability.* The wives complain that their men are poor companions. They come home from work and lapse into bored silence. Once the meal is over they seek the company of other men or sit with their eyes glued to TV. The most bitter complaints are from wives who say that their husbands are scintillating when they are with other people, but utterly dull at home. These unhappy women do not ask why they lack the capacity to draw out the social graces that their husbands undeniably possess.

*Understanding.* How delighted a woman is when her husband anticipates her every need, remembers anniversaries of important occasions and gives her exactly what she wants for her birthday! What wives are seeking here is recognition of their womanhood, and of the *difference* this implies. The woman knows that her basic role in her relationship with her husband, from the most superficial to the deepest levels, is that of *response.* Unless he can act in ways that bring out her responsiveness, she cannot function as a woman. Therefore, she wants to be assured that he recognizes her femininity and understands the peculiarities of temperament and mood that go with it.

*Fairness.* Many wives complain that their husbands keep them short of money while making liberal provision for their own indulgences. Or that they grumble about the quality of the food or the furnishing of the home, without seeming to realize that the wife is doing all that can be done with the allowance she is given. What lies behind this complaint, I think, is the feeling many wives have that their husbands unconsciously treat them as inferior beings, or that they exercise their role as head of the house unjustly.

*Loyalty.* One wife puts it like this: "When my husband and I are out with others, he is continually making fun of me, ridiculing me, humiliating me. That doesn't make a good marriage." Another complains that her husband criticizes her in front of the children. Women have traditionally been in a vulnerable position in relation to their men, who have usually been physically stronger, economically and socially more powerful. Thus, it has always been important for a wife to feel that her husband won't let her down.

*Honesty.* The wife who catches her husband concealing the truth from her can no longer feel secure. If she knows he lies, she is soon wondering what he is doing, where he is going and whom he is seeing when he is out of her sight. Her real fear is that there may be some other woman in his life. A close relationship like marriage becomes unworkable if it is not based on truthful and straightforward communication between husband and wife.

These, in the opinion of women who were asked to consider the question, are the virtues they would look for in a husband. It is interesting that the qualities they listed are of two different types. The first four are concerned with the man's attitude and approach to his wife. The last three are concerned with the man himself—his integrity, his character. The two kinds of qualities are, however, closely linked. It is inconceivable that a man who is by nature unjust, unreliable and dishonest could in any real and sustained way be tender, courteous, companionable and understanding toward his wife. If the women had approached the problem objectively, they might have realized this and put character first. But they clearly responded emotionally, thought first of their own needs, and then realized that only a certain kind of man would be able to meet those needs.

These women are really saying that the perfect husband is a good man who knows how to express love. If all men were like this, most marital problems would cease to exist. For that matter, if all men—and women—were like this, most *human* problems would cease to exist!

### VISION

Gallantry deepens every relationship. It can polish a marriage to a new luster. My friend Marge told me that on her fortieth birthday she was, like many women, deeply depressed. She knew that happy, productive years lay ahead, but in the excessive value placed on youth in our society, she had lost her perspective. She said nothing of this to her husband at breakfast, but after he left she gave way to tears. She foresaw graying hair, deepening wrinkles, a struggle to remain slender. By the time her husband returned she had regained a degree of calm, but the ache persisted. After dinner he said, "Come and look at your presents."

They had always exchanged practical gifts and she suspected he had sneaked in the new vacuum cleaner they needed. But to her amazement she unwrapped a pair of jeweled boudoir slippers and a lace negligee with matching gown. "He didn't explain why," she said, "and he didn't have to. I knew what he was trying to imply: 'You're beautiful, you're glamorous.' And the odd thing was, I began to feel that way." —*Elizabeth Byrd*

# Too Tired to Love

*Condensed from the book: Women and Fatigue—*
*A Woman Doctor's Answer*

MARION HILLIARD, M.D.

A happy bedroom takes on the attributes of a sanctuary for a married couple. Within these four walls, husband and wife reach the height and the depth of the expression of their life together. If they both feel that this is a resting-place for them to keep returning to, their children will also feel it.

I remember rushing home after school as a child and shouting for Mother, as every child does, and then running upstairs to Mother's and Father's big bedroom and finding her sitting by the window, sewing. She could have sewed downstairs in the living room, or even in the kitchen, but we all came to feel that this room was a sanctuary to her—the place where she was most at ease in her home. Any bedroom can be happy if a woman will learn that her happiness comes about differently from the way her husband's does. This takes knowledge, search, patience, humor and love. It is rare for a couple to achieve their dreams when they first marry.

What things detract from the happy bedroom? The first and most important is fatigue. No doubt about it, a happy married life takes energy! When a woman is tired out, her emotional life is at a dead level. A sense of defeat and disillusionment follows when she begins to doubt her ability to love and to make love. Girls who are about to marry should understand this. Too often they are tired out at the beginning of their marriages, exhausted from the bridal showers, the shopping and the many decisions which accompany this important step. One young patient of mine called me the morning after her wedding, weeping inconsolably.

"Last night wasn't anything like I thought it would be," she said. "It was my fault. What shall I do? I couldn't seem to *feel* much like making love. I just wanted to go to sleep."

"I know the trouble," I said. "You were so short on rest up to your wedding that you had to fall apart when it was over. Your husband is probably exhausted, too. Take it easy, let nature take its course, and in forty-eight hours you'll both be laughing about it." The girl came to see me on returning from her honeymoon. She said that she and her husband had talked the matter over. He had been tired out, too, and he had been worried for fear the fiasco had been *his* fault. Then they did a sensible thing: they blamed the whole thing on fatigue and forgot about it.

After the honeymoon, as family demands on her energy multiply, many a wife develops a take-it-or-leave-it feeling about lovemaking. Some women, afraid of becoming pregnant because they don't want to give up their jobs, frequently use fatigue as an excuse. Others, when ten or twelve years of marriage seem to have worn off the glamour, will develop "symptoms" to serve them. I have had women bring me lengthy lists of complaints, hoping they could tell their husbands, "The doctor says I can't." On the other hand, many wives have come to me to find out how they can get their husbands interested in a sex life again. One patient complained, "Honestly, all he thinks of is his job and getting ahead in the world. I want another baby so badly, but he seems indifferent."

"Give him time," I counseled. I knew that the couple had

had a particularly difficult experience with their first child, and it was easy to understand that the husband might not want to repeat such a trying time very soon. Eventually she did get pregnant again, and this time the whole thing went more easily.

The months after a new baby comes home can be a crucial time for a marriage. When a mother comes to me for a final examination after she has had her baby, we talk about the resumption of her sex life with her husband. Something new is going to develop in their physical relationship, I explain. As they go back and pick up this part of their life together, they will feel a great tenderness which can keep growing throughout their marriage. But often the patient will say, "I am just too tired to start yet."

"You may be," I say to her, "but I doubt that your husband is. Your love together is just as important now as it ever was, and you must take care of it. You feed your child so it will grow in stature. Just so, it's up to you to nurture your marriage and see that the child grows up in a happy home."

In most marriages, at some time, a husband or wife will refuse lovemaking because of distraction, excitement or, most likely, personal hurt. This is a powerful weapon because it touches the innermost sensitivities of the partner. But it is a weapon a husband or wife should never use. To do so is a sin against the spirit.

A favorite patient and friend of mine whose husband had died when her two children were babies came into my office after an interval, engaged again and completely transformed by her new happiness. But a year later she was back, her blood count down and her spirits low. There was a blank, life-isn't-fair look in her eyes. "He doesn't pay his bills," my patient's inventory of injury began, "and he drinks a little too much. He has had two jobs in a year. I'm afraid to quit mine because we need the money." To top it all, her children by her previous marriage were becoming problems; her new husband refused to discipline them, and he took sides with them when she tried to. Finally she said, "How can I respond to his lovemaking when I feel the way I do?"

Situations as tough as this have been faced by thousands of women: the expectation that a man will support them and make a home for them is not realized; they had hoped to be protected, but find that they must be the strong ones. This is a time to count up one's assets and realize that one's desire to make a marriage work is meeting a supreme test.

"You knew he was a risk when you married him," I said. "And you can't sit in judgment on him now. You must accept him for what he is—a lovable, happy-go-lucky companion. You ask me how you can respond to his lovemaking. I say you can go further than that. You can know the finest love of all—compassion. You can comfort him, for he knows his limitations and he loves you."

"But it's not fair," she said. "I have to work all day and then come home and get dinner while he stops to have a drink with his friends."

"Of course it's not fair," I agreed fervently. "It never will be. But, first of all, I want you to regain your vitality of last year." My friend was worn out with thinking and judging. I knew she should be still for a while and let love catch her up again. She would find that a love full of compassion and giving can be a more wonderful, truer love because it is built on knowledge and acceptance and not on false expectations. Before she could achieve this, however, she had to overcome the fatigue that saps all vitality from love. "When you come from work," I told her, "make yourself take time to get some nourishment, put your feet up, let the drive of the day slip away while you find out what happened at school. Your children will love to find you listening again. As soon as this resting place is happier and more peaceful than a nearby bar, your husband will come home quickly, too."

It is sad to me that some women note that they feel indifferent to lovemaking and stop there. To create a happy bedroom, they need to understand that making love with their husbands is only partly a physical phenomenon. It engages the mind and heart as well as the body. For her own sake, and her husband's, a woman must work to create that atmosphere of love which is a communication of body, mind and, particularly, heart—so that lovemaking becomes, again and again, a renewing of the whole human being.

### WIFE'S ANSWER

*A* friend of mine read an article in The Reader's Digest called "Too Tired to Love". My friend thought his wife should read it so that they might mutually benefit. That night when dinner was finished, the dishes washed and put away, and the children bedded down, he hopefully broached the subject.

"Honey," he said, "there's a wonderful article in The Reader's Digest called 'Too Tired to Love'—"

"Don't bother me," his wife interrupted. "I'm too tired to read."
                                        —*Milt Josefsberg*

*O*n his fiftieth wedding anniversary an old gentleman gave his recipe for marital happiness: "I've always tried to treat Ma in such a fashion that if I died, it would take more than a hot-water bottle to replace me."                —*Industrial News Review*

# Can Marriage Counseling Help?

NORMAN M. LOBSENZ

**T**his year more than one million couples will seek the help of marriage counselors. Yet most of these men and women have only the fuzziest idea of what marriage counseling is. Moreover, hundreds of thousands of other couples whose marriages might be improved by guidance will avoid counselors out of fear or ignorance of what is involved. Thousands more will toss away their time, money and often their marriages by going to incompetent or out-and-out quack counselors.

It's not surprising that this confusion exists. Marriage counseling is a comparatively recent idea. The first service in America to use the term "marriage counseling" was founded in New York in 1929, by Drs. Hannah and Abraham Stone. It is the aim of this article, based on talks with outstanding authorities on marriage counseling, to provide a clear picture of what the average couple can expect from counseling.

Perhaps the biggest single misconception is that a counselor gives advice. Time and again a client will ask, "What should I do?" Unlike a doctor, a counselor does *not* prescribe a remedy. What he does try to do, says Dr. Emily Hartshorne Mudd, one of the first marriage counselors in the United States, is to help couples "come to grips with their problems, so they can work them out themselves." The counselor does not blame, judge or take sides; he tries to help a person analyze his marriage. A counselor has been described as a blank paper on which one draws a picture of his difficulties; one can then stand back and view them in new perspective.

"I've had hundreds of couples say, 'Just tell us which of us is right,'" says Dr. Robert A. Harper of Washington, D.C., former president of the American Association of Marriage Counselors. "My answer is that there is no right or wrong side in marital disagreement. There are only *different* sides. Differences can often be understood, even removed. But first we must try to understand those different feelings." According to Dr. David R. Mace, a veteran marriage counselor, it is natural for a wife or husband to want to find out who is "at fault" when things go wrong. "To become aware of one's own contribution to the problem is hard," he says. "The marriage counselor encourages one to talk about his marriage until he becomes aware of his own part in the problem."

The case of a couple whom I'll call the Carters is a good example of how a counselor gets this process started. Mrs. Carter pictured herself as a perfect wife. But her husband, she said, was "an ineffective slob." Mr. Carter, surprisingly, agreed; he wanted to know how to be a better husband. When the counselor interviewed Mr. Carter alone, he said, "Why do you blame yourself so much? Maybe your wife sets impossibly high standards." Carter digested this, then answered, "She does make herself a martyr, doesn't she?" From this small beginning the counselor was able to get the couple to develop new insights into their behavior, and to use them as a base for building a better marriage.

A counselor's most important tool is the ability to ask questions that will make the client reexamine his own feelings and motives. The counselor can then guide a client out of despair and self-pity, help him to understand what is happening and why, and point out possible solutions to the problems.

Most practitioners prefer to see husband and wife separately, with an occasional joint session. Sometimes a husband or wife will refuse to coöperate. But counselors generally find that if the counseling begins to effect changes in one person, the other will come around. Counseling can be useful even if one mate boycotts it completely. The guidance given to a husband or wife alone, one authority states, is often sufficient to help the marriage survive.

There is no way to tell how long counseling will take. A simple problem may be cleared up in a few sessions. (A session usually lasts about fifty minutes.) A serious situation may require once-a-week sessions for a year or longer. The client is never committed to a fixed number of sessions; he may withdraw at any time. Only quacks promise "immediate results." Experts estimate that 70 percent of all clients are helped by counseling, 25 percent show no change, and 5 percent find their marriages worsened. Success doesn't necessarily mean that a reconciliation has been effected. Sometimes a counselor judges his work well done if a client realizes that his marriage should be ended.

A façade of symptoms—arguments over money, relatives, child rearing, friends—usually masks the basic problem of emotional immaturity that is at the root of most marital maladjustment. But many counselors consider another element equally responsible: the inability of husbands and wives to communicate their feelings to each other. The Reverend Arthur M. Tingue, executive director of the American Foundation of Religion and Psychiatry, tells of a marriage in crisis in which the husband had to attend a funeral in another city. He asked his wife if she wanted to go along. "If you want me to," she replied. "Well," the man said after a moment's silence, "I'll go alone."

The husband had *wanted* his wife to accompany him. She had *wanted* to go. But the wife, not sure that the husband really meant his invitation, had tossed the decision back to him. He assumed that she was turning him down. And so a couple who had wanted to express their mutual love and need wound up feeling that each had been rejected.

Sex discord is not, in itself, a major cause of marital unhappiness. It is more often a symptom of other tensions. Studies by the Philadelphia Marriage Council have shown that sex was the focal problem for only 15 to 19 percent of the couples.

Marriage counselors have a variety of backgrounds and training, but they all generally take one of three basic approaches. In one, the counselor deals primarily with the problem in the marriage relationship. For example, a wife complains that, although her husband earns a good salary, he flies into a rage if she buys anything beyond basic necessities. The husband in turn complains that his wife is a miserable housekeeper and doesn't know how to handle money. If both these complaints are true, the counselor may concentrate on getting husband and wife to understand how money can be used as a weapon, a reward or a punishment. The counselor may work out a budget for the couple and arrange for the wife to improve her housekeeping via a course in home economics.

In the second approach, the counselor concentrates exclusively on the personality problem of one of the partners. It may be, for instance, that the husband's attitude toward money is a neurotic symptom. By depriving his wife of money, he is expressing his hatred of women. Through counseling, the husband may eventually gain the insight necessary to change his behavior.

The third approach—subscribed to by the majority of counselors—tries to combine the other two. Dr. Aaron Rutledge, director of the Training Program in Counseling and Psychotherapy for the Merrill-Palmer Institute in Detroit, told me most counselors think that "to deal with the marital problem and not the personality, or with the personality and not the problem, is the surest way to wreck a marriage."

A great deal of informal counseling is done by ministers. Critics charge that ministers are likely to be more inspirational than analytical, that they are often too close to those whom they counsel to be objective. But many seminaries have added courses in counseling; many ministers are getting clinical training in top counseling centers. The bulk of professional marriage counseling is done by caseworkers in public and private welfare agencies. The Family Service Association of America says that more than half the 400,000 cases handled by its 319 agencies annually are marital problems. "The big advantage that family-agency counseling affords," says Henry Freeman, executive director of the Family and Children's Service in Pittsburgh, "is that it can deal with many aspects of a marital problem simultaneously.

"We had a case recently in which a wife was seeking help to keep her husband from leaving her. The couple were having money difficulties as well as emotional difficulties; their children were doing poorly at school; the man was in trouble on his job." Whereas a private counselor might work only with the husband and wife, the resources of the family agency were called into play on several fronts—to help the children by explaining the situation to school officials, to help plan for a bank loan to get the family through the financial squeeze, and so on. Group counseling is showing promise. In this new technique, several couples will meet at intervals to talk with one another about their problems. A trained counselor listens and occasionally guides the discussion. Group counseling offers lower fees, a shorter waiting period and definite therapeutic advantages for certain kinds of people.

One of the hurdles that marriage counseling must surmount is the difficulty in establishing professional standards that will draw a clear line between the legitimate counselor and the quack. The American Association of Marriage Counselors, which today has approximately 500 members, has set basic requirements for practitioners. These include a graduate degree in a field dealing with human problems (such as psychology, sociology, social work, theology, medicine), plus several years of clinical experience in providing marriage counseling.

Because no one has to get a license to practice counseling, however, there is no way to enforce these standards. The shortage of qualified practitioners leaves a vacuum that misguided zealots or quacks rush to fill. The charlatans can usually be identified by: their self-advertising (legitimate counselors are not permitted to advertise); their promises of immediate and complete solutions for all problems; their insistence that clients "sign up" for a certain number of interviews; their excessive fees; their emphasis on sex; their theories with pseudoscientific names; their refusal to give details of their training. The following national agencies have information about legitimate marriage-counseling facilities in your community: American Association of Marriage Counselors, 27 Woodcliff Drive, Madison, N.J. 07940; Family Service Association of America, 44 E. 23 St., New York, N.Y. 10010. In most areas, information can also be obtained from your doctor or minister, or from community organizations such as the United Fund, Community Chest, Community Welfare Council.

What can the average husband and wife expect to gain from their sessions of marriage counseling? Each counselor with whom I have spoken gives essentially the same answer: personal growth. "By growth," says Sanford Sherman, of Jewish Family Service of New York, "I mean a widening of emotional horizons, a maturing of personality. As one person said to me after counseling, 'I still have my troubles, but I'm learning how to handle a marriage. Most of the time I even enjoy it!'"

## BREVITY

*T*he late Dr. Randolph Ray, rector of the Little Church Around the Corner, didn't believe in giving young couples long-winded advice on marriage. His usual parting speech was a terse, nine-word affair. "Now," he would tell them with a smile, "don't both get mad at the same time!"              —*Robert Stein*

## HEAVENLY SCROLL

*T*hat eternal problem for East and West alike—how to be happy though married: There was once, says a Chinese tale, a household so happy that for nine generations none of its members had left it, except the daughters that marriage perforce took away. The fame of such domestic bliss reached the ears even of the Celestial Emperor. He sent to inquire the secret. The old father of the house, taking paper and brush, painted many characters, then handed his answer to the imperial envoy. But when the Son of Heaven unrolled it, there was nothing there but the character for "Patience" repeated a hundred times.              —*F. L. Lucas*

84

## Chapter 4/The Merry War Between Men and Women

*Do married people fight? Of course they do. Does this*
*mean they are not in love? Of course it doesn't.*
*The more you care about somebody, the madder you*
*can get with him or her—temporarily.*
*The bonds of matrimony are not meant to be broken,*
*but there are times when they can be stretched a little.*
*Here some of America's best-loved humorists and most*
*provocative commentators offer some diabolical advice*
*on how to harass your spouse and stay married.*

## How to Fight with Your Wife

J. P. MC EVOY

I can remember when I was
little how my mother used to go on about "the patience of a
saint," but it wasn't until I grew up that I learned most
saints were never married. So how could they possibly know
anything about patience? Then I wondered why Mother
never mentioned the patience of a father. Now *there's* patience for you. Oh, yes, Mother was patient. But Father was
patient about all the things Mother was patient about—and
in addition he was patient about Mother.

Mother used to say, too, that a soft answer turneth away
wrath, but I always thought Father's system—a gay answer
—was better. Later I discovered the best system of all, and I
don't mean no answer; for you don't get anywhere in mar-

ried life not having an answer. You only get accused of being an old sourpuss. No, the secret of a happy married life without quarrels is always to have an answer, but be sure it doesn't make any sense. Nothing infuriates a woman as much as to be cornered with Reason or—unforgivable sin— fenced in with Truth.

It was a Chinese traveling in this country who evoked the magic formula which makes quarreling almost impossible for my wife and me. One day, late for his train, he rushed over to the baggage room in Grand Central Station, threw his check on the counter and demanded his bag. The attendant couldn't find it. As precious minutes went by, the Chinese began jumping up and down with inarticulate rage. Finally he couldn't stand it any longer. His train was going—his bag was nowhere to be found—and he pounded the counter with his fist and yelled: "Pretty damn seldom where my bag go. She no fly. You no more fit run station than godsake. That's all *I* hope!"

Before hearing this, when anything of mine got mislaid around the house, which was every time my wife tidied up, I used to scream like a wounded banshee. But now I merely yell, "Pretty damn seldom where my papers go!" In the old days my wife used to come back snappily with, "If you put your papers where they belong, you'd know where to find them!"—which is sheer nonsense, as any husband knows who has ever tried it. I found the only answer to such an unreasonable remark was, "You no more fit run house than godsake!"—which put her in her place until she learned to retort, "That's all *I* hope!"—stopping all argument dead.

In the silly old days I used to moan, "Why don't you fill out your check stubs properly? What is this—$2.20, or $22, or $220? Why can't you keep your balance straight?" Now I just say, "Pretty damn seldom where my money go. She no fly." And I get just as far as I ever did—which was exactly nowhere. As for the children, we never quarrel any more about who is spoiling which child, and the dreadful things we are doing to their future—as if we knew anything about it. One of us—it doesn't matter who—merely looks at the other and says in a resigned way, "You no more fit run children than godsake!" Which nobody can deny.

Well, there it is. Pretty damn seldom where your happiness go. She no fly. But if you don't try this next time instead of quarreling, you no more fit run marriage than godsake. That's all *I* hope.

➔ ◆ ⬅

### THEY STAY MARRIED

"Whenever I got angry," related Mrs. Houdini, wife of the famous magician, "Houdini would leave the house, walk slowly around the block, then open the door and toss his hat into the room. If it was not thrown out again he would enter. On one occasion, my bad temper made me obdurate to his overture. He had shattered two electric light bulbs and at my outburst left the house hastily. When he tossed his hat in, I promptly flung it out. The performance was repeated, at intervals, until finally Houdini vanished for an hour. Then a messenger appeared with an envelope on which was written: 'To be delivered in a hurry to Mrs. Houdini, then Exit Rapidly.' Within were these formal words:

" 'Mr. Houdini wishes to inform Mrs. Houdini that the first globe fell out of his hand, but the second one slipped. He wishes to convey his sorrow and promises that the one that fell will never fall again.—Friend Husband.'

"One couldn't be angry long with a husband like that."

—*Harold Kellock*

# A Man Does the Darnedest Things

JEAN KERR

I feel a bit of a fraud to be picking on men, when I always pretend to be so crazy about them. And, deep down inside, I *am* crazy about them. They are sweet, you know, and so helpful. At parties, men you've barely met will leap to their feet to tell you that you've got the wrong end of the cigarette in your mouth. And when you are trying to squeeze into a tight parking place there will always be some nice man driving by who will shout, "Lady, you've got a whole *mile* back there!"

But, charming as men are, we can't pretend they're perfect. It wouldn't be good for them, and it wouldn't be true. For marrying one is like buying something you've been admiring for a long time in a shop window: you may love it when you get it home, but it doesn't always go with everything else in the house. One reason for this is that most men insist on behaving as though this were an orderly, sensible universe, which naturally makes them hard to live with. The other reason they're hard to live with (I know this sounds illogical) is that they're so *good*. Perhaps I can clarify that by listing a few of their more intolerable virtues.

*A man will not meddle in what he considers his wife's affairs.* He may interfere at the office, driving secretaries to drink and premature marriage by snooping in file drawers and tinkering with the duplicating machine. Back home in the nest, he is the very model of patience and *laissez-faire*. He will stare at you across the dining-room table (as you

simultaneously carve the lamb and feed the baby) and announce, in piteous tones, "There's no salt in this shaker."
What a wife objects to in this situation is not just the notion
that Daddy has lived in this house for thirteen years without
ever discovering where the salt is kept. It's more the implication that only she has the stamina and animal cunning necessary to pour the salt into that little hole in the shaker.

*A man remembers important things.* It really is remarkable the fund of information he keeps at his fingertips: the
date of the Battle of Hastings, the name of the man who
invented the printing press, the formula for water, the
Preamble to the Constitution, and every lyric Larry Hart
ever wrote. It is obviously unreasonable to expect one so
weighted down with relevant data to remember a simple fact
like what size shirt he takes, or what grade Gilbert is in, or
even that you told him fifteen times that the Bentleys were
coming to dinner. A woman just has to go through life remembering for two. As an example of this, I was recently
told about a wife who, from time to time, pinned a tag on
her husband's overcoat. The tag read, "Please don't give me
a ride home from the station. I have my own car today."
This technique wouldn't work with my husband: he usually
forgets his overcoat and leaves it on the train.

*A man will try to improve your mind.* Operating on the
suspicion that women read nothing in the newspapers except fashion ads, the average man takes considerable pains
to keep his scatterbrained wife *au courant* with the contemporary political situation. We get the following dialogue:

"Did you read Walter Lippmann today on the shake-up
in the Defense Department?"

"No. What did he have to say?"

"You should have read it. It was a damn good piece."

"Well, what was the gist of it?"

"Where is that paper? It should be here someplace."

"It isn't. It went out with the garbage."

"That's too bad. It would have clarified everything."

"I'm sure. But what was he saying?"

"Oh, he was against it."

*A man allows you to make the important decisions.* Because he has such respect for your superior wisdom and technical know-how, he is constantly asking questions like, "Does this child need a sweater?" or, "Is that baby wet?" Personally, I am willing to go through life being the court of last appeal on such crucial issues as bedtime (Is it?); cookies (Can he have another?); rubbers (Do they have to wear them?); and baths (Tonight? But they took one last night!). But, just between us, I have no confidence in a man who wanders to the kitchen, peers into the icebox and asks plaintively, "Do I want a sandwich?"

*A man will give you an honest answer.* If you say, "Honey, do you think this dress is too bright for me to wear?" he'll say, "Boy, it sure is."

*A man believes in sharing.* Men are all advocates of togetherness, up to a point. They will agree that it is "our house," "our mortgage" and, of course, "our song." It is interesting, however, to observe the circumstances under which items that once were "our" joint concern suddenly become *your* exclusive possessions. For instance, a man will return from a stroll through "our backyard" to tell you, "Honey, I think your daffodils are getting clumpbound." Or, on another occasion, "I see that the hinge is off your medicine chest." This policy of dissociating from anything that is out of order reaches its ultimate confusion with statements like, "Hey, your man is here to fix the chimney."

*A man doesn't want you to worry.* Since he supposes, and quite correctly, that you worry a great deal about his health, he will go to any lengths to spare you the least alarm about it. He will say casually, "Well, I almost keeled over in Grand Central Station today."

"Good Lord," you will say. "What happened?"

"Nothing. I leaned against a pillar. I didn't fall down."

"But, honey, what happened? Did you feel faint? You didn't have a terribly sharp pain in your chest, did you?"

"Oh, no. Nothing like that."

"Well, what do you mean you almost keeled over?"

"Oh, I guess it's that foot again."

"What foot again? Which foot?"

"The one that's been numb since last summer."

"Your foot has been numb since last summer?"

"Now it's more like the whole leg."

"Good heavens, let's call the doctor. This very minute!"

"Why?"

"Why? Are you out of your mind? Because there's something the matter with your leg, that's why!"

"There you go, flying off again. I'm sorry I mentioned it."

*A man idealizes his wife.* This is another way of saying that he hasn't really looked at her in fourteen years. To get me a housecoat for my birthday, my husband will make the unthinkable sacrifice of entering the awesome portals of some posh lingerie department. There, as I reconstruct the scene later, he selects the slimmest, trimmest little salesgirl on the floor and announces, "She's about your size." Naturally, I have to take the thing back and get myself a housecoat four sizes larger. But on second thought, perhaps I shouldn't complain about that. If you stop and think, it's really rather charming of him.

# Husbands: The New Servant Class

RUSSELL LYNES

"I wish I could," my friend said on the phone, "but I'm up to my elbows in diapers." My friend is the father of two, the more recent one very recent indeed. I had asked him to play tennis, and when I hung up, my feeling was not one of surprise or pity; it was one of shame. I didn't say to myself, "The poor hen-pecked fellow." I said, "Well, I guess I ought to be doing my household chores, too." The narrow-gauge train of thought that this set in motion led me into elaborate speculation about the nature of husbands and the recent changes in their behavior. How did it happen that my friend was diapering and I thought I ought to be waxing or dusting? What would my father have thought about this? I laughed out loud.

Bernard De Voto once said: "What every career woman needs is a good wife." That was a number of years ago. Now, in cities and suburbs especially, every woman, regardless of her notions about a career, takes it for granted that when she marries she gets a package deal—a husband who is also a part-time wife. To call him a wife is, perhaps, to put it too bluntly. He is rather more servant than wife, though the distinction is sometimes a fine one. The roles of the husband and wife are becoming less and less sharply differentiated. Whereas it was once a question of: "Who wears the pants in this family?" it is now a matter of pants all around, and the children are as likely to cling to Father's apron strings as to Mother's. Man, once known as "the head of the family," is now partner in the family firm, part-time man, part-time mother, part-time maid.

If you are in any doubt that this is so, let me produce for you what are known as "the findings" of our favorite oracles, the pollsters. Crossley says that more than a third of the husbands in several Northeastern states do the dishes, clean house and look after the children, and more than half of them do a lot of the shopping. The Gallup Poll insists that 62 percent of American husbands are intimate with dishwater and about 40 percent help with the cooking.

How, I wondered as I put my tennis racket back in the closet, did women get into this frame of mind and men into this fix? What sort of men are we turning into, with our aprons and dishpan hands? If it is anybody's fault, whose fault is it? Actually, the revolution goes back to the time before the turn of the century when the business-career woman got a fingerhold in man's world. Imperceptibly at first, the distinctions between man's world and woman's world began to blur. Men stopped giving their seats to women on buses and taking off their hats when women entered elevators. "If they are going to compete in our world," men reasoned, "then they should be treated as men."

From the man's point of view, this was a major tactical blunder. He ought to have realized that he should preserve at all costs such distinctions as remained between men and women, and he should have kept the line clear as to what was expected of each. But once he had allowed the social differences of the sexes to be played down, it is only logical that he should ultimately have found himself assuming some of the functions of women.

The gradual shrinking of the servant class also explains part of what has happened. Two world wars, with attendant well-paying defense jobs, emancipated the cooks and maids and butlers, and ever since that time the number of women in domestic service has steadily dwindled. Now, with more than 23 million women employed, less than 10 percent are in domestic service. Something had to fill the undusted and unwashed gap between the career woman and her home. As more married women have taken jobs, more mechanical gadgets have been invented to lighten the housework. Some-one, however, had to help run the gadgets for the women who worked. And now we begin to see the answer to the question of how men got into their present fix.

The American male is a sucker for anything that whirs or hums or lights up, and women know this. Men, with their supposed superior knowledge of mechanical things, were con-sulted for the first time on the purchase of expensive pieces of domestic equipment, and before you could say "Change the filter after each using," they were running them. As domestically unskilled labor, husbands came to pride them-selves on being able to operate machines which were so de-signed that they practically ran themselves.

Vanity has also played its part. More often than not, the man with the waxer whining at his feet is so employed be-cause his wife has either suggested that he might not be clever enough or strong enough to do the job, or because she has implied that nobody could do it as well as he. ("Darling," she says, "I suppose it's too big a job for you, but . . ." or "Would you mind? Nobody can make it glisten the way you can.") But vanity, the scarcity of servants and the flood of gadgets tell only part of the story. After World War II, millions of veterans went to school on the GI bill. Many of these men were married, and in order to make ends meet, young wives got jobs. Father, who had learned to make beds, darn socks and police up in the Army, was left with his books and his babies and his broom. He became not only a wife, but a mother. Those were the days when men used to gather in the self-service laundry and swap stories as they once had in the corner bar. Thus, a strange new domestic pattern emerged.

At the same time we have become devoted to what Frederick Lewis Allen called "the cult of informality." With nobody to cook and serve dinner at a given hour, we eat when we please and where we please—in the living room, in the backyard, in the kitchen. The tables, you might say, have been turned into trays on the lap, the sit-down dinner has become a feast of squat-and-scramble. Some member of the family is always on his feet fetching something from the kitchen. Father no longer sits and is waited on. And Mother is no longer the lonely slave in the kitchen. She is now, at worst, a slave among slaves.

In many respects, the man in the apron has no one to blame but himself. It has been men, we must remember, who have invented, promoted and sold the mechanical gadgets that now enslave them, though they did it in the name of making the little woman's burden lighter. Also, it is men who have fought for the shorter work week so that they might, as it has turned out, have longer weekends to clean out the cellar and paint the shutters and more hours in the evening to help with the dishes. They have made their own beds, and now they must lie in them—and the chances are that they must make them again in the morning.

*T*he woman's work that's never done is most likely what she asked her husband to do.
                                                      —*Franklin P. Jones*

# The Power Men Have over Women

MARYA MANNES

**T**he power men have over women is that they wear neckties, use shaving cream and are usually bigger than we are. They are not necessarily brighter, but they usually have us where they want us. Like a man with a dog. The dog sits at the feet of the man, waiting for three things: a look, a touch and a word. He wants these more than a bowl of food; he'll do anything for them.

Now, the dog is no more a slave than we women are. Like some of us, he can be very independent indeed, leaving home for the day to chase rats or rabbits, quite able to feed himself and to survive the rough-and-tumble world outside. But his disposition—like ours—his well-being, his sense of security still depend on the look in the eye, the touch of the hand and the sound of the voice of the man he returns to at night. But the silly male fool is often unaware of how much a look, a touch, a word, can hold for a woman. Nor does he seem to have any idea at all of the degree to which their absence can make her cross, resentful, tiresome.

Let's take the eye first. Why should I look at you? the husband says; there isn't anything I don't know about you, there's nothing to look at. He does not mean it unkindly. You live with a woman or a picture for ten years or more, and how often do you look—really look—at that woman or picture? Yet the female is starved for more recognition: the direct glance that says, I know who you are; you are there.

It's not a question of ardor (although the warm eye is

certainly preferable to the fish eye); it is a direct engagement, forging an intangible bond between man and woman. If you want to know what tragedy is, and the death of love, look at the countless married couples sitting in public places, their eyes never meeting. Not because the woman does not look at the man—she searches, hoping against reality—but because the man does not look at her. Each sits alone, encased in a plastic bag of indifference. It is clearly easier for a man to look at something that is beautiful and new and exciting than at something that is familiar and possibly fading. But he forgets that the familiarity and the fading are part of his doing, and that a woman is invested with beauty and excitement by his attention. We bloom under it; we die without it.

Now for the hand. A woman who is not touched may exist as a person but not as a woman. Here again I am not talking of ardor. It is the exceptional man who, after fifteen years of marriage and a long day at the office, can lunge at his wife and cover her with passionate kisses. No, women— even the most spirited—are much humbler than that. An occasional hand placed fondly on the shoulder, an arm in arm, a brief kiss on the cheek; things like these make us so happy that we wonder why some men forget them. Are they really that much trouble and effort? We are lovable if we are loved, and part of loving is touching.

We need words, too. Not only the comfortable exchange of thoughts and gossip, cozy and welcome as that is, but, once in a while, words that are beamed (like the look) directly at us. Gentlemen, you have heard it before and you shall hear it again: when we wear a new dress, and you notice it, say *something*. One phrase will do: "Nice color," or "Not bad," or "Wow!" If you don't say anything, we count it a failure. You don't know what power this silence has over us. We brood. It doesn't matter how good we think our taste is, how sure we are of our fashion sense; your silence can shatter our confidence. We would rather have you say, "Isn't that a little too tight?" than nothing at all. We'd rather be mad than ignored. There is nothing in the world that makes a woman walk more proudly and gaily than the verbal pat. Wise men know this.

The men who have wit must know what power this, too, can exert on a woman. Make her laugh and you've made her helpless. Women are far more likely to be enslaved on a long-term basis by a homely man who is funny than by an Adonis who isn't. In fact, the higher the sights of a woman, the freer her intelligence, the more she values intelligence in men. It exerts a compelling fascination that many men are still slow to recognize, since they confuse it with rivalry or competition. It is woman asking the most of man so that she can pay him homage. The strong, silent man is powerless beside the witty, articulate man. The right word is a mighty weapon. Of course, all these powers of men over women emanate from one premise: caring. If men don't care, they don't look or touch or speak. And if they don't look or touch or speak, they shouldn't be living with us anyway.

But here we come, I think, to the old and lingering inequity between the sexes. Everything in the long history of the male has conspired toward his self-assurance as a superior being. Everything in the long history of the female has conspired toward her adaptability to him, whether as wife, lover or mother. We are bred to care for what he thinks, feels and needs more than he is for what we think, feel and need. There is no valid comparison between a man's economic support of a woman and her hourly involvement in caring for him. We worry more when he looks seedy than he does when we do, because we notice him more. We worry more when he looks bored at a party than he does when we do. (He doesn't see it, anyway.) We concern ourselves daily with what he would like to eat, whom he would like to see, where he would like to go.

And this remains true even now, with all this talk of equality and emancipation, and in spite of the very real evolution of women into complete human beings. For there can be no love without this caring and catering by women. The difference now is that it is voluntary: not the price of room and board, but the tender of love, freely given.

### THE POWER WOMEN HAVE OVER MEN

*W*omen have power over their mates when they are touchable anytime anywhere. When the men are around, wise women sport crushable hairdos, wear nonsmear lipstick, nonwrinkle clothes, and they know how to turn off the stove the moment they are being hugged in the kitchen.  —*Reader's Digest reader*

*D*uring the Depression of the 1930's I met a girl—small, slender, perhaps 110 pounds. Some said she was beautiful. I could not tell. For you see, I was in love. For nearly a year she played the line deftly, surely, keeping the slack reeled in, never applying enough tension to break the silk; then one quick sweep of the net, and I was caught.

Now, six babies and half as many decades later, she is pudgy and graying. Some might say she is dowdy. I cannot tell. You see, I am in love. For nearly thirty years she has played the line deftly, surely, keeping the slack reeled in, never applying enough tension to break the silk; and heaven holds the sweeping net.

—*Reader's Digest reader*

# The Female Should Not Play Dumb

HANNAH LEES

he other day, searching for
something in a book of quotations, I came to the heading
WOMAN. Sixteen of the first twenty-one quotations tore
woman down. Six of those sixteen suggested that she is a
good deal more attractive when she keeps her mouth shut.

"It is thy place, woman, to hold thy peace and keep within
doors," said Aeschylus back in the fifth century B.C. "When
a woman inclines to learning, there is usually something
wrong with her sex apparatus," said Nietzsche a century ago.

From the moment women are old enough to give a
thought to love, they are constantly told: *Men can't stand
knowledgeable women. Men can't stand having a woman
disagree with them.* And since any woman would rather be
loved than be right, she plays safe—and dumb. Surveys
taken on college campuses reveal that almost half of women
students play dumb when they want to interest a man. An
unusually pretty college girl I know is always in a panic
before each new date, for fear the man will find out she is
on the dean's list. When I asked what she is afraid of, she
looked at me pityingly. "I don't want to scare him off."

"What do you talk about, then?" She grinned, but wryly.
"Oh, how wonderful he is. If I can just get *him* talking,
we're all right."

Does it have to be this way? Millions of women today
have gone to college. At least one wife out of three is a wage
earner. Thousands of women who call themselves "just

housewives" manage the family finances, direct charity drives, take part in local politics, belong to book clubs and go to the theater and concerts. Women may even be somewhat ahead of men culturally, because—thanks to men—they have more time to spend on culture. To make a deliberate effort to conceal all the information, ideas and experience we have acquired seems a terrible waste.

I am not suggesting that women should be above *wanting* to be attractive to men, but is this really the best way to do it? How can you charm any man—or even get to know him —when you are knocking yourself out not to be yourself?

Of course, men have hungry egos. They probably do need to feel superior to women. But they so obviously *are* superior in so many ways. They have made a comfortable country for us to live in. They make discoveries and write books and produce plays and movies, all for our enjoyment. If many of them feel that for a woman to know more than they do on a subject is close to stealing their pants, it's high time women helped them find out that this isn't true. Some experts say that the sight of a knowledgeable woman takes millions of men back to those early days when Mother knew everything. But I suspect that when this happens it is the aggressive way she flaunts her knowledge that frightens men. There are ways to be aggressive without being horrid.

I was fascinated watching the French and Italian women in a North Italian resort one summer. They couldn't have acted more aggressively garrulous, and the men they were with couldn't have acted more enthralled. Every woman I watched did much the same thing. She leaned forward, looking the man straight in the face, and opened her eyes wide in what was almost a caricature of absorption. But the general atmosphere of unafraid communication was enchanting.

Sometimes they were obviously arguing some point—but not with hostility—just because it was fun.

Over here, how often do you see a woman challenging a man with a gleam, instead of blood, in her eye? If we get onto anything serious, it is with *deadly* seriousness and the earnest anxiety to make a point. There is nothing wrong with wanting to make a point, but there is a lot wrong in being earnest and anxious about it. It's summed up in the adage about catching more flies with molasses than vinegar.

A woman I know has a job that involves persuading people to adopt the reforms she is working for; frequently she must fight the men who oppose them. She is an intellectual, and never for a minute pretends she isn't, but it has often made me grin to hear her talking to some man on the phone. "What do you think of our program?" she will ask. "Are you going to get us an appropriation this time?" in a tone which might have been saying, "I loved last evening. Can't wait to see you Saturday." Sometimes she says, "Ah, come on. You don't really think that. You're too smart." You get the feeling that she finds every man she talks to fascinating.

One strong-minded woman used to have a rough time with men who resented her for being contentious. Then one day a man came up to her at a party and said amiably, "Shall we wrestle awhile?" She braced herself. "What do you mean?"

"You like a good argument. So do I. Let's go, but no slugging." And he launched into a discussion of Tennessee Williams. They talked practically all evening. Once or twice when she got heated he said, "Hey, quit slugging."

"That was fun," she told him when they parted.

"Sure was," he said, and added casually, "—best kind of sublimated sex play I know."

"I have often thought of that," she told me recently, "and I haven't had real trouble with a man since. I guess I've learned to wrestle like a lady."

We might as well face it: there is, and always will be, a battle of the sexes. Men and women cannot help trying to one-up each other. It probably goes back to when the first man dragged the first woman off by the hair, and the first woman found ways to make him stick around and help her bring up the children.

Today the battle is fiercer than ever, with woman meeting man on so many of his own grounds. Men are bound to be confused by our not being the possessions we have historically been. It is as if a nice cozy fur rug they are used to having warm their feet suddenly got up off the floor and said, "Talk to me." The fact is that when the average man meets an intelligent woman who considers herself his equal, fur is apt to fly. But can men survive only if we *yes* them eternally? I don't believe it. People grow through meeting challenges, and women can find ways of challenging men so that it is fun for both of them.

### THE TRUE PERSONALITY

*A* girl of my acquaintance never wore her glasses on dates during college, although without them she was practically blind. She also put a severe restraint on a rather sarcastic wit, lest she deflate male egos and be unpopular. Finally, tired of being demure and groping, one night in her senior year she announced: "From now on I am going to be myself, and they can take it or leave it." It made her, in my opinion, a more confident and attractive person. It happened that that night she was my date. Six months later she was my wife. —*T. F. James*

## Chapter 5/The Inner Circle: Man, Woman, Child

*The family is the oldest social unit in the world.*
*It is, in fact, society in miniature. And it is the awesome*
*responsibility of each generation to pass on the torch*
*of civilization to the next. A child does not*
*belong to the two people whose union made his existence*
*possible. He is only on loan to them during his*
*formative years. But during those years the twig is bent,*
*and that is the way the tree will grow.*
*What to do? What not to do? Here are some helpful*
*thoughts from a group of sensitive people who have*
*looked deeply into family problems.*

## There's No Substitute for Parents
MORTON M. HUNT

With so many agencies devoted to child training and development these days, thousands of parents are beginning to doubt their own importance. They seem willing to surrender to others their most precious right—that of passing along to their children the family's spiritual and moral heritage. I have discussed this tendency with dozens of youth specialists and found most of them greatly concerned. "Perhaps we have failed to get across the best of our findings," say these experts. "There is *no* substitute for parents." It is the parents' influence—for good or for bad—that forms the child's character.

If, for instance, a child is habitually late, never does his homework, and loses his valuables, his parents may send him to camp in the hope that "they" will teach him a sense of responsibility. Such parents underrate their own influence. As one Scout executive put it, "All the camp training in the world is of no avail if, when the child gets home, he is again allowed to become overly dependent on his parents." It may seem like the act of a loving mother to pick up after Junior, to feed his dog when he forgets, to buy another watch to replace the one he lost. Certainly it's quicker and simpler than getting Junior to do these things for himself. But the gift of a new watch is tinselly compared with the gift of an inner guide to conduct. The parent who would give the finer gift cannot buy it cheaply or expect to have it given the child by outsiders.

It is the same with honesty. Schools cannot teach children to be honest when there are conflicting values at home. While making a study of classroom cheating in a Midwestern community some years ago, Dr. Howard Lane, then of New York University, let the children grade their own papers, checking later to see how many answers had been changed. A group of children from well-to-do middle-class homes, shockingly enough, were proved to have cheated far more than a group of reform-school kids. Why? Because in the "good" homes, while honesty was given lip service, success was the main goal. The children had seen their parents tell lies to promote their interests, give flattering welcomes to people they despised and do a hundred similar things. Under such circumstances honesty simply doesn't "take."

What can make a child grow up to be callous, selfish or cruel? Many things, most of them within the home. Psychologists agree that a basic liking for people can be created or prevented *during the child's first year of life.* If an infant is always handled gently, fed when hungry, comforted when miserable, he begins to get a fundamental trust in others and an unshakable liking for human beings. Parents who are impatient, easily angered or too busy to spend time with their children are building characters with sand. It is the child's love of his parents that makes him want to adopt their best traits and learn the qualities they urge upon him.

To avoid the bombings of World War II, thousands of London children were evacuated to the country, where they lived in carefully supervised children's communities. Psychiatrists found that the children did indeed learn such aspects of behavior as how to be ingratiating, to yield to authority, to get along with one another. But these qualities were used only to suit the needs of the moment, and were in no way comparable to such deep and permanent traits as generosity, compassion, self-sacrifice. These more profound guides of conscience develop only when children feel stimulated by the power of love to emulate their parents.

Parents likewise play the major role in teaching their children courage—even when they least realize it. For courage, the secure belief that one can face up to problems and new situations, is not something that can be beaten or lectured into a child. It comes by indirection. "Real courage has its roots in the child's feeling about himself, in his sense of worth and self-respect," says Dr. M. Robert Gomberg, former executive director of the Jewish Family Service. "The child who is made to feel too little, too young or too stupid to make his own decisions will not develop courage."

Why have so many modern parents become bewildered about their role? Probably it is because this is a time of change in the patterns of family life. For centuries the family was a self-contained unit. Girls learned from their mothers how to cook and sew. Boys learned from fathers how to plant, hunt, build and defend the home. Along with these skills children learned a set of goals in life and a concept of morality. But now fathers work far from their sons and see them only in leisure hours. Mothers buy precooked foods and ready-made clothing. Having thus lost the old techniques of child rearing, we have not yet found new ones.

This doesn't mean that the job is beyond the abilities of modern parents. It does mean that they must consciously lavish time and ingenuity on the job of child rearing. Take the condition sometimes called "technological unemployment of the young." In the past, when children were an economic asset to the household, they had the unique satisfaction of knowing that they were important to the family's well-being. Today parents must deliberately think up ways to simulate that satisfaction.

Dr. Ray Baber, a sociologist who has studied the family intensively, has advised parents to encourage their children to participate in family decisions. The girl who picks the new wallpaper for her room or the boy who helps decide where the family should spend its vacation not only achieves a sense of importance but recognizes that his wishes—and his reasons for them—may have a real effect on the rest of the family. And from this comes a sense of responsibility.

A parent can't expect his tastes and enthusiasms to be naturally catching. An enthusiasm for such things as literature or music or history must be communicated artfully. Cornelia Otis Skinner tells how her father, the celebrated actor Otis Skinner, made history seem "delicious fun." On a rainy day he might say that if she had been a good girl she could leaf through his costume books—great volumes of colored prints of the clothing of other times. "The way he granted this favor," Miss Skinner says, "made it seem like a special treat, not an obligation, to roam around in the past."

Even when he was performing eight times a week on Broadway, Skinner found time to read aloud at home to his daughter—intoxicating drafts of Shakespeare and Dickens. "But best of all," says Miss Skinner, "was when we used to play historical charades. Someone—usually Father—would act out a famous event, and I'd have to figure out what it was. Mother and I would scream with laughter to watch Father teetering on a chair with his arm tucked inside his jacket, crossing the Delaware. It was just a game—but I got to love both history and acting through it." Not many of us can act out charades to compare with Otis Skinner, but each of us, in his own way, can apply the same principle. It is easier, for instance, to answer a child's questions with flat pronouncements than to discuss them with him creatively. Yet through such painstaking discussions children and parents can develop a wonderful closeness.

Dr. Reuben Hill, at the University of North Carolina, accidentally discovered an interesting technique in this respect. One night, as two of his children were climbing into bed, four-year-old David asked him why the moon and stars didn't fall down, like the snow. Hill decided to pass the buck to seven-year-old Judy by asking, "What do you think?" Judy bubbled over with ideas, and soon David was chiming in with suggestions of his own. From then on, this "What do you think?" game became a nightly routine. The subjects included sex differences, digestion, death, heaven, poverty. The children thus acquired a wealth of new understanding. "With us, and with friends who tried it," says Dr. Hill, "the game became a shortcut to all sorts of meaningful issues."

There are no hard-and-fast rules about passing on important values to your children. Each parent must find his own way. Allen Funt, creator of the TV show "Candid Camera," equipped his cellar with a splendid workshop, but he found it kept him away from his two small children just when he should be with them. If he let them wander around in the workshop they got underfoot, were bored and often came dangerously close to his power tools. So Funt built each child a small workbench near his own, complete with an assortment of pint-size (and safe) tools. Soon all three were working assiduously and happily together, each on whatever he wanted. The children's efforts may not have produced triumphs of cabinetmaking, but there were permanent by-products—patience and persistence, for example, and comradely sharing.

There are hundreds of ways to be a good parent. With the complications of modern living we can't expect parenthood to be an effortless and unconscious process. We must give our best to the task, just as we would to any important creative work. And the reward is unlike any other in life.

### TEST OF STRENGTH

**M**en who came up "the hard way" usually try to make things as easy as possible for their children, thus denying them the discipline of struggle and self-establishment that worked so well in their own cases. Such parents remind me of the kindhearted amateur who raised butterflies as a hobby. He was so touched by the difficulties they had in emerging from the cocoon that once, out of mistaken kindness, he split a cocoon with his thumbnail so that the tiny inmate could escape without a struggle. The butterfly was never able to use its wings.   —*Charles F. Kettering*

# Help Your Child to Wonder

RACHEL CARSON

**O**ne stormy autumn night when my nephew Roger was about twenty months old I wrapped him in a blanket and carried him to the beach in the rainy darkness. Out there, just at the edge of where-we-couldn't-see, big waves were thundering in, dimly seen white shapes that boomed and shouted and threw great handfuls of froth at us. Together we laughed for pure joy—he a baby meeting for the first time the wild tumult of Oceanus, I with the salt of half a lifetime of sea love in me. As Roger passed his other birthdays, we continued that sharing of adventures in the world of nature that we began in his babyhood—a sharing based on having fun together rather than on teaching. I made no conscious effort to name plants or animals or to explain to him, but just expressed my own pleasure in what we saw. I think the results have been good.

We let Roger share our enjoyment of things people frequently deny children because they are inconvenient or because they interfere with bedtime. We searched the shore at night for ghost crabs, those sand-colored, fleet-legged beings rarely glimpsed in daytime, our flashlight piercing the darkness with a yellow cone. We sat in the dark living room before the picture window to watch the full moon riding lower and lower toward the far shore of the bay, setting all the water ablaze with silver flames. The memory of such scenes, photographed by his child's mind, will mean more to him in manhood than the sleep he lost.

A child's world is fresh and new and beautiful, full of wonder and excitement. For most of us that clear-eyed vision is dimmed or lost before we reach adulthood. If I had influence with the good fairy who is supposed to preside over the christening of all children, I should ask that her gift to each child be a sense of wonder so indestructible that it would last throughout life, an unfailing antidote against the boredom and disenchantments of later years, the sterile preoccupation with things that are artificial, the alienation from the sources of our strength.

If a child is to keep alive his inborn sense of wonder he needs the companionship of an adult who can share it, rediscovering with him the joy, excitement and mystery of the world we live in. Parents often have a sense of inadequacy when confronted with the eager, sensitive mind of a child. "How can I teach my child about nature—why, I don't even know one bird from another!" they exclaim. I believe that for the child, and for the parent seeking to guide him, it is not half so important to *know* as to *feel*. Once the emotions have been aroused—a sense of the beautiful, the excitement of the unknown, a feeling of sympathy or admiration—then the wish for knowledge will follow.

Wherever you are and whatever your resources, you can still look up at the sky—at its dawn and twilight beauties, its moving clouds, its stars by night. You can listen to the wind, whether it blows with majestic voice through a forest or sings a many-voiced chorus around the eaves of your house or the corners of your apartment building. You can feel the rain on your face and think of its long journey, its many transmutations, from sea to air to earth. Even if you are a city dweller, you can find a park or a golf course where you can observe the mysterious migrations of the birds and the changing seasons, or ponder the mystery of a growing seed planted in a pot of earth in the kitchen window.

Exploring nature with your child is largely a matter of becoming receptive to what lies around you. One way to open your eyes is to ask yourself, "What if I had never seen this before? What if I knew I would never see it again?" I remember a summer night when I went out on a flat headland all but surrounded by the waters of the bay. The night was so still that I could hear the buoy on the ledges out beyond the mouth of the bay. Once or twice a word spoken by someone on the far shore was carried across on the clear air; a few lights burned in cottages. Otherwise there was no reminder of other human life. I was alone with the stars: the misty river of the Milky Way flowing across the sky, the patterns of the constellations standing out bright and clear. Once or twice a meteor burned its way into the earth's atmosphere. It occurred to me that if this were a sight that could be seen only once in a generation, this little headland would be thronged with spectators. But it can be seen many scores of nights in any year, and so the lights burned in the cottages. An experience like that can be shared with a child, even if you don't know the name of a single star. You can drink in the beauty, and wonder at the meaning of it all.

And then there is the world of little things, seen all too seldom. An investment of a few dollars in a good hand lens will bring a new world into being. Some of nature's most exquisite handiwork is on a miniature scale, as anyone knows who has applied a magnifying glass to a snowflake. A sprinkling of sand grains may appear as gleaming jewels of rose or crystal hue, or as glittering jet beads, or as a mélange of Lilliputian rocks. A lens-aided view into a patch of moss reveals a dense tropical jungle, in which insects large as tigers prowl amid strangely formed, luxuriant trees. Pond-weed or seaweed put in a glass container and studied under a lens is found to be populated by hordes of strange beings.

Senses other than sight can prove avenues of delight and discovery. Down on the shore early in the morning, Roger and I have savored the smell of low tide—that marvelous evocation combined of many separate odors, of seaweeds and fishes, of tides rising and falling on their appointed schedule, of exposed mud flats and salt rime drying on the rocks. I hope he will later experience, as I do, the rush of remembered delight that comes with the first breath of that scent, as one returns to the sea after a long absence. Hearing requires more conscious cultivation. I have had people tell me they had never heard the song of a wood thrush, although I knew the bell-like phrases of this bird had been ringing in their backyards every spring. Take time to listen and talk about the voices of the earth and what they mean—the majestic voice of thunder, the winds, the sound of surf.

No child should grow up unaware of the dawn chorus of the birds in spring. He will never forget the experience of a specially planned early rising in the predawn darkness when the first voices are heard. Perhaps a few cardinals are uttering their clear, rising whistles, then comes the song of a whitethroat, pure and ethereal, with the dreamy quality of remembered joy. Off in some distant patch of woods a whippoorwill continues his monotonous night chant, rhythmic and insistent. Robins, thrushes, song sparrows, add their voices. In that dawn chorus one hears the throb of life itself.

On a still October night when there is little wind, find a place away from traffic noises, then listen. Presently your ears will detect tiny wisps of sound—sharp chirps, sibilant lisps and call notes. They are the voices of bird migrants, apparently keeping in touch with others of their kind scattered through the sky. I never hear these calls without a sense of lonely distances, a compassionate awareness of small lives directed by forces beyond volition or denial, a surging wonder at the sure instinct for route and direction that so far has baffled human efforts to explain it.

What is the value of preserving this sense of awe and wonder? Is the exploration of the natural world just a pleasant way to pass the golden hours of childhood, or is there something deeper? I am sure there is something much deeper, something lasting and significant. Those who dwell among the beauties and mysteries of the earth are never alone or weary of life. Whatever the vexations of their personal lives, their thoughts can find paths that lead to inner contentment and to renewed excitement in living. Those who contemplate the beauty of the earth find reserves of strength that will endure as long as life lasts. There is symbolic as well as actual beauty in the migration of the birds, the ebb and flow of the tides, the folded bud ready for the spring. There is something infinitely healing in the repeated refrains of nature—the assurance that dawn comes after night, and spring after winter.

In my mail I once found a letter from a reader who asked advice on choosing a seacoast spot for a vacation, a place wild enough that she might roam beaches unspoiled by civilization, exploring that world that is old but ever new. Regretfully she excluded the rugged Northern shores. Climbing over the rocks of Maine might be difficult, she said, for an eighty-ninth birthday would soon arrive. As I put down her letter I was warmed by the fires of wonder and amazement that still burned brightly in her youthful mind and spirit, just as they must have done fourscore years ago.

# Do Children Run Your Home?

SIDONIE MATSNER GRUENBERG, WITH LLEWELLYN MILLER

**F**amily and friends had gathered to admire the firstborn in a young family. One guest, the father of three teen-agers, pointed to the sleeping infant. "He looks helpless, but don't be fooled," he said. "There lies a potential tyrant. He is plotting right now to run you and this house for the next eighteen years."

He was joking, but there is truth in his warning. It is natural for children to test their power over parents and use it to the limit if they can get away with it. I have yet to know a child—from toddler to teen-ager—who did not make an all-out effort at some stage to run his home.

There is cause for concern only when parents do not understand the vast difference in benefits to everyone between a home managed with the whole family's interests in mind and a home managed exclusively for the children. Families are happiest and most secure when parents are in firm control. The following examples should help you see to what extent, if any, your children are running you and your home.

*Were they babied too long?* Janie, at four, is an expert in the use of the tantrum to dominate her home. When she was a baby, one of her parents rocked her to sleep each night, having read how important Tender-Loving-Care is. As she grew older this became a storytelling session—a rewarding time for all, until the parents realized that Janie was prolonging it, especially when they had other plans. The first time they delegated the storytelling to a baby-sitter, Janie was outraged. Before the violence of her temper they gave in and stayed home long enough to soothe her to sleep. That was all Janie needed. Now the parents accept only after-dinner dates, and their own guests are often disconcerted by a long-delayed dinner while either host or hostess disappears to talk Janie to sleep. These parents are confirming Janie's idea that to act like a demanding baby long after infancy pays off handsomely.

Stevie is twelve, but in a different fashion he, too, is still making a baby's autocratic demands for attention. He bursts in from school, shouting for his mother to help him find skates, peanut butter or whatever. "I'll just get him under way," his mother says indulgently, leaving her guests or dropping her work at the crack of his whip.

*Is it easier to indulge than to discipline?* Diana is thirteen. In the division of family chores, her job is to wash the dinner dishes. She is at the telephoning stage, and the minute the meal is over she is on the phone. After half an hour of chatter, friends arrive and she rushes for the door. "You haven't done the dishes," her mother reminds her. "Oh, mother! My friends are *waiting* for me! Do I *have* to?" So her mother says affectionately, "Oh, well—go ahead, darling."

One of Terry's chores is to help his father wash the car on Sunday afternoon. But he has delayed doing his homework, and there isn't time to wash the car, do homework and see his favorite television show. "It's a keen show," Terry says. "If I miss it today I'll never have another chance to see it! And I've *got* to do my homework! Do I have to do the stupid old car right now?" Dad wants to be loved. "Okay, go watch your show," he agrees. And he washes the car himself.

"They are only young once, and it's so easy to keep them happy," these parents tell each other, not realizing that the child who is allowed to run his home is not learning the meaning of responsibility and the importance of mutual help.

*Is it easier to serve than to train children?* Eight-year-old Tommy is expected to clean the tub after his bath. But he dawdles, and after twenty minutes the tub is only moderately clean, the room is a shambles and the other children are late starting their baths. Tommy's mother has her hands full at the end of the day. "Stand aside, darling. I'll do it myself," she says, rather than take the time to train him to finish properly.

Lila and Ann run in from school full of a plan to make fudge. The mother agrees—"if you'll promise to have the kitchen cleaned up by five." When it is time to start dinner, sticky pots and plates are all over the kitchen. It is easier for Mother to clean up the clutter herself; but if she does, these children will be inclined to think, as they grow older, that Mother should continue to clean up after them.

*Are you afraid of a showdown?* Louise, thirteen, came down to breakfast Saturday morning wearing lipstick and eye shadow. Her father says, "Go straight upstairs and wash that stuff off!"

"Oh, Father! Don't be so old-fashioned. *Everybody* wears makeup! Mother, do I have to be treated like a baby?"

"Well, I certainly don't think you are old enough to wear any to school," her mother says uncertainly, afraid to say "No" and hoping to stay on both sides—an impossibility in this kind of showdown. The argument that followed this tacit encouragement was anguishing.

*Parents have to work as a team.* If they pull against each other, children quickly learn to play the deadly game of divide and conquer. Many parents fear they will lose their children's love by crossing them. But only by helping children curb their impulses, and by guiding them to better uses of their energies, can parents gain that love. Children have a right to be heard—but we can be authoritative without being authoritarian.

The family is a unique character-building institution. No other arrangement can take its place because it gets there first, has continuity and works by love—three important advantages in developing responsibility and consideration. In a well-adjusted family, parents don't live *for* their children. They live *with* them, happily interdependent, with no one member of the family using power unjustly at the expense of the others.

### REBELLION

**A**ffection, indulgence and humor alike are powerless against the instinct of children to rebel. It is as essential to their minds and wills as exercise to their bodies. If they have no reasons for it they will invent them. It is hard to imagine families limp enough to be always at peace. Wherever there is character there will be conflict. The best that parents and children can hope for is that the wounds of their conflict may not be too deep or too lasting.

—*Carl Van Doren*

### HUSBANDS FIRST

**W**e have been subjected during the last few years to a propaganda barrage emphasizing the child's need to be loved. It is time to restore the balance with equal propaganda for the need of husband and wife to love each other. Children will outgrow much of their need for affection and demonstrativeness—the husbands won't.　　　　　　　　　　　　—*Paul Popenoe*

# What *Not* to Tell a Child About Sex

ARDIS WHITMAN

For several decades "modern" parents have tried to give their children all the facts about sex, honestly and forthrightly, as casually as if they were talking about arithmetic. Has it worked?

It is hard to find evidence that the current generation is a whit wiser in any more profound and meaningful sense than were the generations of the past. Nor have we learned to take care of the very problems that sex information might be expected to solve. Illegitimacy rates have risen markedly in recent years; the number of children found suffering from deep emotional damage is on the increase; innumerable surveys show that young people are desperately uneasy and uncertain about how they should behave with one another.

Can it be, then, that there is something wrong with our basic premise that information is the answer? A number of thoughtful people now believe that this *is* wrong. They believe that while the facts are necessary and important, they are no cure-all, and that we should stop our exclusive concentration on *what* we tell our children about sex, and start paying some attention to *how* we tell them. Troubled by the results of our twentieth-century bluntness, psychologists increasingly emphasize four don'ts for parents.

*Don't tell the story of sex matter-of-factly, as if you were talking about the weather.* Why should we be "scientific" and detached about something that we don't feel in the least detached about ourselves? When we pretend that *we* have no feelings about the subject, what else can our children think but that it's a subject unrelated to feeling? Naturally we find it difficult to talk about sex as if it were nothing special. It *is* special. No subject in the world is more sensitive and more laden with emotion.

*Don't tell children too much too soon.* Children aren't alike. While three-year-old Johnny is plying his mother with questions, it may turn out that Bobby, at the same age, couldn't care less. Moreover, adults are often astonished to discover that the child didn't understand at all what to them seemed so clear. They forget how strange the information is, and how little experience children have with which to receive it. Mrs. Selma Fraiberg, child psychotherapist, has told of a six-year-old boy who planted a package of cucumber seeds beside a telephone pole "so's me and Polly can have a baby next summer." And his parents had been *so* explicit!

But even if the child could understand, would this mean that he should have it all at once? "The modern child is often jaded at fourteen," says the distinguished child psychiatrist Dr. Hilde Bruch. "He knows so much, he has nothing to wait for. Parents should leave a child something to find out, to learn about when the time comes, so that he may have a sense of the miraculous and joyous instead of merely an anxious curiosity."

No doubt it is a good thing to know the human anatomy. No one can deny that we are physical creatures. But we are a great deal more than that. Love between a man and a woman is—and always will be, one hopes—a matter of the heart and spirit, and no chart has been invented which can teach that. Answer your child's questions, but don't use every passing query as a springboard for telling him all you think he will ever need to know. When three-year-old Lucy asks where babies come from, ask her to tell you where *she* thinks they come from. Then you'll be less likely to tangle your fact with her fantasy, and you'll know better how much fact is needed.

*Don't violate your own privacy.* So hectored have parents been by the demand that they be "frank" that many have transgressed their own natural feelings of modesty in the name of sex education. One "enlightened" mother was upset because she didn't feel comfortable when nude in front of her children. A father was disturbed because his four-year-old daughter wanted to watch him at the toilet. He felt he should satisfy her curiosity but admitted that he didn't want to. Many psychiatrists today feel that such "immodest" behavior is unwise and possibly dangerous. Often it arouses a premature erotic interest, and may also produce a serious conflict in the child who senses that his parents aren't behaving naturally. Parents should stop feeling that there ought to be no secrets between themselves and their children.

*Don't think of sex education as a cataloguing of dangers.* To be sure, there *are* warnings that we must give our children. But let's keep them as few as possible, lest we make our children as mistrustful of beauty and tenderness as our Victorian forebears were of the physical aspects of love. Sex is not primarily a pitfall, but one of life's great joys. What fun it seems when we first take a child to see the zoo, or when he first sees snow falling! Couldn't it seem the same when we first tell him about the miracles of birth and love? The truth is that a child may get a better sex education from parents who never once open their mouths on the subject but who clearly love each other and are sensitive to the rights and dignity of others, than from all the textbooks and anatomical information in the world.

A child learns best about sex from parents who love him and each other and are considerate of each other. He learns about it when he is taught to communicate his feelings to those he loves, when he is given the chance to exercise tenderness toward what is small and dependent, when he is taught to respect the reserves and the longings of another person, when he learns that discipline and self-control are part of the search for everything we treasure. A wise old neighbor of mine said once, "Colts and young ones—they learn best in a green field."

We'll be wise to give our children more of the green fields of life, fewer of its clinical facts. We'll be wise to let them approach the wonder of sex gradually, for the best things in life always come to meet us little by little, as we grow in wisdom to understand them.

*I* would rather have all the risks from free discussion of sex than the greater risk run by a conspiracy of silence.

—*Dr. Cosmo Gordon Lang*

## "WHERE, MOMMY?"

*T*he modern child quizzed her mother as to her own origin, and was given the traditional answer: "God sent you."

"And how did you get here, Mother, did God send you, too?" "Yes, dear." "And grandma?" "Yes, dear." "And great-grandma?" "Yes, dear." "Do you mean to say, Mother, that there have been no sex relations in this family for over two hundred years?"

—*Mary Ware Dennett*

*I*f an inquiring child is put off with a lie, the parent loses a certain degree of respect. —*Lee Alexander Stone, M.D.*

# Do You Overwhelm Your Kids?

DANNY KAYE

**H**ow many parents, I wonder, have had to learn the hard way, as I did, how delicate the relationship is between an adult and a child, and how easy it is to distort it? Like so many other children, my daughter Dena is growing up in a family where her father is frequently away from home; and, like so many other fathers, I tried to make my homecomings compensate for these separations. I'd arrive with joyous shouts and a suitcase full of presents, sweep Dena into my arms and smother her with plans for the next day, the next week. I'd hug her close, trying to make up for the lost time, the missed love. But my exuberance just didn't seem to be contagious: at each reunion she responded less. And I didn't know what to do about it.

Then in the spring of 1954, when Dena was seven, I was faced with a protracted absence from home. A U.N. official had said to me, "We're trying to help some children grow up instead of dying at the age of eight or ten, and we'd like you to give us a hand." He asked me to tour the medical and nutritional stations maintained by the United Nations Children's Fund and the World Health Organization, and with a camera crew shoot a color film to be titled *Assignment—Children*.

I delayed telling Dena about the trip as long as I could. Then suddenly at bedtime on a Sunday evening she looked me in the eyes and said solemnly, "You're going away."

"Well . . ." I said. "Yes." While I had stalled and

searched for the best way of breaking the news, she had seen the truth and spoken it. "When?" she asked gravely.

"Not for a whole week. And we'll have a ball during that time. A beach party every day, if you'd like. How about it?" "All right," she said, but without enthusiasm. Dena had already gone away from me.

We opened our tour by joining a mobile U.N. vaccination unit in India, traveling from one small village to another. The children were naturally awed and frightened when we arrived with our needles, and my job was to win their friendship and confidence. For me to be introduced to them as a movie star was obviously ridiculous. These children didn't know what a movie was. If I exploded upon them with a big fanfare, they'd only see a bigmouthed redhead who made a lot of noise in a foreign language and invaded the great sense of privacy all children have.

I quickly learned to move in quietly, letting them come to me. I'd wander through a village and sit down on the ground some place, certain that curiosity would eventually lead the children to me. When they got close enough I'd make a funny face and there'd be giggles. Soon someone would make a funny face back and we'd have a fine contest going, with everyone laughing and relaxed. Then I'd clap hands and start a follow-the-leader game that took us down lanes and around the pagodas, to end up before the doctors. The children submitted to the injections, comforted because they saw in me a reflection of themselves. Thus the adult world was suddenly not quite so overwhelming.

I remembered this lesson when I went to entertain patients in the children's ward in Mysore Province in south-central India. It was a day when the very land seemed fevered. Twenty iron cots lined the walls of a stifling room, and at the far end was an upright piano. The children paid no particular attention to me as I walked down the aisle between the beds, nor did I to them. Standing beside the piano and tapping the beat out lightly, I hummed a song to myself. A couple of little boys glanced at me curiously, then turned back to the beads they were stringing.

My accompanist whispered to me, "Belt one out! Wake 'em up!" I shook my head. "Give me 'Blue Skies,' real easy."

This time I sang the lyrics instead of humming, but quietly, again as if to myself. Several children were gravely watching me now, and by the time I had started the third song a few of the more venturesome had climbed out of bed and come over to the piano. When I finished the song we stared at each other for a moment of dignified silence; then I made a face and they laughed. It was that laughter that brought every child in the room to attention and soon into the party. *Their* laughter made us friends, not mine. They came to me, and on their own terms.

But somehow I didn't see how this lesson applied to my relationship with Dena. Not until I witnessed little Kirim and his parents, and their ordeal in a primitive hospital in central India. Kirim was delicate boy of five, brought in for surgery. He was given an anesthetic, operated on and placed in a crib to regain consciousness. Throughout the entire procedure his parents stood reassuringly close by, where, until the anesthetic took over, he could see their calm dignity, their outward appearance of serenity.

I was nearby when Kirim finally opened his eyes after the operation. If I'd been his father I'd probably have joked and laughed and tried to make the boy smile. But as I watched the boy look up at the familiar and loved faces of his father and mother, I suddenly realized how wrong I would have been—how deep was their wisdom. They spoke his name and touched his hand, but gave no display of their own concern and emotion. During the following hours they talked only when Kirim wished to talk, laughed only when he did, were silent when he was silent. They let *him* decide how much attention he needed, how much love he wanted displayed, and when. They were a great reservoir of strength he could dip into at will.

After my tour had covered 40,000 miles, I turned at last homeward. Through my memory ran an endless parade of little faces, black ones, brown ones, tan and yellow and golden ones. Now I wanted only to see one small pink and white face. As I stepped from the plane, my wife and daughter greeted me with the reserve that comes from a long separation. I kissed them warmly—but quietly—and the three of us left the field hand in hand. I wanted so to walk doubled over with my face thrust against Dena's, forcing upon her my attention, my love, my accumulated sense of loss. I wanted to hold her tight, to squeeze out of her the admission that she had missed me. . . . I wanted it all now, this instant!

But at last I knew better. She would take her own time before accepting me again as part of her life. Usually it required about a week, and the more I bounded at her, I realized now, the slower it would be.

During the drive from the airport Dena's mother and I talked casually about things that had happened at home during my absence. Intuitively my wife understood what I was doing, and together we tried to emphasize not the interruption in our lives but the continuity. We talked as if I had gone away only yesterday. Dena participated in the conversation, but tentatively, cautiously.

At home we had supper on the terrace and were sitting

quietly over coffee when Dena suddenly threw her arms in the air and cried, "How about a beach party tomorrow?"

"Hey!" I cried in response. "How about that!" I opened my arms to catch her as she launched herself at my neck. It had been but three hours since my plane landed.

Since that day I have tried never to drive my daughter from me by overwhelming her with my own moods. And I've learned that this principle doesn't just apply to long separations. Even coming home each evening after the day's work like so many other fathers—I return with some calmness, holding my emotions in reserve to see what her needs may be. I try to be her reservoir of strength. Someday, when she's older, I'll tell my daughter why her father changed. Then she will understand what we owe to Kirim and his parents.

### THEIR OWN LIVES

God knows that a mother needs fortitude and courage and tolerance and flexibility and patience and firmness and nearly every other brave aspect of the human soul. But because I happen to be a parent of almost fiercely maternal nature, I praise *casualness*. It seems to me the rarest of virtues. It is useful enough when children are small. It is important to the point of necessity when they are adolescents. The young on their way to maturity long for privacy, physical and spiritual. They resent being too well understood, and they abhor having their emotions dragged into the light. Mothers who can forbear to pry and question, who have the self-possession to let children weather their own storms, who, above all, respect confidences but do not demand them, will find those same confidences being given without demand. And their children will be stronger persons. Or so one hopes.

—*Phyllis McGinley*

# Teaching Your Child Religion

HARRY EMERSON FOSDICK

he religious training of a child inevitably begins in the home the day the child is born. A child reared in fear under parents who rely on fright to achieve order will be predisposed to be afraid of any God in whom he may believe. Another child, reared in an atmosphere of trust, will find the love of God a congenial idea.

Whether a child shall grow up to regard life with suspicion or with confidence, to be deceitful or straightforward, contentious and grasping or coöperative and loyal—these and other basic characteristics are early determined by the treatment he receives, and obviously they enter into the essential quality of his spiritual life in general and of his religion in particular. When parents, therefore, say that they are not teaching religion to their children, they are deceiving themselves. They cannot help teaching religion.

A further truth becomes evident as the growing child passes out of infancy into youth: Religion is imitated rather than learned. In the long run no teaching of religion in a home matters except that which expresses the way of living that the home practices. In a family where generosity reigns, where differences between Jew and Gentile, Protestant and Catholic, white and colored, rich and poor, learned and ignorant are lines across which appreciation and goodwill run freely, in both word and action, religious teaching will be the elucidation of a kind of life visible to the child's eyes. It will be readily assimilated, and it will sink deep.

This same truth holds about the more intimate matter of teaching children to pray. Of course, the real way is not to teach them to pray at all, but to pray with them. Parents should also see that prayer soon becomes a matter from which they should keep hands off, trusting that the child will know by observation the value of prayer to people whom he himself has loved and admired. Religion is something that only secondarily can be taught. It must primarily be absorbed. Only when religious teaching is an outward explanation of what is first of all an inward and experienced way of living, does it carry through.

After these two initial stages have been passed, in which the child's basic emotional reactions have been set and his family's religion or irreligion absorbed, there is sure to come the period of conscious questioning. Many parents are upset and distressed by this. They have taken it for granted that they had the right to hand on to the child their own religion. It is often difficult to persuade them that the rise of impatient and even distracted questioning is a sign of intellectual life, and is to be expected.

Robert Browning, as he himself says, was "passionately religious" when he was a boy, and he certainly was nobly and undiscourageably religious when he was a man, but in between came the upset when he questioned everything and called himself an atheist. This must have been a very disturbing phase for Browning's parents. But Browning was finding that in religion Goethe's words are especially true: "What you have inherited from your fathers you must earn for yourself before you can really call it yours."

The attitudes of parents toward this fact are interestingly diverse. Some are so much impressed by it that they feel all definite teaching of religion to their children to be impertinent intrusion; and they try to keep the child's mind neutral until, coming of age, he can choose for himself. The attempt is uniformly unsuccessful. The child's mind never stays neutral. From primitive and inescapable questions— such as who made the world or what happens when our friends die, to curiosity about habits of worship—the child's mind is bound to take a religious bent one way or another. Parents cannot put off their responsibility in this matter.

Some parents go to the opposite extreme. They endeavor so to indoctrinate the child's mind with their own conceptions of religion that he never can escape them. Often fear is powerfully employed in this class of teaching, and I find grown people still laboring under an ingrained dread of thinking for themselves. In this way children are taught to associate doubt with sin, questioning with treachery against God, and so the child's mind is bound hand and foot to start with, forestalling the first motions in the direction of religious independence. Wise parents will, I think, adopt neither the policy of neutrality nor that of dogmatic dragooning. Instead, two major considerations will control their method and behavior.

First, they will take it for granted that the child's religion must be his own; that he will in all probability come to the time when he will question what he has been taught, will rethink it, will alike retain, reject and adjust it, and that no parent should wish him not to. In view of this, the parent will desire above all else to teach the child from the beginning as little as possible that he will need to unlearn.

The way parents lie to their children in matters of religion is to me a constant and shocking astonishment. Here is a mother who tells me that in answer to her four-year-old's question as to where God is she has said, "In heaven"; and in reply to the further inquiry as to where heaven is she has said, "In the sky." This mother has now waked up to the fact that these heedless answers were downright falsehoods. She did not believe what she said. And she did not, apparently, comprehend that teaching the child an idea of God set in such an incredible framework of imagination was the surest way to have that child say someday that she did not believe in God.

The New Testament says that God is love; that where love is, God is also, dwelling in those who are lovers of their fellows; that God is spirit, surrounding and interpenetrating us so that He lives in us and we live in Him. Some parents seem to think such an idea of God too rarefied to be taught to children. On the contrary, it is adults who commonly are too crass to understand it, while children can grasp it more easily than they can any other. Most parents condescend to their children when they talk about religion. They never need to do so.

The second item in a wise parent's program logically follows: When questions begin to come, the parent will deal with them honestly. If he knows the answer, he will give it as he sees it. If he does not know the answer, he will say so. In any case he will scrupulously tell the truth. This advice may seem superfluous. The fact is, however, that many parents shamelessly tell falsehoods about all the deepest matters of life, from camouflaging the facts about sex to doling out sophistries about the Bible. An honest agnostic who takes his son into his confidence, talks over with him the solemn problem of life as if they two were intellectual comrades facing an elemental mystery and trying together to see some sense in it, will have a much better spiritual result than a believer who dodges the real questions, assumes certainty he does not

131

feel, gives answers he himself does not understand and, in general, pretends.

We have been dealing with the religious training of children within the home, but it is an unhappy home that must solve the problem without the coöperation of the church. Religion is both individual and social. It is an inward, mystical experience, but if it is wholesome it overflows in fellowship. No man can be completely religious all alone.

The tendency in many American homes today is to neglect those factors in religious training for which the church chiefly stands. In doing so they overlook an educational factor which psychologists are constantly emphasizing: Children learn by doing. Telling a little child a truth is the worst way to teach it to him. Let the child, if possible, do something that involves the lesson; let him act as though it were true. The popular undervaluing of outward religious acts is thus thoroughly bad psychology. Granted that ritual in worship can become formal, empty and stiff. Nevertheless, with all its dangers it is an absolute necessity. We cannot train children in the spirit of religion if the appropriate activities of worship and devotion are forgotten. This truth especially applies to the rearing of a child. Let him be trained as early as possible not only in ethical behavior but symbolic behavior, such as bowing in thanks before meals, kneeling at family prayers, joining in the worship of the church.

To be sure, all this can quite easily be made dry as dust. Some churches and some ministers are murderers, not makers, of beauty in worship, and render repellent what should attract the soul toward God. Happy the homes where, as in some families I know, being made to stay home from church is one of the most dreaded punishments in the parents' entire arsenal.

# The Dangerous Pressures on Childhood

NORMAN M. LOBSENZ

When I was a boy most parents asked little more of their children than that they be "good" or "well behaved." Anything beyond that, such as high marks in school or being elected to head a team or a club, was a bonus. Today's children, however, are under pressure to be smart, to be popular, to be star athletes if they are boys or the *femmes fatales* of dancing school if they are girls. To achieve these successes, young people—and I am talking specifically about grade-schoolers, from about six to fourteen years of age—are expected to work hard, to compete. Given grown-up goals, they are urged to think and act like grown-ups. In short, these children are being prematurely forced into a world of adult pressures and responsibilities.

Education is one of the major areas where special pressure is placed on our children. Teachers and guidance counselors tell grim tales about ambitious parents who want their children driven hard in school, demanding more homework for them, advanced classes in science and language. Others place a heavy emphasis on their youngsters' marks even in the early grades. One mother descended upon a school principal in a fury because her third-grader got an "unsatisfactory" in art. "Don't you realize this record will go along with her all the way to college?" the woman said.

Some parents simply cannot wait to get their children started in school. In many school districts a child must be five years old to enter kindergarten; but often a youngster will turn five shortly after the deadline or "cutoff" date. "The mothers of those children put incredible pressure on us to register them before they are five," one principal told me. "I tell them that a child of that age who is even a few months younger than most of his classmates may not yet be up to the others in learning capacity, and thus be made to feel that he is 'dumb.' By waiting, a parent can give his youngster the chance to make a habit of success rather than failure. But all the parents can think of is that the child is 'losing a year.'"

Children become infected with the parental anxiety. Sixth-graders cram for routine tests as if a Rhodes scholarship were at stake. Not long ago three youngsters were caught changing marks on their report cards. Not one of them was failing; they were changing B minuses to B pluses. And a guidance counselor in a *junior* high school reported that the day after a local newspaper printed a list of the fifty colleges rated academically top in the nation, dozens of boys and girls came to him with the list, asking how soon they should apply for admission.

Childhood is traditionally supposed to be a time when one guiltlessly can—and should—go out and do nothing. Yet today's young-old child is often busy from morning till night with club meetings, athletic practice, tutoring, trips to theaters, museums and similar places where he can absorb adult culture, and a multitude of lessons of various kinds— tennis, swimming, bowling, art, horseback riding. My eight-year-old son recently asked a friend of his to come and play after school. The boy pulled out a datebook. "I have swimming class this afternoon," he said. "Tomorrow is piano. But I'm free on Friday, if you are."

Thus childhood's special sense of time, in which minutes

often seem like hours, is forced to yield to the clockwork of pseudo-adult life. Yet, according to psychotherapist Dr. Victor Balaban: "Most of the activities children are involved in lack a sense of need or reason. Many a youngster has real interests that he cannot follow because he is too busy with things he doesn't care about."

Children are under equal pressure to "succeed" on a social level. Parties, dancing and dating begin early in some neighborhoods; sometimes little girls of ten and eleven cry themselves to sleep because they are wallflowers at class dances. For boys, popularity is linked to the number of activities they're in, or to athletic ability. A thirteen-year-old whose father wanted him to be a football star was made to practice every evening for an hour; he was not allowed to play for fun with his friends because, said the father, "he'll pick up bad ball-handling habits."

This substitution of forced growth for natural growth in school, social life and other activities is not a phenomenon limited to middle-class families in suburban areas. Children of all economic and social strata are beginning to feel these pressures in varying degrees. "What were once 'middle-class' aspirations," says Alfred D. Buchmueller, executive director of the Child Study Association, "are now the aspirations of most American families."

It is not surprising that children who live miniature replicas of grown-up lives also undergo grown-up stresses. Counseling services report increasing numbers of emotionally upset children, and that the incidence of physical "stress ailments" among youngsters—ulcers, for example—is on the rise. Specialists in asthma have long known that the illness is psychosomatic for most youngsters—the result of emotional tensions. According to Dr. Robert P. Morris, writing in *The Annals of Allergy,* the mother of an asthmatic child is usually "overambitious for him, and wants him to become an achieving little adult early in order to gratify her own needs."

It is true to some extent, say the experts, that children have to learn to live under pressure. But it is important to differentiate between what is necessary and what is not. "There are certain normal, inherent pressures that every child must meet," says Sanford Sherman, associate executive director of New York's Jewish Family Service. "He must learn to get to school on time, to develop decent table manners, to get along with others. These are all within a child's capacity at one stage of growth or another. But it is when we place him under abnormal pressures—to be brilliant beyond his capabilities, to be a leader when he is not ready for leadership—that he is going to have difficulties."

Some parents ask a child to compete with an impossible ideal. "We don't want him merely to be better than the kid next door," says Sanford Sherman. "We want him to be as smart as the kid next door, as handsome as the one across the street, as athletic as the fellow down the block, as poised as the boy around the corner. We expect him to be the All-American Boy. As a result, the youngster develops both a need to compete and, simultaneously, the feeling that it is hopeless."

Children learn early that success wins acclaim and failure invites reproach. The child who cannot constantly measure up to his parents' expectations rapidly begins to lose his self-confidence, to lose the feelings of self-worth that enable a mature adult to face life with vigor. A parent should encourage his child to accept competition as a fact of life, but only gradually, as the child gains strength to stand up under it.

Although there is no set of rules by which parents can cope with the forces pushing their children prematurely into an adult world, there are a few commonsense guides:

Try to differentiate between the normal pressures that should be placed on children and the excessive pressures that may be only a reflection of inflated parental ambitions.

Make an effort to resist unhealthy community pressure on children to be competitive, successful, conformist. "Many people do not fight these pressures because they think they are alone in opposing them," says Dr. Balaban. Parent-teacher associations and similar groups, if used intelligently as community sounding boards rather than as *kaffee-klatsches,* can help to curtail unhealthy pressures.

Find out exactly how many demands are being made on your child's time, and if he's overburdened help him cut down or cut free. Mrs. Clifford Jenkins, former president of the National Congress of Parents and Teachers, told me, "Ten years ago I suggested that if parents stopped to make a list of their children's activities, they'd realize how little time the youngsters have to themselves for daydreaming, casual play, reading for pleasure, or just to be part of the family. Today the time squeeze has tightened."

Think in terms of long-range goals for children, rather than being overconcerned with the here-and-now achievements. A parent should be aware of the potential within his child—of what he can accomplish in the future in his own way, in his own good time. By the same token, however, it's important not to hold out long-range goals to a child as the be-all and end-all. Children are not emotionally mature enough to plan for a distant future. You cannot expect a grade-schooler to set his sights on college, on a career or on marriage.

Most important, a child must know that he is loved for himself, even if he fails or does not compete at all. The paradox is that the youngster pressured to achieve a form of maturity in childhood may end as an adult failure, but the youngster who is given love and understanding without this pressure gains the kind of emotional security that will help to make him a successful adult.

In short, a child will grow up in inverse ratio to the amount of undue pressure exerted upon him to do so. Instead of rushing him into a synthetic adulthood long before he is ready, we must give him time and freedom to develop according to his own pace and abilities. We must get used to seeing him as a person in his own right, rather than as an appendage of ourselves to be used for our own satisfactions. We must give him back his childhood.

### PAR FOR THE COURSE

*A* week before school opened, I walked the route my first-grader son would take to school. I walked slowly and it figured out twenty minutes. But when he walked it alone, he was ten minutes late the first two days of school. Puzzled, I walked with him the third day. The twenty minutes was all right, as far as it went. But I'd failed to consider such side trips as:

Tracking down a trail of ants from a sidewalk into a lot.

Critical inspection of a display of trinkets and bicycles in a store window.

An educational pause to watch a man change a tire.

Swing around half a dozen phone poles.

Friendly overtures to three stray dogs and one brown cat.

In short, I had forgotten I was six years old once myself.

*—San Diego Tribune*

# Chapter 6/The Tides of Spring—Adolescence

*They live in a new world between childhood and
adulthood, now facing one way, now the other, not sure
of which way they want to go, not really sure of
anything. Each one is a paradox: sometimes awkward
but always appealing, shy but also brash, stubborn yet
reasonable, reckless and cautious, loving and resentful,
foolish and wise.*

*They are conservatives because something in them
dreads being different. They are rebels because
something in them knows that each generation must
break away from the one that precedes it. They study,
and their minds leap far ahead of their emotions.
They think, and their emotions color everything.
We don't even have a good word to describe them.
"Adolescent" is clumsy and cold. "Teen-ager" is too
often a term of reproach. They are a trial to us at times,
but a wonderful trial. They are our children.
They are the unfolding future. Above all, they are people.*

## Plain Facts About Adolescence
PETER BLOS

**E**arly in the second decade
of life, every boy and girl enters the stage of sexual maturation—adolescence. The physical changes in the body have a
profound effect on the total personality—emotionally, intel-
lectually and spiritually. Adolescence is a time when child-

hood dependencies and ways of life are abandoned, more or less for good. This cannot be achieved without conflict and confused feelings—moodiness, loneliness, self-doubt. Each adolescent must begin to find his own identity, his own place in relation to work, to citizenship, to his spiritual and moral commitments. Each must learn the intimacies of loving and being loved in preparation for the adult role of husband or wife, father or mother. It takes years for this transition to adulthood to approach a degree of stability.

Adolescence makes its appearance gradually. Between the ages of nine and twelve—the period of preadolescence—the child loses some of the charm and tractability of childhood; he begins to gripe about accustomed routines at home, to resist rules and challenge regulations. His language and habits become sloppy. His attention and concentration suffer; his homework becomes an ordeal. In every way preadolescents and parents get on each other's nerves.

The child at this age is at war with time. He never begins anything soon enough and refuses to accept help in planning. Boys enter the "gang" stage, are full of adventurous play and fantasy, become secretive about life outside the home. They avoid girls and prefer to play among themselves. Girls behave either as tomboys or as "little women," eagerly engaged in teasing the opposite sex. It is the function of adolescence to bring order and direction into these fitful beginnings of "growing up." Puberty, the period at which sexual maturity is reached, begins with hormonal changes in the reproductive system; these in turn initiate secondary changes. Boys develop facial hair and change of voice; girls show a rounding out of the hips and growth of the breasts.

The adolescent swings rapidly from independence to dependence and back; he is fearful one day, overconfident the next; he is moody, oversensitive, never quite sure what he wants, apparently wanting quite opposite and irreconcilable things. At about fourteen or fifteen another change appears. The child is still unstable, moody, unpredictable, battling with adult authority and with himself—yet in many ways he is more grown up. His interest in the opposite sex has been awakened and is openly expressed.

At this stage the growing child can be as meticulous about his appearance and manners as he was careless a few years before; he is considerably more responsible; he may throw himself into work with new vigor and direction. He still lapses into introspection and uses childish patterns of problem-solving—bragging, swaggering, sulking—but he is making an attempt to solve his problems on a more mature level.

Because the adolescent is deeply engaged in a struggle for emotional emancipation from his parents, their help is resisted rather than sought. Often a teacher or other adult serves as the adolescent's model. With the advent of sexual maturation, the young person's love needs are directed away from his family to members of the opposite sex outside. The fact that the adolescent begins to withdraw his affection from the persons closest to him makes him lonely and intensely self-centered. During this period sexual expression is normal, and adolescents usually engage in sexual experimentation in some form. Necking, petting, sex play are common. Masturbation among boys is almost universal before adult sexuality is established. (The alleged physical consequences of masturbation we used to hear about—such as sterility or idiocy—are now fully disproved by medical science as complete myths.)

Through experimentation the adolescent discovers his own powers and emotions, his own capacities, interests and desires. Gradually he arrives at a self-chosen code of conduct and morals. It is a paradox that the moral personality which eventually emerges after adolescence often bears a close resemblance to the idols of the past—the parents—which the adolescent seemed so determined to discard and disown. Young people hope to discover utopia, a world better than the one they inherited from their elders. If they cannot create it and sustain their idealism and hopes, then they may try to wrench adult privileges from the older generation by force. They rush ahead disregarding obstacles, yet they are easily discouraged by the magnitude of the struggle toward maturity. Great optimism and pessimism alternate; these swings of mood result in an extreme show of independence, of apparent cynicism, opportunism or callous antiemotionalism. An understanding adult is the only safe bridge for an adolescent as he moves from childhood to adulthood.

The loving parent desires to spare his child the anguish and errors of his own youth. But this is possible to only a limited degree. We cannot protect our children from the exigencies of their own lives and their own growth. Life starts anew with each generation; and life's lessons must be learned anew by each person, in his own way and through his own experience. An adolescent thus has to make many wrong decisions in order to learn. If allowed to do this in minor situations (which jacket or dress to wear to school, at what time to cut the lawn), more important demonstrations of rebelliousness may be avoided.

But no matter how much care is exercised, clashes between the generations are inevitable. The challenge of adolescence to parental authority can be resolved only by a sincere respect for differences and the need for compromise. Adolescence is a profound learning experience for both parent and child. A parent should realize that, since his own youth, changes have taken place in the dating code, clothing styles, party styles, recreation and language patterns.

However the adolescent behaves, he still very much needs his parents. More than anything else, the adolescent *needs his parents' trust in his essential goodness*. And the parent still bears the responsibility for his adolescent child.

⇀◆↽

### ASK NO RETURN

*N*o one has a right to say to another: "Because we belong to each other as we do, I have a right to know all your thoughts." Not even a mother may treat her child in that way. All demands of this sort are foolish and unwholesome. In this matter, giving is the only valuable process; it is only giving that stimulates. Impart as much as you can of your spiritual being to those who are on the road with you, and accept as something precious what comes back to you from them. —*Albert Schweitzer*

### THE CHANGEOVER

*T*he point at which your child becomes an adult is a marvelous and miraculous thing. One day you are battling over everything, you feel the scornful lift of the eyelid, the dreadful arrogance of adolescence. Suddenly it changes. You find yourself at ease, talking together as two who have a basic love for each other. The stress and strain are gone, there is comradeship, new and strange and fine. It is an experience as lovely as the first white tulip in the spring. —*Gladys Taber and Barbara Webster*

*A*merican youngsters tend to live as if adolescence were a last fling at life, not a preparation for it. —*Time*

# Conduct Code for Teen-Agers

JEAN LIBMAN BLOCK

**J**udge Theodore Knudson's fifteen-year-old daughter Kay invited sixty classmates to a party after the season's big basketball game. Sixty arrived, but that was only the beginning: by 11:30 more than two hundred teen-agers, many of them strangers to the hostess, were dancing, playing records, milling through the house. The judge and his wife ran relays from the kitchen to the recreation room to keep the uninvited kids supplied with soft drinks and snacks. When the judge got up next morning he was even more displeased. For daylight revealed a carton of empty beer cans in the driveway. And nearby lawns turned up a basketload of beer cans and an empty fifth of vodka.

The neighbors weren't surprised. Their children had had troubles at parties of their own. One neighbor told how teen-age crashers had broken into his liquor cabinet. Another told of a car "borrowed" and wrecked by teen-agers in a nearby community. Still another had been shocked when a group of fourteen-year-olds refused to go home until 1:30.

Such skirmishes between parents and children had been on the increase in the pleasant suburban community of St. Louis Park, Minnesota. For the past few years things have been different. Party-crashing and adolescent drinking have diminished. Youngsters are saying to parents, "Expect me home about eleven. I'll call if I'm delayed." This astonishing truce went into effect in the fall of 1956, when St. Louis Park became the first city in the state to adopt the Minnesota

Teen-Age Code. The code—unique in that it is statewide—is a guide to help parents and teen-agers find their way through the stormy growing-up years. Judge Knudson, as chairman of the Governor's Advisory Council on Children and Youth, sparked the movement.

The code opens with this basic rule: "Parents should know where their sons and daughters are while away from home, what they are doing and with whom they are spending their time." In two sections, one for junior-high and the other for senior-high age levels, it covers such controversial ground as parties—to be held at home if possible; party-crashing—outlawed; use of car—based on mutual agreement; sensible hours; appropriate dress; respect for the rights and property of others; smoking—forbidden by law under eighteen; and drinking—illegal under twenty-one.

The rules, in rough form, were drawn up from many community codes by the Youth Conservation Commission, a state agency concerned largely with the prevention of delinquency, and submitted in May 1956 to 370 youngsters from all parts of the state attending a conference of the Governor's Advisory Council on Children and Youth. They tore the code apart and took it home to discuss with their families and friends. Their comments, mailed to the commission, indicated overwhelming teen-age support for a code.

Most surprising was the number of youngsters who proposed *tightening* code provisions. "Is there a state law to prosecute parents who make alcoholic beverages available to minors?" a girl from Faribault demanded. There is such a law, and the code now warns irresponsible adults that they may be charged criminally for serving alcohol to other people's children. Revised by the youngsters, the code was next checked over by the three hundred adult members of the

Governor's Advisory Council. Then copies were mailed to every PTA president, school superintendent and student-council president in the state. Adults and teen-agers in each town were urged to study the code, talk it over, change it, reject or adopt it as they saw fit.

Key provisions of the Minnesota code were the following:

A parent, or some other responsible adult, should be at home when teen-agers entertain, but should allow the youngsters a sensible measure of privacy.

"Lights out" games have no place in a well-ordered party.

Young people and their parents should agree in advance on a definite time for getting home from dates.

Young people should come directly home from an evening out unless other plans have been approved by parents.

Parental consent for the privilege of driving should be based on: (1) possession of a driver's license; (2) young people's proof of ability to control themselves and the car.

Riders have a share in the responsibility for safe driving. Dares from riders have been responsible for many deaths.

Young people should understand that it is not a disgrace to decline an alcoholic drink.

Suggested times for terminating social affairs on non-school nights range from ten o'clock for the seventh-grade age level to one o'clock for high-school junior and senior formal dances.

Since 1956 more than 50,000 copies of the code have been mailed out to interested groups in almost every state of the Union, and to other countries as well. Wherever the code is up for consideration, unprecedented crowds turn out. "In many places," says Dr. Hyman Lippman, St. Paul psychiatrist, "parents and young people are getting together for the first time to find out what each expects of the other."

In St. Paul the Women's Institute took the initiative in making the entire city code-conscious, blanketing it with 40,000 copies and getting radio disk jockeys to read excerpts on their programs. "My husband is overseas, and I was having a hard time with my fourteen-year-old daughter," a mother told me. "But now, with the code posted in the kitchen, whenever a touchy question comes up we both say, 'Let's look at the code.'" "I never before had a convincing answer for the familiar 'everybody's-doing-it' argument," a Duluth father declared. "But from the code I've learned that everybody is *not* doing what my youngsters say they are; I can put my foot down."

Minnesota does not claim to have found an easy answer to the teen-age puzzle. The code won't reach the grossly negligent parent; neither will it make a civilized gentleman of a confirmed rowdy. But, as Orville L. Freeman (Minnesota's governor when the code was drawn up) put it, "The code is a constructive action toward solving many of the problems facing young people and their parents today."

### THE PROTECTIVE "NO"

*T*een-agers often are relieved when their parents say, "No!" Although they put up a big show of wanting more freedom, they are comfortable in the knowledge that strong, supportive arms surround them. They want protection against their own impulsiveness and foolishness. I learned this when our daughter, a high-school freshman, presented a fervent and well-rehearsed plea to fly to a university dance. The answer was a flat, "No—you're not ready for such a trip." To my surprise she responded, "I don't think so either, but I just thought I'd try."

—*Ann Landers*

# Let's Allow Our Teen-Agers to Work

WILLIAM G. LONG

In a twenty-two-year period as a judge I heard 50,000 cases involving boys and girls picked up for everything from playing hooky to murder. To my sorrow, many more boys and girls were being brought in during recent years than when I first took office. I have had a chance to study their situations, and I think I have discovered one reason behind their behavior that may also contain an antidote. I have yet to see a really serious offender whose trouble was not caused to a large extent by *idleness*. On the other hand, I have seen many whose lives were salvaged through plain, old-fashioned work.

It is my considered judgment, therefore, that most young people who get into tangles with the law today do so because they have nothing else to do. Laborsaving devices in the home have made family "chores" for youngsters largely a thing of the past. And antiquated, so-called "child-labor" laws make it difficult, if not impossible, for the average youngster under eighteen to take a useful job. Thus, many adolescents are forced into idleness.

Our child-labor laws were originally enacted to prevent the exploitation of children in sweatshops, factories and mines, and to protect their morals. In times past, unspeakable evil was committed upon childhood, and in certain areas this continues even today. It still is desirable that laws psotect young workers. But times have changed. Technical progress has made many unwholesome child-labor practices unprofitable. The rising level of the civic conscience has created new protective measures outside the law. Our laws have now gone past the point of common sense.

For example, a husky, mechanically inclined sixteen-year-old boy was arrested for "borrowing" an automobile—not to take a joy ride in it, but to dismantle it so that he could find out how it worked. While he was on probation, he tried his best to get a job as a mechanic's helper but was blocked by the law requiring him to be eighteen. So he falsified his age, got the job and is now one of the most successful mechanics in his community. Why should the law make it necessary for a kid to lie in order to get an honest job?

I do not advocate abolition of any law really necessary to protect child welfare. But necessary protective measures need not be so restrictive that they drive youngsters into idleness, mischief and eventually crime. The irony of it is that the very qualities that would contribute to their success as good citizens—energy, love of adventure, ingenuity and capacity for leadership—make adolescents the most effective and dangerous criminals. Some very fine people believe that youngsters can just "play" themselves into happy and constructive citizenship; and so they go all out for *more* playfields, *more* camps, *more* recreational facilities. These things, of course, have real value—up to a point. But we must not overlook the virtue of old-fashioned toil during the habit-forming period of life.

I recall three boys who were at loose ends in our community and were giving all of us officials a pretty bad time. We found a God-fearing, hard-working farmer and his wife who took them in and, with love and understanding, worked and guided those wild kids through high school and on through college to distinguished citizenship. Another youngster, committed to a vocational school, came back later to thank me: "Judge, I learned the printing trade, have joined the union, have my own car without stealing it and am going to be married next month."

I particularly recall a seventeen-year-old boy who had been a veritable one-man crime gang for years. We had exhausted every treatment at our command and finally, in utter defeat, I committed him to a state mental hospital. There he followed his old pattern for several months—rebellious, mean, cruel, bitter. But one day a miracle happened. He was on a farm work gang; the tractor broke down and someone suggested that this kid try his hand at fixing it; he did, and quickly got it started. Now, if any kid on earth were a motor expert, *he* surely was: he had demonstrated many times in my court that he could "hot-wire" a car and start it as fast as I could start one with a switch key. The foreman half facetiously dubbed him "tractor foreman." The kid accepted the new title seriously and was allowed to service the tractor thereafter. His attitude and personality changed completely. In a few months he was paroled. He is now constructively working at his own self-sustaining job—"prognosis good."

Having grown up where and when productive work for youngsters was looked upon with favor, I resent the current philosophy which seems to classify all jobs for kids as potentially dangerous rather than beneficial. The arbitrary requirement that "working papers," proof of birth date and a lot of other time-consuming evidence must be submitted as a prelude to allowing an ambitious boy or girl to perform honorable work strikes me as symptomatic of an underlying concept that there is something inherently questionable in a youngster's having the opportunity to work at all.

Under our Washington state law, no minor under fourteen can work without a permit from a Superior Court judge, even in a business owned and operated by the youngster's own parents—unless that business is covered by State Industrial Insurance. Most work by youngsters under sixteen must be performed between 6 a.m. and 7 p.m., except during summer vacations. Many other states have comparable restrictions. Yet those same kids can go to night baseball games, sit in late movies, attend dances, or squint at horror scenes on television far beyond the curfew hour for any productive work. This puts a premium on idleness. Surely there must be some more sensible method of protecting children from the evils of child labor; and there must be a way to untangle the terrific maze of inconsistent technical details in the many laws which must be correctly interpreted before an employer runs the risk of employing an adolescent without fear of drastic penalties.

Is the state of Washington the only horrible example? By no means. Look at the Walsh-Healy Public Contracts Act. This federal law makes it legal for a boy under sixteen or a girl under eighteen to work for a company supplying materials for the U.S. government if the contract is under $10,000. But if the company should get a contract involving just $10,001, it would have to fire all boys under sixteen and all girls under eighteen, or be an outlaw. What kind of hocus-pocus is that?

I'm glad to say there appears to be nationwide concern over this matter. The New Jersey State Grange some years ago resolved: "Many of the causes of juvenile delinquency can be traced to the inability of a child to find employment between the time he leaves school at the age of sixteen and the age of eighteen, when he is permitted to enter industry."

Philadelphia is continuing a wartime school-work program. Robert C. Tabor, Director of the Division of Pupil Personnel Counseling, testified before the U.S. Senate subcommittee on juvenile delinquency: "The value of the program prompted us to continue it. Not only did it reduce the number of dropouts (from school), but young people found a new sense of importance when they could contribute to the family's resources. They learned initiative and responsibility. Discipline problems all but disappeared."

Iowa City, Iowa, has a community-wide project to provide constructive work for youngsters during school vacation. Berkeley, California, has a plan for organized work and organized recreation aimed at helping fourteen- to seventeen-year-old boys and girls both during the summer vacation months and the school year.

If I were given responsibility for revising our archaic child-labor laws, here is what I would suggest that we do:

Eliminate all unreasonably restrictive laws which require youngsters in their teens to register and obtain working papers before they can take normal jobs.

Let boys and girls, with their parents' consent, accept suitable jobs in any appropriate field. It is ridiculous that young boys can have newspaper routes and deliver groceries by bicycle, but cannot work in newspaper offices or grocery stores.

Unify all state and federal labor laws so that what is a legal job for a youngster in one state is not illegal in another.

There should be agencies and community committees specifically designed to find and develop job opportunities for youngsters who want to work. It is through work, rather than play alone, that young people can avoid the physical and moral flabbiness which comes from idleness, and toughen their spiritual muscles sufficiently to carry the responsibilities of adult citizenship.

# The Perils of Promiscuity

*Condensed from the book: A Woman Doctor Looks at Love and Life*

MARION HILLIARD, M.D.

Adolescent boys seem to have a compelling need to prove their manhood. The means differ in every neighborhood. Sometimes a boy can prove himself by scoring a touchdown while draped with enemy tacklers, sometimes by driving a battered convertible at a speed approaching that of sound. Most of the so-called wildness of youth is the necessity to demonstrate daring in order to satisfy the developing sensual appetite.

The phoniest proof of manhood that can be devised—and some teen-age societies demand it—is the physical act of love. A boy believes he must prove himself by succeeding with the town child-harlot or with some older woman. There is real danger inherent in this. The boy certainly will be awkward, and it is possible that he will fail in this initial attempt. Such failure may frighten him. He may even suffer from impotence afterward—psychological impotence is a demonstrable fact. Parents must help their sons find a more acceptable method of proving themselves.

But parents, who know so well how to administer a boy's allowance, how to regulate his homework, how to get him to remember to tuck in his shirt, are prone to mishandle the problem of his sexual urges. Some parents assume the situation is adequately covered with a curt "don't"—which is disastrously unhelpful. Others carefully explain that a boy and

153

girl have the power to start a life, a power too magnificent to be used casually as a toy. This is better, but it also falls short. Adolescent boys need to know that promiscuity is habit-forming and can make a shambles of their adult lives. Promiscuity is not the indulgence of confident, capable men, but of men who have been defeated. It doesn't attract men of achievement, but men looking for achievement.

Promiscuity destroys, much as a narcotic does, blacking out disappointments and making a man feel nine feet tall—and it has the same hangover the next day, with the disappointments still unsolved and the man even less able to cope with them. The promiscuous man is not oversexed at all; he's undersexed. He's not looking to give something, but to get it.

This desolate pattern can be set in adolescence. A boy must not indulge himself in his youth if he wants to be a coherent, secure adult. He might keep in mind that gluttons don't enjoy the taste of food. An adolescent boy can check on his own incipient gluttony by means of a bit of introspection. When he contemplates his date for the evening, is he considering the reward he will get for his investment? Does he choose her with his mind on getting the most return? This is downright immoral.

A youth should also understand his own biology. Throughout the life-span, the male urge for sex is much stronger than the female. It is the boy who will light the bonfire. The best prevention of burns is to make certain that the location prohibits the fire getting out of hand. A good place for the good-night kiss is on the girl's doorstep; the boy goes home pleasantly tingling. The worst place is a parked car on a lonely road; he may go home full of terror and guilt. A boy must appreciate that the act of love can only be debased, possibly forever, by trying to make it a "manly" achievement.

# Why Driver Education Is a Must

PAUL W. KEARNEY

In today's motorized society, 36 percent of all American youths who die between the ages of fifteen and twenty-four are killed in automobile accidents. This shocking toll—four times higher than that exacted by the worst disease in this age group—indicates an epidemic of major proportions. Nevertheless, the only effective antidote thus far devised—driver education in high schools—is under attack in many communities and has even been abandoned in some.

The attack comes partly from school administrators who regard driver education as a "frill" that interferes with academics, partly from taxpayers who don't want to pay the cost and partly from other citizens who sincerely believe that driver education is largely useless.

For example, a few years ago Los Angeles almost lost the most effective phase of its long-established driver-education program. The standard DE course provides for thirty mandatory hours of group instruction in the classroom, plus a minimum of six elective hours of individual training behind the wheel. The latter is highly essential—and expensive. In 1960, opponents of driver education in Los Angeles mounted a determined campaign against in-traffic training. But after the budget and finance committee voted tentatively to drop the practice program, local citizens and officials requested a special meeting of the Board of Education at which they could express their views. Friends of the program rallied support from safety organizations, city and state police, women's clubs, the PTA and insurance companies. Impressed by the facts presented at the meeting, the board agreed to continue the course for one more year and to make a careful study of its merits. On the strength of this evaluation, completed in 1961, the board voted five to one not only to continue practice-driving but to expand it.

In Pittsburgh, Pennsylvania, the story was sadly different. There, opponents succeeded in keeping driver-education courses out of the schools. Schenectady and White Plains have had controversy over DE, but in these New York cities, fortunately, the programs were retained. In Arizona and Utah, threats to driver education were overcome by public opinion. These are only a few random illustrations of the widespread and continuing resistance to the program—a program which *does* save lives and money.

Perhaps the most meaningful proof of this fact was shown in an Illinois study released in September 1963. Of the young drivers included in the study, 339,944 had had no high-school driving course, while 176,832 were DE graduates. Analysis showed that the untrained youngsters were involved in 493 traffic violations and 111 accidents per thousand drivers. The corresponding figures for the DE group were 171 and 56.

But the most convincing evidence that driver education is effective comes from insurance companies, whose rates are based on case-hardened actuarial experience. As fathers and mothers know, liability rates for their sons are very high. (In many states, girls under 21 are now being added to the group who must pay higher premiums.) Yet virtually all of the leading insurance firms grant discounts of 10 to 15 percent for boys and girls, sixteen through twenty years of age, who have passed a high-school driving course meeting national standards.

The Insurance Information Institute estimates that the students now in public high school who will reach driving age without having taken a standard DE course (currently 61 percent) will pay an extra $343,857,296 in liability premiums in their first five years of driving. And these insurance savings are only part of DE's potential economies.

The National Safety Council estimates that automobile accidents in 1962 cost an average of nearly $700 each, and statistics show that drivers under twenty-five were involved in 5,700,000 of these mishaps. If we could cut this total of youthful accidents by even 10 percent, we would save an added $399 million. And the Illinois study indicates we could do far better than 10 percent if DE were universal.

These savings add up to many times the amount we are now spending on driver education—or would spend even if 100 percent of our high-school students were included in the program. Harder to estimate, but far more important indeed, are the potential savings in young lives, broken bodies and heartaches.

If DE is so effective, why the widespread opposition? Some of the strongest resistance has come from educators who feel that driving courses only add to the already back-breaking load of instruction and activities. They have a point; but the fact is that students and teachers already find time for a whole gamut of nonacademic activities. Why not replace some of these with lifesaving DE?

Regular studies need not suffer. Students from Evanston Township High School, in Illinois, have won a high reputation for scholarship during the past twenty years, yet the school still finds time to give driver education in the classroom to all sophomores each year. A number of cities—Chicago and Los Angeles, for example—schedule some individual training periods for evenings, weekends and even during the summer. Last summer, the demand for DE was so heavy in Oklahoma City that five centers with nineteen teachers were needed to accommodate the twelve hundred students who wanted to take the course. In short, where there's a will there's a way.

A more valid criticism involves the often mediocre preparation of driving teachers. Obviously, the answer to this problem is to improve the quality of instruction rather than to abandon the course, and some of our more alert teacher-training institutions are pointing the way. A first-class job of preparation is now being done by Pennsylvania State University, New York University, Michigan State University, the University of Illinois and others.

New and ingenious mechanical aids are helping to provide better instruction. An exciting device called a driving simulator now makes it possible for one instructor to handle twelve to sixteen students simultaneously in a realistic simulation of actual driving in traffic. During the 1963-64 school year, some four hundred schools employed this device with excellent results. Although a typical classroom installation of twelve simulators costs around $20,000, important economies result. Wichita, Kansas, by investing some $40,-000 in simulators, is now training 1600 students at an annual saving of $21,000.

Moreover, the advantages of the simulator extend far beyond economy. "It's a relief," said one youngster in Los Angeles, "to know that I can make my learning mistakes where they can't hurt anybody. This is real basic training that would be impossible in traffic."

Another innovation which enables the student to familiarize himself with driving problems under safe conditions is the off-street driving range. Here, one instructor, aided by a walkie-talkie or a public-address system, usually handles around ten student-drivers at a time. The driving range is now employed in a number of states.

To ease the financial burden on schools and to encourage wider adoption of DE programs, twenty-four states are now allotting financial aid for this purpose. In a dozen other states, legislation is pending. Interestingly, this money need not come from state educational funds. California, which pays its school districts up to $45 per student, collects the money by adding $2 to every fine of $20, or fraction thereof, for moving traffic violations. Several other states recently have adopted this practice. Others add from 50 cents to $2 to the driver's license fee or to the cost of car licenses, or make a higher charge for license examination.

In the end, doubtless, driver education will be mandatory in all of our high schools. In the meantime, laggard communities will continue to pay a higher toll than necessary both in money and in death on the highways.

❧ ◆ ☙

### SPLIT PERSONALITY

Driving a car is supposed to be a pleasure. In a recent poll, 88 percent of the persons interviewed agreed that it is. But it is a peculiar form of pleasure. In many respects a car fulfills the same function as that drug which the upright Dr. Jekyll took to transform himself into the diabolical Mr. Hyde. The same young man who will wait in line for hours to buy World Series tickets bristles with impatience at every red light he encounters on the highway.

—*Réalités*

# The Values of Young People

*Condensed from the book: Self-Renewal*

JOHN W. GARDNER

**J**acques Barzun of Columbia University tells about the little old lady who complained that "the modern thunderstorm no longer clears the air." It's an attitude that is not confined to little old ladies, or to meteorological subjects. Listen to these melancholy lines:

> To whom can I speak today?
>   The gentle man has perished,
>     The violent man has access to everybody.
> The iniquity that smites the land
>   It has no end.
>     There are no righteous men,
>       The earth is surrendered to criminals.

The writer's nostalgia for an older, gentler, more righteous time strikes us as very modern. But the poem was written by a man contemplating suicide some four thousand years ago, in the time of Egypt's Middle Kingdom!

It is an abiding characteristic of man to believe that the old virtues are disappearing, the old values disintegrating, the old, good, stern ways no longer honored. Many people today seem to think that our morality, our devotion to virtue and justice resemble a reservoir that was filled long ago (vaguely, about the time of our grandfathers) and has been seeping away ever since. But our grandfathers thought that the reservoir had been filled by *their* grandfathers and had seeped away ever since. And their grandfathers thought the same. Why, then, isn't the reservoir empty?

The answer is that the moral order undergoes regeneration as well as decay. Men are always corrupting the old symbols, drifting away from the old truths. But while some are losing their faith, others are achieving new spiritual insights; while some grow slack and hypocritical, others bring a new meaning and vitality to moral striving. And that is how most of us play our role in reshaping our society's values. The Swiss philosopher Amiel said: "Every life is a profession of faith. Every man's conduct is an unspoken sermon that is forever preaching to others."

Young people do not assimilate values by learning words (*truth, justice* and so on) and their definitions. They learn attitudes, habits and ways of judging—in personal transactions with their family or associates. They do not learn ethical principles; they *emulate* ethical (or unethical) people. That is why young people need models of what man at his best can be. Each generation, presented with victories that it did not win for itself, must itself rediscover the meaning of liberty, justice—"the words on the monuments." A generation that has fought for freedom may pass that freedom on to the next generation. But it cannot pass on the intense personal knowledge of what it takes to win freedom.

In some cases young people find that the moral precepts their parents offer are no longer relevant, or are contradicted by the parents' behavior. This is not catastrophic. The first task of moral renewal is to strip hypocrisy from cherished ideals. Young people, with their freshness of vision and rebelliousness of mood, are very well fitted to accomplish that.

One of our most difficult problems is to make it possible for young people to participate in the great tasks of their time. They have found a few constructive outlets recently, notably the Peace Corps, but such opportunities are rare. Nineteenth-century New England lads might be sailing captains in their late teens; but in a complex technological society the stress is on long training and experience. All too often, when we seek to evoke the moral strivings of the adolescent today, the best we can do is to invite him to stand sentinel over a drying reservoir.

Instead, we should be telling young people the grim but bracing truth that it is their task, facing the dilemmas and catastrophes of their own time, to *re-create* the cherished values in their own behavior. We should be telling them that each generation refights the crucial battles and either brings new vitality to the ideals or allows them to decay.

In short, the moral order is not something enshrined in historical documents, or stowed away like the family silver. It is a living, changing thing, and never any better than the generation that holds it in trust. A society is continuously re-created, for good or ill, by its members. This will strike some as burdensome, but it will summon others to greatness.

### THE FREE MAN

*L*iberty isn't a thing you have been given as a present. You can be a free man under a dictatorship. It is sufficient if you struggle against it. He who thinks with his own head is a free man. He who struggles for what he believes to be right is a free man. Even if you live in the freest country in the world and are lazy, callous, apathetic, irresolute, you are not free but a slave, though there be no coercion and no opposition. Liberty is something you have to take for yourself. There is no use begging it from others.

—*Ignazio Silone*

## II

*No man ever lived who did not feel, at times, that he was
condemned to go through life handcuffed to a stranger.
That stranger is himself, the mysterious and unpredictable
companion with whom he must share every thought, every
emotion, every experience. Clearly, then, if this inevitable
partnership is to succeed, a man must know how to live
on good terms with himself, how to manage and control and
sometimes improve himself. "Make it thy business to know
thyself," said Cervantes. "Which," he added, "is the most
difficult lesson in the world."*

# HOW
# TO LIVE
# WITH
# YOURSELF

# Chapter 7/Awareness—the Greatest Gift

*A stupendous Creation surrounds us*
*—infinite form, infinite variety, infinite beauty.*
*The more intense our awareness of this vast Complexity,*
*the more alive we are.*
*Here six eloquent apostles of awareness*
*plead with us not to let our senses grow dim or our*
*minds dull and unresponsive to the miracles that*
*surround us.*
*"Open your eyes and your hearts," they cry, "for the*
*more points at which you touch Reality, the more*
*fulfilled you will be!"*

## Stop, Look and *See!*
**JOHN KORD LAGEMANN**

Helen Keller was once asked what she thought was the worst calamity that could befall a person. She replied, "To have eyes and fail to see." I thought of her words a while ago when I watched a TV program in which photographer Ernst Haas demonstrated some techniques used by artists for seeing, for making the world more visible. One device is simply "framing." The world is too big to take in all at once. To make sense and beauty of it we have to look at small parts of it selectively, shutting the rest out, much as a photographer does when he peers through his viewfinder. In short, frame it.

I visited Ernst Haas at his studio and looked at the pictures on his walls. They included strikingly dramatic forms, patterns, compositions, found in the most commonplace subjects—and many of them had been taken while the photographer was walking at random through the streets of New York City. "No matter where you go, you are surrounded by pictures," he told me. "The trick is to recognize them. Look." He crumpled a large sheet of wrapping paper and threw it on the floor. I saw only a formless mass. But then Haas moved a frame over it—a piece of black cardboard with a rectangular opening—and I began to see interesting patterns of light and shade which had escaped me before.

We stepped outside into the city street. At first I saw nothing of note. But when I used the cardboard frame, pictures leaped to the eye. A dribble of paint on the pavement made a striking free-form design. I framed another picture, one that resembled an ancient cave drawing, on the wall of an old building where children had been busy with chalk.

"Look," Haas said, and nodded toward an elderly couple who, climbing the steps of a brownstone house, had paused for a moment to watch a young couple swinging by. An ordinary enough scene but, viewed in an imaginary frame with all else excluded, it made a picture of unusual force.

To enjoy such mental snapshots requires no camera, nothing more than the will to look, observe and appreciate. And the "frame" can be scaled to any size you like. Sometimes it's fun to "see small." Did you ever, for example, peer deep inside a lily? Or observe the starburst in the center of a wet ice cube? William Blake wasn't exaggerating when he said it was possible "to see a world in a grain of sand, and a heaven in a wild flower."

A simple way to help you see small is to carry a pocket magnifying glass. I discovered this on a country walk one summer with Dr. Robert M. MacIver, distinguished sociologist, who used his pocket glass to find unsuspected design, form and color in leaves, pebbles, shells, mushrooms, feathers and seeds. The glass, he remarked, "greatly extends the scenery." At one point our walk led to a beach, where I picked up a handful of wet sand and looked at it through the glass. I saw something I'd never noticed before: the grains, each with its thin coating of water, never actually touched one another! "That," my companion explained, "is why sand never changes and is never ground to powder, no matter how long it's pounded by the waves."

Too often we see only what we expect to see and miss what is really there. We look at our reflection every day and take it for granted in a closeup view that face and mirror image are the same size. But put a dab of soap on your finger and draw the outline of your face in the glass. You will find that the oval you have drawn is only half the actual size of your face. Step back as far as you like and look again. The mirror image of your face will still fill the oval.

If you were painting trees, what color would you make the trunks? Nine out of ten people would make them brown or black. Those are the conventional colors. In reality, tree trunks are purple, gray, yellow-green—just about every color *except* brown or black. "I don't try to teach my students to draw the model," said painter Maurice Sterne. "Anyone can be taught to do such things. I try to teach them to see. It is not technique but vision that creates art."

One reason why Sherlock Holmes delights us is that he sharpens our awareness of significant detail. He notices a badly cleaned pair of boots Dr. Watson is wearing and deduces that his friend has been walking in the country *and* has a careless scullery maid. He knows that the killer who wrote a word in blood on the wall near his victim must be *over* six feet tall, because the word is six feet from the floor and "when a man writes on a wall his instinct leads him to write about the level of his own eyes."

Sir Winston Churchill was another who always took pride in his gift for the significant detail. On a wartime inspection tour of the British naval base at Scapa Flow, the prime minister kept looking at a dummy battleship and a dummy aircraft carrier moored in the harbor to deceive German bombers. Suddenly he said, "I know what's wrong with those dummies: there are no sea gulls around them. That would be noticed immediately by enemy planes." He ordered food to be thrown out to attract gulls.

An easy technique that helps the trained observer see more sharply and retain what he sees is the double take. He forms a first impression, then verifies this impression by looking again. In a busy restaurant I know, the checkroom girl depends on memory alone, and does it "by looking at everybody twice." Try it yourself and you'll be surprised how much more you see on the second look. Glance at a dollar bill, for example, then close your eyes and try to visualize it. Many of the details will be blurred. Now give it a second look, and again visualize it. Do you notice how much more sharply you see the details?

Carl Van Doren, summering in Connecticut, told of visiting a neighbor, Matthew Bradford, a retired Yankee farmer, half blind, living alone on a wooded hillside. "Do you see that cloud shadow coming toward us?" Bradford asked. "If you watch, you will see how these shadows keep the valley always changing. Some days they are very leisurely. Today they go like the wind. They are my moving pictures."

"As I looked," said Van Doren, "another shadow broke

over the ridge of hills, rolled down the long slope, turned the row of maples a darker green, swept solidly across the swamp and meadow and went by us with what I almost thought was a swish. I half caught my breath. Similar shadows must have been breaking over us all afternoon and I had not noted them. A quiet old man who could barely see small objects at hand still saw so much that he had, for me, added a new spectacle to nature."

The wonderful power of seeing the world in one's own unique way is what gives the artist his style. It is the result of what Ernst Haas calls "dreaming with your eyes open," one of the most rewarding seeing devices of all. Children use it well. "Oh, look, Mummy, there's a rainbow in the gutter," a little girl tells her mother—where her mother might see only a dirty oil slick.

All of us possess this ability to "dream with our eyes open." But in growing up we usually suppress it out of fear of being thought different. We ought to lay aside these fears occasionally and see the beauty around us. "Seeing is believing," the maxim says. But, more than that, seeing is living. The more vividly you learn to see, the more alive you are.

### THE TRAVELER

An admirer inquired of Henry Thoreau whether he had traveled much. Thoreau's unhesitating answer was: "I have traveled widely in Concord."

And it was Thoreau who derived the word "saunter" from "Sainte Terre," or Holy Land, so that a saunterer, he said, was one who made every walk a pilgrimage to the Holy Land that lies about us, hidden from the dull, habitual eye.

*—The Christian Science Monitor*

# Are You Living or Existing?

STUART CHASE

There seems to be an ascending scale of values in life, and somewhere in this scale there is a line—probably a blurred one—below which one more or less "exists" and above which one more or less "lives."

What does it mean to be alive, to live intensely? I do not know what life means to other people but I do know what it means to me, and I have worked out a personal method of measuring it.

Take the days as they come, put a plus beside the living hours and a minus before the dead ones; find out just what makes the live ones live and the dead ones die. Is it possible to catch the truth of life in such an analysis? The poet will say no, but I am an accountant and only write poetry out of hours.

My notes show a classification of eleven states of being in which I feel I am alive and six states in which I feel I only exist. These are major states, needless to say. In addition I find scores of substates which are too obscure for me to analyze. The eleven "plus" reactions are these:

I seem to live when I am creating something—writing this article, for instance; making a sketch, working on an economic theory, building a bookshelf.

Art certainly vitalizes me. A good novel, some poems, pictures and operas, many buildings and particularly bridges affect me as though I were taking the artist's blood into my own veins.

The mountains and the sea and stars—all the old subjects of a thousand poets—renew life in me. As in the case of art, the process is not automatic—I hate the sea sometimes—but, by and large, I feel the line of existence below me when I see these things.

Love is life, vital and intense. Very real to me also is the love one bears one's friends.

I live when I am stimulated by good conversation, good argument. There is a sort of vitality in just dealing in ideas that to me is very real.

I live when I am in the presence of danger—rock-climbing, for example.

I feel very much alive in the presence of genuine sorrow.

I live when I play—preferably out-of-doors at such things as swimming, skating, skiing, sometimes driving a car, sometimes walking.

One lives when one takes food after genuine hunger, or when burying one's lips in a cool mountain spring after a long climb.

One lives when one sleeps. A sound healthy sleep after a day spent out-of-doors gives one the feeling of a silent, whirring dynamo. In one's vivid dreams I am also convinced that one lives.

I live when I laugh, spontaneously and heartily.

In contradistinction to these moments of "living" I find these states of "existence":

I exist when I am doing drudgery of any kind: washing dishes, answering most letters, attending to money matters, shaving, dressing, riding on streetcars, buying things.

I exist when attending the average social function—a tea, a dinner, listening to dull people talk.

Eating, drinking or sleeping when one is already replete, when one's senses are dulled, are states of existence, not life.

Old, monotonous things—city walls, too familiar streets, houses, rooms, furniture, clothes—drive one to the existence level.

Sheer ugliness, such as one sees in a big-city slum, depresses me intensely.

I retreat from life when I become angry. I exist through rows and misunderstandings and in the blind alleys of "getting even."

So, in a general way, I set life off from existence. It must be admitted, of course, that "living" is often a mental state quite independent of physical environment or occupation. One may feel, in springtime for instance, suddenly alive in old, monotonous surroundings. Then even dishwashing becomes eventful and one sings as one shaves. But these outbursts are on the whole abnormal.

My notes show that in one week, of the 168 hours contained therein, I only "lived" about 40 of them, or 25 percent of the total time. This allowed for some creative work, a Sunday's hike, some genuine hunger, some healthy sleep, a little stimulating reading, two acts of a play, part of a moving picture and eight hours of interesting discussion with friends. I believe that I could deliberately "live" twice as much in the same 168 hours, if only I would come out from under the chains of necessity, largely economic, which bind me.

It may well be that the states of being which release life in me also release it in most human beings. Generally speaking, one's salvation is bound closely with that of all mankind— the ratio of living growing with that of the mass of one's fellow men.

# "Every, Every Minute"

JEAN DALRYMPLE

**M**any years ago when I was very young and on the threshold of a life which was to turn out to be crammed full of, to me, fascinating work, people and pleasures, I was overcome by discouragement and a deep depression. Today I would be sent to the psychoanalyst's couch, but at that time I was sent to the theater.

The play was Thornton Wilder's *Our Town*, and it was my old friend Frank Craven, its star, who led me to the matinee. The magic of Wilder's compassionate wisdom switched on a light in the dark room of my mind.

It happened late in the play where Emily—whose short life in Grover's Corners we had followed—had died in childbirth but was allowed to return to earth to relive her twelfth birthday. For the first time Emily really saw her mother and father in their simple goodness and love for her, and could realize the myriad small details which make up our daily life. Unable to bear the loveliness and pathos of this long-forgotten day, she suddenly called out:

"It goes so fast! We don't have time to look at one another . . . take me back—up the hill—to my grave. But first: Wait! One more look. Good-bye, good-bye, world. Good-bye, Grover's Corners . . . Mama and Papa. Good-bye to clocks ticking . . . and Mama's sunflowers . . . and new-ironed dresses and hot baths . . . to sleeping and waking up. Oh, earth, you're too wonderful for anybody to realize you. Do any human beings ever realize life while they have it?

Every, every minute?" And Frank Craven, playing the Stage Manager, answered, "No."

Right then and there, I too saw how fast life goes, how we really do not take the time to look at and know one another; to appreciate the rain and wind as well as the sunshine, to accept the disappointments and defeats with grace since they make the achievements and the victories count. All simple things in my life became its true beauties; the reasons for my discouragement and depression became unimportant.

They still are, and I have made a conscious effort to realize life, every, every minute of it, from that day on. Do you? Try to. It is surprisingly rewarding.

✦

## JOY OF THE SENSES

**D**id you know that in Japan you may be invited to a moon-viewing party, at which no conversation is expected? You merely sit in subdued but elegant surroundings and watch the moon rise, *and* stretch your appreciative abilities.

The Japanese, of course, in their controlled appreciation of nature go to some extremes that could well seem bizarre in the West. They have parties to watch and celebrate the fall of the first snow of winter—the suddenly different aspect it gives to the countryside, the softening of contours, the change in the quality of light and shadow. They go out to the country on a summer night to listen—not comment on, just *listen*—to "insect-music." I was once invited to a party where all the ladies sat around in a reverent hush while pieces of different kinds of wood were carefully brought to a glow over a charcoal brazier and then handed around on separate trays so that each of us could smell them. We caught the subtle differences in the fragrances of peach, cherry, pine, balsam and other woods.                    —*Santha Rama Rau*

## Chapter 8/The Rewards of Self-Improvement

*Every one of us knows in his secret heart that he*
*could be a better person—more tolerant, more unselfish,*
*more generous, more kind. None of us ever fully lives*
*up to his ideals, but the encouraging thing is this:*
*improvement is always possible.*
*Sometimes willpower will do it. Sometimes*
*prayer. Sometimes a sermon. Sometimes words on a page.*
*"Our chief want in life," said Emerson, "is someone*
*who will make us do what we can." Here some experts*
*tell us how to do just that.*

## Be Honest with Yourself!
**T. F. JAMES**

**E**very American applauds
the honesty that storekeeper Abraham Lincoln practiced
when he trudged miles to return a customer's change. But
this kind of honesty, toward others, cannot compare in importance to being honest with ourselves.

Lack of self-honesty can be profoundly damaging. "Failures in self-honesty," says psychotherapist Dr. Albert Ellis,
"are at the root of almost every emotional and mental disturbance." Industrial psychologist Dr. Frederick F. Gaudet says,
"Again and again, promising men ruin their careers because
they are poor judges of their own abilities and aptitudes."
Veteran marriage counselor Emmanuel Hallowitz, assistant
professor of psychiatry of the Albert Einstein College of

Medicine, declares, "In almost every disrupted marriage there is, on both sides, self-deception." On the other hand, the ability to look at yourself hard and honestly—admitting both the bad and the good—is the most powerful untapped source of human energy.

Consider a man whom we shall call Paul McKenzie. At forty he began drinking too much. Life seemed to have lost its savor, yet he could not understand why. He had a good job; his wife was devoted; his children were healthy. Then one day as McKenzie reached toward his liquor cabinet, he glimpsed himself in the mirror. He saw a face he had almost forgotten, with traits of character, hints of strength, signs of weakness that were all new to him. McKenzie slammed the liquor cabinet shut and spent the next five hours writing an exhaustive and ruthlessly honest analysis of himself.

It turned out to be the most profitable five hours' work he had ever done. For the first time he saw himself as too ambitious and aggressive for the job he was holding. The disciplines of a large company chafed him. So he organized his own public-relations company, which has been extremely successful. More important than financial returns, however, is the enthusiasm with which he now lives and works.

The emotional rewards of self-honesty are its more potent dividends. A mature self-knowledge greatly reduces the anxiety with which men live. Dr. Carl Rogers, well-known psychotherapist, noted in his counseling that people with emotional problems had a very low opinion of themselves. But once they experienced the counselor's acceptance of them *exactly as they were,* with all their shortcomings, a very positive change took place. Soon they were admitting not only their faults but their good points. From self-acceptance, it was only a short step to emotional health.

In his book *The Creative Years*, Reul Howe tells about a meek, timid teacher who was put in charge of a class of incorrigibles. One boy in particular, fourteen-year-old Joe, delighted in throwing the class into an uproar. One afternoon in desperation the teacher kept Joe after school and asked him why he was making her life so miserable. For a moment he looked sullenly at her, and then replied, "Because you're such a sucker for it."

"I know I am," she sighed. "I've always been afraid of people like you, and yet I'd like to be able to help you. Don't you want anyone to love you or help you?" To her amazement, the bully broke down and poured out to her the story of his misery and poverty and loneliness. "Her honesty as a person," Howe says, "called forth the truth from this confused and resentful boy." Her power to accept herself, with all her fears and weakness, became her power to accept him. This in turn made it possible for him to accept himself.

Unfortunately, self-honesty is rare. Analyzers of the national psyche have pictured millions of Americans as "other-directed"—looking to the goals and ideals and ideas of others for guidance, rather than within themselves. This kind of thing distorts the individual, frustrates his inborn hunger for "personalization." He is forced constantly to dodge what he really thinks and feels—and yet in the end he cannot avoid it, because it is the deepest, most important concern of his life.

How can you check on your self-honesty? Dr. Gordon Allport, Harvard psychologist, suggests examining your sense of humor. Can you laugh at yourself—truly, genuinely laugh? If so, you probably have a good idea of what you are really like.

Dr. Gaudet recommends writing a thorough self-analysis, not as an end in itself but as a kind of check. "A good friend should be able to help you decide whether your list of traits and abilities is objective. If you do not have a friend from whom you can ask such help—that, in itself, could be a sign that you are not being honest with yourself." Self-honesty is not easy to achieve, nor is it something we win overnight. It is something we must work toward, slowly. Certainly no one should spend all his time probing his inner motives. But we can at least try to be honest about a selected set of goals. One important area is work.

Why does a person get himself into a muddle by choosing the wrong job? "Because he has his eyes fixed on the accidentals rather than the essentials," says Jerry Fields, a New York employment counselor: "the salary, the glamour or prestige a certain job offers. He doesn't stop to ask himself whether he really wants to do that kind of work, or how well it fits his capabilities. As a result he may spend years in a futile effort to gain success, when half this effort made in a field better suited to his talents and temperament would yield twice the progress."

Sometimes failure can make us more honest about our careers than success. One of the happiest men I know quit a good job as a newspaper editor to spend two years toiling on a novel. He sent the finished product out to publishers, and got back nothing but rejection slips. But when I sympathized with him, he said, "I don't regret a day of those two years. When my book failed, I realized I just was not a novelist. You can't imagine how *free* I felt." He went back to work, unburdened by doubts about his destiny, and is now a top magazine editor. His favorite advice to someone who complains that he has a frustrated dream is: "Try it! Even if you find you don't like it, or aren't any good at it, you've gained in self-knowledge. Then you can knuckle down to working at something you *are* good at."

As an industrial psychologist, Dr. Gaudet sees another common type of job problem: where a man becomes troubled when he does not advance rapidly. Dr. Gaudet advises that before he plunges into an orgy of self-blame, he should ask some basic questions: 1. Does he really want to advance? Many people do not. They are satisfied with the work they are doing. 2. Is it his own desire to advance, or someone else's?—his wife's, for example. 3. Is he willing to pay the price of advancement? The higher a man goes, the longer his working hours. "Advancement," Dr. Gaudet says, "is not synonymous with happiness, nor even with success. It should be the result of a drive from within."

Almost all the experts I have talked with agree that in searching for self-honesty the greatest danger is the human tendency to castigate oneself. Too many equate self-honesty with self-condemnation. But genuine self-honesty includes an appraisal of bad *and* good. We need to recognize our weaknesses; we must also recognize our potentialities so we can develop them.

The goal of self-honesty has been summed up by Dr. Carl Rogers in the phrase: "the open self." The person who achieves mature self-knowledge is no longer afraid of life. He can accept all his experiences and feelings, whether of grief or of happiness, of love or of guilt. "He recognizes," says Rogers, "that it rests within himself to choose his way of living, the only question that matters being: Is this a way which is deeply satisfying to me, and one which truly expresses me?"

Being honest with yourself is more than a formula for success on the job or in marriage. It is a way of life.

# Never Stop Learning

JAMES A. MICHENER

he war had passed us by on Guadalcanal in 1945, and we could see certain victory ahead. Relieved of pressure, our top officers in the South Pacific Force could have been excused if they loafed, but the ones I knew well in those days used their free time to educate themselves in new fields. One carrier admiral studied everything he could get on tank warfare. The head of our outfit, Vice Admiral William Lowndes Calhoun, spent six hours a day learning French. I asked him about it. "Admiral, what's this big deal with French?" "How do I know where I'll be sent when the war's over?" he replied.

A few nights later I happened to participate in an officers' study group. As we were breaking up, the leader asked me, "By the way, Michener, what are you studying?"

I had been studying exactly nothing, and as I walked back to my quarters, the challenge implicit in his probably idle question touched in me a profound response. That very night I started work on something that I had been toying with for months. In a lantern-lit, mosquito-filled tin shack, I began writing *Tales of the South Pacific*.

I know now that the good work of the world is accomplished principally by people who dedicate themselves unstintingly to the big, distant goal. Weeks, months, years pass, but the good workman knows that he is gambling on an ultimate achievement which cannot be measured in time spent. Responsible men and women leap to the challenge of jobs that require enormous dedication and years to fulfill, and are happiest when they are so involved. This means that men and women who hope to make a real contribution to American life must *reeducate* themselves periodically.

In the United States the average man (let's leave out doctors and highly specialized scientists) can expect to work in three radically different fields before he retires. The lawyer is dragged into a business reorganization and winds up a college president. The engineer uses his slide rule for a while, then finds himself a sales expert and ends up in labor relations. The schoolteacher becomes a principal, later on heads the town's automobile agency.

I have been the typical American in that I have had widely scattered jobs: teacher, businessman, soldier, traveler, writer. No college education could give me specific preparation for any of these jobs, but mine did inspire me with the urge to reeducate myself constantly.

By fantastic luck, I got to Swarthmore College, outside Philadelphia, just as it was launching an experiment. At the end of my sophomore year the faculty assembled a group of us and said, "Life does not consist of taking courses in small segments. A productive life consists of finding huge tasks and mastering them with whatever tools of intelligence and energy we have. We are going to turn you loose on some huge tasks. Let's see what you can do with them."

Accordingly, we were excused from all class attendance and were told, "Pick out three fields that interest you." I chose logic, English history and the novel. The faculty said, "Go to the library and learn what you can about your fields. At the end of two years we'll bring in some experts from Harvard and Yale whom you've never seen, and they will determine whether you have educated yourself."

What followed was an experience in intellectual grandeur. The Swarthmore professors, realizing that when I was tested they would be tested, too, helped me to gain as thorough an education as a young man could absorb. When the two years ended, the visiting experts arrived and for a week they queried, probed and heckled. At the end one of the examiners said to me simply, "You have the beginnings of a real education." He was right: it was only the beginnings. If my education had ended then, I would have proved a useless citizen. But what I *did* learn was how to learn, how to organize, how to educate and reeducate myself.

From my own experience and observation, I realize today that it is not so much the education that counts: it's the self-reeducation—the discipline that keeps a man driving toward hard and distant goals, the human values he believes in.

Specialization is not enough; what the world needs for the big jobs—historically, culturally, morally—are well-rounded *human* beings. I remember a day in 1942 when the U.S. Navy was hungry for talent. Four of us were shivering in our shorts in a small room. A grim-faced selection committee asked the first would-be officer, "What can you do?" and the man replied, "I'm a buyer for Macy's, and I've trained myself to judge very quickly between markets and prices and trends." The board replied, "Can't you do anything practical?" And they shunted him off to one side.

When the board asked the next man, a lawyer, if he could do anything practical, he had to confess, "I can weigh evidence and organize information." He was rejected.

I was third and when I answered, "I know language and a good deal of history," the board groaned and I went shivering away. Then the fourth man said boldly, "I'm a college-trained engineer, and I can overhaul diesel engines." The committee practically made him an officer right on the spot.

But this is not the end of the story. When the war was over, the Macy's buyer was assistant to the Secretary of the Navy, in charge of many complex responsibilities requiring instant good judgment. He had given himself courses in naval management and government procedures and had become a top expert. The lawyer wound up as assistant to Admiral Halsey, and in a crucial battle deduced logically from intelligence reports just where the Japanese fleet had to be. He came out covered with medals. I got the job of naval secretary to several congressional committees who were determining the future of America in the South Pacific.

What was the engineer doing at the end of the war? He was still overhauling diesel engines.

### THE MIRACULOUS

"**I** have learnt nothing from life," wrote Omar Khayyam, "except my own amazement at it." It would be a sad thing if we, in our age of miracles, were to lose our sense of the miraculous. It is surprise, curiosity and love which rejuvenate the mind.

—*Harold Nicolson*

### SET NO LIMITS

**D**on't run away from adventures of the mind which you find hard to understand. Keep an open mind for the things "practical" people say won't work. Perhaps we have more "senses" than we think. For thousands of years electricity was all around us and we could not use it. How can we be sure there aren't powers of the mind which we understand as little but could as well if we knew how?

—*Ardis Whitman*

# Seven Ways to Improve Memory

HENRY C. LINK, PH.D., AND ROBERT NORMAN

f course the memory can be improved. It can be improved vastly. It can be improved by anyone with normal intelligence. Moreover, the methods by which it can be cultivated are all founded on practical common sense. Every experience in life makes an impression through one or more of the senses on some of the cells of the brain, or other nerve centers. The problem of memory improvement is to emphasize these impressions and to file them away in such an orderly manner that many will remain intact. The clearer the impressions, and the neater your mental storehouse, the easier it will be to remember.

*Repetition is the most elemental—and least interesting—method of memorizing.* You can learn and remember almost anything if you have the patience to repeat it often enough.

*Bring as many of your senses as possible to bear on what you want to remember.* Suppose you were exhibiting an apple to a person who had never seen one before. If he looked at the apple he would carry away a certain impression of it. But if he lifted it, smelled it, tasted it, he would carry away a clearer and more lasting memory. The scientific reason for this is that the impression you receive through the sense of sight is recorded on an entirely different cell from that transmitted through touch or any other sense. All cells of the nervous system are connected, however, so that the more impressions you get of a thing, the more strings you have with which to pull it out of the subconscious mind at will.

183

This principle is very important in remembering names and faces. People who do not remember names are usually those who do not hear the name distinctly in the first place or who pay little attention to it. Perhaps they are more concerned with the stranger's appearance, or with what kind of impression they are going to make on him, or with what they will say to him. An employment manager with a poor memory set out to improve this faculty. When any person came to him, he made sure at the start that he knew the name exactly. If necessary, he would ask for the spelling of it. Then he would write the name down and look carefully at it. Thus a definite impression was made on his visual and muscular senses. In his conversation he would repeat the name again and again. Meanwhile he was studying the man's face and expression and mannerisms. Today that manager can meet and call by name ten thousand persons.

*Cultivate the power of attention.* People do not focus sharply and clearly on one thing at a time. In conversation they do not think so much of what the other person is saying as of what they are going to say next. They look at scenery but do not drink in the details.

Men of fruitful intellects and first-rate memories invariably have excellent powers of observation, concentration and attention. Attention means sidetracking everything except the thought or experience you want to remember. Beware of mental hazes as a mariner avoids a treacherous shoal. Note the details of what you want to remember. A bank cashier who had difficulty in remembering people started to study the details of each face. He found that pictures built up thus, with attention to detail, did not fade from his memory.

*Association, when not fantastically overdone, is one of the shortest and surest ways of remembering.* Not long ago I met a Mr. White who told me that he lived at 25 St. Nicholas Avenue. An obvious association struck me: "White—Christmas; Christmas—the twenty-fifth of December—St. Nicholas." Everyone has in his mind many facts to which he can anchor new facts by associations. But remember, the simpler our associations, the less they will burden the memory.

*If you are deeply and genuinely interested, your attention focuses more or less as a matter of course.* Some men are so interested in baseball that they know the names of all the big-league players, their batting averages and so on. Many extraordinary memories can be explained by the element of intense interest. The moral is: Try to develop a genuine, vital interest in the subject you want to remember.

*Gain understanding.* If you do not understand a subject or situation, you cannot be expected to remember it. You must know the logical relations between all the given facts.

*Make a careful and thoughtful selection of the things that it is necessary for you to remember, and turn your mental searchlights on these alone.* No one can remember everything. Many people use a thousand-dollar tool for ten-cent jobs. They try to remember telephone numbers, when it would be much wiser to save their precious mental machinery for more important work. Many things belong in your notebook rather than in your mind. Focus your memory and attention wisely. Do not attempt the impossible at the start. If you can't remember names and faces, select two or three persons whom you wish to remember, and make a deliberate, determined effort to fix them firmly in your memory. Make a note of their names and characteristics. Look these notes over later and re-create in your memory an exact impression of your new acquaintances. Keep up this practice, and you will soon be astonished at the results.

# Make Your Mind Behave

FREDERICK B. ROBINSON AND M. K. WISEHART

**V**isiting an exhibition given by the well-known Brooklyn Etchers' Club, I was astonished to notice that two particularly attractive etchings were signed by a man I had known for years. Until that moment I had not had the slightest inkling that Frederick B. Robinson, president of the College of the City of New York at the time, included etching among his varied accomplishments.

A friend who was with me added that Dr. Robinson had recently become a fair amateur musician. He had done it because certain of his friends had been skeptical of his theory that, within certain limits, a man can accomplish anything he sets out to do. They had suggested that he learn to play the cello within six months. Though entirely unfamiliar with musical instruments, he had given them a "recital" at the end of sixty days. It included Massenet's "Elégie," Pergolese's "Tre Giorni," Handel's "Largo" and Mendelssohn's "Spring Song," all played, as the professional musicians agreed, very acceptably.

Influenced by the belief that in the way this distinguished educator went about learning to play the cello there might be a valuable lesson for the rest of us, I called at his office to make further inquiries about it.

"There is no secret about the small measure of success I achieved," he said. "I worked; I applied myself. The important thing is that I have learned to love the cello. I have bought a real 'old master,' and now look forward to studying under a professional teacher and becoming a fine player."

"Concentration means more to you than to most of us," I said. "Just what *is* concentration?"

"I think of concentration as a kind of stamina, or mental tenacity, the result of a consistent purpose. It is the art of making our minds behave. It requires *choice:* fixing our mind and energies on one thing to the exclusion of others. The men who achieve important positions in life depend less upon their natural aptitudes than on this acquired ability to fix the attention upon any specific problem and to hold the mind to that problem until they have seen it through."

Dr. Robinson went on as follows:

As a practical man, I have found four principles of great use to me in developing and applying my mental powers.

1. A keen and active interest—zest—in the subject or task to be mastered is essential.

2. We must learn to amass in an orderly way the raw materials of our thinking. Get the facts! Stress those which bear on the problem, and subordinate the others.

3. If we want to think and hit hard, we must learn to take it easy. That is to say, the most efficient use of our mental and physical energy is likewise the most economical.

4. There is evidently something in the mind which, after a sustained effort, becomes temporarily exhausted but recovers and goes on trying and trying, so that the ultimate solution of the problem may come in an altogether unexpected way. To a certain extent, we can make the subconscious work for us.

The first principle concerns interest. I made progress in becoming an amateur etcher and cellist because I was naturally interested. But if I had *not* been keenly interested naturally, I feel certain that I could have found ways and means of stimulating the interest necessary to make my efforts effective. It is often necessary to look forward to desired results rather than feeling only the drudgery of the moment.

My second principle is to get the facts. Remember that when the mind is "going in circles," over and over the same matter, without new ideas occurring to us or our conclusions sharpening, the cause is presumably a lack of information on which a definite decision could be based. Successful results cannot be obtained from an effort of the will in a vacuum.

Let me illustrate my third principle: When I was a young man, working under pressure and attempting to accomplish varied tasks in the shortest possible time, I used to rush at them and get "steamed up." Later, I learned that really effective men are completely at their ease even under urgent and distracting circumstances.

There is a judge whose mind I have watched in action. Never disturbed, even in the midst of exciting disputes, he takes things easily, in his quiet way, asking a question now and then. When doing our hardest thinking, there should be a general relaxation and serenity of body and mind, but with a deliberate focusing of the mind and a maximum of intensity in *one* direction.

In my own experience I have found it useful, when I have been working long on some particular question and find myself getting high-strung and tense, to pause deliberately in my speech or thoughts, relax, breathe deeply and simply wait till the tense condition has gone away.

Of equal importance with this principle is another: too long a study of one problem may cause the mind to "go stale." Physical diversion or a change in the form of our mental activity may pave the way for a solution of some long-pondered problem. As students, many of us have had this experience: After working hard at night on a particular problem, we have solved it with ease the next morning. Such work, accomplished by the mind without our consciously directing its activities, would appear to be the very opposite of concentration. But without the concentrated effort that went before, such flashes of insight are not apt to occur.

One of the best exercises I know of for developing skill in concentration, for young and old, is to read carefully a paragraph of a book, then turn the book down and name the essential points covered in that paragraph. Once you can do this with a short paragraph, practice doing the same with a longer paragraph, and then several paragraphs. Or jot down the main points of an address by a speaker, and when the address is over, with these points memorized, develop the speech over again in your own way.

It is well to recall what some of our notable men have said on this subject of concentrated energy. Under these sayings one may see a common denominator of meaning and emphasis: namely, that the great difference between those who achieve and those who fail consists not so much in the amount of time devoted to work by each, but in the degree to which he intelligently applies his powers, mental and physical, to one purpose. Thomas Carlyle said: "The weakest creature, by concentrating his powers on a single object, can accomplish something; whereas the strongest, by dispersing his over many, may fail to accomplish anything."

And Charles Dickens: "The one serviceable, safe, certain, remunerative, attainable quality in every study and pursuit is that of attention. My own imagination would never have served me as it did but for the habit of humble, daily, toiling attention."

# The Fine Art of Keeping One's Head

WILLIAM FITZ GIBBON

Very often we think about the great crises in life, the mighty "moments of truth," and wonder how we would face them. Yet it is the little panics, the pressure squeezes of daily life, that should give us concern. These are the incidents that bring on those mental blackouts which make us appear to be less than we are.

When our word is questioned, for example, instead of stating our case more convincingly, we frequently grow dark-minded and blurt out some reply that we regret later. Or when we match wits in conversation, we may get rattled and subside into banalities. James Thurber once wrote a story based on the witty things he would have said if he had thought of them at the time—an experience we can all understand. Sometimes, under pressure, we say something utterly different from what we intend, like the young man who became so nervous in his boss's office that he asked for a salary raise for someone else.

Our failures to handle the little crises in life can accumulate to destroy the very thing that we all wish for: to be completely ourselves, to show others we are all that we know ourselves to be. Happily, the ability to keep one's head is not something one is born with or without. It is within everyone's reach. As the late William Lyon Phelps of Yale said, "Tranquillity of mind, so necessary for one's happiness and for the accomplishment of good work, can be acquired."

The primary way to learn to handle ourselves well under

pressure is by observing life around us and adjusting to its rhythms. One sure method is to study those who have already mastered this art. These persons are often found in the tensest jobs. Among them are business executives, strike mediators, politicians, baseball pitchers, surgeons. The experiences of such men and women reveal seven keys to the art of keeping one's head in a crisis, and the corollary art of taking the steam out of a crisis as it begins to build up.

*Use Humor*. There is no greater force for breaking tension. In the India-Burma Theater during World War II, British Field Marshal Viscount William J. Slim searched for a way to reassure his staff after a major defeat. "Things could be worse," he began. "How?" asked a voice from the rear. "Well," said Slim, "it could be raining."

Since it is not always possible to think of a humorous remark on the spur of the moment, it helps to keep a favorite story or two in mind to change the atmosphere when it clouds up. The late Vice-President Alben Barkley often used stories in this way, as he did in the U.S. Senate Chamber one humid July night in 1946 when a bitter debate on price control had been going on for almost twelve hours. It was midnight, tempers were short and chances for a decision on the measure seemed remote. Barkley rose from his desk.

"It is a peculiar situation we face," he began. "Those who want no controls are going to vote against this measure. And apparently some of those who want *more* controls are going to vote against it, too. It reminds me of the spinster who went into a furniture store and asked if she could trade in her old-fashioned double bed for twin beds. 'That's an unusual request,' said the clerk. 'What is the object?' 'I live alone,' she replied, 'and every night before I retire I look under my bed to see if a man is there. If I have two beds, my chances will be doubled.' " The *Congressional Record* shows that the measure was approved within the hour.

*Take Your Time.* There is a temptation, under pressure, to act quickly. The baseball pitcher who has just been hit hard by opposing batters feels an overpowering urge to fast-ball the next man at the plate. "You want to throw it by him as quickly as you can," says former Yankee relief pitcher Marshall Bridges. "That's the time you should pick up the rosin bag or talk to the catcher. Delay keeps you from doing something foolish."

A little delay may also bring a missing answer to mind. A friend of mine who teaches English once forgot the author of a play he was discussing, and his class was beginning to sense it. Instead of panicking, however, he kept the conversation going, letting time as it passed coax the answer out of his mind. At last he dropped in the author's name, Sir James Barrie, and remarked with a straight face, "I'm surprised none of you thought of it."

*Don't Dominate.* Trying to get self-satisfaction through "victory" of our ideas or our wills leads to endless tension. Everyone hates to find himself out on a limb. Yet we often force an opponent, a subordinate or an employer into that awkward position by our demands.

"An important factor in my work," says strike mediator Theodore Kheel, "is to keep people from getting out on limbs. One of the ways I do this is by bringing both parties in a dispute gradually up to the point where I suggest a solution. As soon as I raise this suggestion, I turn them away from it. I may talk about my boat—anything to give them plenty of time to think about what's been offered before they speak. Later I draw out their reactions. That technique usually keeps everybody from climbing out to where it's hard to get back. A lot of people have been saved by that boat."

*Consider Motives.* Nothing causes us to lose our heads so quickly as sharp criticisms or insults. I recently asked a psychiatrist how he managed to keep calm in the face of the kind of abuse men in his profession so often receive from patients. "Most of the insults we get are not actually directed at us," he said. "Usually the patient is really angry at someone else—a relative, an employer. He is merely taking it out on us." That is a point we could all make more use of.

"Another thing to remember is that it takes two to have a fight. I remember an occasion when a woman in my office was definitely looking for one. 'All psychiatrists are crazy,' she said. 'That's funny,' I said. 'Driving to work this morning, I was thinking the same thing.' "

*Be Frank.* "If I feel tense in an interview," a Los Angeles newspaper reporter told me, "I say so. That makes me feel better immediately and often relaxes the other person, too. Once when interviewing a government official I couldn't think of anything to break the ice. Finally I said, 'I wish I could think of an icebreaker.' That was enough."

*Be Prepared.* Nowhere was this shown more dramatically than in Astronaut Gordon Cooper's space flight in May 1963. When the automatic aids that were expected to bring in his craft failed, Cooper calmly took over the manual controls—and achieved a most accurate reentry. "I was not overly concerned," he said. The reason: He had practiced every conceivable emergency maneuver over and over. "We had checked, checked and double-checked," said Cooper. "I felt right at home in the bird." Gemini astronauts Edward White and James McDivitt also came down manually in June 1965.

*Look Ahead.* Walter N. Thayer, president of the New York *Herald Tribune,* never enters a conference without having made as good a prediction as he can of what is likely to happen. If it is a day when opposing points of view will be presented, he weighs what the arguments may be, reviews his own stand. If it is up to him to try to sway a meeting he forecasts the possible challenges and makes his position as sound as he can. As a result of educated predictions, Thayer never enters a conference nervously or leaves one angrily. A co-worker calls him "the calmest executive I know."

Keeping your head affects your well-being in more ways than one. Our health, doctors are discovering, is more closely connected with our ability to handle ourselves well under pressure than anyone realized even a few years ago. Their findings have opened a new frontier in medicine. Dr. Hans Selye of Canada, an authority on the effect of stress on health, has discovered that our health may be affected by the supply of hormones—the body's tiny adapters that help us adjust to stress. If we lose our heads frequently in small crises, we produce excesses of certain of these hormones. Dr. Selye has found that these excesses may have a relationship to such diseases as arthritis. "We are just beginning to see that many common diseases," says Dr. Selye, "are largely due to errors in our adaptive response to stress, rather than to direct damage by germs, poisons or other external agents."

But of all those things ensured by our ability to keep our heads, the most valuable is the *harmony of our natures*. As we train ourselves to be frank, to use time and humor as allies, to predict and prepare, and to be considerate of others, then we begin to move clearheadedly through whatever life brings, saying and doing what we intend, being more fully ourselves. We approach the tranquillity that comes when mind and spirit are in team. If that state of being isn't happiness itself, it's surely its next-door neighbor.

# Unlock Your Real Personality

*Condensed from the book: Psycho-Cybernetics*

MAXWELL MALTZ, M.D.

"**P**ersonality," that magnetic and mysterious something that is easy to recognize but difficult to define, is not acquired from without; it is *released* from within.

Every baby has "personality plus." This is because a baby has no qualms about expressing himself. In his own language, mostly crying or cooing, he expresses his real feelings and thus exemplifies superbly the psychological dictum, "Be yourself." He is not in the least inhibited because he is at this stage totally un-self-conscious, and he will remain so until he enters into communication with other human beings.

In all social relationships we constantly receive monitoring signals which govern our freedom of expression. A smile, a frown, a hundred different subtle clues of approval or disapproval, interest or lack of interest continually advise us how we're doing. Such signals can, of course, be helpful. But if you become too consciously concerned about what others think, inhibition results—and poor performance.

"Who are the scholars who get 'rattled' in the recitation room?" asked philosopher William James. "Those who think of the possibilities of failure and feel the great importance of the act. . . . Just as a bicycle chain may be too tight, so may one's carefulness and conscientiousness be so tense as to hinder the running of one's mind."

A famous salesman, author and lecturer recalls that when

he first left home he was painfully self-conscious, especially when eating in a hotel dining room. Why was he so ill at ease? He knew that he knew enough social etiquette to get by. Why had he never felt ill at ease when eating in the kitchen with Ma and Pa? He decided it was because when he was eating with Ma and Pa he was not concerned about producing an effect.

The late Dr. Albert Edward Wiggam, famous educator and psychologist, in his early years was so painfully self-conscious that he found it all but impossible to recite in school. He constantly fought his self-consciousness until one day he realized that his trouble was not self-consciousness at all, but "others-consciousness." He was too painfully sensitive to what others might think of everything he said or did. With this realization, he concentrated on developing *more* self-consciousness: feeling, acting, behaving, thinking *as he did when he was alone,* ignoring how others might feel. It worked, and in time he became a highly successful speaker.

"Conscience doth make cowards of us all," wrote Shakespeare. Conscience itself works in much the same way as an electronic computer. The answers a computer gives are reliable only if correct information has been stored in it before it is given problems to solve. In the same way, if your basic beliefs are sound, conscience becomes a valuable guide in deciding what is morally right and wrong. But if your basic beliefs are not sound, your conscience can be misleading.

For example, self-expression may be morally wrong to the conscience of a person who, as a child, was squelched, humiliated or punished for speaking up or showing off, and thus learned that it is wrong, perhaps, to speak at all. And a child punished for showing anger, or shamed for showing fear, comes to believe that experiencing such emotions is wrong. Yet, properly directed and controlled, anger and fear may be moral or constructive forces. The child who is squelched every time he comes up with an opinion learns that it is right for him to be a nobody. Many people, inhibited by the wrong kind of conscience, take a back seat in any kind of endeavor, even in worthwhile church activities.

If you are among the millions who suffer unhappiness and failure because of inhibition, you should deliberately practice *disinhibition*. You need to practice being less careful, less concerned, less conscientious. When I give patients this advice, they often say, "Without a certain amount of inhibition, civilized society would collapse."

"Yes," I agree, "but the key words are 'a certain amount.' The path to the goal of self-fulfilling, creative personality is a course between too much inhibition and too little."

If you habitually rush in where angels fear to tread; if you habitually find yourself in hot water because of impulsive, ill-considered actions; if you can never admit you're wrong; if you are a loud talker—you probably have *too little* inhibition. You need to think more of consequences before acting.

If, however, you dread new and strange situations; if you feel inadequate, worry a lot, feel self-conscious; if you have any nervous symptoms such as facial tics, difficulty in going to sleep; if you hold yourself in and continually take a back seat—then you probably have too much inhibition. You need to practice St. Paul's advice to the Philippians: "Be careful for nothing," and follow these principles:

Don't wonder in advance what you are going to say. Just open your mouth and say it. Improvise as you need to.

Don't think before you act. Act—and correct your actions as you go along. "We cannot think first and act afterward," said the great contemporary philosopher Alfred North

Whitehead. "From the moment of birth we are immersed in action, and can only fitfully guide it by taking thought."

Stop criticizing yourself. After each action, however simple, the inhibited person says to himself, "I wonder if I should have done that." After he has got up courage to speak, he immediately thinks, "Maybe I shouldn't have said that. Maybe the other person will take it the wrong way." Useful and beneficial self-criticism works subconsciously, spontaneously, automatically. Conscious self-criticism, self-analysis and introspection are good and useful—if undertaken sparingly. But as a continual performance they are defeating.

Make a habit of speaking *louder* than usual. Inhibited people are notoriously wispy-voiced. You don't have to shout and use an angry tone—just consciously raise the volume of your voice. This in itself is a powerful disinhibitor.

Let people know when you like them. The inhibited personality fears expressing good feelings as well as bad ones. Ignore such worries. Compliment at least three people every day. If you like what someone is doing or wearing or saying, let him know it. Be direct. "I like that, Joe." "Mary, that's a pretty hat." And if you're married, just say to your wife, "I love you," at least twice a day.

⇢ ♦ ⇠

### IDENTITY

*T*he more one studies the biographies of men like Washington, or women like Florence Nightingale, the more one feels that they might conceivably have been lost in the crowd. What most of all gives them distinction is that they identified themselves with a cause greater than themselves so that when you think of it you think of them. —*Harry Emerson Fosdick*

# How to Think Creatively

BLAKE CLARK

"Who, me? Why, I couldn't think of an idea if I tried." This is a typical response when anyone is asked to attempt something original. Most of us completely lack confidence in our ability to create. We cling to the belief that we are *born* creative or noncreative, and that nothing can be done about it. This notion has been proved false. Courses conducted in colleges and industry over the past fifteen years have shown that creativity *can* be developed. For example, in one research project, graduates of creative problem-solving classes at the University of Buffalo were paired against comparable students who had not had the classes. The course-takers averaged 94 percent better than the others in ability to produce fresh and useful ideas.

With the same creative-development methods, men of industry are designing machines, and manufacturers are finding more uses for their products. More than 150,000 persons have now taken such courses and are getting demonstrable results. General Electric Company gave a two-year course designed to make its engineers more creative. The 430 who took it between 1937 and 1964 averaged many more patents than others with the same educational background who did not take it. GE sponsors, in addition, similar shorter-term programs which many hundreds of employes have taken. More than a hundred other leading industrial firms now give some form of creative problem-solving courses to managers, supervisors and other employes. At General Motors' AC Spark Plug division in Flint, Michigan, A. L. Simberg, as supervisor of personnel research and development, selected two groups of hourly employes. One group had a high record of good suggestions for plant improvement; the other group's was low. Each received a ten-hour course in creative thinking. During the following year the high achievers increased their number of suggestions by 40 percent, the others theirs by 47 percent.

This does not mean that you can take "ten easy lessons" and become a creative genius. But knowing the principles of creative thinking is a big step toward developing creativity. The rest, says psychologist J. P. Guilford, of the University of Southern California, depends upon "practice, practice, practice." You learn to think more creatively just as you learn to write, paint or play ball, say the experts—by doing it. So course-work consists of solving problem after problem. Classes usually begin with a few mental limbering-up exercises. For example, "How would you arrange four 9's to add up to 100?" the instructor may ask. About one person in ten gets this after wrestling with it five minutes. Try it. The answer is at the end of this article.

How many uses can you think of for a brick, other than for building? Beginners usually come up in five minutes with 6 or 8 ideas, including doorstop, weapon, a weight to hold things down. At the end of a course, after practicing the principles and techniques of creative thinking, they average 15 to 20, including such ideas as a block for ratholes, a whetstone, a stage for a flea circus, and "paint it gold as a Christmas gift for a bricklayer or a goldbricking sergeant."

Alex F. Osborn, a leader in the field of creative thinking, has studied the principles used, perhaps unconsciously, by the great natural-born creators and has shown how to use them. His book *Applied Imagination* is the text used in most creative-thinking courses. What are these principles?

First: *Clearly define the problem.* It sounds obvious, but even seemingly simple problems may not be precisely put. A young mother in a class given by LeRoy Schneider of Roanoke, Virginia, asked, "How can I get my boy to eat his eggs as breakfast?" Others complained of the same difficulty with their youngsters. "Why do you want them to eat eggs?" demanded the teacher. "For the body-building protein," was the reply. Correctly stated, then, the problem became: How can I help my child to get enough protein? Soon, instead of rebelling against eggs, the youngsters whose parents were in this class were getting their protein from food they liked better, such as hamburger or peanut butter.

Second: *Think of all possible solutions.* Good decisions come from a choice among many alternatives. The fertile innovator approaches his problem from every point of view and lets the thoughts come tumbling. Most of us just don't have this fluency, so Osborn has found ways to help us achieve it.

If you want to have lots of ideas, says Osborn, *postpone criticism.* This is the basis on which Osborn initiated "brainstorming," the scheme whereby a group of ten or twelve people suggest as many solutions as possible to a single problem. One person's thoughts stimulate another's to such an extent that a brief, well-conducted brainstorming session can produce an astonishing number of good ideas. The one strict rule is that all criticism must be suspended; no one is to make fun of another's idea.

For example, a group was asked what might be done to save a destroyer at anchor, toward which a mine had already floated so close that there was no time to start up the engines and get away. After many suggestions, one person said laughingly, "Get everybody on deck and blow the mine away!" This patently impractical proposal led another participant to say, "Turn the fire hoses on it and push it back." And this was actually what the crew of one destroyer did when they found themselves in this very predicament off the coast of Wonsan during the Korean War!

Teachers point out that you can brainstorm problems by yourself, by self-quizzing. The late Professor John Arnold, when a member of Stanford's mechanical-engineering department, devised a useful list of "spur" questions, divided into these nine categories:

Other Uses? Major question in this area: "Is there a new way to use as is?"

Borrow or Adapt? Under this heading, we can prime our imaginations with questions like this: "What other ideas might be adaptable?" (Rudolf Diesel got the idea for his engine from a cigar lighter.)

New Twist? A typical question: "What other shape?" (Like the buggy-maker who *tapered* the roller bearing that Leonardo da Vinci had invented four hundred years before.)

More So? The questions under this heading include: "Increase strength?" (Reinforced heels and toes in hosiery.)

Less So? One such question: "Eliminate?" (Example: tubeless tires.)

Substitutes? A typical question under this head: "What replaces?" (Like synthetic rubber during World War II.)

Rearrange? One such question: "Transpose cause and effect?" (As doctors do in diagnoses.)

Reverse? Sample question: "Do the opposite?" (Elias Howe perfected his sewing machine by designing a needle with the hole at the bottom instead of at the top.)

Combine? Most ideas are combinations of other ideas. A typical brainduster along this line: "Combine purposes?" (Benjamin Franklin, to avoid changing from one pair of spectacles to another, cut the lenses of each in half and stuck the halves together, with the reading lenses below. Thus he invented bifocals.)

Third: *Forget the problem for a while.* Teachers encourage students after a long period of seemingly fruitless work to turn the problem over to the subconscious. Here our infinitely complex computers make mysterious calculations and then, suddenly, in a day or a week or a month, an answer may pop into the mind.

George Westinghouse worried for years over ways to bring a long string of railway cars to a simultaneous stop. The answer came in a flash the moment he read that compressed air was being piped to drillers in mountains miles away: he would pipe it along his line of cars and stop them with an air brake. But such inspirations come after long preparation and thought. Other things being equal, the person with the most knowledge in his field will be the most creative in it.

Fourth: *Evaluate the ideas; select the best; act upon it.* The problems thrown at students vary with the subject matter of the course. Men in Dr. Harry Hansen's class in Creative Marketing Strategy at Harvard Business School attacked actual problems troubling specific firms, studied them for a term and presented suggested solutions to company heads.

More than 40,000 college youths all over the country have taken Creative Thinking in connection with their Air Force ROTC training. They tackle difficult situations faced by officers during, for example, the Korean War. "You're a lieutenant in command of the maintenance squadron at Pusan," says the instructor. "Your job is to keep seventy-five planes in repair for repeated missions. How would you organize your mechanics to keep the greatest number of planes in the air?" One trainee suggested an assembly-line system, with each mechanic checking the same parts every time. The instructor passed the idea on to a maintenance officer, who tried it, liked it and now uses it at his base.

Teachers and students agree that the most important benefit from a course in creative thinking is the change in one's mental attitude. Solving poser after poser, week after week, students gain confidence, stop fearing problems and even come to welcome them. They take on some of the spirit of the late Charles F. Kettering of General Motors, who said that problems are the price of progress. "Don't bring me anything but trouble. Good news weakens me."

Courses are stimulating, but many inventive minds never had one. A homeowner, surprised that a handyman had fixed a complicated machine, said, "Did you read the manual?" "No, I can't read," was the reply, "and when you can't read, you have to think." You don't have to register and sit in a class to think. Anyone can follow the principles Alex Osborn has revealed.

If you have a problem, think it through carefully until you can state it clearly. Then, alone or with the help of family, friends or business associates, invent all possible means of solving it, postponing criticism. When you run dry, apply the checklist of "spur" questions and start the stream again. Write down all your ideas and, after a day or two, select the best. You may have the answer you're looking for.

*Solution to the problem of the four nines on page* 200: $99 + 9/9$.

## Chapter 9 / Slow Down—and Live

*The age we live in has been called the aspirin age.
Certainly it is an age of hurry, tension, frantic
competition. We seldom walk anywhere. We usually drive,
and as rapidly as possible. We hurl ourselves through
life at a breathless pace, trying to keep up with the
people who are trying to keep up with the Joneses. Is it
worth it? Here some thoughtful observers of life argue,
gently but persuasively, that it is not.*

# The Art of Purposeful Pausing
STUART KINZIE

On a liner bound for Europe, I was browsing in the library when I came across a puzzling line by Robert Louis Stevenson: "Extreme busyness, whether at school, kirk or market, is a symptom of deficient vitality." Surely, I thought, "deficient" must be a mistake—he meant "abundant." But Mr. Stevenson went merrily on—"It is no good speaking to such folk: they *cannot* be idle, their nature is not generous enough.'"

Was it possible that a bustling display of energy might only be camouflage for a spiritual vacuum? The thought so impressed me that I mentioned it next day to the French purser, at whose table I was sitting. He nodded his agreement. "Stevenson is right," he said. "Indeed, if you will pardon my saying so, the idea applies particularly to you Americans. A lot of your countrymen keep so busy getting things done that they reach the end of their lives without ever having lived at all."

On the other side of me was a fragile little Chinese scholar from Hong Kong. "True," he said. "When there is no time for quiet, there is no time for the soul to grow. The man who walks through a countryside sees much more than the man who runs." He smiled and waved a fine-boned hand. "Sometimes, when you have a task to do, try doing it tomorrow instead of today. In the end, maybe you will get more done—because maybe you will live longer!"

It was advice that sounded like heresy to me. I had crammed my life full, prided myself on never having an idle moment. But now I began to experiment with a little purposeful pausing. And slowly I began to see that this change of pace actually enhanced the excitement of living. I slowed myself down to the point where a breathless awareness of everything gave way to a truer appreciation of essentials: the landscape ceased to be a blur and became a countryside with detail, color, dimension and depth.

One surprising discovery was that pausing can increase efficiency. I found that if you deliberately put off a task for a day or two, you are often likely to do it better. Waiting sometimes dispels the tension that results from an imagined urgency, and so you make fewer mistakes. When you get around to working on the problem, often you find that certain elements of it have already been solved by your subconscious mind.

Another advantage of pausing is that it gives you a better chance to make a decision that is morally right. Following the TV quiz scandals in 1959, a central figure was quoted as saying, "All my life I've been in a hurry." The remark is significant. He was hurrying so that he had no time to read the signs on the boundary dividing honesty from dishonesty.

Still another discovery I made was that leisureliness, tranquillity, little periods of deliberate aimlessness—these things draw people together. Fishermen know this sort of comradeship well. But you don't have to be a fisherman to achieve it. Try spending an hour with your husband or wife just sauntering along the street, window shopping. Or hunt for pine cones or acorns in a wood with the children (children are instinctive pausers). The ancient prohibition against work and organized entertainment on Sunday was designed to create this atmosphere of spiritual harmony. When you practice the art of pausing, you are really scattering fragments of Sunday throughout the week. Many top executives now give themselves a half hour after lunch when they take no phone calls. One man I know, whenever he's faced with an endless series of visitors, arranges for a three-minute interval between appointments. He leans back, puts his feet on the desk and stares out the window. If his mind goes blank, so much the better—it will be all the fresher when the next visitor comes in.

Anyone who will step back and take a look at his way of life can find ways to slow down without resorting to tranquilizers. Why shouldn't the busy housewife, between chores, kick off her shoes, lie down on the sofa and daydream for a few minutes? If her conscience tries to intrude, it should be sent on an errand. When she gets up she'll find that a lot of energy has flowed back into her.

Pausers are not time-wasters; they are time-users. Thoreau's solitary reflections around Walden Pond produced the insights that made him famous. It was Thoreau who said, "The swiftest traveler is he that goes afoot"—a remark that might well be the creative pauser's motto.

To be sure, pausing can be overdone. Lying in bed that extra five minutes is delightful; an extra hour might be not only dull but disastrous. Sooner or later most of us have to get up, go to the office or get the children off to school, attend to the endless mechanics of living. But we will do these things better if we have the emotional balance and the controlled energy that come from deliberate slowing of the pace.

Why not try it? All it takes is a little "won't" power. Make up your mind that you won't be hurried, you won't be rushed, you won't—necessarily—do it now.

### TIME FOR THE SOUL

*A* friend of mine, a distinguished explorer who spent a couple of years among the savages of the upper Amazon, once attempted a forced march through the jungle. The party made extraordinary speed for the first two days, but on the third morning, when it was time to start, my friend found all the natives sitting on their haunches, looking very solemn and making no preparation to leave. "They are waiting," the chief explained to my friend. "They cannot move farther until their souls have caught up with their bodies."

I can think of no better illustration of our own plight today. Is there no way of letting our souls, so to say, catch up with our bodies? If one thinks over the sort of life led in innumerable homes a generation ago, our immense speeding up in the process of living today is clear. People then, as we say, "had time." Now no one "has time."  —*James Truslow Adams*

*F*olks used to be willing to wait patiently for a slow-moving stage coach, but now they kick like the dickens if they miss one revolution of a revolving door.  —*Ed Wynn*

# Pick More Daisies

DON HEROLD

Of course you can't unfry an egg, but there is no law against thinking about it. If I had my life to live over, I would try to make more mistakes. I would relax. I would be sillier than I have been this trip. I know of very few things that I would take seriously. I would be less hygienic. I would go more places. I would climb more mountains and swim more rivers. I would eat more ice cream and less bran. I would have more actual troubles and fewer imaginary troubles.

You see, I have been one of those fellows who live prudently and sanely, hour after hour, day after day. Oh, I have had my moments. But if I had it to do over again, I would have more of them—a lot more. It may be too late to un-teach an old dog old tricks, but perhaps a word of forewarning from the unwise may be of benefit to a coming generation. It may help them to fall into some of the pitfalls I have avoided.

If I had my life to live over, I would pay less attention to people who teach tension. In a world of specialization we naturally have a superabundance of individuals who cry at us to be serious about their individual specialty. They tell us we *must* learn Latin or history; otherwise we will be disgraced and ruined and flunked and failed. After a dozen or so of these protagonists have worked on a young mind, they are apt to leave it in hard knots for life. I wish they had sold me Latin and history as a lark.

I would seek out more teachers who inspire relaxation and fun. I had a few of them, fortunately, and I figure it was they who kept me from going entirely to the dogs. From them I learned how to gather what few scraggly daisies I have gathered along life's cindery pathway.

If I had my life to live over, I would start barefooted a little earlier in the spring and stay that way a little later in the fall. I would play hooky more. I would shoot more paper wads at my teachers. I would have more dogs. I would keep later hours. I'd have more sweethearts. I would fish more. I would go to more circuses. I would go to more dances. I would ride on more merry-go-rounds. I would be carefree as long as I could, or at least until I got some care—instead of having my cares in advance.

More errors are made solemnly than in fun. The rubs of family life come in moments of intense seriousness rather than in moments of lightheartedness. If nations—to magnify my point—declared international carnivals instead of international war, how much better that would be!

G. K. Chesterton once said, "A characteristic of the great saints is their power of levity. Angels can fly because they can take themselves lightly. One 'settles down' into a sort of selfish seriousness; but one has to rise to a gay self-forgetfulness. A man falls into a 'brown study'; he reaches up at a blue sky."

In a world in which practically everybody else seems to be consecrated to the gravity of the situation, I would rise to glorify the levity of the situation. For I agree with Will Durant that "gaiety is wiser than wisdom." I doubt, however, that I'll do much damage with my creed. The opposition is too strong. There are too many serious people trying to get everybody else to be too darned serious.

# Mastering Tensions
*Condensed from the book: Take It Easy*
WALTER B. PITKIN

**E**motions, attitudes and feelings are explosives. The explosion may be violent and marked to any observer, as when you "lose control of yourself" in a fit of rage. Or it may be violent only within your body, while outwardly you are poised and calm. We appraise an emotion as good if it relaxes us or prevents us from growing tense. Grief, for instance, is surely unpleasant, as a rule; yet we all know the benefits of "a good cry."

The commonest evil result of strong emotions develops somewhere in the digestive tract. Sometimes the throat goes horribly tense. Again it is the stomach which tightens up so badly that it cannot perform the digestive movements. It may be even the colon, whose spasms bring on constipation and ulcers and appendicitis. Such disasters are never brought on by a single emotional shock that passes after a few minutes. They come only after many prolonged tensions of fear, worry or anger have set up a habit in the muscles.

Stomach ulcers which have been caused by tensions induced by worry can often be cured by relaxing. Four Columbia University professors reported that thirty-two such sufferers recovered after listening to a psychologist's lectures on tensions and relaxation. At the end of each lecture the listeners drank cold water. That was the entire treatment. After six weeks all but two were eating what they liked.

Our problem is to discover which emotions and attitudes

lead to restful living. A well-balanced emotional life is vastly more important than a well-balanced intellectual career. Had I to choose between the ability to remain serene through adversities and the ability to speak fluent French or German, I should not hesitate a second.

You are tense. You cannot rid yourself of the plague. You want relief. What can we do for you? First of all, learn to work easily, to cultivate the habit of *restful* attention.

Last year I spent an evening with a man to whom it was my duty to report conditions of the country affecting one of his many businesses. He is a man who has earned enormous wealth. He uses his energies with extraordinary economy. As I began my report, he slumped in his easy chair, closed his eyes and dropped his head upon his chest. He seemed to be in a stupor. I spoke for perhaps forty minutes, during which time he gave no sign of life. As I finished he came to in a flash, asked a few questions and within three or four minutes shaped his final judgment on the whole matter. To do this he had relaxed utterly, cutting off as many irrelevant stimuli as possible, closing his eyes to give his ears right-of-way. He was entirely submissive, and what I had to say found a free path to everything in his memory that related to it.

Edmund Jacobson gives us the paradoxical advice: "Do not *try* to relax! Just stop trying!" He is right, for to try to do anything is to set some muscles in action. *Imitate a restful person,* get the soft, warm, delicious feeling of laziness. One of the oldest and best proved tricks is to lie face down on the floor and, as the children say, "make yourself heavy"—the old schoolyard game of going limp all over. When you have done this well, it is perfect relaxation.

Most of us do not stretch enough. Imitate the cat, which does it with ease and grace. Turn the toes downward, stiffen the arms above the head and straighten the fingers. Stretch until it hurts, literally. Stand up and stretch after every half hour of close eye-work. Walk around. Get fresh air if you can. Hold your arms out straight with one set of muscles while you try to pull them back to the shoulder with the opposing muscles. If you are troubled with eye tensions that do not seem to be accompanied by faulty vision, the tensions may be brought on by oversmoking. For, in many people, nicotine seems seriously to narcotize the small muscles of the eyes, hampering them, especially in close work.

A muscle that tenses and then relaxes in a moment or two never causes trouble. But even a very tiny muscle in an unimportant part of your body, if long tense, becomes a plague. The housewife who works too long at a table too high for her may grow overwhelmingly fatigued and attribute this to overwork. Many typists grow irritable and inaccurate from poor posture or badly placed machines, and the root of the difficulty lies in tiny tensions in shoulders and arms of which the sufferer may not even be conscious.

A few enlightened factory men have mastered the secret of rest in work. They require their employes to knock off once or twice every hour and do something totally different from their assigned tasks. In the spinning department of a Pennsylvania textile mill it was found that workers came and went at the rate of 250 percent (that is, 2½ workers filled each job there in the course of a year), while in the other departments the turnover was only 5 percent. Workers in the spinning department complained of neuritis, foot trouble and melancholia. So rest periods were established. Every two hours everybody was compelled to lie down flat, and relax for ten minutes. The situation was transformed. Melancholia ceased, production rose and for the first time workers began to earn bonuses. At the end of the first year there had been no labor turnover. Every man had stuck to his post!

Some of our most upsetting tensions are caused by fear; and the most devastating fears are fears of the unknown. To be aware of a peril but not to understand it throws the human body into a supreme tension and panic. The very instant you know what the menace is, you begin to ease up. This points to a simple rule. Whenever you find yourself worrying, fearful and tense, stop short and ask yourself: "Well, just what am I worrying about? Of what am I afraid?" And cast about for the correct answer. Then your troubles will be half over. For the very act of seeking the answer itself reduces your tensions somewhat.

Having analyzed the factors that lead to your fears, you can begin to plan intelligently. As soon as you do this, you cease to be frightened. *Knowing what to do next breaks down fear. It dissolves fear tensions and frees the muscles for adaptive behavior.*

When wrestling with a difficult situation that is sure to continue for long, learn to break it down into units of twenty-four hours each. Then deal with each day's task, forgetting utterly the scores or hundreds of days beyond tomorrow. Stop trying to solve the entire problem at once. This is the essence of that rugged old British opportunism which men sometimes call "muddling through." It is one of the soundest rules of mental health ever laid down.

Every normal reader should ponder certain experiments in institutions of New York State, Illinois and Pennsylvania, showing that music works strange miracles upon the shattered mind. A man whose memory had gone blank recalled almost everything clearly, after listening to beautiful melodies. A man who was always fighting his keepers became serene. Many a patient deep in dark introspection rises to sanity as he listens to music, and inmates who join in singing old songs lose their eccentricities, some of them remaining close to sanity for days after such participation.

Normal people benefit from music even more than do these poor broken creatures. Something tense breaks within the listener as the music flows on; some strange release is brought by its magic. Many people have told me that they never knew what utter relaxation was until they caught the trick of snapping off the lights, turning on fine music and then flinging themselves in an abandon of rest upon the bed.

Briefly, the art of relaxation comes with the philosophy of putting pleasure before business. Such a philosophy does not butter our bread, perhaps, but it certainly helps us digest it.

### THE POWER OF PEACE

*R*ealize that you have sixteen waking hours, three or four of which should be devoted to making a silent conquest of your mental machinery. The failure to cultivate the power of peaceful concentration is the greatest single cause of mental breakdown. A few hours out of the sixteen will suffice; only let them be hours of daily dedication. —*Sir William Osler*

### FACING FACTS

*I* do believe one ought to face facts. If you don't, they get behind you and may become terrors, nightmares, giants, horrors. As long as one faces them, one is top dog. The trouble is not to steel oneself but to face them calmly, easily—to have the habit of facing them. —*Katherine Mansfield*

# Boredom and Excitement

*Condensed from the book: The Conquest of Happiness*

BERTRAND RUSSELL

**B**oredom as a factor in human behavior has been, I believe, one of the great motive powers throughout the historical epoch, and is so at the present day more than ever. The desire for excitement is very deep-seated in human beings, especially in males. I suppose that in the hunting stage it was more easily gratified than it has been since. The chase was exciting, war was exciting, courtship was exciting. But with the coming of agriculture, life began to grow dull. In old days, after supper everybody sat round and had what was called "a happy family time." This meant that paterfamilias went to sleep, his wife knitted and the daughters wished they were dead or at Timbuktu. All this weight of boredom should be borne in mind in estimating the world of a hundred years ago.

We are less bored than our ancestors were, but we are more afraid of boredom. We have come to believe that boredom is not part of the natural lot of man, but can be avoided by a sufficiently vigorous pursuit of excitement. Every housemaid expects at least once a week as much excitement as would have lasted a Jane Austen heroine throughout a whole novel. As we rise in the social scale, the pursuit of excitement becomes more and more intense. A wish to escape from boredom is natural; indeed, all races of mankind have displayed it as opportunity occurred. Wars, pogroms and persecutions have all been part of the flight from boredom; even quarrels with neighbors have been found better than nothing.

Boredom, however, is not to be regarded as wholly evil. Too much excitement not only undermines the health but dulls the palate for every kind of pleasure, substituting titillations for profound organic satisfactions, cleverness for wisdom and jagged surprises for beauty. A certain amount of excitement is wholesome, but, like almost everything else, the matter is quantitative. Too little may produce morbid cravings; too much, exhaustions. A certain power of enduring boredom is therefore essential to a happy life.

All great books contain boring portions, and all great lives have contained uninteresting stretches. Imagine a modern publisher confronted with the Old Testament as a new manuscript submitted to him for the first time. What would his comments be, for instance, on the genealogies? "My dear sir," he would say, "you can't expect your reader to be interested in a mere string of proper names of persons about whom you tell so little. You have begun your story, I will admit, in fine style, and at first I was very favorably impressed, but you have altogether too much wish to tell it all. Pick out the highlights, take out the superfluous matter and bring me back your manuscript when you have reduced it to a reasonable length." All the best novels contain boring passages. A novel which sparkles from the first page to the last is pretty sure not to be a great book. Nor have the lives of most great men been exciting except at a few great moments. Socrates could enjoy a banquet now and again, and must have derived considerable satisfaction from his conversations while the hemlock was taking effect, but most of his life he lived quietly with Xanthippe, taking a constitutional in the afternoon and perhaps meeting a few friends by the way. Immanuel Kant is said never to have been more than ten miles from Königsberg in all his life. Charles Darwin, after going round the world, spent the whole of the rest of his life in his own house. Karl Marx, after stirring up a few revolutions, decided to spend the remainder of his days in the British Museum. Altogether it will be found that a quiet life is characteristic of great men, and that their pleasures have not been of the sort that would look exciting to the outward eye.

The capacity to endure a more or less monotonous life is one which should be acquired in childhood. Modern parents do not realize the importance to a child of having one day like another, except, of course, for somewhat rare occasions. The pleasures of childhood should in the main be such as the child extracts from his environment by means of some effort and inventiveness. Pleasures which are exciting and at the same time involve no physical exertion, such, for example, as the theater, should occur very rarely. A child develops best when, like a young plant, he is left undisturbed in the same soil. Too much travel, too great a variety of impressions, are not good for the young and cause them as they grow up to become incapable of enduring fruitful monotony. A boy or young man who has some serious constructive purpose will endure voluntarily a great deal of boredom if he finds that it is necessary by the way. But constructive purposes do not easily form themselves in a boy's mind if he is living a life of distractions and dissipations, for in that case his thoughts will always be directed toward the next pleasure rather than the distant achievement. A generation that cannot endure boredom will be a generation of little men, of men unduly divorced from the slow processes of nature.

Whatever we may wish to think, we are creatures of earth; our life is part of the life of the earth, and we draw our nourishment from it just as the plants and animals do; the rhythm of earth life is slow; autumn and winter are as essential as motion. The human body has been adapted through the ages to this rhythm. I have seen a boy two years old, who had been kept in London, taken out for the first time to walk in green country. The season was winter, and everything was wet and muddy. To the adult eye there was nothing to cause delight, but in the boy there sprang up a strange ecstasy; he knelt on the wet ground and put his face in the grass and gave utterance to half-articulate cries of delight. The joy that he was experiencing was primitive, simple and massive. The organic need that was being satisfied is so profound that those in whom it is starved are seldom completely sane. Many pleasures, of which we may take gambling as a good example, have in them no element of this contact with earth. Such pleasures, in the instant when they cease, leave a man feeling dusty and dissatisfied, hungry for he knows not what. Those, on the other hand, that bring us into contact with the life of the earth have something in them profoundly satisfying; when they cease, the happiness that they have brought remains, although their intensity while they existed may have been less than that of more exciting dissipations. What makes Shakespeare's lyrics supreme is that they are filled with the same joy that made the two-year-old embrace the grass. Consider "Hark, hark! the lark," or "Come unto these yellow sands." The special kind of boredom from which modern urban populations suffer is intimately bound up with their separation from the life of the earth. It makes life hot and dusty and thirsty, like a pilgrimage in the desert. A happy life must be to a great extent a quiet life, for it is only in an atmosphere of quiet that true joy can live.

## Chapter 10/The Hidden Power in People

*Psychologists say that most of the time people don't
begin to live up to their potential. Now and then, in
a crisis, they may call on hidden reserves of strength
and perform incredible feats while the crisis lasts. But
once it is over they become their ordinary selves again.
What is this hidden power in people? Can it be
analyzed? Can it be put to work? Philosopher William
James and Reverend Norman Vincent Peale
are among those with telling answers.*

## Of Course You're Creative!
**MICHAEL DRURY**

For many of us the word "creativity" has a wall around it, and we are on the outside. We
protest that we have no gift, that creativity is for geniuses.

But creativity is *not* the special gift of a favored few, a
burst of light you've either got or you haven't. One of the
most creative people I ever knew was an old woman who
lived on a remote sheep ranch in California. A Chilean, she
had married an American sea captain at sixteen, moved to
his country and learned his language. On that lonely, fog-
swept coast she made a home, a life, an empire both spiritual
and commerical. She bought and sold land, delivered babies,
and cooked for thirty men at shearing time. She bore five
children, and taught them to read and write and ride and to
be as much at home in the ocean as a seal. It made your

blood sing to watch her, at nearly ninety, climb the hill behind her house and face the sun as it went down in the sea.

She was a woman with little education except what she had taught herself, out of need and love and high courage. But by living up to herself and always a little beyond, she had found out what she was and used it freely for herself and others—and that's creativity.

It is false to imagine that creativity just happens. The *capacity* to be creative is inherent in human beings, but the utilization of that capacity is hard work. It is not hobbies or "taking courses" or "keeping busy." Creativity is work that goes somewhere; it is sustained effort toward an ideal.

When Sir William Herschel, the father of modern astronomy, set out to make the finest telescope the world had ever seen, he first had to learn to grind and polish mirrors. After months of work his first mirror turned out to be imperfect. He made two hundred attempts before he produced a telescope that satisfied him. It took Brahms almost twenty years to compose his "First Symphony."

We may not be endowed to build a bridge or write a poem or find a new star, but if we would live our lives deeply and creatively we must work and go on working to show our own view of what it means to be alive. The work itself may be modest, but if it calls forth delight, curiosity, inventiveness, we are using the same forces that genius uses. For creativity is not so much an aptitude as an attitude, and therefore applicable anywhere from making a lemon pie to building a moon rocket. Those people we call talented know this by instinct. The rest of us have to learn it.

The exact process is not known, but perhaps most often creativity begins in response to things greater than ourselves. The wonder of the sunrise, when for an instant you feel the slow, majestic roll of earth; the awe that flickers through you when you accomplish, after all, the task that was too hard; the glimpse into infinity when whole landscapes are mirrored in a puddle no deeper than a plate—these are the stirrings of creativity. Beyond them come reflection, an awareness of awareness, taking notice of our own thought.

In the film version of William Saroyan's *The Human Comedy*, a little boy keeps asking what it is to be afraid. Then, at a carnival, a man in a mask scares him, and after a moment of terror the boy exclaims with delight, "I'm afraid! I know what afraid is!" In a similar way the creative person says to himself, "This I know. This I have seen and felt."

On the heels of awareness is the impulse to *do* something with what we feel and know. Here, sadly, is where many of us go awry. Making and doing turn out to be so difficult that we abandon the attempt. Because an idea or a plan doesn't readily take shape, we conclude that it is no good, that we aren't creative anyway—when, in fact, it takes an enlightened stubbornness to produce anything. Even Mozart, who could conceive whole movements of a symphony in one lightning flash, had to transcribe that flash one note at a time.

Some people insist they have no ideas at all, when what they mean is that they don't have big or revolutionary ideas. But good ideas bombard us every day—from people, travel, reading. Anyone can have more ideas by being hospitable to those he has—using them, trying them out, not discarding them before he has given them a chance. Other people sprout ideas like mushrooms but let the vision drift away because they are impatient with small beginnings. If they can't start impressively, they choose not to start at all. This is deadly to creativity. Helen Keller wrote: "When we let a resolution or a fine emotion dissipate without results, it means more than lost opportunity; it actually retards the fulfillment of future purposes."

Beyond the longing to do or make something to give our feeling form and substance comes the rough work of discipline—a word we don't care much for these days. And yet it is more truly in the small, daily, moment-by-moment discipline that creativity can be seen than in the crowning triumph. The story is told of a woman who rushed up to Fritz Kreisler after a concert and cried, "I'd give my life to play as you do!" And the violinist answered soberly, "I did."

So must we, if we would be creative. Giving one's life means choosing from the multitude of possibilities a certain goal and then working patiently toward it, even when we are tired or puzzled or afraid. It means loving what we do, not just its high points but its day-in-day-out effort. It means sticking to one's own purpose through a thousand storms and fires, from within as well as from without, and experimenting, failing, trying again until both the purpose and oneself are refined and ready.

I know an actor in his seventies who all his life has had only minor roles. One day I asked him about it. "When I was getting on toward fifty," he said, "I admitted to myself that I was never going to be a really big star. There was no other work I'd rather be doing, so I made up my mind to give my best to every job I got, even a walk-on. That way, I've made my own place, and I've had satisfaction that nothing can take away from me." He had realized the deep inner rewards of the creative attitude, something quite different from the desire for applause.

Too often we say in effect, "Tell me how to be creative." The very request is a denial of creativity. The great and transforming truth is that being creative is a discovery—of ourselves, of our own way of responding to life. And discovery implies what no one has known before. It is something one does alone, like getting born or dying, and to recognize and accept that, and stop asking how, is to take the first long step in our own creativity.

⇒ ◆ ⇐

### THE CHINA DOLL

*T*he best years of my life came after what seemed at first a tragedy from which I could never recover. I had been a Dresden China Doll sort of wife. I'd grown up in too much luxury. I knew nothing. And so it happened that my husband ran our home, as well as his own successful business, while I accepted soft, sweet irresponsibility.

Then one day his partner looted the firm and fled. A month later my husband's overstrained heart gave way. And I, ignorant heir to his wholesale butter-and-egg business, walked into his empty office and began to learn things. Friends begged me to sell out for whatever I could get. I was warned that I'd end in bankruptcy. But some invisible force drove me on. I stuck. I studied. I visited bankers and wholesalers and customers, eagerly learning. Every night I fell into bed exhausted. But the Dresden China Doll had come to life at last. After a year I was still horribly in debt. I had lost half the old customers. But I felt at home in the business.

Three years later I was on my feet, sure of myself. I was making almost as much as my husband had earned. Pretty good for an ex-China Doll. More old customers had come back. I ate better, slept better—and joked oftener—than ever before.

I was thirty-nine years old then. Now I'm turning fifty-nine. And I'm still in the Best Years of My Life—the years that have brought out the very best in me.    —*Anonymous, Art of Living*

# The Job Your Unconscious Mind Can Do

SMILEY BLANTON, M.D.

**A**s a practicing psychiatrist, I have listened to just about every human problem under the sun. No two troubles are alike—human nature is infinitely complex. But the people who come seeking help do have one thing in common. Each is struggling to overcome some problem—and failing. Usually in the first visit these people blurt out their frustration: "I've tried everything I can think of, Doctor, *everything*. What on earth shall I do now?"

The advice I often give these people is quite simple, and it never fails to startle them: "Don't try!" Sounds defeatist, doesn't it? But it isn't. After more than forty years of practice, I still find it the best all-inclusive prescription I know.

The reason is this. Within each of us an all-wise Creator has placed a marvelous reservoir of courage, energy and wisdom that we seldom use. This reservoir is the subconscious or, more exactly, the unconscious mind. Like a dynamo it furnishes the power and drive of our lives. This power takes many forms. What we call intuition, for example, is nothing but a "still, small voice" from the unconscious. It is also the unconscious that produces for poets, prophets, scientists—indeed all creative thinkers—their deepest insights.

The power that the unconscious *can* provide is almost limitless; we all know of individuals who, in a crisis, were able to perform incredible feats of strength or endurance. But the circuits that bring the power from the unconscious can be blocked by frustration, tension, anxiety—or by the equally destructive emotions of fear, guilt, hate, sustained anger. And that is what is happening to most of the individuals who seek my help. They are fighting so furiously on the conscious level to solve their problems, and are rendered so desperate by their failure that emotionally they have short-circuited themselves.

Such people have to be taught to trust their unconscious and shown how to use it. Sometimes this is difficult because many are afraid of the uncharted region within and the primitive impulses that lurk there. But such fear is based on ignorance. There is nothing necessarily evil in the unconscious. Even the primitive impulses, understood and rightly channeled, can be used for successful living. But how, then, does a person tap the tremendous reservoir of power that is locked within him? He must develop habits and attitudes that will unblock and deepen the channels between the conscious and the unconscious mind, and let that power flow.

What are these habits and attitudes? They have a familiar ring, because centuries ago religion identified them and nurtured them in man.

First: *Trust and believe in the hidden power within you.* A psychiatrist might say, "Have faith in your unconscious." A minister might say, "Have faith in God." Personally, I see no conflict between the two ideas. Indeed, they may well be the same idea, expressed differently. After all, it was the Founder of Christianity who said that "the kingdom of heaven is within you."

Next: *Be willing to surrender to it.* Get rid of the notion that *you* are all-powerful, that *you* can run your life and solve all problems without help from any source. The advice "Don't try," after you have tried everything, is an invitation to let go, to give up and let the deeper mind take over. The

more complete this surrender, the more remarkable the results. When I was studying the healings at Lourdes some
years ago, I noticed that those who were healed (medically
verified healings did take place) had reached the absolute
end of their resources—physical, emotional, spiritual. They
had done all they could; the doctors had done all they could;
there was nothing left but total surrender to whatever restora-
tive force resided in God or in their own deeper selves.

The third bit of advice that I often give to patients (when
I think they may take it) is perhaps the most effective of all:
*Try prayer.* In prayer, whatever the creed or denomination,
one accepts the concept of a Creator who is the source of life
and to whom one can turn in humility and trust. Here again
the surrender of self is the indispensable attitude: "Not my
will, but Thine be done." When this attitude is truly domi-
nant, the results can be astonishing. Whether you choose to
call it mobilizing the unconscious or making contact with
God, prayer is a channel through which enormous power
can flow.

A fourth method of tapping the power in the unconscious
is this: *Learn the secret of creative relaxation.* The psychiatrist's couch has become a source of endless jokes, but the
idea behind it is valid: to reach the unconscious, tension
must be at a minimum.

Everyone, it seems to me, should have a daily period during which he arranges not to be disturbed, lays aside anxieties and burdens and gives himself up to the creative unconscious. It is best to lie down, if you can, and make yourself as
limp as a wet leaf on a log. If this is not possible, sit in a
chair, close your eyes to remove visible distractions and just
"let go." Such a quiet period, in which the mind says to the
body, "Don't try," is a great energy restorer during the day, a

great tranquilizer before going to sleep at night. If you have problems, you can turn them over to the unconscious to work on while you sleep. And it will work effectively, for it is crammed with all the knowledge you have dropped into it, all the things you have learned during your life and "forgotten." The unconscious is timeless and it does not forget.

A fifth method of releasing the power of the unconscious is: *Use autosuggestion.* Too much, at times, has been claimed for this—loudly asserting that problems don't exist, for example, will not make them go away. Still, it is also true that attitudes *are* more important than facts. And there is no doubt at all that if you consciously look for the best in things, it will act as a tonic for your mind and heart, tending to remove the tensions that stifle the creative unconscious.

I knew a man once, a salesman, who literally breathed confidence into himself. By nature he was shy, but he devised a little trick of autosuggestion that worked wonders for him. When he approached a prospect, he deliberately listened to the rhythm of his own breathing, then imagined that with every exhalation he was breathing out negative ideas, and with every inhalation breathing in positive ones. "I'm breathing out shyness," he would say to himself, "breathing in confidence. I'm breathing out timidity, breathing in assurance. I'm breathing out failure, breathing in success." What he was breathing, of course, was simply air. But his unconscious mind took these signals from his conscious mind quite literally, and in response sent him the very qualities he needed.

Every doctor has seen cases in which a desperately ill patient miraculously recovers because his family needs him and he simply decides he isn't going to die. Again the Bible summarizes it with matchless brevity: "As a man thinketh in his heart [not his conscious mind, notice, but his *heart*], so is he." The thing to remember, then, is this: each of us has, in his unconscious mind, power and strength and courage past all imagining. Sometimes we fail to use this strength because we don't know it is there. Sometimes we delude ourselves into thinking we don't need it. Sometimes we block it with fear or guilt or tension. But it is most assuredly there.

"Don't try," clearly, is not advice to be given (or taken) when a person has made only a halfhearted attempt to help himself or has not really tried at all. But when a full, honest, conscientious effort has been made with no success, then the best thing to do is to stop struggling and let the great creative forces of the universe come to your rescue.

"Having done all," advised St. Paul, "stand!" Stand quietly, he meant. Wait. Relax. Accept the help that will come to you out of the mysterious realm that we psychiatrists call the unconscious—and that St. Paul called God.

### UNCONSCIOUS ANSWERS

**D**r. Hans Selye, whose concept of stress is world-famous, declares: "If all efforts planned specifically to stimulate associative thoughts fail, there is no point in trying to force a solution by sheer stubbornness; it is best to let the problem slip from the sphere of conscious analysis and incubate in the unconscious. At this stage all we can do is to create conditions favorable to imaginative thinking. It seems that, after we have saturated ourselves with all the material necessary for the appraisal of a new correlation, we invariably are too close to this or that aspect of it to see things in their true perspective. An unexpected solution to a problem is most unlikely to present itself while we are making a desperate conscious effort to find it."    —*Executive Health*

# You Are Tougher Than You Think

*Condensed from the book: The Tough-Minded Optimist*

NORMAN VINCENT PEALE

Let's face it, to live in this world you have to be strong. Sooner or later something will hit you—pain, sickness, accident, failure—and when it comes it will rock you, *unless* you have developed some good inner toughness—"tough-mindedness," I call it.

It could be that the world was made as it is, full of problems and difficulty, to bring out this tough quality in human beings. Because you are, in fact, tougher than you think. All the strength you'll ever need to handle *anything* is within you now. It was put there by your Creator, who knew very well what you would be up against in this life—and made you equal to it.

If life seems to be going extra hard for you, ask yourself honestly just where the trouble is. The tendency is to blame other people, or forces beyond your control. But the truth is that your problem is *not* beyond your control; the solution is within you. As Gautama Buddha declared, "The mind is everything; what you think, you become." If you are weak and defeated, the reason may well be that you have allowed failure to dominate your thoughts, creating a deep unconscious belief that you do not have the ability to succeed.

The solution? Reverse the mental image of yourself. This will not be easy; negative mental habits have channeled deep grooves in your consciousness, and your mind will protest a positive reorientation. But you must realize that your mind has actually been lying to you about your real abilities, deliberately causing you to fail. So you must stand up to your mind, dominate it. Don't let it control you. You can always—with God's help—control it.

Young people were once taught this strong philosophy in the schools of America and in homes and churches, too. Such forthright teaching developed a great breed of men; but it has been rather generally abandoned, and a deteriorating softness has been allowed to set in. I call this a crime against human nature. My fifth-grade teacher back in Norwood, Ohio, was George Reeves, a giant of a man whose huge hand was more than once applied forcibly to the seat of my trousers—an act which he considered both beneficial to the student and contributory to the main purpose of education: namely, to make men.

But George Reeves left a lasting impression upon the mind as well as the body. I can recall vividly how he would, in the midst of class, suddenly thunder out, "Silence!" With that he would turn to the blackboard and write in large letters the word CAN'T. Then he would turn around and glare at us. We knew what to do. With united voice we would chant, "Strike the T off the CAN'T." And with a sweeping, powerful stroke he would erase the 'T, leaving the great word CAN standing forth unforgettably.

"Let that be a lesson to you," he would say. "Stop whining that you can't. Remember who you are. You are children of God. You are Americans. With God's help you can overcome all difficulties." Then he would add a phrase I've never forgotten: *"You can if you think you can."*

The defeated mind can hardly bring success out of failure, for it is incapable of perceiving possibilities in hard situations. But the strong person has a mind unclouded by gloom. He realizes the obstacles in a given problem, but he has the ability always to see a chink of light in any darkness, however black. I was reminded of this on a visit my wife and I paid to our daughter Elizabeth when she was a student at Mount Holyoke College. Strolling about the campus, we came to a sun dial on which is the following inscription: "To larger vision the end of shadow is the line of light."

What does that mean? Well, once I took off from New York on a jet for Paris. It was near midnight, or 5 a.m. Paris time. It was a moonless night, and we leveled off at 33,000 feet. It was totally dark, but not for long. Looking east at that great height, I saw a very thin, almost infinitesimal line of light appear on the far horizon where the shadow ended. A short time later and five hundred miles farther on, the radiant dawn in all its glory flared up the heavens. The strong person has this "larger vision" and is therefore able to see the line of light at the end of the shadow. And he never gives up, either. One of the simplest things about all facts of life is that to get where you want to go, you must keep on keeping on.

I once asked Dr. Frank Boyden, headmaster of Deerfield Academy, one of our outstanding schools for boys, how he had managed to build this great institution from practically nothing. He chuckled as he told of his close brushes with bankruptcy over the years. "I'm sure the bank wrote me off a hundred times," he said. "But help always came. Time and again we were scraping bottom, but I knew I was doing something God wanted done: trying to make men out of boys. I put everything in His hands—and I worked my head off." There is truly a tough-minded optimist in action.

I'm told that Frank Leahy, when he was Notre Dame's football coach, wrote a legend in gigantic letters on the locker-room wall. It was the last thing the players saw as they trotted out to the field: "When the going gets tough, let the tough get going."

Write that thought in large letters in your consciousness; practice until it becomes part of you the conviction that there is a God-given supply of strength within you. If you've been taking a dark view of things, muster up your character and look deeply into yourself. Perhaps your spiritual "muscles" have grown soft through neglect; if so, they should be exercised and developed until you can begin to see the bright view. Practice seeing yourself, not as weak and vacillating, but as strong, controlled, purposeful.

Poet Ella Wheeler Wilcox describes very well what right thinking can mean to you: "Man is what he thinks. Not what he says, reads or hears. By persistent thinking you can undo any condition which exists. You can be free of any chains, whether of poverty, sin, ill health, unhappiness or fear." Remember, you can indeed be a tough-minded optimist.

**N**othing splendid has ever been achieved except by those who dared to believe that there was something inside them superior to circumstance. —*Bruce Barton*

### THE LAST STRAW

**M**y cousin Hannah was living through one of those winters when every known calamity descends on the family. She is a buoyant soul, but when her mother broke her hip, Hannah gave vent to a word of bitterness which has become a family byword. "I know the Lord won't send me more trouble than I have strength to bear," she said. "But I do wish He didn't have quite such a good opinion of me!" —*Mrs. Arthur R. Pennell*

# How to Increase Your Energy

*Condensed from the book: The Energies of Men*

WILLIAM JAMES

**E**veryone knows what it is to start a piece of work, either intellectual or muscular, feeling stale—or *oold,* as an Adirondack guide once put it to me. And everybody knows what it is to "warm up" to his job. The process of warming up gets particularly striking in the phenomenon known as "second wind."

Usually we make a practice of stopping an occupation as soon as we meet the first layer of fatigue. We have then walked, played or worked "enough," so we desist. But if an unusual necessity forces us onward, a surprising thing occurs. The fatigue gets worse up to a certain point, when, gradually or suddenly, it passes away and we are fresher than before! We have evidently tapped a new level of energy. There may be layer after layer of this experience, a third and a fourth "wind." We find amounts of ease and power that we never dreamed ourselves to own, sources of strength habitually not taxed, because habitually we never push through the obstruction of fatigue.

Most of us may learn to live in perfect comfort on higher levels of power. Everyone knows that on any given day there are energies slumbering in him which the incitements of that day do not call forth. Compared with what we ought to be, we are only half awake. Our fires are damped, our drafts are checked. We are making use of only a small part of our possible mental and physical resources.

Only the very exceptional individuals push to their extremes. To what do these better men owe their escape from the habit to which the rest of us fall prey—the habit of inferiority to our full self? The answer is plain: either some unusual stimulus fills them with emotional excitement, or some unusual idea induces them, of necessity, to make an extra effort of will.

A new position of responsibility, for example, will usually reveal a man to be far stronger than was supposed. The careers of Oliver Cromwell and Ulysses S. Grant are stock examples of how war will wake a man up. Humbler examples show perhaps still better what effects duty's appeal may produce in chosen individuals. Every case of illness nursed by wife or mother is a proof of this, and where can one find greater examples of sustained endurance than in those thousands of homes where the woman keeps the family going by taking all the thought and doing all the work, sewing, scrubbing, saving, helping neighbors? If she does a bit of scolding now and then, who can blame her?

Despair, which lames most people, wakes others fully up. Every siege or shipwreck or polar expedition brings out some hero who keeps the whole company in heart. Following a terrible colliery explosion in France, two hundred corpses were exhumed. After twenty days of excavation the rescuers heard a voice. *"Me voici,"* said the first man unearthed. He was a collier who had taken command of thirteen others in the darkness, disciplined and cheered them and brought them out alive.

Such experiences show how, under excitement, our organism will sometimes perform its physiological work. But the normal opener of deeper and deeper levels of energy is the *will*. The difficulty is to use it, to make the effort that the word implies. A single successful effort of moral volition, such as saying no to some habitual temptation, or performing some courageous act, will launch a man on a higher level of energy for weeks, will give him a new range of power.

"In the act of uncorking a bottle of whiskey which I had brought home to get drunk upon," said a man to me, "I suddenly found myself running out into the garden, where I smashed it on the ground. I felt so uplifted after this act that for two months I wasn't tempted to touch a drop."

The best practical knowers of the human soul have invented disciplines to keep the deeper levels constantly in reach. The German Prince Pueckler-Muskau wrote to his wife from England in the early 1800's that he had invented "a sort of artificial resolution respecting things that are difficult of performance. My device," he continues, "is this: *I give my word of honor most solemnly to myself* to do or to leave undone this or that. I am of course extremely cautious in the use of this expedient, but when once the word is given I hold it to be perfectly irrevocable. I find something very satisfactory in the thought that man has the power of framing such props and weapons out of trivial materials, indeed out of nothing, merely by the force of his will."

Our energy budget is like our nutritive budget. Physiologists say that a man is in "nutritive equilibrium" when day after day he neither gains nor loses weight. Just so, one can be in what I might call "efficiency equilibrium" on astonishingly different quantities of work, no matter in what direction the work may be measured. It may be physical work, intellectual work, moral work or spiritual work. Of course there are limits: trees don't grow into the sky. But the fact remains that men, pushing their energies to the extreme, may in a vast number of cases keep the pace up day after day, and find no reaction of a bad sort, so long as decent hygienic conditions are preserved. A man's more active rate of energizing does not wreck him, for the organism adapts itself. As the rate of waste augments, so does the rate of repair.

I say the *rate* and not the *time* of repair. The busiest man needs no more hours of rest than the idler. Some years ago Professor George Patrick of the University of Iowa kept three young men awake for four days and nights. When his observations on them were finished, the subjects slept themselves out. All awoke from this sleep completely refreshed, but the one who took the longest to restore himself from his vigil slept only one-third longer than was regular with him.

It is evident that our organism has stored-up reserves of energy that are ordinarily not called upon—deeper and deeper strata of explosible material, ready for use by anyone who probes so deep. The human individual usually lives far within his limits. In rough terms, we may say that a man who energizes below his normal maximum fails by just so much to profit by his chance at life.

### PERFECT FOCUS

In one of the laboratories in Washington, D.C., is a burning glass which measures three feet across. When it is hung in the window, it converges thirty-six inches of ordinary sunshine in one tiny point of flaming radiance. The point is hotter than a blowtorch, so hot that it will melt its way through a steel plate as easily as a heated needle will burn a hole through tissue paper. Three feet of common sunshine—but perfectly focused. An ordinary mind, disciplined to concentrated effort, is capable of achievements quite as impressive. —*James Gordon Gilkey*

# The Importance of Feeling Inferior
*Condensed from the Book*

MARIE BEYNON RAY

On a June day the new streamlined Broadway Limited stood flashing its flanks in a Long Island railroad yard. Suddenly bulbs exploded, cameras clicked, the crowd surged. A man in athletic trunks stepped out on the tracks, hitched a chain to the observation car, pulled. The whole seventy-two tons of steel followed him along the track. He was forty-seven years old and his name—Angelo Siciliano.

Angelo was raised in Brooklyn slums, son of Italian immigrants. At sixteen he was "a ninety-seven-pound runt, pale, nervous and a prey to bullies." One Saturday he went with settlement-house boys to the Brooklyn Museum. There Angelo sat transfixed by the statues of Apollo and Hercules. The group leader informed him that for these statues young Greek athletes had been models. That evening Angelo Siciliano clipped a series of exercises from a newspaper and began making himself over in the likeness of a Greek athlete. He started inventing his own exercises, pitting one muscle against another, and presently—there was no doubt about it —Angelo was beginning to bulge in all directions. He became "the world's most perfectly developed man," "the possessor of the true classic physique, a blend of Hercules and Apollo." These are titles held by Charles Atlas.

He posed for the statue of Alexander Hamilton in front of the Treasury Building in Washington. For George Washington on the Washington Square Monument in Manhattan. For "Sorrow" on the banks of the Marne. And for many others. Isn't it obvious that Angelo Siciliano became Charles Atlas *because* he was once a ninety-seven-pound runt, the prey of bullies?

Gertrude Klasen was born within sound of London's Bow Bells, a cockney from her first yell. Her father was a drunkard and a singer in low music halls. At thirteen Gertie went to live with him and his mistress in one room divided by a curtain. He was "in the theater" and that's where Gertie wanted to be. Playing bit parts, she was soon being told she looked almost like a lady. She went to see Miss Italia Conti, a well-known coach. Miss Conti assured her that, though she might learn to look and act like a lady, with her raucous voice and cockney accent she'd never fool anyone. That was all Gertie needed. From being wistful, she became determined. She haunted the premises until finally Miss Conti consented to take her on.

You may have seen this same Gertie in George Bernard Shaw's *Pygmalion* on Broadway, in the role of Eliza Doolittle, the flower girl who in a flood of cockney bawls out a lady for the rude behavior of her son. That was Gertie, uttering her native woodnotes wild. What Professor Higgins did for Eliza in the play is exactly what Miss Conti did for Gertrude Klasen: by the simple process of phonetics she transformed her into Gertrude Lawrence, as perfect a lady as ever graced the British stage.

With this start Miss Lawrence rose to become a dashing figure in international society. For poverty she substituted wealth. For cockney speech, exquisite diction. For emotional insecurity, the stability of marriage to a devoted husband. Even Gertrude Lawrence herself recognized that her whole life was motivated by a "wrong side of the tracks" complex.

These two people, each with a different goal, achieved those goals because of a strong feeling of inferiority in their childhood. This is not the exception. It is the rule.

No one succeeds *without* an inferiority complex. No one succeeds *in spite* of an inferiority complex. Everyone who succeeds does so *because* of an inferiority complex. Fortunately, everyone has an inferiority complex.

When Alfred Adler was a small boy, he awoke one morning to find a brother dead in bed beside him. To this terrible experience he reacted in character with the man he was to become. He decided to be a doctor so that he might fight death.

Early in his medical career Adler stumbled upon a sequence of phenomena which was to lead to his becoming a great discoverer of facts concerning the human mind. Examining cadavers, he noted conditions which had not before attracted particular attention. He discovered a heart enlarged well beyond normal size and noted that the obstruction of a valve had prevented blood from reaching the lungs in sufficient quantities. Had the heart perhaps increased in size in order to make up this deficiency?

In a body from which one diseased kidney had been removed he noted that the other kidney was considerably larger than normal. Where one lung was weakened by disease he might find the other had developed more power. Wasn't it logical to suppose that it was endeavoring to make up for the lost efficiency of the other? Upon broken bones he remarked that the bone had formed a tough callus. Was this to make the bone stronger than before? These phenomena happened so regularly as to make it appear that the body had a law of its own: to replace a minus with a plus.

Now he pushed his searches further. He began visiting art schools and testing the eyesight of the students. He discovered that over 70 percent of the students had more or less serious deficiencies of sight. Why had they elected to build a career around a defective organ? He learned that as children they had sensed their inadequacy and had made a special effort to see better than others. They had trained their observation, their pleasure in seeing, to the point where they took a more than average interest in the visual world.

Adler now dug into the biographies of great artists and discovered that many of them had suffered from deficiencies of sight—that Albrecht Dürer squinted and Adolph von Menzel was so shortsighted that he was forced to bring his canvas within a few inches of his eyes; that Edouard Manet had severe astigmatism and Franz von Lenbach only one eye. Why had so many individuals with poor eyesight elected to become artists? Was this perhaps the same law at work that he had observed in his dissections: that nature endeavors to compensate for a bodily deficiency?

He went on to study the blind and confirmed that their hearing, touch and smell were unusually keen. And the aural deficiencies of such musicians as Anton Bruckner, Robert Franz, Friedrich Smetana and Ludwig van Beethoven seemed at least in part to account for their extraordinary intentness on the beauty of sound.

Adler in his investigations had passed imperceptibly from biology to neurology and from neurology to psychology— from compensation for organic deficiencies on a biological level to compensation for bodily defects on a psychological level. But so far the types of compensation he had noted had all been unconscious. The human will had played no part.

He now began investigating less obvious cases. There was

Louis Pasteur, who, with the speech areas of his brain destroyed by a stroke, had slowly and painfully fought his way back to speech by a powerful effort of the will, developing new speech centers in the brain. He turned up hundreds of similar cases—famous strong men who had been weaklings in their youth, record-breaking milers who had been cripples, prima ballerinas who had had polio, great singers who had been consumptives. Struggling desperately to overcome their disability, they had developed a superior ability. This was not blind nature at work—this was human will.

It began to look as though this was some sort of law, as though human beings often accomplished what they did because of an initial disability, as though humanity needed a hurdle in order to jump—and that the higher the hurdle, the bigger the jump. Man alone of all the animals is conscious of his own inadequacy. He alone has an inferiority complex. He alone attempts to compensate for it. That is why he is man. Thus Adler reasoned.

Of course, you may go through life haunted by a vague sense of inferiority without ever recognizing the cause. But if you try, you can discover it and come to grips with it. Just take yourself apart, admit the most damning facts about yourself and try to put the pieces together again in a more satisfactory pattern. Admittedly it's difficult. But in the labyrinth that is you, you can still find your way—if you hold a clue.

And there is a clue. The way Adler put it was this: Ask yourself, "What is my goal in life?" Every human being, he held, has a goal. Formulated in infancy, it is at first no more than a vague desire to dominate. Throughout life the ultimate goal remains the same for all of us—superiority, prestige, the esteem of our fellowmen. Our goals represent a compensation for some real or fancied deficiency. The purpose of the inferiority complex—to spur us to compensation.

But the average human being must choose a goal within his reach and not seek an unattainable one by daydreaming. In the world of daydreams every girl is a ballerina, a glamorous debutante, a movie star, an opera singer; every boy is a test pilot, an orator, a foreign correspondent, a criminal lawyer; and all these glittering goals are achieved effortlessly, through the dreamers' natural gifts, which they never doubt they possess, rather than by hard work, which they hope to avoid. They choose the goals which flatter their egos without ever considering their ability to attain them. Since they are incapable of reaching them, and make little effort to do so, their sense of inferiority steadily increases. The remedy? To shift the goal. It may be humiliating to admit that one is never going to be a Lindbergh or a Garbo, but that with hard work one can become a darned good public accountant or private secretary. Yet in the end this is far more satisfying than a dream that never comes true.

A puny lad named Carnegie dreamed of being a football hero. A college football coach finally convinced him that he was more the type for a water carrier. Digging around in the ruins of his dreams, the young man came up with the surprising discovery that what he really wanted was the applause and popularity attached to being a football star. He switched to public speaking, for which he had a small talent, and eventually founded a famous school of public speaking and wrote a book called *How to Win Friends and Influence People*. By shifting his goal from the impossible to the attainable, Dale Carnegie not only overcame his own inferiority complex but helped millions of others to overcome theirs.

Goals set impossibly high lead by slow stages from idealism to frustration to demoralization. Psychologists recognize this process as fertile soil for all sorts of disorders. The remedy is to adjust our sights to meet the realities.

The goal we choose must be conducive to self-esteem and the esteem of others. Since the ultimate goal of all our efforts is to raise ourselves in the estimation of our fellowmen, this condition is axiomatic. Anytime we fail to win this dual approval we can feel the cold ripples of inferiority beginning to lap around our feet.

Granting that you have an inferiority complex or two and that you'd like to cash in on them, can you? It is hard, yes. Impossible? Human experience would seem to show that it is not. The possibilities of achievement through compensating are illustrated in the lives of some of the world's greatest men and women. We cannot read the biographies of Darwin, Keats, Stevenson, Byron, Wagner, Dostoevski, Aristotle, without realizing that their characters and lives were molded by their disabilities; that men like Alexander, Napoleon, Nelson, D'Annunzio were stimulated to seek military glory because of their small stature; that men like Socrates, Mirabeau, Voltaire were goaded into developing their extraordinary abilities by their extraordinary ugliness.

The stumbling block is not the impossibility of changing ourselves, not even the difficulty of changing—it is that we don't *want* to change. Let someone or something else change —then you'll see how well adjusted *we* are. But once a person begins seriously to explore his own ego, he discovers attitudes which he has always endeavored to conceal from himself, and he realizes that he can change them.

In order to make such changes we must first change our interpretation of past events. If in childhood we formed the opinion that every man's hand was against us because our father's was and we have in consequence taken a hostile attitude toward the world, if we have been filled with self-pity because of some childhood disability or situation, and feel that the world should protect us and forgive us for everything as our mother did—then we must now realize that these are false interpretations and we must change them. Once we discover the meaning we have given to life, and the causes behind it, we hold the key to our personality and to the possibility of altering our lot.

Let us assume that you have reached the point where you earnestly desire to make certain changes in your way of life. You are persuaded that the inferiority complex is the key to these changes. You realize that it is not, as you may have suspected, a liability but an asset. What it can do for you depends upon how much drive you will put behind it.

Until this motivating force in human nature was discovered and named by Adler, we were like men fighting in the dark. Many used this force blindly and emerged victorious. Today anyone can use it with full knowledge of what he is doing—and there will be more victors.

If the compensation we seek is to be satisfactory, it must be positive, not negative; it must be an expression of our own independent thinking and acting; it must be conducive to self-esteem and the esteem of others; it must be socially responsible and valuable.

The time to start is *now*. With this key to understanding yourself, a whole new life can open up to you. You will refuse any longer to be humiliated by an inferiority complex. You will decide to put it to the use for which it was obviously intended and to which successful and happy people have always put it. You will no longer be ridden by it but will ride it, even if a little uncertainly at first, toward your destination of a richer, fuller life.

# Chapter 11/The Quest for Inner Peace

*Peace of mind, peace of soul . . . throughout the
ages saints and sinners, philosophers and mystics, great
minds and simple ones have proclaimed such peace
the only true happiness, and have sought it in a
thousand ways. We know what some
of the enemies are: fear, guilt, envy, malice, anger.
But inner peace is more than just the absence of these.
Here seven men and women look deep into their own
lives—and offer their hard-won wisdom to anyone who
will pause long enough to listen.*

## The Need for Sanctuary
MARGARET BLAIR JOHNSTONE

Many of us think that to
seek sanctuary in time of trouble is to take cowardly flight
from reality. But it is not that. Rather it is flight *to* reality.
For when life's violence threatens and we do not seek sanctuary, it is then that we become escapists, dodging anxieties
and scurrying among confusions. Like sparrows crossing a
highway by hopping, we do not realize that we have the
power to rise above the danger coming at us from all sides.

Sanctuary is, in fact, special strength. It gives more than
refuge and release; it gives *renewal*. Essentially, sanctuary is
a means of finding the power to face life on lifted wings. It
is this power which enables men to "renew their strength
. . . mount up with wings as eagles . . . run and not be

weary . . . walk and not faint." All of us have access to this power. Sooner or later that which is weak in us cries to lay down a burden on Someone stronger. When that Someone gives us strength to bear our burden triumphantly ourselves, then we have found sanctuary.

We need not turn to some enchanted island, remote from daily living, to find our place of refuge. One of the most misinterpreted verses in the Bible is the familiar "He leadeth me beside the still waters; He restoreth my soul." Most of us think the still waters were placid lakes or quiet meadow brooks. Not so! They were part of torrential mountain streams where day in and day out the shepherd had to lead his flock. But here and there he managed to find "waters of quietness"—some pool alongside the fierce mainstream. And we too can find, right along life's mainstream, the still waters that will renew our minds.

Sanctuary may be no further away than your own backyard. Ever since Eden some men have come "nearer God's heart in a garden than anywhere else on earth." A student once pointed out that the decisive element in the discovery of the law of gravitation was not so much the falling apple as the garden. Newton was alone in the quiet of a garden when he saw his great truth. The mountains and the sea are perennial places of sanctuary. "When things get thick, I turn my back on my busy kitchen and gaze at the mountain scene framed by my window," says a mother fortunate enough to be able to lift up her eyes unto real hills. But a professor I know has no such view. So he has a color transparency of the sea in the east window of his city apartment.

There are times when one can reach sanctuary simply by going into one's room and shutting the door. A friend who is a social worker lives in a settlement house, where her single window looks out on a littered alley. Her life is an endless routine of pavement-pounding, tenement-stair climbing, grievance-hearing and monotonous record-keeping. One night I paused at her door to leave a message. She invited me in. I found her small room aglow with candlelight. "This is how I keep my sanity," she explained. "Every night for fifteen minutes I light these candles. To me the most serene thing on earth is a lighted candle."

Some find renewal in the act of serving. The next time you are hounded by fear or stymied by despair, try going to your local hospital ward. You can't talk to the sick? Then leave a bouquet of flowers. Or stop in on that housebound old man across the street with some small gift that will bring him pleasure. You may find sanctuary even in a lunch hour. Music can recharge you when you are mentally beaten or nervously exhausted. "I take twenty minutes for lunch, the rest for feasting on Brahms," says a busy editor.

You can find sanctuary by immersing yourself in a tub of warm water. One of the oldest rites is ablution: the ceremonial washing away of life's soil and stain. Hydrotherapy is one of the modern techniques for purging tension and pain. There are still other ways. One woman who reared a large family and ran a boardinghouse as well was asked how she remained so composed. "Well," she said, "you know that big rocking chair in my room? Every afternoon, no matter how busy I am, I rock awhile and empty out my brains."

Sometimes, however, we need to empty out more than our brains; we need to pour out our soul. This is the time to rediscover the fact that "strength and beauty are in His sanctuary." You can find them by stopping at church before facing the humdrum of a busy day. Or you may discover them when you kneel in a hospital chapel to pray for a dear one.

There come times to all of us when, in our desperate need, no holy ground in nature, no lonely place apart, no sanctum of man seems to give sanctuary. Then what? When disaster strikes on British navy vessels, "The Still" is instantly blown. It means: "Prepare to do the wise thing." When the signal is piped, few men know the wise thing. But in the moments of calm enforced by that signal they find it. Each man calculates his position and checks his resources. By observing "The Still," they rout confusion and frequently avert catastrophe.

So with our personal emergencies. Few of us know the wise thing instantly. "If only I could *know* what to do!" we cry, forgetting that the order of procedure is: *Be still!* No matter how little you *know,* or even how little you think you have faith to believe, the next time you need sanctuary stop instantly all feverish activity and do what those who have found sanctuary do: *"Be still* and know. . . ."

Countless hard-pressed men and women find in religion their "place of certain shelter" when their hearts cry for spiritual sanctuary. We are again laying hold on the central reality that all religion offers: "God is our refuge and strength, a very present help in trouble."

### THE ART OF FORGETTING

*H*ow should one proceed if troubled by memories which one knows ought to be dismissed from the mind but which obsessively haunt it? Keep away from every place likely, by association, to revive unhappy memories. Besides thus weakening the chain of associations that would help to hold miseries in remembrance, make it a point to develop an entirely different chain —and go into it with enthusiasm.          —H. *Addington Bruce*

# Retreat—to Go Forward

JOHN KORD LAGEMANN

For centuries, monasteries and convents have opened their doors to men and women who felt the need to withdraw temporarily from the world and deepen their faith. Today a modern version of this age-old religious practice has become a widespread movement crossing all sectarian lines. More and more people are learning what an intensely moving personal experience it can be to "make a retreat."

For two or three days, usually over a weekend, they withdraw to a secluded place with a small group to study, meditate and take spiritual inventory of their lives. Here they rediscover religion as something to be lived as well as professed. The majority return to everyday concerns with a feeling of renewed strength, purpose and self-understanding.

In recent years churches have been swift to adapt retreat practice to the needs of ordinary people with jobs and families. Before World War I the only full-time retreat house for laymen in the United States was Mount Manresa, the Jesuit center on Staten Island in New York harbor. Today there are more than three hundred Roman Catholic retreat centers. The growth of the Protestant retreat movement, pioneered by Episcopalians, Lutherans, Methodists and Quakers, has been no less phenomenal. "The movement is snowballing," says Dr. Samuel Emerick, director of the interdenominational Yokefellow Institute in Richmond, Indiana. "I'd estimate that over 50,000 Protestants made first retreats in 1964. It looks as if their number may double this year."

What's behind this increased interest in retreats? "After the last war there was a tremendous widening of church membership," says Dr. John L. Casteel, of Union Theological Seminary. "The retreat movement represents the *deepening* of religious feeling. There is a growing hunger for greater personal participation in the quest for a meaning in life. For many it isn't enough to sit and listen to a sermon. They want a chance to ponder and ask questions."

Some retreats are for special groups or occupations—vestrymen, doctors, lawyers. Many are for men only or women only, but a growing number are for married couples. Retreats are held in summer camps, schools and resort hotels, as well as in specially built retreat houses. The late Major Edward Bowes, of radio's Amateur Hour fame, left his Hudson River estate at Ossining, New York, to the Lutheran Church for a retreat center. In the San Bernardino Mountains of California, Sky Forest, a lodge built by the late oilman Herbert C. Wylie, is now a Presbyterian retreat house. In contrast, Yokefellow Retreat House is a converted cow barn; and Kirkridge, founded by Dr. John Oliver Nelson, director of religious field work at Yale Divinity School, is a farmhouse and hunting lodge near Bangor, Pennsylvania.

Some centers hold retreats that last a week. The shortest retreats are "quiet days" or "quiet evenings" offered to those who feel the need to pause for a few hours to get their spiritual bearings. Fairly typical, however, is the weekend experience of Bill and Helen Marshall.

On a Friday afternoon Bill, a young engineer, and Helen, pregnant at the time with their first child, drove from their home near Princeton, New Jersey, to Pendle Hill, the Quaker Study Center in suburban Philadelphia. They had made reservations two months previously and, at the suggestion of Pendle Hill board chairman Dr. Douglas V. Steere, philosophy professor at Haverford College, had done some advance reading in the New Testament, Thomas à Kempis' *Imitation of Christ* and Evelyn Underhill's *The Spiritual Life*. Now, equipped with work clothes, the Marshalls looked forward to this weekend as a chance to seek answers to the age-old questions, "Who am I? Why am I here?"

At Pendle Hill, in a colonial mansion set in parklike grounds, the opening dinner had a pleasant, get-acquainted atmosphere. Afterward, in the big living room, each retreatant introduced himself. There were twenty-three altogether, including four married couples, a widow, a retired lawyer, a young minister and two college students. Dr. Steere spoke informally about the retreat rhythm: silent work, prayer, study. He invited members to visit him privately if they felt the need to talk. The rule of silence began as the men and women bowed their heads in prayer. On the way to their rooms the Marshalls and several others stopped by the Quiet Room to pray for a time. By 10:30 everyone had retired.

Rising bell next morning was at seven. Before breakfast the retreatants visited the Quiet Room for prayer and meditation. Three times during the day the group met in the living room to receive spiritual instruction—brief, informal religious talks by Dr. Steere. Part of the morning was spent at tasks such as spading a garden plot, clearing brush, repairing and painting screens. So the weekend passed—in quiet meals, silent worship, physical labor, walking, reading, religious instruction and counseling. At 10:30 Sunday morning the retreatants met to confer with Dr. Steere. They were free now to break silence in order to share their thoughts and insights with the group. The Marshalls and several others chose to remain silent. "It grew on us," Helen said later. "We hated to break the spell."

Recalling what the weekend had meant to her, Helen said, "If I had just three days to live, I think this is the way I would want to spend them." Bill stressed the value of the silence: "I went out to do chores with a man I'd never seen before. After a few hours we felt as companionable as if we'd known each other since boyhood. There was no need to close oneself against the demands of another's talk, no urge to compete or conceal. I've never felt so free to be myself."

Now Bill and Helen are experimenting with "silent periods" in their own home. "We've settled more differences with the quiet hour than we ever did with talk," Helen told me. "Maybe it's because so many of our differences are merely verbal in the first place."

"Because of its flexibility, the term 'retreat' is sometimes misapplied to get-togethers which are really conferences or weekend vacations with religious overtones," Dr. Nelson told me. "But more and more the trend is toward the basic disciplines of meditation and worship. Whether the retreat is Protestant or Catholic, the underlying purpose is identical— to purify oneself, to regain a sense of direction and communication with God and to return to everyday life strengthened for its duties."

Retreats often close with an "evaluation session." Most participants express satisfaction at coming closer to self-understanding. A few say that they were disappointed because "nothing happened." Retreat leaders warn against expecting miracles. "How much a person gets out of retreat depends on how much he brings to it in terms of maturity, receptivity and self-discipline," says Dr. Casteel.

What impels people to make a retreat? "Some men and

women look on it as an annual spiritual checkup," says the Reverend Robert I. Gannon, S.J., former Fordham University president. "They want to find out where they've slipped, where they need tightening up." Some who are troubled by doubts make a retreat to give their faith a last chance.

Going on retreat does not of itself solve anything. It simply helps people to face life more realistically by removing distractions and pressures. "A man will come in on Friday, troubled and full of uncertainty," Father Gannon told me. "By Sunday the air has cleared. The man is smiling easily. He has had a chance to reflect and to pray in silence. He has found hope and strength for renewing the battle of life."

⇒ ◆ ⇐

### FROM A TIN-CAN GULLY

**I**f you have no sanctuary, you may be able to create one. I had a neighbor once whose life had not been joyous. In her later years, she cleared out a little ravine behind her house. Freeing a spring of accumulated junk and dirt, she rolled a log beside it, for a seat, and in an old stump she scooped out a bird bath. She pulled up coarse weeds, and grateful wildflowers sprang up to reward her. Rats left, squirrels moved in, and what had been a tin-can gully was transformed into a leafy sanctuary. "Just getting rid of all that rusted wreckage did my soul good," she said. She has never spent a cent upon her sanctuary and never spent an hour there without rewards.

Whatever the sanctuary, be sure to keep it sacred to its purpose. For in a world engulfed by hate and destruction, only one pinnacle rises above the flood—the high impregnable rock of the individual spirit. From this citadel comes only the reassuring voice of the inner sentinel: "Believe and hope; something may yet be won."  —*Henry Morton Robinson*

# Live in Day-Tight Compartments

*Condensed from the book:*
*How to Stop Worrying and Start Living*

DALE CARNEGIE

In the spring of 1871 a young man, then a medical student at the Montreal General Hospital, who was later to become the most famous physician of his generation, picked up a book by the Scottish essayist and historian Thomas Carlyle and read twenty-one words that were to have a profound effect on his future: "Our main business is not to see what lies dimly at a distance, but to do what lies clearly at hand."

The secret of his success, Sir William Osler told a group of Yale students some forty years later, was not any special quality of brains, but what he called living in "day-tight compartments." Just as a great ocean liner can be shut off into watertight compartments, he said, so we should shut the iron doors on the past—the dead yesterdays—and the future—the unborn tomorrows. The load of tomorrow, added to that of yesterday, carried today, makes the strongest falter. The only possible way you can prepare for the future is to concentrate with all your intelligence, all your enthusiasm, on doing today's work superbly today. Remember, said Osler, that The Lord's Prayer teaches us to ask only for *today's* bread. Today's bread, he went on to point out, is the only kind of bread you can possibly eat.

Many men have rejected the counsel of Jesus to "take no thought for the morrow" as a counsel of perfection or a bit of

255

Oriental mysticism, not realizing that His words were translated more than three hundred years ago, when the word "thought" frequently meant anxiety. Of course, that advice doesn't mean not to *plan* for the morrow. During the war our military leaders *planned* for the morrow, but they could not afford to have anxiety. "I have supplied the best men with the best equipment we have," said Admiral Ernest J. King, who commanded the United States Navy, "and have given them what seems to be the wisest mission. That is all I can do."

Arthur Hays Sulzberger, chairman of the board of the New York *Times*, told me that he was never able to banish his worries and find peace until he had adopted as his motto the words from a church hymn:

> Lead, kindly Light . . .
> Keep Thou my feet. I do not ask to see
> The distant scene; one step enough for me.

"Think of your life as an hourglass," an Army doctor told a GI who had worried himself into a case of combat fatigue. "The thousands of grains of sand in the top of the hourglass all pass slowly and evenly through the narrow neck in the middle, one grain of sand at a time. You and I and everyone else are like this hourglass. When we start in the morning, there are hundreds of tasks which we feel we must accomplish that day, but if we do not take them one at a time and let them pass through the day slowly and evenly, we are bound to break our own physical or mental structure." That bit of advice, the young man wrote, not only helped him physically and mentally during the war but has also helped him since in business. "Instead of getting taut and nervous, I remember what the doctor told me. 'One grain of sand at a time. One task at a time.' By repeating those words again and again to myself, I accomplish my tasks efficiently without the confused and jumbled feeling that once almost made a wreck of me."

We are all standing this very second at the meeting place of two eternities of the past and the future. We can't possibly live in either of those eternities even for one split second; but, by trying to do so, we can wreck both our bodies and our minds. So let's be content to live the only time we can possibly live: from now until bedtime. "Anyone can carry his burden, however hard, until nightfall," wrote Robert Louis Stevenson. "Anyone can do his work, however hard, for one day. Anyone can live sweetly, patiently, lovingly, purely, till the sun goes down. And this is all that life really means."

One of the most tragic things I know about human nature is that all of us tend to put off living. We are all dreaming of some magical rose garden over the horizon—instead of enjoying the roses that are blooming outside our windows today. "How strange it is, our little procession of life!" wrote Stephen Leacock. "The child says, 'When I am a big boy.' But what is that? The big boy says, 'When I grow up.' And then, grown up, he says, 'When I get married.' But to be married, what is that, after all? The thought changes to 'When I'm able to retire.' And then, when retirement comes, he looks back over the landscape traversed; a cold wind seems to sweep over it; somehow he has missed it all, and it is gone. Life, we learn too late, is in the living, in the tissue of every day and hour."

John Ruskin had on his desk a simple piece of stone on which was carved one word: *Today*. And while I haven't a piece of stone on my desk, I do have a poem pasted on my mirror where I can see it when I shave every morning—a poem that Sir William Osler always kept on his desk—written by the Indian dramatist Kalidasa:

### Salutation to the Dawn

Look to this day!
For it is life, the very life of life.
In its brief course
Lie all the verities and realities of your existence:
   The bliss of growth
   The glory of action
   The splendor of beauty,
For yesterday is but a dream
And tomorrow is only a vision,
But today well lived makes every yesterday
      a dream of happiness
And every tomorrow a vision of hope.
Look well, therefore, to this day!
Such is the salutation to the dawn.

So, if you want to keep worry out of your life, do what Sir William Osler did and shut the iron doors on the past and the future. *Live in day-tight compartments.*

### MOMENT BY MOMENT

*T*here is only one world, the world pressing against you at this minute. There is only one minute in which you are alive, *this minute*—here and now. The only way to live is by accepting each minute as an unrepeatable miracle. Which is exactly what it is—a miracle and unrepeatable.     —*Storm Jameson*

# How to Cope with Criticism

**NORMAN VINCENT PEALE**

nly two things in life are certain, Benjamin Franklin once remarked: death and taxes. But there is one other unpleasant certainty: criticism. No one escapes it entirely. And often our careers, our emotional stability, our happiness depend on how we react to it.

There are really two kinds of criticism: the gentle, tactful, constructive variety (which no one gets much of!) and the blunt, harsh, hostile kind. I can speak with wry authority about this second kind. For years everything in my life went fairly well. Then some very vocal critics of my writings and my ministry appeared. When the storm arose, I didn't know how to handle it. I had to learn—the hard way! What I learned mainly is that if you're a sensitive person, and an honest one, you can't just brush criticism aside or pretend it's not there. You have to face up to it on three levels: the emotional, the rational and the practical.

Controlling your emotional reaction is the hardest. Criticism is a direct attack on your self-esteem. So it is all too easy to react with resentment and anger. But this just makes you more vulnerable; if all you do is resent your critic, you are only poisoning yourself. The first step, then, is to *force* yourself to be dispassionate. This is never easy, but it can be done. I once went to see Herbert Hoover, surely one of the most unjustly maligned men of our era. "Mr. President," I said, "how did you keep from being embittered by all that criticism during your Presidency?"

"Well," said Mr. Hoover, "I can think of two possible answers. In the first place, I'm an engineer, trained to anticipate problems. I knew that sooner or later every one of my predecessors had had to face a barrage of criticism. So, when I moved into the White House, I was prepared. That was one thing. The other," he said gently, "is that I'm a Quaker." I knew what he meant: Quakers believe in an inner quietness, a peace that will come if you empty your heart of resentment and bitterness. When a man has this God-given inner calm, he is not likely to be disturbed by man-made storms.

The Bible says, *pray* for your critics; bless them that hurt you. This may seem preposterous to someone smarting under the lash of undeserved criticism, but the amazing truth is that it does relieve the hurt. If you force yourself to pray for your critic, you cannot simultaneously brood about the injury that has been done to you.

Yet another way to steady your emotions under attack is to reflect that strong men and women have always been criticized. If your life has any vitality at all, if you are determined to get things done, and especially if you blaze new paths, you are going to encounter hostility and opposition. The greatest Man who ever walked this earth was bitterly criticized, finally crucified by contemporaries who could not stand the impact of His revolutionary ideas. Abraham Lincoln once said, "If I were to try to read, much less answer, all the attacks made on me, this shop might as well be closed for any other business. I do the very best I know how, the very best I can. If the end brings me out all right, what is said against me won't amount to anything. If the end brings me out wrong, ten angels swearing I was right would make no difference."

The second step in coping with criticism is to be rational. Take up the criticism and examine it objectively, for as Theodor Leschetizky, the great piano teacher, remarked, "We learn much from the disagreeable things people say, for they make us *think;* whereas the good things only make us glad." Ask yourself honestly if there is any truth in the criticism. Beware of self-excuses or rationalizations; if you give in to these, you may just compound the original error. If you are forced to the conclusion that whatever your critic is saying is the truth, the best thing to do is admit it. This in itself will silence him. After all, if you agree with him, what more can he say? Besides, it is astonishing how readily people will rally to the side of someone who can admit that he has been wrong.

Another rational approach is to examine the qualifications of your critic. Is he reputable and sincere? If so, you had better not dismiss his words too readily. Has he reason to be spiteful or jealous? Then perhaps you can dismiss them. Dignified silence is often the best reply to slander. Sometimes, of course, if the criticism is false and damaging, you *must* reply to it. But it is best simply to state the facts, not to try to retaliate.

Another thing to remember: When criticism finally reaches your ears, it may well have become exaggerated. There are always people who enjoy the excitement of a feud and will throw gasoline on the flames if they can. "Come on," they say, in effect, to the victim of the criticism. "Put up a fight!"

You must be wary of these not-so-innocent bystanders. A few years ago, the dean of a famous divinity school made a speech in which he said some very harsh things about me. When reporters swooped down on me, clamoring for a reply,

I didn't even know what the dean had said. One of the reporters was more than happy to tell me. I was upset, but I took a deep breath and said that my critic was an eminent man whose judgment I respected. I added that therefore I had better reexamine my message and my methods, and that if I found any error I would do my best to correct it. I'll never forget the expressions on those reporters' faces. They had been looking for a battle—and they were unable to stir one up.

Trying to deal with criticism rationally brought me to one other conclusion: Not everyone is going to like me—or you. Just as some people rub us the wrong way for no particular reason, so we rub some others the wrong way. If you face this simple truth, you will not be unduly disturbed by a certain amount of unpopularity.

Is there anything on the *practical* level that you can do in dealing with criticism? Yes. You can try to help your critic. For criticism is a two-edged sword, and often it is the poisoned edge that cuts the person who wields it. Gossip, for example, is nothing but criticism motivated by jealousy or insecurity. Small people often find it easier to tear someone else down than to try to build themselves up. But what is their reward? No one trusts them. In the end, no one believes them.

The Bible commands us to return good for evil. This is not pious nonsense; kindness *is* stronger than malice. My father once told about a reporter he knew who covered William McKinley's campaign for the Presidency of the United States. His newspaper was violently opposed to McKinley, and he was to travel on the train with the candidate and send back negative stories at every opportunity. At first he did—and McKinley knew it. But one bitterly cold afternoon the reporter fell asleep huddled on the green plush seat of the unheated car. McKinley came by, stopped and spread his overcoat over the man. When the reporter awoke and found out what had happened, he sent a telegram to his newspaper announcing his resignation from his job. He couldn't go on maligning a man big enough to answer his criticisms by befriending him.

Constant critics are often warped and unhappy people, clutching at false importance, trying to cover up their own inadequacies by pointing out the failings of other people. The Christian thing to do when you encounter hostility in another person is to try to get behind the anger, to understand what causes it and to remove the cause for the other person's sake as well as for your own.

As Disraeli once remarked, "It is much easier to be critical than correct"—so there will always be plenty of critics in the world, some well intentioned, others cruel. You can defend yourself against the unkind ones by learning to control your emotional reactions, by adopting a calm and rational attitude and by honestly trying to help your critics to rid themselves of their anger. But, in the last analysis, your best defense is your own day-to-day conduct. It is keeping your moral standards high. It is having a clear conscience. It is living a life without any necessity whatever for deception or for lies or for concealment.

⇢✦⇠

Criticism is something you can avoid by saying nothing, doing nothing and being nothing.                    —*Anonymous*

Public opinion is a weak tyrant compared with our own private opinion. What a man thinks of himself, that it is which indicates his fate.                    —*Henry David Thoreau*

# Finding Yourself Again

ARTHUR GORDON

Not long ago I came to one of those bleak periods that many of us encounter from time to time, a sudden drastic dip in the graph of living when everything goes stale and flat, energy wanes, enthusiasm dies. The effect on my work was frightening. Every morning I would clench my teeth and mutter: "Today life will take on some of its old meaning. You've got to break through this thing." But the barren days went by, and the paralysis grew worse. The time came when I knew I needed aid.

The man I turned to was a doctor. Not a psychiatrist, just a doctor. He was older than I, and under his surface gruffness lay great wisdom and compassion. "I seem to have come to a dead end," I told him miserably. "Can you help?"

"I don't know," he said slowly. He leaned back, crossed his arms and gazed at me thoughtfully. Then, abruptly, he asked, "Where were you happiest as a child?" "As a child?" I echoed. "Why, at the beach, I suppose. We had a summer cottage there. We all loved it."

He looked out the window and watched the October leaves sifting down. "Are you able to follow instructions for a single day?" "I think so," I said, ready to try anything.

"All right. Here's what I want you to do."

He told me to drive to the beach by nine the following morning. I could take some lunch, but I was not to read, write, listen to the radio or talk to anyone. "In addition," he said, "I'll give you a prescription to be taken every three hours." He tore off four prescription blanks, wrote a few words on each, folded them, numbered them and handed them to me. "Take these at nine, twelve, three and six."

"Are you serious?" I asked. He gave a short bark of a laugh. "You won't think I'm joking when you get my bill!"

The next morning, with little faith, I drove to the beach. It was lonely, all right. A northeaster was blowing; the sea looked gray and angry. I sat in the car, the whole day stretching emptily before me. Then I took out the first of the folded slips of paper. On it was written: *Listen carefully*. Why, I thought, the man must be mad. He had ruled out the radio and human conversation. What else was there? I raised my head and I did listen. There were no sounds but the steady roar of the sea, the creaking cry of a gull, the drone of some aircraft high overhead.

I got out of the car. A gust of wind slammed the door with a sudden clap of sound. Am I supposed, I asked myself, to listen carefully to things like that? I climbed a dune and looked out over the deserted beach. Here the sea bellowed so loudly that all other sounds were lost. And yet, I thought suddenly, there must be sounds beneath sounds—the soft rasp of drifting sand, the tiny wind-whisperings in the dune grasses—if the listener got close enough to hear them.

On an impulse I ducked down and, feeling faintly ridiculous, thrust my head into a clump of sea-wheat. Here I made a discovery: If you listen intently, there is a fractional moment in which everything seems to pause, wait. In that instant of stillness the racing thoughts halt. For a moment, when you truly listen for something outside yourself, you have to silence the clamorous voices within. The mind rests. I went back to the car and slid behind the wheel. *Listen carefully*. As I listened again to the deep growl of the sea, I found myself thinking about the immensity of it, the stupendous rhythms of it, the velvet trap it made for moonlight, the white-fanged fury of its storms.

I thought of the lessons it had taught us as children. A certain amount of patience—you can't hurry the tides. A great deal of respect—the sea does not suffer fools gladly. An awareness of the vast and mysterious interdependence of things—wind and tide and current, calm and squall and hurricane, all combining to determine the paths of the birds above and the fish below. And the cleanness of it all, with every beach swept twice a day by the great broom of the sea. Sitting there, I realized I was thinking of things bigger than myself—and there was relief in that.

Even so, the morning passed slowly. The habit of hurling myself at a problem was so strong that I felt lost without it. Once, when I was wistfully eying the car radio, a phrase from some forgotten author jumped into my head: "Silence is the element in which great things fashion themselves. . . ."

By noon the wind had polished the clouds out of the sky, and the sea had a hard, merry sparkle. I unfolded the second "prescription." And again I sat there, half amused and half exasperated. Three words this time: *Try reaching back.* Back to what? To the past, obviously. But why, when all my worries concerned the present or the future? I left the car and started tramping reflectively along the dunes. The doctor had sent me to the beach because it was a place of happy memories. Maybe *that* was what I was supposed to reach for: the wealth of happiness that lay half forgotten.

I found a sheltered place and lay down on the sun-warmed sand. When I tried to peer into the well of the past, the recollections that came to the surface were happy but not very clear, so I decided to experiment: to work on these vague impressions as a painter would, retouching the colors, strengthening the outlines. I would choose specific incidents and recapture as many details as possible. I would visualize people complete with dress and gestures. I would listen (carefully!) for the exact sound of their voices and their laughter.

The tide was going out now, but there was still thunder in the surf. So I chose to go back twenty years to the last fishing trip I made with my younger brother. (He died in World War II, and was buried in the Philippines.) I found now that if I closed my eyes and really tried I could see him with amazing vividness, even the humor and eagerness in his eyes that far-off morning.

In fact, I could see it all: the ivory scimitar of beach where we were fishing, the eastern sky smeared with sunrise, the great rollers creaming in, stately and slow. I could feel the backwash swirl warm around my knees, see the sudden arc of my brother's rod as he struck a fish, hear his exultant yell. Piece by piece I rebuilt it, clear and unchanged under the transparent varnish of time. Then it was gone. I sat up slowly. *Try reaching back.* Happy people were usually assured, confident people. If, then, you deliberately reached back and touched happiness, might there not be released little flashes of power, tiny sources of strength?

This second period of the day went more quickly. As the sun began its long slant down the sky, my mind ranged eagerly through the past, reliving some episodes, uncovering others that had been completely forgotten. For example, when I was around thirteen and my brother ten, Father had promised to take us to the circus. But at lunch there was a phone call. Some urgent business required his attention downtown. We braced ourselves for disappointment. Then we heard him say, "No, I won't be down. It'll wait."

When he came back to the table, Mother smiled. "The circus keeps coming back, you know." "I know," said Father. "But childhood doesn't." Across all the years I remembered this, and knew from the sudden glow of warmth that no kindness is ever really wasted, or ever completely lost.

By three o'clock the tide was out; the sound of the waves was only a rhythmic whisper, like a giant breathing. I stayed in my sandy nest, feeling relaxed and content—and a little complacent. The doctor's prescriptions, I thought, were easy to take. But I was not prepared for the next one. This time the three words were not a gentle suggestion. They sounded more like a command. *Reexamine your motives.* My first reaction was purely defensive. There's nothing wrong with my motives, I said to myself. I want to be successful—who doesn't? I want a certain amount of recognition—but so does everybody. I want more security than I've got—and why not?

Maybe, said a small voice somewhere inside my head, those motives aren't good enough. Maybe that's the reason the wheels have stopped going round. I picked up a handful of sand and let it stream between my fingers. In the past, whenever my work went well, there had always been something spontaneous about it, something uncontrived, something free. Lately it had been calculated, competent—and dead. Why? Because I had been looking past the job itself to the rewards I hoped it would bring. The work had ceased to be an end in itself; it had been merely a means to make money, pay bills. The sense of *giving* something, of helping people, of making a contribution, had been lost in a frantic clutch at security.

In a flash of certainty I saw that if one's motives are wrong, nothing can be right. It makes no difference whether you are a mailman, a hairdresser, an insurance salesman, a housewife—whatever. As long as you feel you are serving others, you do the job well. When you are concerned only with helping yourself, you do it less well. This is a law as inexorable as gravity.

For a long time I sat there. Far out on the bar I heard the murmur of the surf change to a hollow roar as the tide turned. Behind me the spears of light were almost horizontal. My time at the beach had almost run out, and I felt a grudging admiration for the doctor and the "prescriptions" he had so casually and cunningly devised. I saw, now, that in them was a therapeutic progression that might well be of value to anyone facing any difficulty.

*Listen carefully:* To calm the frantic mind, shift the focus from inner problems to outer things.

*Try reaching back:* Since the human mind can hold but one idea at a time, you blot out present worry when you touch the happiness of the past.

*Reexamine your motives:* This was the hard core of the "treatment," this challenge to reappraise, to bring one's motives into alignment with one's capabilities and conscience. But the mind must be clear and receptive to do this—hence the six hours of quiet that went before.

The western sky was a blaze of crimson as I took out the last slip of paper. Six words this time. I walked slowly out on the beach. A few yards below high-water mark I stopped and read the words again: *Write your worries on the sand.*

I let the paper blow away, reached down and picked up a fragment of shell. Kneeling there under the vault of the sky, I wrote several words on the sand, one above the other. Then I walked away, and I did not look back. I had written my troubles on the sand. And the tide was coming in.

# Humility—Balance Wheel of Life

MICHAEL DRURY

**M**y mother lives on a mountain, where in summer the stars are as big as chrysanthemums and, to my city-trained eye, almost frighteningly close. One night a number of years ago, as we stood under them, simply looking, I was moved by what I supposed at the time was humility to say, "Doesn't it make you feel insignificant?"

"No," my mother answered, "only grateful to be included in such a universe." There was amusement in her tone, and I saw that she was laughing gently at my fuzzy notion of humility, what it is and what it does for one. I realized that it is *not* the job of humility to make us feel small, but to expand our capacity for appreciation, awe, delight; to stand silent before all that we do not know—and then to get on with the work of finding out.

Humility so often seems vaguely desirable but not really attractive. It might get one into heaven, but it won't promote a raise in pay. It sounds somewhat spineless, incompatible with intellect and a vigorous spirit. I have had to learn that the reverse is true. The figures we commonly hail for their humility—Jesus, Socrates, Lincoln, Gandhi, Einstein—were never timorous souls, but men of strong destiny with a fierce determination to carry it out. Humility is not self-disparagement; it is a tough, free, confident characteristic.

It does not saturate a personality, but flavors it. Theodore Roosevelt was a man of immense tempo, something of a bull in a china shop at times, barging exuberantly into almost every avenue of life. Yet he could say cheerfully, "Nobody can accuse me of having a charming personality"—a remark much closer to true humility than a long face and a pious bringing together of the fingertips. The late Fiorello LaGuardia, New York's colorful mayor, was famous for his candid acknowledgment of a blunder: "When I make a mistake, it's a beaut." Neither of these men confused humility with dimming his own light; rather, admitting the voltage, they could also admit that it was sometimes ungovernable.

The Ozark Mountain people have a saying, "A man don't know nothing he hasn't learned." We all start from the same degree of nakedness and ignorance and, as Abbé Ernest Dimnet—author of *The Art of Thinking*—pointed out, even genius depends on the data within its reach, the information that comes from what others do and have done. Shakespeare made use of the playbooks. Mozart is said to have taken the opening theme of the overture to *The Magic Flute* from a Clementi sonata. Bach borrowed both inspiration and thematic material from the music of contemporaries. None of this makes these giants any less towering, because none of them pretended anything else. They knew that every man's work stemmed from all that had gone before and, if it had any merit, transcended the source and itself became part of the reservoir. This was pure humility.

Nowhere is humility more revealed than in what has been called "tender consideration of the ignorant." Some years ago the motion-picture director Alfred Hitchcock, about as cocksure a man as may be found, was filming scenes in a slum area of New York. The weather was surly, and at one point the whole crew sat around for several hours waiting for the sun. Then a filthy old man sidled up to Hitchcock and said,

"Hey, I'd like to make a suggestion." Hitchcock replied, without irony, "Yes?" The derelict spat. "You pay them guys by the hour, don't you? You could save a lot of dough if you rigged up some artificial light." The director explained briefly the different requirements of indoor and outdoor film, and why he couldn't mix the two kinds of light. Then the bum nodded. "Got ya, chief," he said, and shuffled away.

When an aide remarked, "That was decent of you," Hitchcock shrugged. "Ideas come from everywhere," he replied, "including left field. You have to listen or you're lost." This went beyond kindness. It took account of the human potential, however low the lamp might be burning.

As a reporter, I was once assigned to cover a speaking tour of a political figure. It was April in the Southwest, and overnight the weather turned from winter to spring. Our man got beguiled by the idea of a picnic, but the schedule was too crowded to rent a car and drive it into the hills. So the women in the party had a local restaurant pack a lunch, and we surprised him with a spread on the shaded lawn of the county courthouse. When time came to leave, the politician began collecting all the papers and empty cups that had blown about, and disposed of them in an ashcan. He did it as casually as he might have picked up a used towel in his own bathroom; but it told me more about him than a whole barrage of questions might have. Humility doesn't ask what is the decent thing to be done; it does the decent thing by instinct and without fuss.

At the same time, humility is more sophisticated than it may seem. A great actress once provided a brilliant opportunity to a young actor of promise who dazzled everyone during rehearsals and then, on opening night, made a terrible blunder. Filled with remorse, he was sitting numbly in his dressing room when the actress swept in. "I've ruined my career," he said bitterly. "I've let you down. I might as well quit." The actress grew icy. "Just who do you think you are that you should not make mistakes?" she demanded. "I make them; we all make them. Only God does not err, my young friend, and you are not God. You will go back on that stage and you will do well!" And he did.

To admit a mistake is one thing, but to assume a position above the possibility, even the necessity, of erring is to set oneself on a pedestal. At a national convention of Boy Scout officials in Chicago a few years ago, a young Scout delivered a brief speech. He stumbled badly. Quickly, however, he said into the microphone, "Oops, I goofed," and shared the audience's laughter. Then he went on from there. That is the difference between humility and groveling. It is *going on from there* that marks the genuine article, not the permanent wearing of sackcloth.

Humility is necessary and useful for the same reason that a lead keel is useful on a racing sloop: it keeps us from tipping over. The faster the sailboat, the more essential a finely balanced keel. The mechanic or the housewife may not be in as much danger of capsizing as the prime minister or the opera star, but each needs humility in proportion to his speed. It takes equanimity to view another's good and not be swayed off course either by envy or by admiration. The neighborhood child who is plainly superior to one's own child; the man who is elected company president when you were in line for it; the teammate who keeps walloping homers over the fence when you are in a slump—life is filled with such people, and it takes genuine humility to keep them in perspective, neither too high nor too low. *Humility is poise.*

We should not expect total humility from ourselves or from others, any more than we expect total wisdom. To be truly humble takes a working knowledge of who and what one is, and this requires experience—which in turn requires time. The art cannot be mastered in a matter of three weeks. As Sir James M. Barrie knew and said, "Life is a long lesson in humility."

### SCALED TO SIZE

George Washington Carver, Negro scientist who achieved wonders with the humble peanut, used to tell this story:

When I was young I said to God, "God, tell me the mystery of the universe." But God answered, "That knowledge is reserved for Me alone."

So I said to Him, "God, tell me the mystery of the peanut." Then God said, "Well, George, that's more nearly your size." And He told me.                                        —*The Liguorian*

### MODESTY AND CONCEIT

Modesty is not incompatible with justified self-confidence, or with knowledge of and joy in true capacity and achievements. Absorption in one's work is not necessarily absorption in oneself. As a young man—her press agent—I once heard Lillian Russell allude to her beauty. I suppose that I looked shocked, for Miss Russell turned from her mirror, smiled at me, and said, "You think that's conceit, but you're wrong. After years of being pictured and written about everywhere, it wouldn't be possible for me not to know that God gave me more than average comeliness. Certainly conceit would show itself in pretending that I *didn't* know."                                        —*Channing Pollock*

# Living with Your Regrets

MARGARET CULKIN BANNING

hree times in the past year I have been bereaved by death. Each time a stinging swarm of regrets has risen from the inevitable loss. Some of these were small and unimportant, such as a regret that a letter had not been written, a visit or gift which might have given comfort had been overlooked, a journey postponed which now never could be taken. But other regrets were so painful that they made my life hard to bear for many months.

I was bitterly sorry that I had given to my own interests time and energy which could have been devoted to companionship. I regretted every time that I had been impatient or lacked understanding. And each of these times was like a melancholy record that my mind kept playing over and over again. Why had I not shown greater gratitude to one person, and to another the constant love that had actually been deep in my heart and mind?

Such things added up to a pile of obsessions which I carried around until I was almost exhausted. Then one day it was necessary for me to face another person who was meeting a like deep grief. I said to him, almost involuntarily, because I knew the effects of such experience so well, "Please do not allow yourself to regret things which cannot be changed now. It is futile. It will destroy your work. It will make you good for nothing!" Giving this advice to someone else made me even more conscious of what I was doing to myself. I began to try to evaluate this feeling called regret. I felt that I must find out whether it was merely a self-inflicted lash upon the mind, a form of morbidity or a vanity. Did it, or could it, serve any useful purpose?

Regret is certainly one of the most common emotions. Nearly everyone I have talked to about it admits being sorry for something in his past or present life. But some people handle their regrets much better than others do. Without dismissing their regrets, they have learned to live with them. For many, regrets seem to become good tools with which to build a better future. My mother used to quote this maxim:

> For every evil under the sun,
> There is a remedy or there is none.
> If there is one, try to find it,
> If there is none, never mind it.

That homely instruction is just as good as it ever was. It makes the sound and necessary distinction between *vain* regret and *useful* regret. Vain regret is to be sorry for the irrevocable. Poets have often made that state of mind romantic: the lover sighing for rejected love. But to brood over what cannot be changed can be as tiresome as it is fruitless. An unmarried and successful business woman over fifty years old has a habit of saying to her friends, "I shall always regret that I never had a child." Perhaps she never had the opportunity to marry. Possibly she made a wrong choice of careers. But she is now too old to bear a child, and her regret is a completely vain one. She could, but does not, channel it into benefactions for the children of other people.

A politician in my district is certain to bring almost any conversation around to his regret that he did not run for the Senate some years ago. At that time there was an unexpected landslide for his party and he certainly would have been elected. But he did not enter that campaign, and now political leadership in the state has so changed that his opportunity to become a Senator is gone. His regret is not only useless—it has blocked his adjustment to public service which would be less distinguished but still valuable.

False regrets are even more obnoxious than vain ones. These are the ones which continually dwell on the loss of imaginary talents, imaginary lovers and imaginary fortunes. They stem, of course, not from real remorse but from thwarted vanity. "I should have kept up my music," one woman complains to anyone who will listen. "If I had, I could be on the concert stage today." What she could regret to more avail are the facts that she is overweight and lazy. If she corrected these faults, she would be a happier woman. Her singing would never have brought her fame, for the talents so regretted exist largely in hopes and dreams. But they become lodged in the mind and, like a gallstone, create a permanent irritation. The people who regret careers for the sake of which they never submitted to training or discipline are a sorry legion.

Imaginary love affairs also cause much needless regret. Many husbands are all too familiar with the "If I had only married—" beginning of a sentence, and wives are not immune to the same kind of regrets in the glances of their husbands. These regrets, like the ones for talents which never existed, have a tendency to become chronic. They make homes uncomfortable and quarrelsome. They break up marriages.

The fortunes which are regretted run into billions. The "I could have made" group was particularly large after the last great boom and depression, but plenty of its old members and descendants are with us today. They chant, "If I had bought that stock at twenty-four, I would be a rich man today." This kind of regret has never shown a profit or supported a household. A man of genuine ability in my acquaintance began to regret long ago what he had not made in the previous year when he was only thirty years old. He has lived on to petulant failure, longing for money he never had. Men and women of extraordinary accomplishment have learned to free themselves from the shackles of regret; they have learned, as Eleanor Roosevelt once said, never "to clutter up one's mind with might-have-beens." Yet their lives show, as do all distinguished careers, an *awareness of mistakes*, and the use of them to redirect conduct and patterns of living.

I found out for myself that it was necessary to turn my back forever on some regrets. (I shall never let myself regret the passage of time because that is irrevocable. There is nothing to be gained by beating one's head against the wall of life. I shall cease to regret happenings in my past which cannot be changed.) But I found there were others which could be put to good use and built into the future. When I faced the definite mistakes and blunders I had made, I had practical examples of what not to do again, and that gave me a path to follow.

Regrets are as personal as fingerprints. In my own case I am especially sorry for the times when I have carelessly or deliberately withheld encouragement from others. I regret most bitterly the times when I have injured delicate feelings or inflicted pain. Once many years ago I impatiently sent a little girl out of my room. She fled in tears and I have never forgotten the incident. For the little girl died not long after and I had given an hour of unhappiness to her short life. My deep regret should evidence itself in more patience with other children.

I regret today the way I have spent some of my time in the last ten years. I could have used it to much more advantage. I have gone to far too many pleasureless, noisy parties. I have cut short days in the country and had too few evenings to read or listen to music. I regret I have never seriously studied foreign languages. I am self-employed and I regret I have not been a considerate or wise employer. I have always demanded too long a working day. I regret every worry I have caused members of my family, especially the ones who are gone. These regrets, I hope, are not entirely vain ones. For I can do something about them and with them. It may be too late for me to master foreign languages, but I can make it possible for others in my family to learn them while they are young. I can administer my time so as to eliminate much of the waste. I can stop worrying people.

It is neither idle nor morbid to consider what we should be sorry for, and to sort out those regrets which can be carried through remorse to amendment. It is one way to discover—and continually to rediscover, for regrets are a perennial crop—the kind of person you are. Discarding what is vain or false, facing the facts that should truly disturb your conscience, is worth whatever time it takes or pain it may cause. It can pay to the future what you owe to the past.

## SMILING THROUGH

Someone has said that regret can do the mind and body more harm than a prolonged drunk. As for crossing bridges before we come to them, and worrying lest they may collapse, that is the quick way to death.                                   —*Bruce Barton*

## Chapter 12/Changed Attitudes
## Mean Changed Lives

*"Attitudes," said a great American psychiatrist, "are more important than facts." Of course they are. A handicap is a fact. A hardship is a fact. A disaster is a fact. But where one person is defeated by a handicap, another is stimulated. Where one merely complains about hardship, another fights to eliminate it. Where one is paralyzed by disaster, another rises to the challenge. There is nothing inevitable about attitudes. They can be changed, and anyone can acquire new ones. All you have to do is discard the old.*
*And here are six areas where you can begin!*

## The Chance to Grow
ARDIS WHITMAN

The class reunion was in full swing. For the tenth time someone said, "I'd have known you anywhere—*you haven't changed a bit.*" "But it isn't true," I said. "We've all changed. Peter over there is the only one who hasn't." It was no compliment. Peter really did look the same, but why? He was doing the same thing he had done the year after graduation—holding down a minor job in the family business which demanded no particular effort of him. Somehow, without even knowing it, he had been shunted into a backwater of life.

None of us really wanted to be like Peter. Nevertheless,

what we voiced so wistfully was the most common of all human dreams: to stop life in its tracks, to hold on to what we cherish, to keep change away from us and all we love.

How we cling to youth and hate the coming of middle life! How we dread to leave an old home, to leave old friends and make new ones! But change is as inevitable as the turning of the seasons and the tides. To try to keep it from our door is to try to shut out life itself. For everything that is alive is in constant change. As our cells die and new ones replace them, as our very personalities change, so do we live. How much regret we could spare ourselves if we would regard change for what it is—a chance to grow.

It is when we *fail* to change that we fall behind in living and our spirits age. Perhaps you can remember a time in your own experience when for a while nothing much happened—nothing to disturb you, nothing to bring you joy. Time passed, but you stood still. "I felt as if I were the date stamp at the post office," a friend who had fallen into such a slough said to me. "All that happened was that every morning someone changed the date." Eventually the sameness ended. Something happened, and suddenly your life changed. And whether the change was good or bad, the hours of its coming loom larger in your memory now than years of quieter living. Even now you can recall how, in spite of the wrench it gave you, the discarding of an old way of life made you feel young again.

I know a marriage, made in great love, which paled and withered because there were too many business cares, too much money and no time for each other. The marriage would have dissolved, I think, except that a disaster wiped out the husband's business. The couple were poor once more —as they had been early in their marriage—and they bought a little home in the country and started an orchard. They worked on the orchard together for long hours every day. Soon they were a happy partnership again.

Some rare people know instinctively that change is life asserting itself, and they renew themselves by keeping pace with it. I have a friend in her late seventies who is off to Spain this summer. "I'm really going to enjoy it," she writes, "because last winter I took some courses at the university in Spanish art and history!" Why can't we all be like that? Why do most of us, instead, grow inflexible, fall into ruts? Often we are miserable with things as they are, yet when new experience breaks into our lives we hang back. Why? Partly it is inertia. By twenty-five, wrote the philosopher William James, we are almost literally "a bundle of habits," and we use the phrase "settled down" as the very symbol of maturity.

But the biggest reason we don't adapt to change is what Gilbert Murray, the great British classical scholar, once called man's "failure of nerve." After a certain point, early or late, most people seem to lose their youthful daring and to draw back from risk. "I always wanted to build houses," a cabdriver told me. "I worked with a builder one summer, and I was never so happy. But there's an awful lot to learn on that job, and a million things can go wrong. I *know* I can drive a cab, and I don't have any worries. Let somebody else build the houses."

When we suffer such a failure of nerve, staying put is our defense against disappointment. Perhaps it would work if we really *could* make our lives stand still. But we can't. Our only choice is how we will face the inevitable changes which come to us. The best way to face them is to welcome them. Above all, learn to extricate yourself from the bondage of the past. Keep it as a treasure in your heart, but don't waste time longing for its happiness. Changes are sure to come, and it is possible to prepare oneself to meet them. How? Just as the athlete readies himself for competition by a rigorous training schedule, so we, too, need to exercise our "change muscle." Purposely we should rethink our habits, our customary ways, making small changes whenever we can, to keep us mentally and spiritually limber. As Alfred E. Perlman, president of the New York Central Railroad, once said, "After you have done a thing the same way for two years, you should look at it carefully. After five years, look at it with suspicion. After ten years, throw it away and start over."

When, after years of housekeeping, Adeline Reynolds began her new career as an actress at the age of seventy, she felt that her old ways of life would not do for this new one. So she learned to sleep on the floor, took lessons in swimming, horseback riding, tap-dancing, fencing. "I keep myself limber by always learning something," she said when she was in her eighties.

Perhaps all of us cannot alter our lives so radically, but we can day by day make small adaptations to keep us flexible and venturesome. Experiment with your daily schedule. Do in the morning what you formerly did at night, and vice versa. Work all night; get up at dawn. Go by yourself where you are used to going with others, or with others where you are used to being alone. Walk where you usually ride. Go twelve hours someday without eating. Try, above all, to do without as many things as you can. One thing that most pins us in ruts is our fondness for habitual comforts.

Practice flexibility, and you will be astonished to discover how eventful your days become. You will always feel young, for you will be keeping up with life rather than letting it pass you by.

# Don't Be Afraid to Be Different

STUART KINZIE

When I was a child, my parents sent me to summer camp. Part of each camper's uniform was supposed to be a Boy Scout hat, low-crowned, wide-brimmed, to be worn every afternoon when we lined up for inspection. But my parents, through some catastrophic oversight, sent me off instead with one of those U.S. Army campaign hats, vintage of 1917. It was wide-brimmed, all right: when I put it on, I was practically in total darkness. As for the crown, it seemed to rise half a mile straight up in the air. Whenever I wore this monstrosity, instead of being an inconspicuous boy, I became a freak. Or so I thought.

Looking back now across more than thirty years, I can smile at the memory. It was no joke at the time, though. I was miserable—utterly, abjectly miserable—simply because I was different from the others. There must be few of us who cannot recall some such childhood episode, and fewer still who do not carry some of this deep-rooted fear of being different into adult life. But if we value leadership, achievement, maturity, we have to overcome this childish concern.

The rewards of differentness are easy enough to see. No matter what field you choose—science, entertainment, business—the demand is for *individuals,* whose performance is above average and therefore different. At any dinner party, the liveliest and most attractive guest is the one whose observations are stimulating because they are different. I have no doubt that a man's earning power parallels almost exactly his capacity to produce new ideas, to show unusual persistence or energy, to take chances—to be different.

The fear of being different, like most fears, tends to diminish when you drag it into the light and take a good look at it. At the bottom of such fear lies an intense preoccupation with self. That Army hat, back in my childhood, might have caused some momentary merriment or teasing, but the whole thing was too trivial to have lasted long. I was the one who kept it alive by agonizing about it. Recognize this self-consciousness as a form of egotism, and you are not so likely to be victimized by it. Some of the hostility that you shrink from is probably imaginary.

Another way to minimize the fear of being different is to remind yourself, if you do run into resentment or ridicule, that few pioneers escape being laughed at or criticized. Most of the great religious leaders of history, for example, have been nonconformists. Christ defied authority, as when He healed sick people on the Sabbath. He upset convention, as when He sat down to dinner with publicans and sinners.

People don't object to differentness nearly so much as they object to the attitude of superiority that so often goes with it. General Billy Mitchell's concept of air power, four decades ago, was prophetic—and correct. Unfortunately, he was unable to conceal his conviction that anyone who disagreed with him was a fool. As a result, his hopes were thwarted.

So be as different as you like, but be tolerant of your neighbor who does things his way. If we all granted to one another the right simply to be ourselves, we would be different enough. When Henry Thoreau was eight years old, someone asked him what he was going to be when he grew up. "Why," said the boy, "I will be *I!*" He was, too—and it's what we remember him for today.

# Do You Act Your Part?

MAUD SCHEERER

**A**fter the excitement, gaiety or tragedy of a fine play or movie, haven't you felt that the experience was more real than the actual events of your own existence? If acting is so much more real than routine living, and so much more exciting, why shouldn't all of us cultivate the art on a larger stage, our world? I am convinced we should. For years I have taught the principles of acting to persons preparing for a stage or movie career. The more I work with these principles, the more I am convinced that they have significance for us in daily living.

I don't for a moment mean that you should cultivate affectations. On the contrary, I suggest acting as a means of genuine self-expression and release. When President Wood of Stephens College asked Maude Adams to come and teach dramatics there he made it plain that he did not expect her to turn out stage stars. "Rather," he said, "I want you to teach them how to control and direct their emotions."

Superficial playacting—pretending to be something you are not—is as easily detected in life as on the stage. Real acting is a matter of making outwardly apparent the thing you feel true within. It is a matter of projecting yourself imaginatively into a situation and then letting action and speech luminously interpret what you feel.

Few of us are conscious of the satisfaction we could get if we accepted and played heartily the varied daily roles that life gives us. Usually we go from one situation to another with no change of pace or manner. Or we typecast ourselves as does the actor who plays butlers so well he is always cast for a butler role. A competent executive may typecast himself by carrying over into the home the personality that he has used all day in business. He arrives home: a new role and a new scene. He may dump the office and its problems right out on the dining table, dishing them up with his wife's well-served dinner. He may miss entirely the cue of appreciation, or affection, or relaxation, that suits the healing atmosphere of the home. If, however, he can see that the home scene calls for an entirely different technique of acting—a release from his business troubles, a change of feeling followed by a change of voice and manner as well as dress—then both he and his partners in the scene will get vastly more relish out of it. The person who enters any situation determined to play up to its every implication finds that it has a far sharper meaning than one who merely drifts aimlessly into it, lugging his humdrum self along.

The actor enters a scene with purpose and directness, eliminating all that does not relate to the immediate problem. If you try this, you are not content with aimless geniality or vague irritability, but you set yourself to show specifically the friendliness or indignation that fits your part. You may be worried about home situations while attending to business, but if you use the actor's methods of concentration you will rule out concerns that do not affect the job of the moment.

Obviously this practice means that we enter every situation with all our forces marshaled, not unused or scattered over a lot of lingering worries. It means too that by integrating our personalities around the role of the moment we can avoid incongruities and ineffectualities—things that are out of character, as when a man putting up an aggressive argument uses a whining or pleading voice.

One delightful role that every woman is called upon to play is that of hostess. Properly acted, it can be glamorous. Yet consider the number of hostesses who permit a dozen and one things to deflect them from the part. Some give all their attention to the cooking and planning, and are too tired to incarnate hospitality. Others are too eager to make an impression. Most women think only of the etiquette of the affair and miss entirely the spirit of their central role.

Dame Sybil Thorndike, the great English actress, once explained to a group of young actresses that the reason the stage was so splendid was that ordinary incidents of everyday living became a symbol on the stage. Pouring tea is no longer just pouring tea; it becomes the spirit of sociability, the symbol of hospitality. If you can translate this sense of symbols into life, the rewards will be immense.

You will be surprised to find how the inner embodiment of a role actually creates a new outward appearance. I remember once being asked to a party when I realized that I had no dress suited to the occasion. I considered not going at all. Then I decided to use the actor's art and dress my mind as best I could, to go and put my whole being into acting the role of guest. I let appreciation of the party, the hostess, the other guests take possession of me. The odd part of it is that the compliments I got that evening were on the dress I wore.

To feel and behave in a manner appropriate to the scene is far more important than to dress appropriately. Often I have seen girls applying for jobs who are handicapped by concern about their looks and what they are going to say. I want to tell them, "Dress the part as best you can, but the chief thing is to fill your clothes with the person you intend to fill the position you are applying for. Practice telling what you have to offer—skill, experience, knowledge and, above all, interest. State each with its own quality, not cloaked with either apology or conceit."

Were there no other advantage to be gained, acting in daily life would be worthwhile for the detachment it affords. Good acting is always dispassionate. It calls for poise, balance and control, and hence helps you to draw apart from a situation and view it both as a participant and spectator. Only the dispassionate person has full mastery, whether in social conversation, family discussion or business conference.

This impersonal quality in good acting has the value of making you more acutely aware of other persons in the scene. The best acting is done with a full awareness of your partner's role. Every contact we have throughout our day—from good-morning to the elevator man to the last good-night —may be made pleasanter by skillful use of this principle. Our lives can be drab if we allow them to become habitual —zestful if we act up to our role and our partners.

To those who protest that such histrionic displays are affected and unnatural, it can only be replied that all of our behavior is, in the broad sense, unnatural. Talking itself does not come natural with us; why not go on and talk in a way that expresses the role we feel best suited to the occasion? Such acting is not a matter of imitating another person. We may think that the charm, grace and vivacity of some actress dwell in her mannerisms. But to copy these externals is only to become an affected imitator. The true technique is to make the most out of every good trait you yourself possess. Technique is not a putting-on, it is a drawing-out process. It is making your everyday speech and movement, gesture and manner, habits of thought and feeling, good instruments and tools to use in expressing yourself in your many relationships. Not just to "get by" but to be wholly effective.

This idea of acting your part in life adequately, with truth and assurance, gives you an incentive to improve your voice and speech, carriage and posture, manners and habits of facial expression. In Shaw's *Pygmalion,* we have an insight into the transforming power of technique. It requires a kind of self-discipline that is cultural and thus draws out the individual's potentialities. You can't improve the speech without improving the person. And there are more ways of speech than words.

Posture can say: I am tired. I am discouraged. I am careless. I am alert. I am timid. I am a great guy!

Walk can say: I pound the pavement. The earth is my springboard. It's a long, hard road. I must not miss the surprises of the way.

Facial expression may say: I am disappointed. I am interested in you. I am a worrier. I have a sense of humor.

Voice quality may tell that you are a nagger, a whiner, a comfort, a mouse or a lion.

It's your own choice whether you slump into the less prepossessing of these alternatives, or create for yourself the role —the personality—that springs from the others. A certain pose may gain the effect we desire, and if it does, it is as legitimate to use it as it is to seek the apt word—and equally effective. The crowning principle of good acting is simplicity —economy of action and movement, restrained emotion, controlled thinking. Simplicity in acting is using just enough of all your powers to convey your intent and elicit the right response from the listener.

Simplicity is not to be confused with easiness. Simplicity is a certain fine clarity, even austerity. The person of great learning speaks simply, a person of great wealth dresses simply, a person of fine eloquence talks simply, an actor of rich technique is simple in his acting. But this great quality is hard-earned and represents the deepest honesty. It cannot be put on, it cannot be pretense; it is the expression, the making actual of the truest within us.

Every day, as we play the series of roles that life demands of us, we can employ these principles of acting. The wise father needs a correct sense of his various roles in daily affairs. When as an executive he has a problem to solve, he must have the actor's dispassion and detachment. At a business luncheon with clients, awareness of the scene and his partners in it are of the first importance. Back home in the evening he must understand that the role calls for good humor and simplicity and perception, for the attentiveness that marks him as the wise father.

Whether we like it or not, all of us must act: we must express outwardly what we feel within. The question is whether we do it poorly or well, whether we are content to be puppets operated by the strings of habit, or whether we shall consciously and skillfully portray our full role in each new scene or relationship. The thing to aim for is a cultivated technique of self-expressiveness by means of which your feelings, reactions, thoughts or wishes can be honestly and effectively conveyed.

⇒ ✦ ⇐

## OUT OF THE MOUTHS OF BABES

*M*y neighbor's two youngsters have built a clubhouse in their yard. On the wall, in childish letters, a list of club rules is posted. No. 1 reads: "Nobody act big, nobody act small, everybody act medium." —*Jack Denham*

# Take a Holiday from Caution

ELIZABETH BYRD

**F**red Gordon walked into his office that spring morning as he had done every working day for sixteen years. He looked out over New York's sooty rooftops, but he was dreaming beyond them—of an abandoned farm he had seen years before, eighty green miles up the Hudson River. "You can't," said his caution. "You're an accountant, not a farmer. You can't start a new life at fifty-four." "You can," argued his young heart. "You have no dependents. Only habit ties you here."

By noon Fred had resigned his position and was packing. That afternoon he was off on the great adventure of his life. It was more than three years ago that Fred made his decision. When I last saw him I asked if he had regretted it. He said, "I regret I didn't do it long ago." Few of us can run away as Fred did; jobs, family and community responsibilities take precedence. But we *can* adventure out of our ruts, and the first step is to analyze our use of caution. The function of caution is to protect us. Unfortunately it often enslaves us, forbidding us to do what we long to do.

As a little girl I was habitually timid, missing out on many of the small, exciting adventures of childhood. Suddenly, in my thirties, I realized that I had never accomplished anything I *really* wanted to do. I wanted to write. Writing for a living is a gamble. When I planned my first book, a long historical novel, I saw that it would take at least three years. Most books earn less than $3000 for the author, and I had no assurance of publication. Friends begged me to think of the book as a hobby. Take a job, they said, and write on the side. It was sensible advice, but I hesitated. Then I chanced on an essay by Ralph Waldo Emerson which echoed my deepest convictions: "When you find that prudent people do not commend you, adhere to your own act, and congratulate yourself that you have done something strange and extravagant. . . . Give your heart a holiday from caution."

My holiday from caution meant a very inexpensive apartment, cheap clothes and a diet of beans and spaghetti. But it also meant enormous satisfaction and a growing certainty that when you feel deeply about something you should not compromise. Luckily, the novel was successful. But, beyond that, the experience opened new vistas. And it made me thoughtful about cautious behavior.

Besides crippling our enterprise, inflexible caution may also blight our emotional relationships. Many people never trust a new acquaintance. Such cynics are fearful of "being taken." I think that they *are* being taken—by their own unwarranted skepticism. In a Maine village a band of gypsies rattled into town in red-and-yellow wagons. One storekeeper hid expensive groceries under the counter. "If we don't watch, they'll steal us ragged," he said.

But another left his merchandise easily accessible. "Don't the gypsies steal from you?" I asked. "No," he said. "They steal only from folks who expect it. I haven't expected it for fifty summers, and I ain't expectin' it now."

"What will people say?" is perhaps the most inhibiting type of caution. Children are naturally free of this fear, and also of snobbery, until some adult, with dubious wisdom, cautions them about making friends.

I happened to be visiting Selda and Peter Marchand

when they were planning a birthday party for their six-year-old Pete. "The one I want most at my party," Pete said, "is Liam." Liam worked at the town dump—a big, red-bearded Irishman who, Pete told us, knew more about knights, giants and leprechauns than anybody else. Selda frowned, but Peter said, "Go ahead, son. Ask whomever you like."

Selda told me later, "My first impulse was to worry about what people would say. But later I realized how shallow and snobbish my attitude was. Liam's stories and magic tricks were the hit of the party. More important, we came to cherish his friendship."

Some parents display another sort of caution: nagging worry about their children's health, about some vague tragedy that "might happen." Such cautions provide fertile soil for habitual anxiety and hypochondria.

As a child at camp I was roused at three o'clock one morning by a counselor, who said, "Let's go for a walk in the woods." Mindful of warnings never to get my feet wet, I started to put on heavy socks and sneakers. "No," Dorothy said, "it's more fun barefoot." I followed her meekly through half a mile of dripping pinewoods. When we reached the lake, bright moonlight sparkled the water to a sheet of diamonds. A loon called—an eerie laugh that still haunts me. Dorothy, with a flair for the dramatic, told me the wild, romantic tale of an Indian princess who had died here at Mad Squaw Lake. When I think of that summer I treasure above all else those venturesome hours.

Often people need our help, but we harden our hearts for fear of financial loss or social embarrassment. When we do, we are shutting our doors to life itself. In January 1957 three alcoholics who had once been derelicts had only four dollars —and a dream. They wanted to convert a vacant nightclub into a rehabilitation center where desperate men could find help toward food and lodging, and where their wives and children, panicky and hopeless, could come for guidance.

"We hesitated a long time before approaching the landlord," Buford Peterson told me. "We hadn't yet raised enough money to pay the first month's rent. And we waited in despair for him to ask the obvious questions about security and bank references, for we had absolutely nothing but blind faith." To their astonishment, the landlord also acted on blind faith. Unquestioningly he granted them a lease. Today the Fellowship Center at 190–34 Jamaica Avenue in Hollis, Queens, in New York City, is a monument to four men whose holiday from caution has helped thousands.

When we meet a situation that demands faith in another person, we must trust our intuition. My father has always believed that people strive to live up to our best opinion of them. Once when I visited him in Kentucky his handyman, Will, drove me home from the movies. I had forgotten my door key, and Dad wasn't in. Will asked me for a bobby pin, and within seconds the door was open.

"How on earth did you do it?" I asked. "If I couldn't have picked this lock, your father would have been mighty disappointed in me," Will said. "After all, it used to be my business." "Locksmith?" I asked. "No," he said with a touch of professional pride. "Burglar."

My father's trust in Will had created a chain reaction that often happens when people adventure with faith. Today Will has his own hardware store and is active in helping other ex-convicts, who in turn help others. Holidays from caution are likely to be contagious. How far can we afford to journey on such a holiday? Bernard Baruch advised, "When in doubt, follow your heart."

# Get Involved!

MORTON M. HUNT

**R**ecently a young friend of mine was the only witness to a traffic accident. While visiting in Washington, D.C., she saw a carful of teen-agers crash into a truck. The teen-agers blamed the truck driver, but my friend volunteered to testify in his behalf. It would cost her several further trips down from her home in New York, but she wanted to see justice done.

When she told her Washington hostess about the incident, she was greeted with the familiar rejoinder: "Oh, for goodness' sake, why did you *get involved?*"

Every day you hear decent, well-meaning persons restating Cain's position, "Am I my brother's keeper?" in such clichés as "I don't want to get mixed up in it," or "It's not my affair." Such statements tell us something about the time we live in. Many people are too fearful of hurt or rebuff to invite others into their lives. But in a world that is increasingly too big and too complicated, we desperately *need* to get involved if we are to live our lives fully.

Years ago, when I first moved to New York, I bought a small apartment in a coöperative building. Shortly thereafter we co-op owners had our first general meeting and, because I spoke out, someone nominated me for president. Reluctantly I accepted. Friends told me I was foolish. "Why get involved?" they said. "You'll have plenty of headaches and no thanks." True enough, I did have headaches. As unpaid president for two years, I was plagued by budget problems, noisy wrangles and irate fellow owners ringing my doorbell about leaks or insufficient heat.

Yet the final balance showed a huge profit for me. I learned things about business and law—and human nature —which have been useful to me ever since. I also learned much about myself—that I am not a good administrator, for one thing. Best of all, I found among the tenants some whose warm friendship has enriched my life ever since. Time and again I have been astonished at rediscovering how great are the rewards of human involvement—when you take the trouble to help a stranger, to protest against an injustice, to assume a civic responsibility or to enter on the rare and wonderful risks of a new friendship. And you are seldom snubbed when you reach out in sincerity.

The personnel manager of a large firm told me that he supported a student-exchange program financially, but hesitated to get involved personally because of the adjustment it would require for his family to assume responsibility for a foreign student. Then he decided to chance it. He took a Japanese high-school student into his home for a year. "That boy became a member of the family," he told me. "He says he has two sets of parents, Japanese and American, and we feel we have another son. Through him our community found a new and rewarding interest in Japanese customs and culture."

The moral imperative to "get involved" is applicable in the tiniest and the largest of our daily considerations, in everything from helping a neighbor all the way to *caring* about the state of the world. In little daily deeds that add up impressively, each of us can contribute to the world we live in—and to our own life. Every little act of genuine involvement, in fact, encourages the growth of the identity beyond the Me to the We, intertwining us with other selves until the thread of each life is no longer a single strand but a part of the fabric of humankind.

A friend of mine was riding on a bus when a gang of noisy youths started taunting an elderly woman who had asked them to stop shoving. "Everyone else in the bus looked out the windows, or straight ahead, as though they couldn't hear the kids saying fresh things about her," he told me. "So did I, at first. Then all at once—I don't know quite why—I thought, *How dare I keep out of this? This is part of the world I live in.* So I turned and snapped out at them, 'Haven't you young people any parents? How would you like someone to treat your own mothers the way you're treating this lady?' To my astonishment, they looked sheepish and fell quiet. I found myself shaking all over, but for the rest of the day I felt warm inside because I had not left a good deed undone."

Is it not curious how the times of most intense involvement with other people stand out in our memories as the times when we were least frightened, least bored, least pessimistic about life itself? In his book *Humanity and Happiness,* Georg Brochmann dwells on the strange fact that he was never so happy or so vibrantly alive as during the wretched years of the Nazi occupation of his beloved Norway. For that was a time when, despite sorrows, hardships and constant danger, he and his fellow patriots in the underground were bound to one another by a sense of high purpose and mutual trust. Many of us experience such nostalgia for the war years, when we were closer to our countrymen than ever before or since.

No one can deny that getting involved means taking a chance. The person you fall in love with may hurt you terribly, the quarreling friends you try to reconcile may turn their joint anger upon you, the drowning man you try to save may pull you under with him. Yet in avoiding hurts and disappointments we become cold, inhuman. British author C. S. Lewis, in his book *The Four Loves,* says, "If you want to make sure of keeping it intact, you must give your heart to no one, not even to an animal. Avoid all entanglements, lock it up safe in the coffin of your selfishness. But in that casket—safe, dark, motionless, airless—it will change. It will not be broken; it will become unbreakable, impenetrable, irredeemable."

For specimens of the unbreakable heart, look to those philosophers of ancient times who tried to attain serenity by schooling themselves not to care deeply about mortal or perishable things. Anaxagoras, when brought word of his son's death, maintained an icy calm and said merely, "I never supposed I had begotten an immortal."

Today we pity the recluse who barricades himself in a house full of junk or riches; in his self-imposed isolation we recognize the symptoms of profound emotional illness. And, indeed, most of the 518,000 patients in America's mental hospitals can be defined as people who have found it necessary to retreat from normal human involvement.

What we fail to notice is that we ourselves often do the same thing in lesser degree. Every widow or widower who finds excuses for staying at home and avoiding the effort of seeking out new friends, every citizen who dislikes the way things are being run but does nothing about it—all these are doing the same thing. All deliberate noninvolvement is a limitation of growth and health. That is why men who are wiser than Anaxagoras have willingly faced the chance of pain, knowing, as Tennyson wrote after a bereavement,

'Tis better to have loved and lost
Than never to have loved at all.

Think whom you admire. It is likely to be a person with
an abundant heart. We admire Dorothea Dix, for instance,
who retired from schoolteaching at thirty-nine to repair her
health and to enjoy peace and quiet—and then learned
about the desperate condition of America's mentally ill.
Abandoning all thoughts of herself, she spent the next
thirty-six years vigorously campaigning to get the mentally ill
out of chains and jails into more humane surroundings. Far
from weighing upon her, this immense responsibility gave
her health, strength and cheer she had never known.

For responsibilities are not just dead weight, but the most
precious freight we can carry—a cargo that makes our journey through time a valuable expedition, and not just an idle
passage toward death. Deep commitment to other persons
seems to stave off the shrinkage of old age. The great senior
citizens of our times—Winston Churchill, Bernard Baruch,
Konrad Adenauer, Herbert Hoover, Carl Sandburg, Albert
Schweitzer, Eleanor Roosevelt—remained vital through
their unceasing involvement in the world around them.

Bertrand Russell, as hearty and alive as any man in his
nineties, says that in his youth he was melancholy and unhappy because he was given to brooding about himself.
Then slowly he learned to fasten his attention on other
persons. "The happy man," Lord Russell wrote, "is the
man who has free affections and wide interests, who secures
his happiness through these affections and interests and
through the fact that they, in turn, make him an object of
interest and affection to many others."

And thus the great secret about involvement is that, quite

300

literally, it is life itself. Noninvolvement is a limbo, a vacuum. Andrew Marvell was ostensibly only wooing a reluctant lady when he wrote,

> The grave's a fine and private place,
> But none, I think, do there embrace.

He was also hinting at a deeper truth: that living and embracing are part of each other, while privacy—noninvolvement—and death go hand in hand. The eighteenth-century philosopher Johann Fichte said the whole thing in nine words: "The I," he wrote, "is not a fact, but an act."

And just how does one go about putting this philosophy into action? For myself, I think first of some of the obvious do's and don't's. Don't hurry past people in trouble; *do* take a chance on helping strangers. Don't sidestep painfully or deeply felt topics of conversation; *do* care how others feel. Don't think of reasons to justify keeping your distance from neighbors, business acquaintances or distant relatives; *do* reach out and strive to know them. Don't be content to "let George do it," whatever it is; *do* care about your home, your town, your nation enough to try to improve them. In sum, don't be everlastingly careful. *Do* get involved!

❧ ✦ ☙

### THE FLAMING SPIRIT

*E*nthusiasm is the thing that makes the world go round. Without its driving power nothing worth doing has ever been done. It alleviates the pains of poverty and the boredom of riches. Apart from it joy cannot live. Therefore, it should be husbanded with zeal and spent with wisdom. To waste it is folly; to misuse it, disastrous. —*Robert Haven Schauffler*

# A Whim a Day
from "Topics of the Times"
THE NEW YORK TIMES

For refreshing one's zest for living, for leaving behind one's vexing problems and irritations, or for opening new horizons, there is nothing like doing things "at whim." Writing a letter to a complete stranger who has done something praiseworthy, walking over that hill one has always meant to explore, wandering through an old cemetery, going to an auction, rereading an old book of poems or essays, building a birdhouse—all, if done "at whim," can be rewarding.

But the way of the whim is not easy, for the world is full of whim-puncturers. Children and gardeners know all about this because their whims are constantly being shot down by dreadfully logical people to whom the thought of buying a banana split an hour before dinner, or replacing a nuisance of a hedge with a stone wall, is unsettling and therefore undesirable. Also, whims have a way of breaking sharply from established routines and may upset carefully calculated family budgets. But this is all to the good, now and then. It is easy to confuse routine with efficiency and to grow stodgy; whims were designed expressly to prevent solidification of the spirit. Someday perhaps the medical profession will recognize the special healing qualities of whims and include among its prescriptions one that reads, "Take a whim at least once a day." Surely this is excellent advice, all things considered.

# III

*Reality is what our five senses tell us of the universe*
*that surrounds us. We must learn to live with*
*it because we live in it. This in itself is both a challenge*
*and a delight. There is the challenge of making a*
*living, of carving a niche for yourself, of winning a*
*place in the sun. There is the challenge of adversity,*
*of illness, of pain. There are the delights of music,*
*literature and art, of people, places and things.*
*To all of these we are introduced when we are born,*
*and we live with them until we die. It's like being given*
*free tickets to a marvelous play. Here we sit, each of us*
*at the center of his own consciousness. And every*
*morning, miraculously, the curtain rises. . . .*

# HOW
# TO LIVE
# WITH
# REALITY

# Chapter 13/The Excitement of Getting Ahead

*"The secret of success," said Disraeli, "is constancy to
purpose." True enough—persistence does count. But
there are other secrets, too. Henry Kaiser, one of the
most successful men of our time, thinks there are
seven ingredients—and you will find them listed in the
pages that follow. Thomas J. Watson of the vast International Business Machines Corporation gives a discouraged
young man his formula for rising to the top. Ideas worth
studying, all of them, if you believe, as Robert Browning did, that "a minute's success pays the failure of years."*

## Imagination—the Secret of Success
*Excerpt from the book: Streamline Your Mind*
JAMES L. MURSELL

Imaginative power is the
chief characteristic of the supremely successful career. Lincoln was a great statesman because he had a clear vision of
what the American Union could and should mean. The emi-
nence of industrial and business leaders has been due to
their imaginative vision, which revealed to them new possibilities, new programs, new modes of organization and action. Newton, Einstein and Darwin have set the patterns of
human thinking because from the stuff of their minds they
wove a new texture of ideas and interpretations.

On a much humbler level, too, imagination is the key to
success. If you want to write fiction or drama or poetry, this

above all is the secret you must learn. Perhaps your aim is to concoct some original entertainment for your friends: again you are facing a job for the imagination. The advertising man or the sales manager achieves success by his ability to think of new combinations and new avenues of approach to old problems. The executive is most valuable who can conceive of new patterns of function and new strategies.

Fortunately, imaginative power can be developed.

You can develop it if you follow the trail whose landmarks psychology can map. In governing the imagination you must specialize with ever-growing power along definite lines. *Give your mind wholeheartedly to a certain line of interest.* Ideas do not come to us haphazardly. If we do nothing but sit and wait for them we shall never in all our lives do anything but sit and wait.

*Cultivate the notebook habit,* or better still a card file. Always keep cards or a notebook in your pocket. Whenever any suggestion comes to you, whether from reading or conversation or meditation or dreaming, jot it down on a separate card or a separate page of the book. Once a week go over your ideas. Give your mind a chance to ramble and explore. See if any brand-new suggestions occur to you. And write down anything that comes. If this is kept up systematically for a year, you will have accumulated a good deal of stuff that looks like junk. But do not throw it away. You never know when an idea, like lightning, may run zigzag through such a mass of material and fuse it into an effective unity. Without the use of a system you would have missed it. And remember that it only takes one really good suggestion to multiply any man's effectiveness manifold. Lastly, you will have trained yourself to be on the lookout for new notions, new combinations, new and valuable thoughts. A notebook may not suit your personality at all. But it is the principle, not the detail, that I want to present. Do not just hope for good ideas. Go out and try to scare them up.

*Seek for definite and concrete starting points* for any imaginative undertaking. Do not let your mind wander helplessly over the entire universe hoping for something to turn up. Be businesslike. Start a process of directed and determined search. Many a great piece of music has begun with nothing but two or three notes or a simple rhythm. The man of genius picks up hints from here, there and everywhere. They are points of growth. Sometimes very slowly, sometimes very swiftly, ideas and images and thoughts coalesce about them. You must set yourself to coax ideas. You must poke about to unearth them in their hidden lairs. This is where the notebook habit can help you enormously. Find some solid, concrete point from which to start. In itself the germinal idea may be trivial. It may seem exceedingly remote from the business in hand. But it is very necessary.

Then *practice the art of imaginative experimentation.* Consider every conceivable combination of circumstances for your sales campaign, or your administrative setup. Never mind if some of them seem silly or impossible at first glance. Maybe a wild notion can be tamed and made to do good work if you do not reject it too soon. In this work of imaginative experimentation knowledge and experience count for most. Some people have supposed that mental creation means making something out of nothing at all. But knowledge that has been assimilated and is part of you is the vital substance of imaginative construction. One cannot think well about any subject unless one knows it well. Facts are always the best possible prompters of ideas. So if you find yourself stuck for new ideas, turn to facts. Here is your best chance of finding new expedients, new lines of action, new modes of treatment. There is a definite relation between the amount of knowledge people possess and their ability to think creatively and originally.

Whenever imaginative construction has begun, *push it through to a conclusion* of some kind. Even though the grand new scheme for your party will never be tried out, develop it in full and get it into black and white. *This* plan may be a failure, but the definite completion of a piece of work has a most beneficial effect. Half-baked projects are bad for your mind.

*Don't quit your job when you quit your desk.* Carry, not the routine, but the wider issues of your job along with you. Treasure and utilize opportunities to be alone. They are chances to transform yourself from a *routine* specialist into a *creative* specialist. Consider how your job might be altered beneficially. The proper use of periods of free time is one of the great secrets of imaginative success.

Such are the suggestions which psychology has to offer for imaginative self-direction in any and every field. By them you can fashion your imagination into a streamlined, swiftly moving instrument, economical of power, capable of most valuable service.

❖ ◆ ❖

### CAN AND CANNOT

*I* don't want men of experience working for me. The experienced man is always telling me why something can't be done. He is smart; he is intelligent; he thinks he knows the answers. The fellow who has not had any experience is so dumb he doesn't know a thing can't be done—and he goes ahead and does it.
                                        —*Charles F. Kettering*

# Seven Keys to Achievement

WILLIAM J. LEDERER

In Hawaii they say that a falling coconut will never strike the bald and shiny head of Henry J. Kaiser, because the tempestuous builder and improviser never stands in one spot long enough. At eighty-three, Kaiser dashes around with the velocity of a teen-ager who has a hornet in his britches. With no thought of retirement, he recently built a community for 50,000 people in a previously barren area of Hawaii; and he is planning his future projects: an international medical center and a system for helping backward countries to develop.

Kaiser is noisy and flamboyant. He attacks every project with ferocity and glee. When he inspects a construction job he flays his arms like a windmill, while shouting orders and questions to everyone within visual distance. His organization sprawls over the world. It annually grosses around a billion dollars. Watching him at work recently, I found it hard to believe that as a young man Henry Kaiser was a failure. In 1895, when, at thirteen, he first started looking for a job, people in his home town of Sprout Brook, New York, shook their heads. Who would want to employ a fellow like him? Frail, painfully shy, he fouled up everything he attempted. By trial and error over the years, however, Kaiser stumbled upon a formula which he claims guarantees success to anyone who has the courage to apply it. "Anyone who observes my seven principles can't help but be a success." Kaiser carefully explained his principles to me.

*Most people use only one tenth of their total capacity for work and original thought. Harness your full powers and you will be amazed at the results.*

At sixteen, the then out-of-work Kaiser timidly approached the proprietor of a photographic studio. "Mister," he said, shaking with fright, "I want a job. I think I can triple your profits in two months."

"You can do *what?*" laughed the proprietor.

"Yes, sir. If I *don't* triple your profits, I'll work for nothing. And if I succeed, I want half of the extra profits."

"You triple the profits and I'll make you my partner," said the owner, amused.

"At first," Kaiser told me, "I was scared. I really didn't think I could do it. But I had made a commitment, in front of witnesses. Now I had to act. First I posted signs saying that we gave one-day photo service. The boss said this could never be done. I assured him that I could do the extra work, and I did. I worked sometimes until four o'clock in the morning. The boss warned that I'd have a nervous breakdown. But a strange thing happened. Working eighteen hours a day didn't tire me. I had a specific goal. I began enjoying myself. I didn't need as much sleep as previously. Business became so heavy that I had to devise a new studio lighting system and a method of continuous processing. After two months the profits almost quadrupled. I became a partner."

*If you persevere, and push, and hang on long enough, you will wear down the opposition.*

Everyone associated with Kaiser recognizes how powerful a force his persistence is. One of his partners said, "Henry is like a happy elephant. He smiles, and leans against you. After a while you know there's nothing left to do but move in the direction he's pushing." One of the first people to discover this quality in Henry was a hardware proprietor by the name of McGowen. Tiring of the photographic business, Kaiser approached McGowen for a job as clerk. "There's no job opening here," said McGowen tartly. But day after day for two weeks, Kaiser returned. On the fifteenth morning, before McGowen could say no again, Kaiser said, "Mr. Mc-Gowen, just let me show you one urgent matter." Kaiser pointed. "You have several thousand dollars' worth of housewares there. They haven't moved because they're tarnished. I'll shine them for you. . . ."

"Shine the darn stuff. Sell it," McGowen moaned in total exasperation. "Just stop pestering me." Kaiser started the job. But the next day he cornered the boss again. "Mr. Mc-Gowen, it won't work. Shining that stuff is too slow. I want you to hire some boys to help me." Once more McGowen told Kaiser to get out. However, the following morning Kaiser again showed up, this time with the village banker.

"Mr. McGowen," said the banker, "Henry wants to borrow enough money to buy some of your tarnished stock. He doesn't have any collateral but, knowing his perseverance and honesty, I'm willing to lend if the price is right."

The surprised McGowen threw his hands into the air. "All right! All right! Henry, I give up. Go hire yourself twenty boys. I'll put you on the payroll just to get you off my back." Kaiser sold the housewares at a profit and, within three months, was sales manager of the store.

*Decide what your real dreams are—then reach for them. They are closer than you think.*

"Many people," Henry Kaiser says, "have grand dreams. But they feel these dreams are impossible. They shilly-shally around, wasting their time on routine jobs. They spend their energy telling themselves why it can't be done. If you *think* you don't know what you want to do, just ask yourself, 'What do I want most out of life?' That's your dream. And no matter how silly it appears—you can reach it. First announce your dreams. Then look for the ways and means."

How does Henry Kaiser put his own aspirations into hard reality? Here is what his son, Edgar, said: "At the beginning of World War II my father wanted to build ships. Everybody told him it was impossible. So my father called together the staff for an 'impossibility conference.' We listed every reason why we should fail. We had no steel, no shipyard, no experienced shipbuilding personnel, no plans, no money. My father tackled one 'reason for failing' at a time. He had no ship plans and no ship designers. 'Okay,' he said, 'we'll be our own designers.' Having no past experience to restrict his thinking, he devised an original method of ship construction based on prefabrication.

"This assisted us on some of our other roadblocks. The prefabrication system required fewer experienced workers than did traditional methods. As you know, we even employed grandmothers as welders in our yards. The system also meant a less complicated shipbuilding yard, so the problem of getting a shipyard was reduced. The bankers, seeing how our first problems were being minimized, were more inclined to finance us. And so it is: you solve a small portion of the tough parts, and the remainder falls into place. Dad launched a ship a day, about fifteen hundred of them."

*Serve the public. Find projects that fill public needs. The more people who benefit, the better it is for you, too.*

In 1954 the then seventy-two-year-old Kaiser decided to spend a vacation in Hawaii. But he had trouble finding a hotel room. Thousands of tourists had been turned down. "A lot of people want to spend money in Hawaii today," said

Henry. "I'm going to extend my trip and build some hotels."

Some Hawaiian business tycoons laughed when they heard what Kaiser was up to. Where could he build a hotel? The only sites left in the Waikiki area consisted mostly of mud flats and slums. But it was these mud flats and slums that Kaiser bought. He and his partner, Fritz Burns, brought in 30,000 cubic yards of white sand, turning the mud flats into one of the largest and finest beaches in Waikiki. They cleared the slums and laid foundations. Months later, 875 of the 5000 rooms of the Hawaiian Village Hotel were completed. Guests registered enthusiastically, and have ever since. As Kaiser says, "Those who do good for the public usually end up doing well for themselves."

*You seldom accomplish very much by yourself. You must get the assistance of others.*

"I make progress," says Kaiser, "by having people around me who are smarter than I am—and listening to them. And I assume that *everyone* is smarter about something than I am." Kaiser goes about this by constantly seeking opinions. He listens, questions, and listens. When an employe gives him a bright idea, Kaiser usually says, "That's fine. I like it. You've just acquired an extra job. Put your idea into action —starting this afternoon."

It makes no difference who the idea man is; the person who shows the initiative is given added responsibility. One result is that the majority of the sixty Kaiser companies are headed by executives who became managers when they were under thirty-two years of age.

*Achieving success demands total effort. Avoid distractions.*

If you want success you must pay a price. When you have the urge for diversion—social visits, TV, cards, movies, golf —you must evaluate it by asking, "Will this expenditure of time and energy help me realize my present purpose in life?" Success is a selfish taskmaster. Read the biographies of famous people—the Curies, Einstein, Edison, Michelangelo, Paderewski. All of them, and almost all others who have achieved greatness, were at their jobs from first morning light until after midnight. Kaiser is like this, too. Watching him embark on a new project is like seeing a man with blinders on. He only looks ahead—never glances to one side.

*Conduct your affairs as if you expect today to be your last.*

Henry Kaiser is one of the most time-conscious people in the world. Even the five hours he allots himself for sleep are productive. This is what he calls his "idea period," and he always has a pad and pencil next to his bed. People who don't know him are often amazed when he telephones at 3 a.m. "Say, Smitty," comes an almost sinfully cheerful voice. "I've just had an idea. . . ."

Kaiser believes that by saving a few minutes here and a few hours there it is possible to add many years of usefulness to your life. Every morning he mentally lists everything he wants to accomplish before midnight. In the late afternoon he goes over the list. Every project must be completed —just as if Kaiser would not be around tomorrow to take care of loose ends. This practice permits him to start each day "neat and uncluttered."

These seven principles have catapulted Henry J. Kaiser from being a sickly, stammering, poverty-ridden youth to great wealth, vigor, prestige, longevity and happiness. Is it possible for the average person to use these same principles successfully? Henry Kaiser thinks so. "First decide what you want to do, and then have the courage to start toward the goal, no matter how impossible it looks," he says. "If you want to get there badly enough, nothing can stop you."

# The Incentive of Failure

CHARLES WESTRILL

At the age when you're convinced you can twist the world into a pretzel, I left my native Georgia and got a job, a very small job, on a New York magazine. I intended to be a writer. I figured that I would learn exactly what sort of writing was in demand; then I would quit my job, start producing reams of this precious commodity, and shortly retire to the Riviera to hobnob with Noel Coward and Somerset Maugham. It didn't quite work out this way. The things I wrote at night or on weekends came bouncing back with dismal regularity.

Well, if I wasn't cut out to be a writer, I told myself, I could at least take over the magazine business. To hasten this process, every noon I would go to the Automat, buy a bun, take it out to a bench in Central Park and dream great dreams. One day, munching on my bun, I began to wonder why my employer, who owned a whole flock of magazines, didn't translate some of his better magazine articles into Spanish, combine them into a single top-quality magazine, and assign a star salesman—me—to sell it all over Latin America. It was with such a splendid vision that I hurried back to my cubbyhole at the office.

Of course, there might be problems in the form of tariffs, currency regulations and so on. Before approaching the boss with my brilliant idea, I decided to find out about these details. I asked my cellmate at the office if he knew of an authority on Latin America. "Latin America?" he said. "I

314

guess T. J. Watson over at IBM knows as much about Latin America as anyone."

"IBM?" I echoed. "What's that?"

He gave me a look of weary scorn. "International Business Machines. Why don't you go back to Georgia?"

Well, I had never heard of International Business Machines, or this T. J. Watson either. But certainly he had to eat, and if I was careful, I figured, I could afford *two* buns in the park—or maybe even the cafeteria at the zoo. So I called up IBM and asked for Mr. Watson. When a secretarial voice answered, I announced cheerily that I would like to buy Mr. Watson a lunch and pick his brains about Latin America. I'd been told he was an authority, I explained. Friday would suit me best. (It was payday.) We would eat in the park, I said, not specifying the menu. I could pick Mr. Watson up at his office, or we could meet at the zoo.

"The zoo?" echoed the voice, with rising inflection.

"The cafeteria at the Central Park zoo," I said, a bit impatiently. "Will you go and ask him, please?" The voice went away, but soon came back. Mr. Watson would be glad to see me, it said. But he had suggested that I come and have lunch with him. In the light of my finances, this struck me as a first-rate suggestion.

When I walked into the IBM skyscraper on Fifty-seventh Street and asked the elevator starter if he happened to know on which floor someone named T. J. Watson worked, he gave me a queer look and a number. On the designated floor the receptionist summoned a secretary who took me to a waiting room. There another secretary came and escorted me to another waiting room. Each time the paneling grew darker and richer, the pile of the carpet deeper and the reverential silence more profound. So did my conviction that somebody was making a terrible mistake—probably me. The final secretary was a man. "The president will see you now," he said.

"President?" I said hoarsely. But already a massive door had swung open, revealing an office roughly the size of Grand Central Station. At the far end, behind an enormous, polished desk, was a tall, silver-haired gentleman: Thomas J. Watson, Senior, one of the mightiest tycoons in America. On his desk was a small, neatly lettered sign: THINK. I *was* thinking—thinking I should have stayed in Georgia.

He rose with as much courtesy as if I had been a visiting ambassador. "Well, young man," he said, "it's nice of you to drop in. Sit down and tell me what I can do for you." I moved forward and sat down. But I was speechless.

He waved his hand. "Don't let these surroundings bother you. When I was about your age, I was working in a store in an upstate town named Painted Post, trying to sell pianos and organs. Backgrounds change, but people don't—much. Now tell me: What's all this about Latin America?"

My voice came back from wherever it had gone, and I told him about my plan. He listened attentively. I said that I wanted to know what difficulties to expect. He nodded. "It's not a bad idea at all. I'll arrange for you to see the right people after lunch." He touched a button, and a little man appeared with a notebook. On the notebook cover, I noticed, was a word stamped in gold: THINK.

Mr. Watson named the people I was to see. "And while you're at it," he added casually, "see that this young man gets a copy of every magazine published in Latin America." (They came, too. In droves.) "Now," said Mr. Watson, "how about some lunch? I really was tempted to meet you at the zoo. Nobody ever asked me to the zoo for lunch before. But we have our own dining rooms here, in the building, and I'm afraid that the habit of time saving is hard to break."

Mr. Watson and I had a fine lunch. He told me about IBM, its vast worldwide organization, the benefits for employes, the little copybook maxims that he liked to hang on office and factory walls. People didn't notice them consciously after a while, he admitted, but unconsciously they were affected by them. THINK was one of his favorites. AIM HIGH was another. "You were aiming pretty high," he said quizzically, "when you said you wanted to pick my brains. But I like that. That's why I said yes."

I admitted, with a gulp, that when I walked into the building I hadn't the faintest idea who he was. He laughed. "It's a blow to my ego, but probably a healthy one." He looked at me speculatively. "How much salary are you making now?"

I told him. He smiled. "If you'd like to join our IBM family, I think we could do a little better for you than that."

"Thank you, sir," I said, "but machines don't like me. What I want to be eventually is . . ." I stopped. I had about decided that I would never be a writer. But I had a feeling that this man could see right through me anyway, so I told him about the endless rejection slips.

He leaned back. "It's not exactly my line," he said, "but would you like me to give you a formula for writing success?" He hesitated. "It's quite simple, really. Double your rate of failure." I stared at him. This was no copybook maxim.

"You're making a common mistake," he said. "You're thinking of failure as the enemy of success. But it isn't at all. Failure is a teacher—a harsh one, perhaps, but the best. You say you have a desk full of rejected manuscripts? That's great! Every one of those manuscripts was rejected for a reason. Have you pulled them to pieces looking for that reason? That's what I have to do when an idea backfires or a sales program fails. You've got to put failure to work for you." He folded his napkin and put it beside his plate. "You can be discouraged by failure—or you can learn from it. So go ahead and make mistakes. Make all you can. Because that's where you will find success. On the far side of failure."

I did remember. My desk was still full of unsalable manuscripts. And when I presented my grand design for a Latin-American magazine to the boss, he said acidly, "Do you think we have money to put into a crazy scheme like this? Stop bothering me." (Actually, it wasn't such a bad idea. A year or two later The Reader's Digest started its Spanish and Portuguese editions, which today are the most widely circulated magazines in Latin America.)

But that's not the point. The point is that somewhere inside me a basic attitude had shifted. A project turned down, a lot of rejected manuscripts—why, these were nothing to be ashamed of. They were rungs in a ladder—that was all. A wise and tolerant man had given me an idea. A simple idea, but a powerful one: if you can learn to learn from failure, you'll go pretty much where you want to go.

## MAKE A MISTAKE!

**H**ow often we intend one thing and it turns into another! The wrong book comes home from the library and opens a whole new field of interest. I know of a student in college who wandered into the wrong classroom and became so interested in the subject being discussed there that he pursued it and made it his career. I need scarcely add that, being so absentminded, he became a famous professor. It should take the edge off disappointment to remember that half the things that go wrong surprise us by turning out all right. —*Robert Hillyer*

# The Right Way to the Right Job

JAMES NATHAN MILLER

Most people at one time or another are faced with the need of finding a job. Today, with the commercial and industrial scene changing rapidly, people are changing jobs often, and there are many opportunities available. But, however ample his ability, the average job-seeker usually has little knowledge of how to sell that ability on the labor market. There are techniques which can be learned readily, and the jobs go to those who master them. Watch an expert job counselor in action.

Ray A. Ziegler is director of the senior worker division of the Oregon Bureau of Labor. He conducts a two-session night course in Creative Job Search Techniques at Portland Community College. Of 1500 who took the course in its first year, 1200 are now working, and nine out of ten say they owe their jobs to what they learned there. Ziegler meets job-seekers in what was once a high-school classroom. Behind the desks in a typical first session are about twenty students, the youngest a boy of eighteen in a blue zippered jacket, the oldest a housewife in her sixties. There are high-school dropouts, college graduates, skilled and unskilled workers—most of them currently unemployed. At the first meeting Ziegler gets right down to business.

"How many of you filed ten or more applications for jobs last week?" One hand goes up. "When we're done here," Ziegler says, "you'll understand why you've got to do better than that, and you'll know how." Then he analyzes the problem of finding a job, making the process seem as logical as the working of a mathematical formula. Here are the major factors he points out.

*First,* remember that jobs are *always* available at every salary level, because of the constant "churning" of the labor market. U.S. Department of Labor figures for one month showed a turnover rate of 8.9 percent of the labor force. Roughly half of this was created by "accessions," or newly created jobs; a quarter by "quits"; the remaining quarter by layoffs, firings, retirements and deaths. On the blackboard Ziegler shows what this means. "There are 350,000 jobs in driving distance of us right now, in the Greater Portland area. Use a rock-bottom estimate of the turnover rate, say 4 percent. That means 14,000 openings in the next month alone—as available to you as to anyone else."

*Second,* zeroing in on one of these jobs should be an organized, full-time job in itself. To treat job-seeking as a kind of unwelcome semiholiday is not only inefficient but demoralizing. Ziegler emphasizes to his students: "For an employer you work a forty-hour week. Why goof off when you're working for yourself?"

Set a goal of a certain number of applications a week—always making the applications *in person,* not just by letter or telephone. For nonexecutive jobs, an attainable goal is one application an hour, 40 a week; for jobs at the executive level, which require longer interviews and more complicated scheduling, 10 to 12 a week. Don't think that when you've applied once you have that company permanently "covered"; keep going back. Some employers, as a matter of policy, hire a man only after his second or third visit.

*Third,* analyze your experience and ability. Do it ruthlessly and objectively. This is perhaps the hardest part. At the end of the first session Ziegler hands the class six mimeographed questions to be taken home and answered at length. Then at the second session, in a kind of group-therapy technique, the answers are discussed in class. The questions: What things have I done with any degree of success? What things have I done that others have commended me for doing exceptionally well? What jobs have I held? (Describe them in detail.) What equipment can I operate? What are the things that I really like to do? That I don't like to do? "It's amazing what a complete inventory these questions provide of your job potential if you give them real thought and answer them fully," said Ziegler.

Surprisingly, most people find they have *under*estimated their potential. Recent high-school and college graduates, and housewives particularly, tend to feel that they have nothing special to offer. One eighteen-year-old girl, unemployed for nine months, listed on her self-analysis sheet that she enjoyed designing and making her own clothes, that she had often been complimented on her taste, and that she had studied art, design, fashion and advertising art in high school. Her feeling was that plenty of other girls could list the same things. Ten days after taking the course, however, she had a job as an assistant window decorator in one of Portland's department stores.

In the classroom discussion there is no coddling, since the purpose is an objective inventory of each individual's assets and liabilities. A former counterman is forced to agree, once it's pointed out, that four employers in a row couldn't *all* have been prejudiced when they claimed he was antagonizing customers. A man unsuccessful as a salesman is asked why, when he heads his list of dislikes with "meeting strangers," he is in the field at all.

*Fourth,* once you know your potential, decide whether you are now qualified to get full benefit out of it. If not, it may be wise to take night-school or correspondence courses after getting a job—or even go back to school or into the armed services for further training. Ziegler puts it this way: "The average twenty-five-year-old has 80,000 working hours ahead of him; the average forty-five-year-old, 40,000 hours. Multiply your expected number of working hours by your present hourly wage—and then by the hourly wage you could earn if you increased your skills. For young people especially, a year or two or three invested now in self-improvement can pay enormous dividends."

After looking at it this way, many do choose further training. A middle-aged bookkeeper is now aiming for a master's degree in psychology, intending to become a teacher. A twenty-year-old stock clerk upped his lifetime earning potential from $140,000 to $325,000 by taking a three-year course in electronics.

*Fifth,* write a resumé. This is the most important single tool in any job search. (Of those who got jobs after taking the course, 91 percent attributed their success largely to the resumé.) It is simply a one- or two-page typewritten list of your jobs and skills, prepared in such a way as to advertise everything salable. It is drawn up in reverse chronological order, the most recent experience listed first. In class, the resumés are subjected to rigorous group discussion out of which emerge tight, hard-selling documents with the irrelevancies eliminated.

"Their most common fault is too much generality," says Ziegler. "An employer wants to know more than that you were 'a salesman'; were you just an order-taker in an easy line, or did you have to go out and sell hard? Whatever you were successful at should be spelled out." The resumé provides leverage to the job-seeker. First, it makes possible a high rate of applications, since less time is wasted filling out application forms. More important, it allows *you* to set the tone and direction of the interview. Many job-seekers emerge from interviews with the miserable realization that their strongest points were never discussed. A good resumé prevents this.

*Sixth,* study the labor market and its economics. Too many think what they're doing is "asking for a job"; actually they're trying to sell their services—a given quantity of usable energy, of a certain quality, on which the employer can make a profit. You buy a package at the store not as a favor to the clerk but because you want what's in it. An employer hires you for the same reason.

To learn which employers are shopping for what skills, consult such publications as the U.S. Labor Department's "Occupational Outlook Handbook" and "The American Worker's Fact Book," as well as the manufacturers' directories of all companies in a given area—available at the library or local employment-service headquarters.

*Seventh,* know the specific avenues that lead into the labor market. In a recent survey, a thousand employed and unemployed male workers were asked where they looked for jobs. Most gave only these sources: the help-wanted ads in the newspapers, the state employment service, private employment agencies.

"This is only scratching the surface," Ziegler points out. "And those three aren't necessarily the best sources." Some of the others discussed in the course are:

A canvass of plants. "Talk to the workers at quitting time; they'll tell you a lot about a company's hiring practices."

Friends and neighbors. "Employers put personal referrals from employes high on their list of supply sources."

New construction. "Every new office building or factory that goes up needs to be staffed, from air-conditioning maintenance men to building manager. And many of the tenants will be new or expanding businesses, or will have to replace employes who didn't make the move."

Civil service. Government is one of the biggest employers in the country, if not the biggest, employing millions. Therefore merely by the mathematics of the turnover rate the government should have several hundred thousand available jobs at any given time.

High-school or college job counselor. "But don't depend on him alone."

For any field, you can make up your own list: the Yellow Pages, trade papers, a union agent, trade associations—all can give invaluable leads. But the seeker has to work at it. And that, of course, is the heart of the matter.

"I tell the students I'll give them half of what's needed: the knowledge," Ziegler says. "But it's completely up to them to add the other half: the determination and raw energy."

The results of his remarkable course—the people who have gone out and found jobs—are a source of deep satisfaction to Ziegler. "If you get a job for a man you are only answering his immediate problem," he says. "But if you teach him how to get his own job, you've helped him in a fundamental way. You've given him the pride and security that come from self-reliance."

❖

The reason a lot of people do not recognize an opportunity when they meet it is that it usually goes around wearing overalls and looking like hard work.  —*The Christian Science Monitor*

# How to Sell an Idea

ELMER WHEELER

**H**ave you ever approached
your boss with a red-hot idea for increasing efficiency—only
to have him become resentful instead of enthusiastic? Have
you ever offered your wife or the neighbors "good advice"? If
this has happened to you, you know what I mean when I say
that most people resent having other people's ideas forced
on them.

When someone approaches us with a new idea, our instinctive reaction is to put up a defense against it. We feel
that we must protect our individuality, and most of us are
egotistical enough to think that our ideas are better than
anyone else's. There are three tested rules for putting your
ideas across to other people so as to arouse their enthusiasm.
Here they are:

*Rule One: Use a fly rod—not a feeding tube.* Others
won't accept *your* idea until they can accept it as *their* idea.
It was said during World War I that Colonel Edward Man-
dell House was the most powerful man in the world because
he controlled the most powerful man in the world—
Woodrow Wilson. "I learned that the best way to convert
him to an idea," explained Colonel House, "was to plant it
in his mind casually, to get him thinking about it on his own
account."

When you want to sell someone an idea, take a lesson
from the fisherman who casts his fly temptingly near the
trout. He could never ram the hook into the trout's mouth.

But he can entice the trout to the hook. Don't appear too anxious. Just bring your ideas out where they can be seen. "Have you considered this?" is better than "This is the way." "Do you think this would work?" is better than "Here's what we should do." Let the other fellow sell himself on your idea. Then he'll stay sold.

*Rule Two: Let the other fellow argue your case.* He instinctively feels called upon to raise some objection to save his face. Give him a chance to disagree with you—by presenting your own objections. "The way to convince another," said wise old Ben Franklin, "is to state your case moderately and accurately. Then say that of course you may be mistaken about it; which causes your listener to receive what you have to say and, like as not, turn about and convince you of it, since you are in doubt."

Another technique is to sell the other fellow the idea as his, not yours. "You gave me an idea the other day that started me thinking," you begin. At a committee hearing, Tom Reed, for many years Speaker of the House, would remain silent until everyone had had his say, making notes of all objections. When everyone else was argued out, Reed would say, "Gentlemen, it seems to me that what has been said here can be summarized as follows. . . ." Reed would then present *his* ideas—and sell them.

Once movie director Dudley Nichols wasn't satisfied with a scene in one of his pictures. To remedy the situation, he said to Rosalind Russell, the star, "Wonderful, wonderful, but I could see, Miss Russell, when you hesitated that brief instant, that you were thinking about the possibility of playing the scene down a trifle more. Shall we try it once the way you were thinking?"

*Rule Three: Ask—don't tell.* Patrick Henry, another

326

famous idea salesman, was a political unknown when first elected to Virginia's House of Burgesses—but every resolution he introduced was passed. Listen to him in his famous "Liberty or Death" speech and see how he uses questions to get his ideas across: "Our brethren are already in the field— why stand we here idle? . . . Shall we lie supinely on our backs? . . . What is it that gentlemen wish? What would they have? Is life so dear or peace so sweet as to be purchased at the price of chains and slavery?"

Try saying the same thing in positive statements and see how it would invoke antagonism. When you put your ideas across with questions, you give the other fellow a share in the idea. You don't tell him—you ask him for the answer. You're giving him a chance to sell himself.

⇢ ◆ ⇠

### ON HIS WAY!

*T*he lower grades were having a hobby show, and fond parents flocked to view their offspring's handiwork. On each child's desk was an exhibit with a brief description of his hobby. There was the usual assortment of postage stamps, dolls, model airplanes, seashells, paper-match folders and so on.

But the entry that attracted the greatest attention was a display of Christmas cards with this note: "My hobby is selling Christmas cards. A box like this one sells for 25 cents, or five for $1. If you order now, I will get them to you three weeks before Christmas. You can put your order in the box on my desk, or telephone me at WI 4025. Charles Thompson."   —*James M. Sutherland*

*H*erman Grimhoffer of Wabash, Rhode Island, was stuck in an elevator for four hours. Upon his release he had sold the elevator operator a new Cadillac.   —*Matty Simmons*

# Know the Best Moment
STUART KINZIE

I shall never forget an interview I had with that grand old actor, the late Charles Coburn. I asked a stock question: What does one need to get ahead in life? Brains? Energy? Education?

He shook his head. "Those things help, of course. But there's something I consider even more important: *knowing the moment.*"

I remember staring at him, my pencil poised. "What moment?"

"The moment," he said, "to act—or not to act. The moment to speak—or to keep silent. On the stage, as every actor knows, timing is the all-important factor. I believe it's the key in life, too. If you master the art of knowing the moment, in your marriage, your work, your relationship with others, you won't have to pursue happiness and success. They'll walk right in your front door!" The old actor was right. If you can learn to recognize the right moment when it comes, and act before it goes away, the problems of life become vastly simplified. People who repeatedly meet with failure are often disheartened by what seems to be a relentlessly hostile world. What they almost never realize is that time and again they are making the right effort—but at the wrong moment.

"Oh, these quarreling couples," I heard a family-relations-court judge say not long ago. "If only they'd realize that there are times when everyone's threshold of irritability is

328

low, when a person can't stand nagging or criticism—or even good advice! If married partners would just take the trouble to study each other's moods, and know when to air a grievance or when to show affection, the divorce rate in this country would be cut in half!" The judge was saying what Charles Coburn had said: Know the moment. Once, in a penitent mood, I asked my wife which of my smaller failings annoyed her most.

"Your tendency," she said promptly, "to wait until we're about to walk into a party before telling me that my hair is mussed or my dress doesn't look quite right."

Good manners are often nothing but good timing. What is more annoying than to be interrupted in mid-anecdote? Who has not been trapped for what seems a lifetime by the bore who never knows when to leave? Good timing sometimes means doing the unexpected. Down in Georgia a doctor who had arranged for a childless couple to adopt a baby was making some late night calls with his wife. Suddenly he said, "The adoption papers are all in order. Let's go to the hospital and get the baby for Ruth and Kenneth."

"At this hour of the night?" cried his wife. "Why, they're not supposed to get the baby for several days. They'd be scared to death!"

"Ha!" said the doctor. "New babies have a way of arriving late at night—and first-time parents are always scared to death. It'll give them a good, normal start. Let's do it!" So the baby was "delivered" in the middle of the night, the parents were flustered and excited, and it was indeed a memorable beginning.

For a long time I thought that timing was a gift, something you were born with, like an ear for music. But gradually, observing people who seemed blessed with the gift, I realized it was a skill that could be acquired by anyone who cared to make the effort. To master the art of good timing, keep five requirements in mind:

First, keep yourself constantly aware of how decisive timing can be in human affairs, of how true Shakespeare's insight was when he wrote, "There is a tide in the affairs of men which, *taken at the flood*, leads on to fortune." Once you have grasped the full importance of "knowing the moment," you have taken the first step toward acquiring a capacity for it.

Next, make a pact with yourself (a pact you will undoubtedly break at times) never to act or speak when driven by the whirlwinds of anger, fear, hurt, jealousy or resentment. These emotional monkey wrenches can wreck the most carefully developed timing mechanism. At a turbulent public meeting once I lost my temper and said some harsh and sarcastic things. The proposal I was supporting was promptly defeated. My father, who was there, said nothing, but that night, on my pillow, I found a marked passage from Aristotle: "Anybody can become angry—that is easy; but to be angry with the right person, and to the right degree, and at the right time, and for the right purpose, and in the right way—that is not within everybody's power and is not easy."

Third, sharpen your powers of anticipation. The future is not a closed book. Much of what is going to happen is determined by what is happening now. Yet relatively few people make a conscious effort to project themselves beyond the present, gauge future probabilities and act accordingly. This look-ahead capacity is so important in business that many corporations make it a main yardstick for job advancement. But it is just as important in running a household. Will Saturday be a good day for a trip to the beach? Better have cold cuts and sandwich bread on hand just in case. Is your widowed mother-in-law's health beginning to fail? Better face the possibility that she may have to move in with you or be placed in a nursing home. The art of good timing includes knowing the moment when present action will eliminate future trouble or gain future advantages.

Fourth, learn patience. You just have to believe, with Emerson, that "if the single man plant himself indomitably on his instincts, and there abide, the huge world will come round to him." There is no easy formula for acquiring patience; it is a subtle blend of wisdom and self-control. But it is important to learn that premature action can often spoil everything.

The final—and most difficult—step is learning to get outside yourself. Each moment is shared by every living creature, but each person sees it from a different point of view. Really knowing the moment, then, includes knowing how it looks to other people.

A great philanthropist, the late Mrs. John Dibert of New Orleans, told how one night in midwinter, as she was riffling through a magazine, her eyes were caught by a cartoon. In it, two ragged old women were shivering over a meager fire. "What you thinkin' about?" asked one. "About the nice warm clothes the rich ladies will be givin' us next summer," answered the other. Mrs. Dibert, supporter of hospitals, donor to many charities, looked at the cartoon for a long time. Finally she went up into the attic, unpacked trunks, made bundles of warm clothes to be distributed the next day. She resolved to time her charity better, to give, as she put it, "to the ones whose needs are *now*."

As the Old Testament says, "To everything there is a season, and a time to every purpose under the heaven."

## Chapter 14/The Lure of the Lively Arts

*The last few years have witnessed an explosion
of culture in our land. Amateurs are playing in
symphony orchestras. A great many are taking courses in
art appreciation. People are discovering the truth of
Walter Pater's observation that "Art comes to you
proposing frankly to give nothing but the highest
quality to your moments as they pass."*
*Perhaps the surest way to appreciate any of the
arts is to participate in them. In this chapter Mary
Martin urges everybody to sing, Charles Laughton
discusses the pleasures of reading aloud, and the
greatest Englishman of our century tells of the
fascination he found when he took up painting.*

## My Adventures with a Paintbrush
*Condensed from the book: Amid These Storms*
WINSTON S. CHURCHILL

T o have reached the age of
forty without ever handling a brush, to have regarded the
painting of pictures as a mystery, and then suddenly to find
oneself plunged into the middle of a new interest with
paints and palettes and canvases—and not to be discouraged
by results—is an astonishing and enriching experience. I
hope it may be shared by others.

For to be really happy and to avoid worry and mental
overstrain we ought all to have hobbies, and they must all be

*real*. Best of all, and easiest to take up, are sketching and painting. They came to my rescue late in life, at a most trying time.

When I left the Admiralty at the end of May 1915, I still remained a member of the Cabinet and of the War Council. In this position I knew everything and could do nothing; I had vehement convictions and no power to give effect to them; I had enforced leisure at a moment when every fiber of my being was inflamed to action.

And then it was, one Sunday in the country, that the children's paint box came to my aid. My first experiments with their toy watercolors led me to secure, next morning, a complete outfit for painting in oils. The next step was *to begin*. The palette gleamed with beads of color; fair and white rose the canvas; the empty brush hung poised, heavy with destiny, irresolute in the air. Very gingerly I mixed a little blue paint with a very small brush, and then with infinite precaution made a mark about as big as a small bean upon the affronted snow-white shield. At that moment a motorcar was heard on the drive and from it there stepped none other than the gifted wife of Sir John Lavery, the distinguished portrait painter. "Painting! But what are you hesitating about? Let me have a brush, a big one." Splash into the turpentine, wallop into the blue and white, frantic flourish on my palette, and then several large, fierce strokes of blue on the absolutely cowering canvas. The spell was broken. My sickly inhibitions rolled away. I seized the largest brush and fell upon my victim with berserk fury. I have never felt any awe of a canvas since.

This beginning with audacity is a very great part of the art of painting. We must not be too ambitious. We cannot aspire to masterpieces. We may content ourselves with a

333

simple joyride in a paint box. And for this, audacity is the only ticket.

I write no word in disparagement of watercolors. But there is really nothing like oils. First of all, you can correct mistakes more easily. One sweep of the palette knife "lifts" the misfortunes of a morning from the canvas; the canvas is all the better for past impressions. Secondly, you can approach your problem from any direction, beginning if you will with a moderate central arrangement of middle tones, and then hurling in the extremes when the psychological moment comes. Lastly, the pigments are so nice to handle. You can build them on layer after layer, if you like, and can change your plan to meet the exigencies of time and weather. Matching them with what you see is fascinating. Try it, if you have not done so—before you die.

As one slowly begins to escape from the difficulties of choosing the right colors and laying them on in the right places and in the right way, wider considerations come into view. One is astonished to find out how many things there are in the landscape one never noticed before. And this is a tremendous new pleasure that invests every walk or drive with an added object. So many colors on the hillside, each different in shadow and in sunlight; such brilliant reflections in the pool, each a key lower than what they repeat; such lovely lights gilding or silvering surface or outline. I found myself, as I walked, instinctively noting the tint and character of a leaf, the dreamy purple shades of mountains, the exquisite lacery of winter branches, the dim, pale silhouettes of far horizons. And here I had lived for more than forty years without ever noticing any of them except in a general way, as one might look at a crowd and say, "What a lot of people!"

I think this heightened sense of observation of nature is one of the chief delights that have come to me through trying to paint. And if you do observe accurately and with refinement, and if you do record what you have seen with tolerable correspondence, the result follows on the canvas with startling obedience. Then, the art galleries take on a new and—to me at least—a severely practical interest. You see the difficulty that baffled you yesterday; and you see how easily it has been overcome by a great painter. You look at the masterpieces of art with an analyzing and a comprehending eye.

Chance one day led me to a secluded nook near Marseilles where I fell in with two disciples of Cézanne. They viewed nature as a mass of shimmering light in which forms and surfaces are comparatively unimportant, indeed hardly visible, but which gleams and glows with beautiful harmonies and contrasts of color. I had hitherto painted the sea flat, with long, smooth strokes of mixed pigment. Now I must try to represent it by innumerable small separate patches of pure color. Each of these little points of color sets up a strong radiation of which the eye is conscious without detecting the cause. Look at the blue of the sea. How can you depict it? Certainly not by any single color that was ever manufactured. The only way in which that luminous intensity of blue can be simulated is by this multitude of tiny points of varied color all in true relation to the rest of the scheme. Difficult? Fascinating!

I was shown a picture by Cézanne of a blank wall of a house, which he had made instinct with the most delicate lights and colors. Now I often amuse myself when I am looking at a wall or a flat surface of any kind by trying to distinguish all the different tints which can be discerned upon it, and considering whether these arise from reflections or from natural hue. You would be astonished the first time you tried this to see how many and what beautiful colors there are even in the most commonplace objects. Obviously, then, armed with a paint box, one cannot be bored or left at a loose end. How much there is to admire and how little time there is to see it in! One begins to envy Methuselah.

It is interesting to note the part memory plays in painting. When Whistler guided a school in Paris he made his pupils observe their model on the ground floor, and then run up-stairs and paint their picture on the floor above. As they became more proficient he put their easels up a story higher, till at last the elite were scampering up six flights into the attic.

All the greatest landscapes have been painted indoors, and often long after the first impressions were gathered. In a dim cellar the Dutch or Italian master re-created the gleam-ing ice of a Netherlands carnival or the lustrous sunshine of Venice. Here, then, is required a formidable memory of the visual kind. So painting may be a very useful exercise for the development of a trained, accurate, retentive memory.

Again, there is really nothing like painting as a spur to travel. Every day is provided with its expedition and its oc-cupation—cheap, attainable, absorbing, recuperative. The vain racket of the tourist gives place to the calm enjoyment of the philosopher. Every country you visit has a theme of its own, and even if you cannot portray it as you see it, you know it, you feel it, and you admire it forever. But after all, if only the sun will shine, one does not need to go beyond one's own country. The amateur painter wanders and loiters contentedly from place to place, always on the lookout for some bright butterfly of a picture which can be caught.

Painting is complete as a distraction. I know of nothing which, without exhausting the body, more entirely absorbs the mind. Whatever the worries of the hour or the threats of the future, once the picture has begun to flow there is no room for them in the mental screen. They pass out into shadow and darkness. All one's mental light becomes concentrated on the task. When I have stood up on parade, or even, I regret to say, in church, for half an hour at a time, I have always felt that the erect position is not natural to man and is only with fatigue and difficulty maintained. But no one who is fond of painting finds the slightest inconvenience in standing on his feet to paint for even as long as three or four hours at a stretch.

Buy a paint box and have a try. It would be a sad pity to shuffle along through one's playtime with golf and bridge, when all the while, if you only knew, there is waiting for you close at hand the wonderful new world of thought and craft, a sunlit garden gleaming with color. Inexpensive independence, new mental food and exercise, an added interest in every common scene, an occupation for every idle hour, an unceasing voyage of entrancing discovery—these are high prizes. I hope they may be yours.

### THE FINAL TEST

"When I am finishing a picture," Marc Chagall explained, "I hold some God-made object up to it—a rock, a flower, the branch of a tree or my hand—as a kind of final test. If the painting stands up beside a thing man cannot make, the painting is authentic. If there's a clash between the two, it is bad art. That's something I have understood," he added, "only these last ten years."
—*Ernest O. Hauser*

# Everybody Sing!

MARY MARTIN *as told to* CHARLES D. RICE

Why don't more families know the wonderful fun of music? I'm pretty sure the answer is that most people think music is an "art"; that you need good voices; that you have to know the "finer points" and own a piano. But these notions couldn't be more wrong. Enthusiasm counts for more than good voices, and singing unaccompanied (*a cappella,* musicians call it) makes the loveliest music of all.

I can almost hear people say, "That's all very well for Mary Martin, because she has a musical family." But the truth is that as a family we're not trained one bit. And all our favorite stunts could be done by any other family in America. For instance, playing "Crazy Choir." The trick is to sing well-known songs against each other, and if you pick the right songs—"Casey Jones," "Oh! Susannah," "Turkey in the Straw" and "The Arkansas Traveler" are perfect— you'll sound like the greatest quartet in the world. Of course, when people start singing separate songs at once, it may take a few minutes' practicing until everyone gets together on the beat, but the false starts are fun too.

Singing songs of the same harmonic pattern against each other has been going on for centuries. If you want to try it, choose two or more of these combinations:

*Group 1:* "Oh! Susannah," "Turkey in the Straw," "Casey Jones" (chorus only), "The Arkansas Traveler," "Camptown Races."

*Group 2:* "Annie Laurie," "Put On Your Old Gray Bonnet," "Swanee River."

*Group 3:* "London Bridge Is Falling Down," "How Dry
I Am," "Frère Jacques," "Boola-Boola," "The Old Gray
Mare."

*Group 4:* "The Sidewalks of New York," "A Bicycle Built
for Two," "In the Good Old Summertime."

With these to start you off, you'll probably end up with
some combinations of your own.

One of the most charming family customs I know of is the
musical grace. Only a few generations ago grace was sung
more commonly than it was spoken, and I think it's too bad
that we've lost the extra pleasure. The most appealing grace,
I suppose, is John Cennick's:

> Be present at our table, Lord.
> Be here and everywhere adored.
> Thy creatures bless, and grant that we
> May feast in Paradise with Thee. Amen.

It can be sung to several melodies. We used to sing it to
"Old Hundred" and "Genevieve." When our children first
started saying grace, they seemed bored. But when we tried
*singing* it, they were full of enthusiasm.

The idea of rhythm bands for children helps get even the
little ones interested in music. Since rhythm bands are made
up of any handy racket-making objects, there is little real
music involved. But it's a step toward the family band. I ·
can't remember all the crazy instruments we used to play
together at home—tissue paper and combs, ukuleles, kazoos,
eggbeaters, jugs, harmonicas, cowbells, oversize rubber
bands, whistles and skillets. And is there any child so un-

lucky as never to have played in a Bottle Symphony? You collect eight bottles—or glasses—that have especially fine tones and fill them with varying amounts of water until you get all eight tones of the scale. Then you play them with a spoon. You can't expect to become an expert in five minutes —perfection requires at least a quarter of an hour. A close relative of the Bottle Symphony is the Slim-Rim Band. The trick is to dip your finger in water and slide it around the rim of a thin glass. When you get good at it, you can make it ring as though the angels were singing. One family I knew collected the best-sounding glasses in the house and marked them. One day when I was visiting and went to get a drink of water, the mother said, "Oh, Mary, don't use that glass— it's the children's B-flat!"

Did you ever hear of what our family calls "Echo Singing"? One member of the family sings a simple melody, and another follows just a fraction of a beat late. A third person can follow just another fraction late, and the effect is startling: it sounds as though the music were echoing down the corridors of time.

Music in the home, I'm convinced, has to be started by the parents, and the earlier the better. I often hear parents complain that there is so much automatic music today that kids are too lazy to make their own. I don't think it's true at all. They don't sing because they have never heard their parents sing. They don't know that making music is fun because they've never heard their parents treat it as fun.

There is one thing about music that has impressed me all my life: of all the families I've known, the ones that sang at home were always the happiest. I suppose you might argue that they sang *because* they were happy, but I think it works the other way too—a family can be happy because it *sings*.

# It's Fun to Read Aloud

CHARLES LAUGHTON

Once I read passages from Will Shakespeare's *Twelfth Night* to a group of college English teachers. Afterward a young instructor confronted me. "That wasn't quite fair," he said. "You edited those passages to make them livelier."

"But I didn't skip a word," I protested. "Whatever made you think that I did?"

"Well," he replied simply, "this is the first time I ever completely understood the play." I feel certain that his new appreciation of the drama was inspired by the enjoyment of hearing it read. Reading aloud is a well-loved but neglected pastime. These days we may drone through a few bedtime stories for our youngsters, but by and large we regard books as something to be taken silently, swiftly and alone.

I plead for more reading aloud. It is a friendly, quiet and refreshing thing to do. It makes us participants rather than spectators. Instead of sitting by to let the professionals amuse or enlighten us, *we* can get into the act, make contact with new ideas, exercise our imaginations. More than that, it is a shared experience which draws people closer together. Husbands and wives, families or groups of friends can enjoy the comfortable satisfaction that comes from laughing together, learning together—from doing the same thing at the same time, together. There is nothing better than family reading to form a warm bond between parents and teen-agers.

I began reading aloud to strangers during World War II.

Not fit for juggling or singing but anxious to do something, I decided to read to whoever would listen. My first audiences were in Army hospitals. Before long, I met men who pronounced the Bible a dull book, then sat spellbound as we read the old stories together. I saw wounded men, embittered by pain, discover that their troubles were not unique and find solace in the sufferings of Shakespeare's tragic heroes. More recently, on my reading tours of the United States, I have seen the good feeling of companionship grow in crowds of from several hundred to several thousand because we were bent on something together.

How, then, do you begin reading aloud? Many people find taking the plunge the hardest part. Some feel they will be expected to declaim like Fourth of July orators. Others are shy. Dozens of servicemen have told me they wanted to read poems to their wives or sweethearts, but didn't know how to start. To such as these, I say, brace up! *Wanting* to begin is the only requirement. After that, choose a book you're comfortable with. Anything is worth reading if you enjoy it. Time and again, when I have finished reading to groups in private homes, someone will fetch a book and say, "Do you know this?" and then read, far more beautifully than I could, a passage that had special meaning for him. Near the top of my own list of favorites are the Bible, Shakespeare, Charles Dickens, the Fables of Aesop and the witty works of James Thurber. I also like Mark Twain, the short stories of O. Henry, the verse of Rudyard Kipling.

If a volume loses its savor, drop it. Experiment with several books at once, taking a short story from one, a chapter from another, a poem from a third. One couple I know never approaches the end of one book without dipping into the opening chapters of another—a sort of "Coming Attraction," or promise of things to come. Having started, go at your own pace. One quick way to lose enthusiasm for reading aloud is to let it become a nightly chore. But once you start, stay with it. Don't let interruptions cool you off before your author has a chance to get his story under way. Remember that reading aloud takes some degree of concentration. When your attention begins to wander, you've had enough. This is not to say that everyone must sit stiffly alert. Ladies may knit. Gentlemen may overhaul fishing tackle.

As for the technique of reading aloud, above all be natural. Straining for effects sounds affected. Your normal speaking voice will be your best reading voice. Your own interest will lend the best emphasis to the story. Do not end your evening with the closing of your book. When you stop reading, begin talking. Reading aloud is fun in itself, but it is better yet when it prompts lively conversation.

Two young people once told me that they had been reading *War and Peace* for a year and a half. "It's not that we're slow readers," they explained. "It's just that every few pages seem to suggest something fresh to us, and then we're off, talking, thinking, planning. We're not sure that we'll ever finish the book, but we've learned a great deal about ourselves and our life together." This, to me, is how to enjoy reading aloud.

⋙ ◆ ⋘

### BLESSING FROM ABOVE

*A*t a dinner party in Paris where Benjamin Franklin was one of the distinguished guests, the Abbé Raynal asked, "What kind of man deserves the most pity?"

Franklin answered, "A lonesome man on a rainy day who does not know how to read."    —*Edward Frank Allen*

# Get In There and Play

OSCAR SCHISGALL

Twenty years ago, critics lamented that phonograph records and radio were driving out "live" music. Now it appears that the years of good listening have merely whetted our appetite for *making* music. In 1950 the American Music Conference of Chicago counted 19 million amateur instrumentalists. Today the number has skyrocketed to 37 million—about one out of every five of us.

There are now more than 1400 *amateur* symphony orchestras (the so-called "community" orchestras) playing fine music in the United States. Their average size is between 70 and 100 players. One third are located in cities of less than 50,000 population; 10 percent are in towns of less than 10,-000. In Bluefield, West Virginia, players come to rehearsals from as far as 140 miles over mountain roads. In Iowa, people converge from 15 small communities to play with the Waverly Orchestra. Not all these orchestras are "community" in the geographical sense alone. In New York I have heard fine concerts played by The Doctors' Orchestral Society. (I learned that similar medical orchestras exist in many cities.) There is a U.S. Department of Agriculture Symphony, a Greater Cleveland Youth Orchestra, a Boro Park Y Orchestra in New York City. More than 1600 businesses now sponsor symphony orchestras, bands and smaller ensembles, just as they sponsor bowling teams.

One rainy Saturday afternoon my wife and I stopped at a resort hotel in Maine. The weather was keeping everybody indoors, and in the lobby we were greeted by an amateur jazz session. A dozen guests who had borrowed instruments from the hotel orchestra were playing with gusto seldom shown by professionals. As an amateur piano pounder myself, I used to join a group of seven men in so-called jam sessions. We never had an audience; we didn't dare. We played Gershwin and Berlin rather than Beethoven and Tchaikovsky, because they were easier for us. But when we got through a number without *too* many mistakes, there was a sense of exaltation that I have never known elsewhere.

The real community orchestras have some difficulties of course. The chief problem: Where can they find competent conductors? Instrumental groups near big cities can usually find a conductor among the professionals. This advantage is not shared by small communities, however. The American Symphony Orchestra League, which represents more than 800 orchestras, is a source of help. The League, with headquarters in Vienna, Virginia, is supported not only by dues from member orchestras; it has also received grants from the Rockefeller Foundation. To develop talent the League has enlisted some of the nation's leading conductors to give free seminars for students. Remote community orchestras send their promising conductors to attend these sessions.

But when we speak of the 1400 community orchestras in the United States, we have merely touched the surface. The count made in 1964 showed 49,000 bands, 6000 orchestras and 8000 jazz bands in United States schools. More than 12 million young people of school age are studying an instrument. New teaching techniques, which introduce a novice to melodies rather than to scales, help make the study of music more popular. So it is hardly surprising that the country now has more than 500,000 music teachers. The school music teacher today is likely to be an enthusiastic young person with a college degree in music and a sufficient budget from the board of education to provide *free* instrumental training for any student who wants it. His students put on concerts, light operas, choral performances.

Amateur musicians sometimes find extraordinary ways to indulge their love of playing. At Bowdoin College a group of students formed a "brass ensemble" to revive seventeenth-century German "tower music." This music, composed for brass instruments, was played from the towers of old castles and churches. For almost three hundred years these compositions faded out of musical repertoires. Then twentieth-century trumpets began to blare the old melodies from the towers and rooftops of Bowdoin College. "Those of us on campus were a captive audience," one student said to me, "but we seemed to get as much fun out of listening as the trumpeters got out of playing."

You never know where you will find amateur musicians. Not long ago, in a New York taxi, a friend was telling me how he had paid his way through Harvard by playing a saxophone in a five-man band that entertained at weddings, parties and so on. He was dilating on how much pleasure this had given him when the taxi driver interrupted with, "Mister, you ain't kidding. There's nothing like making music. I work out of a Bronx garage, and we got half a dozen guys there that formed a combo. I'm on the drums. Two-three times a week we get together after work, and you know something? Most of us would rather play than eat!"

By far the most popular instrument among amateurs is the piano (over 22 million Americans play it). I would have guessed that the violin was second—and I would have been wrong. The recent rise of "country" music and the continuing appeal of folk singers like Burl Ives have had their effect: the second most popular instrument is now the guitar, with 7½ million devotees. Woodwinds come third, brasses a close fourth, and stringed instruments other than the guitar, fifth. Altogether, Americans in 1964 spent 744 million dollars for instruments, sheet music and accessories. But the boom is not instrumental alone: singers appear to outnumber instrumentalists. There is scarcely a music-loving community in the country that doesn't have its choir, glee club, or oratorio society. Besides these, there are operatic workshops and amateur theatrical troupes which produce some 4300 musical plays every year—from Gilbert and Sullivan to Rodgers and Hammerstein.

Add up the various elements of what is happening, and it's clear that the United States has become the most music-loving nation on earth. Walt Whitman must have been using the eyes and ears of a prophet when, a century ago, he cried, "I hear America singing!"

### HEAVEN-BENT

"*D*ear Mrs. Bowen," a reader once wrote to me. "Not long ago I read a quotation where you said that if you died and turned up somewhere, you would know it was heaven when Mozart came forward and told you, 'Mrs. B., I am so glad you are here. I have just written 258 new string quartets, and we badly need a second fiddle.' "

The quotation was letter-perfect, and my correspondent went on to say she had given the matter much thought. "In case you get there first," she added, "please mention me for the cello position, if it isn't already filled. I promise to practice all I can in preparation."                           —*Catherine Drinker Bowen*

347

# Take Music Instead of a Miltown

GEORGE R. MAREK

**T**hat morning I was sure the end of the world had come. My boss had fired me; and, with the pessimism of youth, I knew I would never find another job. I was marked for failure. (I was nineteen years old.)

That evening I had a date to meet a friend at Lewisohn Stadium to hear the New York Philharmonic. Job or no job, I decided to go. At first, as I sat there, the music merely lapped against the stone wall of my anxiety. But with the final number of the program, the First Symphony of Brahms, I began to listen in earnest. As the music reached me, I reflected that I had heard the symphony often before, that I was probably to hear it often again under different conditions—and that it always had been, and would be in the future, the same satisfying music. *It* did not change; only *I* did. I was impermanent; the symphony was permanent. I drew comfort from this. I measured the event of the day more calmly. Was it as important as all that? Couldn't I do something about it? As I walked home, the dull blanket of despondency weighed less.

Since then, I have often marveled at the power that lies in music to raise the spirits, to comfort shaken nerves, to serve as a rope on which hope can lift itself. I am, of course, not the first to marvel. Most of us remember Congreve's "Music hath charms to soothe the savage breast." Horace spoke of music as "the healing balm of troubles." "I feel physically refreshed and strengthened by it," said Coleridge. Even

Goethe, who was not particularly musical, said that music made him unfold "like the fingers of a threatening fist which straighten, amicably."

Music may be used in two different ways—for listening and as background. The first way is the road taken by the music lover. He need not be able to tell a fugue from a fandango. But to him music is an experience that grips his mind and tears at his heart. He cannot remain indifferent.

How does one become a music lover? There is but one way: listen to music! Only direct experience, not study or explanations or props will lead you to music. I have two suggestions for the beginner. First, listen to the *same* composition often, until you can respond to it emotionally. Do not expect to encompass a symphony at first hearing. And do not be discouraged or feel guilty if, while listening to an unfamiliar symphony, your attention wanders. Initially, absorb from it as much as you can—and coast through the rest. There will come a time when the clouds roll away. In music, the familiar is the enjoyable. Don't dart from one composition to the next. Stay with it!

Second, choose—in the beginning, at least—romantic music. This is repertoire that begins with Beethoven and ends with Sibelius and that, in its wide orbit, includes the most popular works—those of Schubert, Brahms, Dvořák, Tchaikovsky, Verdi, Wagner, Berlioz and a dozen other composers of the nineteenth century. Such music, with its rich coloring, its exuberance, its sweetness, its exciting oratory, makes an immediate appeal.

But it is not safe to predict what *you* will like. We do know that people tend to respond more easily to Chopin and Puccini than to Handel or Haydn. Yet your experience may differ. I know one woman whose enthusiasm for music flared when she became acquainted with Scarlatti and Vivaldi. She happens to be very modern in her tastes, and possibly these early-eighteenth-century products furnish a counterbalance.

Of all the arts, music is the freest. Most music does not "mean" anything—except in its own world and on its own terms. But because it has little to do with what we call real life, it can effectively take us away from our own lives, from our nine-to-five worries. Because music travels on winged feet, it can make us forget where the shoe pinches.

The other way of using music is as background accompaniment, which can be like a tepid bath in which you induce a drowsy reverie. You hardly listen to what you hear, any more than you consciously listen to the surf of the sea. Almost any kind of music can be used for such a purpose, though most people prefer a smooth blend of sound. We meet such music in the most unlikely places—in the dentist's office, in the airport and the bus depot, at the meat market.

In factories, such music helps to relieve the boredom of routine labor. So it does in the home: women mix the sound of violins with the sound of the dishwasher. But mental processes—creative or calculating—seem to be aided as well. El Greco hired musicians to play for him as he painted. Many men, thinking their problems through, like to have the radio or the phonograph going. Many background-music records help to calm nerves and assuage fatigue.

John Oldham, England's favorite satirist of the seventeenth century, dropped his doubts when he wrote:

> Music's the cordial of a troubled breast,
> The softest remedy that grief can find;
> The gentle spell that charms our care to rest
> And calms the ruffled passions of the mind.

# Chapter 15/The Anvil of Adversity

*"Man that is born of woman," wrote the gloomy author
of the Book of Job, "is of few days, and full of trouble."
An overpessimistic view of life, perhaps, but certainly
trouble does come—like death and taxes—to all of us.
How we face it depends on many things: our courage,
our endurance, our philosophy of life—and the size
of the trouble. But a man's reaction to adversity
is often the true measure of the man. Here are discussions
of the grimmest problems that plague our society: mental
illness, alcoholism, divorce, incurable disease. Each
writer has something helpful to say. And the noted
minister, Harry Emerson Fosdick, points out hopefully
that trouble can sometimes be a friend.*

## What Is a Nervous Breakdown?

ROBERT O'BRIEN

An attractive young couple
moved to our suburban town from another state. They had
two small children, and were expecting a third. The husband commuted to the city, leaving early and not returning
home until late evening. The mother's day was filled with
endless errands, household chores and the care of two frisky
youngsters. Gradually the stresses of her life began to take
their toll. Her moods swung from despair to brittle gaiety,
and back again. One minute she would sit staring dully out
the window, the next she would be frantically cleaning the

garage or attic. One morning as she prepared for a shopping trip she suddenly dreaded leaving the house. Her heart pounded. The dread rapidly spiraled into panic. On the verge of hysteria, she phoned her husband and begged him to hurry home. He found her locked in a bedroom, weeping.

Not long ago, a brilliant young advertising man I know was promoted to be vice-president of his firm. His ambitious wife was delighted. He, however, felt just the opposite. Underneath, he didn't want the increased responsibility. But how could he admit it? Everyone would think him weak. He grew moody and depressed. He had trouble sleeping. One spring day his gaze traveled out the open window of his nineteenth-floor office. Slowly he froze with horror. The space, the languid air outside, seemed to beckon him. He stared in terrible fascination at the open window, struggling with an almost overpowering impulse to jump. A jangling phone came to his rescue. He stumbled and took a taxi forty miles home. He called his doctor and went to bed. . . .

Doctors used psychiatric terms to describe these different illnesses. But the term that seemed to satisfy relatives and friends was more general. They called both cases "nervous breakdown." Most of us would say the same. Just what is a nervous breakdown? Since nerve tissue never mechanically snaps, or "breaks down," does the term have any validity? Several doctors I talked with dismissed it as a "vague catchall." Others defend it. The main reason for the term's usefulness, doctors are coming to understand, is that all nervous breakdowns have certain elements in common.

The core of the nervous breakdown is *anxiety,* a condition of heightened tension accompanied by an overpowering feeling of apprehension without apparent reason. We all have anxieties. Their causes are usually forgotten. But the duplication of a once frightening circumstance may call these nameless fears from the depths of our unconscious mind to fill us with baffling dread and terror. I once knew a newspaperman who broke down on the death of his mother. Psychotherapy uncovered a long-buried terror that he'd felt as a child whenever his parents had left him alone in the house. When his mother died and "left him behind" once more, it had all swept back with crushing force.

Another common element in all breakdowns is the failure of defense mechanisms. Early in life most of us learn ways of protecting ourselves against situations that cause anxiety. The most common defense mechanism is rationalization. A man rationalizes his heavy drinking by telling himself that he's just being sociable, for example. Another technique is "displacement." Here the upsetting emotions we feel toward one person are concealed by working them off on another. For instance, a salesman hates his boss but can't admit it, so he picks fights with his wife. Other methods of warding off anxiety include denial, a blind refusal to admit that problems exist; and repression, an unconscious but purposeful "forgetting." Sometimes defense mechanisms perform more or less effectively for a lifetime. But frequently, when tensions and fears pile up overwhelmingly, the defense mechanisms fail and the anxiety bursts through. It is then that the person "breaks down" into helplessness. In our stressful society, this is happening with disturbing frequency.

All breakdowns have a common denominator: the man can't go to work (or the housewife can't keep house). But they are rarely the sudden, dramatic crack-ups that they often seem to be. "If anything is typical," one doctor told me, "it is that a nervous breakdown is the end result of a gradual decline taking place over weeks or even months. *It is a pro-*

353

*gressive inability to cope with anxiety.* And the warning symptoms are clearly visible, all along the way."

All breakdowns are caused by stress—often physical and social as well as mental. There is a limit to human tolerance of stress, and every man has his breaking point. If mild physical strain (such as lack of sleep) is added to a severe neurosis —or if very heavy physical and social strain (such as overwork and family trouble) is added to a minor mental stress —an individual may break down. *How* he breaks will in large part be determined by his underlying psychological weaknesses.

How can we tell when we are heading for trouble? The first sign is generally a prolonged feeling of being vaguely unwell, "below par." At the same time, we may experience annoying physical ailments: tenseness, restlessness, persistent fatigue, insomnia. We may develop more crippling symptoms: severe headaches, palpitation of the heart, dizziness, gastrointestinal disorders, muscular pains. These symptoms serve a purpose, according to Dr. Francis J. Braceland, chief psychiatrist of the Hartford (Connecticut) Institute of Living. They give us an excuse to avoid stressful situations—a noisy party, a difficult conference, an appointment.

A warning symptom more readily apparent to others than to ourselves is a marked change in personality—either an intensification of a character trait or an abrupt reversal in behavior. A shy person may become more shy; an outgoing person may become exuberant and rattle on endlessly about unrealistic schemes. On the other hand, a person who has been neat and orderly all his life may grow careless and slovenly. The important fact is the change itself. If the emotional disturbance develops unchecked, the next step may well be the breaking point.

What are the chances of avoiding a breakdown? Excellent, authorities agree, particularly if the disturbance is recognized and resolved in its early stages. Says Dr. Alan A. McLean, staff psychiatrist for International Business Machines Corporation: "In most instances, changes in behavior occur quite early in the development of an emotional illness. The altered behavior pattern usually affects the individual on the job. The alert foreman or manager may be able to detect it. If the patient obtains immediate treatment, he can usually straighten out his problems without prolonged time off from work."

Once a breakdown occurs, recovery depends on the complexity and depth of the disturbance, the patient's desire to get well and the adequacy of treatment. In the case of the advertising man who was promoted to vice-president, a few days of rest and self-appraisal and a long talk with his family doctor opened his eyes to the necessity of asking for his old job back—and he was cured. A dozen interviews with a psychiatrist, combined with more help and understanding from her husband, enabled the housewife to meet her problems more maturely.

Most breakdowns can be "cured." But it is better not to have one in the first place. So if we recognize in ourselves symptoms that are making us, or others, unhappy, we should seek immediate help. A good place to start is the family doctor or clergyman. In the early stages of emotional trouble, a candid talk with a sympathetic listener may be all we need.

As individuals, we might try to handle better the stresses of life. Says Dr. John Donnelly of the Institute of Living, "Every problem of frustration which is faced realistically and dealt with in an organized way adds to the strength of the personality. Every failure from which a lesson has been learned provides both an experience and an asset which increases our capacity to meet new problems."

When stress is unavoidable, we can give ourselves a break by keeping it simple. If we're starting out on a new and unfamiliar job, we don't pick that week to give up smoking. If we find that we're getting wound up over a worrisome problem, the best thing to do is to take time out—see a movie, go away for the weekend—and come back to the problem with a relaxed mind.

In work and in play, we must try to recognize our limitations. A writer once told me, "The most important day of my life was the day I stopped trying to set the world on fire, and accepted myself—the good and the bad, the strength and the weaknesses—for what I was. I've been a happier man, a more understanding father and a more useful citizen ever since."

These seem like little things, and they are. But they help us accept a truth that may have been hard to learn as children—that there is nothing, really, to be afraid of. As we learn this, we grow in faith, we grow in strength and, most important, we grow in our capacity to love.

### HORSE SENSE

*O*nce upon a time we had the good sense to realize that periodic despair is normal, that squabbles between husbands and wives or parents and children are unavoidable, that not everybody is intended to live in bliss unending. We even had enough horse sense to realize that anyone who is happy all the time must be mad. One indication of good health is precisely the capacity to be unhappy when reality warrants it—to be unhappy without anxiety, apology or defensiveness. —*Leo Rosten*

# The Mysterious Medicine for Alcoholics
PAUL DE KRUIF

Thirty years ago, alcoholism was among the most hopeless of human afflictions. The millions suffering from it were largely untouchable by the science of medicine. Today there's a reversal in their dreadful fate. More than 350,000 ex-drunks are now engaged in fighting their common enemy—alcohol—and are leading productive lives, many of them better citizens than those of us who can take it or leave it alone. This astounding victory had no medical origin; the victims themselves were their own first doctors. Their medicine is not chemical. Their curious weapon against alcoholic doom is an utterly abject humility. They have one commander, not human, only God —God as each of them individually understands Him.

They have absolutely no organization and reject all outside donations. They follow a strict rule: the names of none of them must be publicly known. Sacrifice and humility— these are the secrets of their death-fighting power. Such is the fellowship of Alcoholics Anonymous.

In 1934 there was only one, lone A.A. He was a brilliant man, as alcoholics often are, but despite his brains he had fought a losing battle against the bottle, often ending up literally in the gutter. He was on his way to commitment for alcoholic insanity. The beginning of the salvation of this "Mr. Bill," as A.A.'s call him, was a spiritual mystery. He was befriended by a former drunk, "Ebby," who assured him that the one medicine for alcoholics was a simple belief in

God. A surrender to God: "Thy will, not mine, be done."
What made Ebby a bit offbeat as a missionary was that,
although sober then, he couldn't stick to his own medicine.
He couldn't stop drinking for good.

Bill, a confirmed atheist himself, was hardly a candidate
for Ebby's theoretical therapy. All he had was a desperate
desire to stop drinking. Once, drying out in a hospital (he
knew this was a temporary expedient), Bill felt his depression deepen unbearably till at last it seemed as if he'd sunk
to the bottom of the pit. Suddenly he found himself crying
out, "If there is a God, let Him show Himself! I'm ready to
do anything, anything!" All at once the room seemed lit up
with a great white light. Bill was in ecstasy. It burst upon
him that he was a free man, free from his demon. All
through him there was a wonderful feeling of a "Presence."
Then he became frightened. His scientific education told
him, "You're hallucinating. Better call a doctor." It was provi-
dential that he confided his vision to Dr. William Duncan
Silkworth, for many years physician-in-chief of the Charles
B. Towns Hospital in New York City. "Dr. Silky," out of his
vast experience, knew well that there was no medical hope
whatever for most alcoholics, and this had stirred his compassion for down-and-out drunks. "I'm crazy, Doc," said Bill, in
a panic. Dr. Silkworth probed him with questions. At last he
said, "No, Bill, you're not crazy. There's been some basic
spiritual event here."

Bill now remembered a book he'd read in his sad search
for a cure. It was *The Varieties of Religious Experience*, by
the psychologist William James. James taught that true religious experiences have a common denominator of pain,
suffering, calamity, complete hopelessness. This "deflation at
depth" had to come, said James, before any victim was ready

for God's medicine. And that was exactly what had happened to Bill before his illumination.

Bill, nothing if not a promoter, now wanted to tell other alcoholics about his experience. He envisioned beginning a chain reaction among them. "I started out after drunks on jet propulsion," says Bill. "It was a kind of twin-engine power drive—one part genuine spirituality, and one part my old desire to be a No. 1 man, a big shot." Bill's drunk-fixing turned out to be a flop. At the end of six months, none of the scores of inebriates he'd tried to bring to see God had sobered up. "Look, Bill," said Dr. Silkworth, "you're having nothing but failure because you are *preaching* at these alcoholics. You've got to deflate these people first. Give them the medical business. Pour it into them about the sensitivity of their bodies that condemns them to go mad or die if they keep on drinking." They'd listen if it came from another alcoholic, Dr. Silky said. And *then* Bill might suggest the God medicine to them.

That got Bill his first convert, a physician in Akron, Ohio —Dr. Bob. Then these two got busy working on others. That 1935 summer in Akron, out of many attempts, Bill and Dr. Bob converted just one more alcoholic. The three of them were the first group of A.A.'s. By 1939, Bill and Dr. Bob proudly counted a total of some one hundred absolutely down-and-out drunks now dry. They presumed to write a book, *Alcoholics Anonymous*, to celebrate this unparalleled achievement. The book was built around what they called twelve steps leading to sobriety. We'll boil them down:

Have a real desire to quit.

Admit you can't. (This is the hardest step.)

Make a rigorous confession of personal defects.

Resolve to help others.

Ask for God's ever-present help.

Accept and acknowledge that help.

At first, the medical profession was dubious about a method that seemed "in no sense scientific." But more and more doctors began to come to the aid of Bill and his exbibulous band. Distinguished psychiatrist Dr. Harry Tiebout, of Greenwich, Connecticut, had completely failed to cure alcoholic patients—*scientifically*. Then one of his patients, a deeply alcoholic woman, came to him after her first A.A. meeting: "I think I have the answer. I'll never drink again, doctor." And she hasn't.

This woman and other recovered people told Dr. Tiebout of their accepting a higher power—namely, God. But first, the A.A.'s taught them, they had to acknowledge their own helplessness; they had to admit they'd hit bottom. The trouble with typical alcoholics is that they're arrogantly sure they'll "lick this booze business" themselves. Not until they finally find they can't, Dr. Tiebout saw, do they hit bottom. Then they can choose: to go down to insanity or death—or to start up toward God. When they choose God, they don't want to drink anymore. It is as simple as that. "The miracle of A.A. was now clearer to me," says the doctor. "Hitting bottom became my therapeutic goal with alcoholics."

Bill and Dr. Bob and their converts counted more and more recoveries. By recovery they meant sobriety—total, complete and permanent. After six years the number had mushroomed to more than 2000, and by the end of the seventh year, to 8000. One reason for this astounding growth is, in the words of famed neuropsychiatrist Dr. Foster Kennedy, of New York, "Every cured drunkard is a missionary to the sick." They thank God for saving them by doctoring others.

No A.A. need be anonymous to family, friends or neighbors. But before the public—press, radio, films and TV—the revelation of identity is not for them. Why? Bill explains it simply. The A.A.'s are really a new kind of person. To gain enough humility to stay alive they have had to give up what have been characteristics common to most of them—excessive ambition and pride—and quit their crazy contest for personal prestige. Anonymity is only another word for humility, the spiritual key to their way of life.

Now members of the medical profession gave A.A. high praise, recognizing it as the real treatment for alcoholics. And the doctors referred problem drunks by thousands to Alcoholics Anonymous. But where in the early days all recovered alcoholics had to begin at total bottom, as strictly skid-row bums, now physicians began to ask the A.A. brethren an embarrassing question: "Just how deep is bottom? How do you recognize an early alcoholic? If we knew that, we could begin to raise the bottom."

Bill explained that the first sign is a loss of control of drinking. Many, perhaps most, people who drink have some experience with intemperance. But the potential alcoholic realizes he's beginning to get drunk at the wrong time— when the consequences could be painfully damaging. Using this sign, physicians have been able to discover incipient drunks by thousands and thousands. Doctors tell such patients that the fact they haven't yet lost their jobs doesn't mean they aren't in danger, and send them to join a group of A.A.'s. There are 11,000 such groups in the United States and Canada, and in 90 countries overseas. Their telephone numbers are listed under Alcoholics Anonymous in local telephone directories. Inquiries may also be sent to P.O. Box 459, Grand Central Station, New York, N.Y. 10017.

With such a resounding success, how does it happen that

A.A. is still utterly without organization? No hospitals, no paid trained experts. A.A. remains a loosely knit fellowship of more than 350,000 members meeting in little groups to sustain one another against their affliction. The doors of their meeting places are always open to victims no matter how far gone. They try to lift up all who fall, which many do. Why has their fellowship insisted on staying poor? "John D. Rockefeller, Jr., must be thanked for that," says Bill. "We once asked him for funds for hospitals and a big organization. Mr. Rockefeller was deeply moved. But he said, 'I'm afraid money would spoil this thing.' He rejected the plea flatly."

An associate of Rockefeller had said, "Why, A.A. is first-century Christianity!" And of course we all know that first-century Christians changed the world—without money.

❖

### THE ALCOHOLIC'S NEXT TWELVE HOURS

*Just for today* I will try to live through this day only, and not tackle my whole life problem at once. I can do something for twelve hours that would appall me if I felt that I had to keep it up for a lifetime.

*Just for today* I will be happy. This assumes to be true what Abraham Lincoln said: "Most folks are about as happy as they make up their minds to be."

*Just for today* I will adjust myself to what is; and I will not keep trying to adjust everything else to my own desires.

*Just for today* I will look as well as I can, dress becomingly, talk low, act courteously, criticize not one bit.

*Just for today* I will be unafraid. Especially I will not be afraid to enjoy what is beautiful, and to believe that, as I give to the world, so the world will give to me.     —*Just for Today*

# Divorce Is No Solution

NINA WILCOX PUTNAM

**D**ivorce has become an American bad habit, indulgence in which seldom secures either happiness or emotional freedom. Recently I asked a world-famous psychiatrist why divorces so rarely bring about the rosy future expected of them. "When two people have been irresistibly drawn together, it is love," said he, "and that cannot be dissolved!"

He spoke a simple, basic truth. You can never be wholly free of someone you have once loved. Separation will not unravel the skein of emotion tangled in your memories. What, then, can we do, instead of divorcing when the task of marriage seems impossible? Personally, I believe that happiness is only a part of love, and that its residue lies in the feeling of completeness which comes when a man and woman meet life as a unit. If we can accept this and work at it, divorce will seldom be necessary.

Many times during our years of marriage my husband and I have thought of divorce. Yet ours has become one of the most truly successful marriages I know. In our marriage we have faced down almost every conceivable ground for divorce: jealousy, bad personal habits, poverty, family interference, difference of religion, even a seeming physical incompatibility. And always one or both of us have taken time out for reflection, with the result that a better, stronger relationship has sprung from the ashes of our anger. I believe that in any marriage *time* is "of the essence." The ability of people to live through their differences ultimately gives marriage a foundation like the Rock of Gibraltar.

I have experienced two divorces. These earlier marriages might have been successful if I had really tried. In the first, my own intolerance was as great a fault as the man's offense. The second divorce came about because my subsequent incredible loneliness had driven me into a hasty alliance unfair to both of us. A marriage such as my second can easily lead to a chain of divorces in which the desperate and misguided seeker after happiness discards one marriage after another, like a child biting into and throwing back morsels of candy.

I was sincere enough in wanting my divorces, yet on each occasion, when the wish crystallized into reality and I had to sign papers, I was miserably unhappy. Almost all divorcing people experience this last-moment reluctance; and it is well known that Reno echoes with more unhappy gaiety than any other spot on earth. My two divorces left me only a dubious liberty, and the more or less equivocal position of the divorcée. A divorcée, remember, is fair game to many men.

My present marriage was not the calm, reasonable procedure which might have been expected, but a love match. Yet that in itself was no sure augury of success; but now I realized that divorce cannot be used as a gateway to happiness. I knew it was not so much a question of *whom* I married as of *how* I married, since the person you find yourself married to does not exist before marriage, nor are you the same individual who stepped so willingly into the greatest crucible known to humanity. I was aware that one has to get used to a whole set of unfamiliar habits in any new mate, that false quarrels come of this, and that the entire awkward age of marriage must be lived over again. Yet this marriage was going to last, even though its awkward age continued for a decade. I had no formula for success, but *I decided to give this marriage the time necessary for its success.*

Another thing I had learned was that the building of a marriage is much like the building of a house. Recalling the skeleton frames of my previous, unfinished homes, I could see how simply many of my building problems could have been solved; how a wall here was unnecessary, a gap there could have been filled, a window thrown into a dark room to let in the sunshine. This time I determined that no matter what happened I would sustain sufficient courage to perfect my new structure and make it stormproof. I was also alert to another pitfall which can entrap one into divorce: bad advice. Divorced women especially like to pull married women down into their own well of loneliness. They seem to feel, perhaps unconsciously, that each time another woman gets a divorce their own decision has been bolstered. These malcontents do an incredible amount of mischief.

Another spurious cause for divorce is silly pride after a quarrel. Thousands of divorces are based on nothing more important than a willful determination not to change one's mind. It is often better to acknowledge a fault, of which one is not guilty, if in doing so you can bridge some torrent of recrimination. Hundreds of quarrels which may mislead to divorce could be avoided by remembering that one's wife or husband can also be a friend, if offered the common courtesy and consideration extended to an outsider. Lastly, but importantly, the status of sex in marriage *can be adjusted to the requirements of both concerned* and should be adjusted unashamedly. In this enlightened day, when information is available both from dignified literature and your own family physician, there is no excuse for continued sexual incompatibility, except the existence of some actual deformity.

Undoubtedly there are situations in which divorce is justifiable, but these are seldom the ones given. If she says, "I left him because he didn't let me have enough money," or he says, "She took all my money," both are lying. Money is an excuse for the break, *never the cause of it,* for money alone will not separate two people who know it cannot purchase understanding. Even infidelity is not without possibility of reconciliation. Many a person who has refused divorce in spite of this humiliating transgression has lived to forgive a grateful prodigal who has learned a bitter lesson.

Divorce is easy, and so we do nothing about it. We thereby gloss over the fact that divorce frequently drives women into taking lovers, men into having mistresses; that it makes emotional orphans out of normally healthy-minded children. We accept it as part of our community ills. The result is an increasing disregard for the dignity of marriage, especially noticeable in the casual attitude of the oncoming generation. In a survey of 125 youngsters between sixteen and twenty which I conducted, 85 percent declared they were not afraid of marriage, because: "If it doesn't work out, there is always divorce."

The increased leniency of public opinion toward divorce may have been beneficial to certain innocent victims of hopeless marriages. But when it is carried to a point where the thought of divorce prefaces an increasingly large number of marriages, it is time for protest. Approximately 800,000 Americans a year now sever their marital ties. Each year, for every four marriages performed, one is dissolved.

Why cannot more of us try out the simple expedient of staying married, of giving the vaccination of marriage time to take? For when it does, the healed spot, though it be a scar, is a symbol of success.

# The Modern Housewife—
# Emancipated or Trapped?

JHAN AND JUNE ROBBINS

"**P**roblems? *What* problems?"
The young husband we were talking with suddenly lost his
temper. "My wife is well educated and in perfect health.
We have three fine children and a home of our own. My
wife has sixteen push-button machines to do her housework.
She has a car. I take her out to dinner. We give parties and
go on vacations. What's more, all her friends and neighbors
have the same advantages. No women in the world's history
have ever had it so good! I'm getting sick and tired of hearing about the problems of today's married woman!"

Many young American husbands feel this same sense of
resentment and impatience. More important, young married
women all over the country are puzzled and embarrassed by
their own symptoms; even as they complain, they feel that
they have no right to be doing so. A New Haven, Connecticut, psychologist who specializes in problems of young married couples told us that most of the wives who come to him
begin with the statement, "I'm ashamed to say this, but . . ."

These women are among our most intelligent and able
young wives and mothers. Why, then, are they so anxious
and dissatisfied? In the course of a survey we have found that
the answer seems to lie in one or more of these expressions:

I am constantly worried about doing or saying the right
thing.

I want people to think that what I'm doing is important.

I feel pushed and pulled; most of the time I'm under terrible pressure.

I have no time for myself, no life of my own. [A Pittsburgh housewife told us, "I feel like a pie cut up in six pieces being served to a dinner party of ten."]

This does not sound like the emancipated American woman the civilized world has been taught to envy. Nor indeed is it. Today's housewife is struggling with an impossible number of next-to-impossible, conflicting tasks. She is told that a good mother nurses her babies and stays "close" to her children. Her cooking must bear a personal touch. She is warned that she must be trim, slim and sexually attractive if she expects to hold her husband. It is strongly hinted to her that her husband's job advancement may depend on her ability to make herself charming and to entertain gracefully. Community culture, youth activities, charitable good works and the advancement of education all are loaded largely on her shoulders.

And finally she still has the burden of all the domestic chores—washing, ironing and cleaning—except that today she performs these tasks in lonely isolation, helped by cold, inflexible machinery. Certainly the automatic washer-drier is one of the greatest laborsaving devices of all time. But what has the modern woman done with the four or five hours a week she used to spend at the washtub? Chances are she is working on one more committee, helping out with a prekindergarten art group, or collecting for the town swap shop.

"A film made of any typical morning in my house would look like an old Marx Brothers comedy," one mother of three confessed. "I wash the dishes, rush the older children off to school, dash out in the yard to cultivate the chrysanthemums, run back in to make a phone call about a committee meeting, help my youngest child build a block-house, spend fifteen minutes skimming the newspapers so I can be well informed, then scamper down to the washing machine. By noon I'm ready for a padded cell. Very little of what I've done has been really necessary or important."

"I thought if I could just get all my children into full-time school," another young mother said, "I would be free. What I didn't realize is that the minute your children step out into the community, the community grabs you by the throat. My commitments to outside activities have eaten up all the leisure I looked forward to. Some of these activities seem worthwhile. Many are not. But if you beg off, you're considered lazy or incompetent."

Some observers believe that it is in the kitchen that our culture has played its sorriest trick on modern woman. A survey conducted in 1955 by a leading women's college reported that women spend seventy-eight hours a week doing housework. Of this time 20 to 25 percent is devoted to cooking, serving, washing dishes, planning menus and shopping for food. These figures may come as a shock to many thinking readers. What about canned goods? Frozen foods? Prepared mixes? Paper plates and napkins? The answer seems to be that American women have used the time saved by inventions and conveniences to raise their standards of performance rather than to contribute to their leisure.

Says Anthony DeMarinis, executive director of Family and Children's Service of Greater St. Louis: "Some women who come in to see me can remember that in their childhood the family lived during the week on milk, cornbread, oatmeal and slab bacon. That's what made roast beef and apple pie taste so good on Sunday! Today's housewife, however, feels compelled to serve a tasty variety of three-course meals throughout the week. Ideally, each evening meal is presented on a table graced with fresh flowers, good china and bright linen. Of course, few women manage to live up to this standard, but their failure is felt as a great frustration."

One cause for modern woman's exaggeratedly high standards is what scientists call "social mobility." Many young families now move in social circles quite different from the environment in which they were reared. This presents particularly painful problems for women, who are traditionally the guardians of social structure and family hospitality. A minister in Boston told us, "A young married woman whose girlhood social manners were learned at church functions is suddenly thrown into a cocktail-drinking suburb. A woman whose mother used to entertain only on religious holidays or at family weddings finds herself throwing weekend parties around a barbecue pit. It is all very confusing."

Social mobility also makes it hard to form lasting friendships that sustain social and moral values. When today's young mothers were girls, their mothers had close friends and confidantes who would lend furniture, recipes, or "spell you out" in nursing a sick child. Today, in a society where people move around so much, enduring female friendships seem to be a thing of the past.

In her social life today's young mother is no better off. She rarely throws a party for the people she honestly wants to see. Either she "owes somebody" or she is entertaining her husband's business associates. Thus the young wife wrestles with inner and outer conflict. She says that she has freely chosen to be a wife and mother, but she resents the fact that the tasks of homemaking and community activities engulf her completely. Is there an easy escape? Most of the advisers we talked with say no.

Norman W. Paget, executive director of the Family Service Agency of San Bernardino, California, has summed up the situation this way: "Modern woman's problem is to narrow her field, reject cheap outside pressures and let her family know from the very beginning just what league she wants to play in. The woman who tries to be all things to all people and nothing to herself is betraying her intelligence, her sex and the very humanity which she is supposed to be particularly able to defend."

## POLICY DECISION

*M*y wife applied for an accident policy and listed her occupation as "Housewife." She received a letter from the mutual insurance company saying, "We are sorry to have to tell you that your present occupation is *not* in the nonhazardous group to which our membership must be restricted. We hope you will let us know if you change to less hazardous work in the future."

—*Paul Alley*

## REST CURE

*W*hen I went to baby-sit for a young couple with twins five weeks old, I found the wife haggard and exhausted. Assuming she was going out, I asked her where she could be reached. She pointed to the bedroom. "That's my forwarding address," she said. "But I don't want to be disturbed."

Five hours later she emerged, wearing a pretty dress and looking completely refreshed. At that moment her husband arrived home and let out a surprised, appreciative whistle. When I left, each of them was holding a baby and chatting happily.

—*Stephanie Gerrard*

# When Doctors Play God

LOIS MATTOX MILLER

A few years ago a famous physician and medical educator handed me a folder of letters which, he said, dealt with the "most difficult problem the doctor must face: whether to prolong life—and suffering—in the face of inevitable death." The letters were from doctors and nurses, and from the children of aged and dying parents whose last days had been unmercifully prolonged by the "miracles" of modern medicine. They all asked the same questions:

Are we justified in applying "extraordinary" or "heroic" measures merely to sustain a spark of life in an old, hopelessly ill patient whose time to die has come unmistakably? How long is the physician obliged to continue this struggle when there is no hope of recovery and death is inevitable? What about the emotional and financial strain this imposes, for no good purpose, on the patient's family or friends? Is the doctor really prolonging "life," or is he only prolonging the act of dying?

When I had finished reading the letters, the physician anticipated my obvious question. "These people are *not* advocating euthanasia, or mercy killing," he said. "Euthanasia, literally 'easy death,' is the deliberate termination of life, and is forbidden by medical ethics, religious codes and the law. What is involved here is the very opposite—*dysthanasia*, which means difficult, painful, undignified death. Specifically, it is the deliberate postponement of merciful death for days, weeks, sometimes years, when everyone knows that the borrowed time will be spent only in misery."

The cases this doctor cited had a tragic sameness: An old man with cirrhosis of the liver is deep in hepatic coma and obviously dying; the medical team at his bedside succeeds in bringing him out of the coma—only to await the fatal hemorrhage or still another coma that will bring death. A seventy-year-old patient with advanced and rapidly spreading cancer develops pneumonia; penicillin cures the pneumonia and restores the patient to the longer ordeal of dying from cancer. An eighty-year-old woman who has spent years in a nursing home, suffering from a complex of chronic ills and mentally blank, has a heart attack; she is rushed to a hospital, placed in an oxygen tent, fed intravenously, given heart stimulants, started on heparin, subjected to a battery of tests. Within forty-eight hours she is dead—but her family has a whopping hospital bill.

"This is an old problem," the doctor said. "But it has grown more acute in recent years. Modern medicine has lengthened the average life-span, and we have a greatly increased population of old people. Because we are better able to cope with the chronic ills and degenerative diseases that come with old age, most of these people are alert, vigorous, capable of enjoying their later years. That's the bright side.

"But there is another side. Today we have many old folks who are only technically among the living. They are 'vegetables' lying in hospital beds, barely breathing in oxygen tents, their wasted bodies nourished through nasal tubes, their bladders drained by catheters. We have drugs to stimulate the faltering heart, drugs to restore consciousness, drugs to ease pain. But death is still a part of life and we cannot forestall it indefinitely. We can only prolong the process of dying.

Someone has said that we have merely developed a new way of dying—slow passage via modern medicine."

Since then I have discussed this problem with scores of physicians, surgeons, nurses, hospital administrators. Everyone agreed that the problem is acute, but few were willing to be quoted for publication. "No matter how cautiously we speak, we're bound to be accused of advocating euthanasia," said the dean of one medical school. I reminded him of my friend's distinction between euthanasia and dysthanasia. "I agree," he said. "But does the average layman know the difference?"

"The profession is partly to blame," said one surgeon. "There are zealous doctors who feel obliged to keep on fighting for the last faint heart flutter. We all know that Hippocrates pledged physicians never to use a drug to produce death, but we seem to have forgotten that he also forbade the administration of remedies to those beyond hope."

Dr. Walter C. Alvarez, emeritus consultant in medicine of the Mayo Clinic, believes something should be done to "moderate the zeal of some physicians who like to keep treating strenuously long after all hope for a cure has gone. . . . For thirty-five years I have begged young physicians not to do everything *routinely*, but always to stop and think and ask themselves, 'Will what I am now ordering do the patient any good?'" Dr. Alvarez recalled that the late Dr. Alfred Worcester of Harvard told how, in his first year of practice, he had made tremendous efforts to prolong an old man's life. "But actually he had done this at the cost of making the old man unhappy and uncomfortable," Dr. Alvarez says. "He decided never to do that again."

In 1940 Dr. Worcester wrote a classic book, *The Care of the Aged, the Dying and the Dead*. "Modern methods of resuscitation are most decidedly out of place where by disease or accident the body's usefulness has ended," he said. "Especially is this true when resuscitation would only renew the patient's suffering. Such attempted defiance of nature is even less justifiable than are efforts for prolonging life when the inevitable approach of death offers merciful release. Yet in both these ways many of our profession seem duty-bound to do their utmost. They ought to know better. The dying ought to be allowed to depart in peace."

Most of the physicians with whom I discussed the problem emphasized that they were speaking only of patients who are old, incurably ill and obviously dying. The question of prolonging life is quite different when the patient is young or middle-aged. "Every good physician knows that in most cases of serious illness in childhood he must keep fighting for a cure until the very end," says Dr. Alvarez. "Young adults who are dying will be reluctant to go before they have had a chance to live. Men and women a little older can be much distressed at having to go and leave a greatly loved spouse. Less distressing, usually, is the problem of slow death when it comes to the aged whose race has been run. Older persons who for years have suffered the tortures of a failing heart or crippled joints or a series of strokes are often glad to go, and some keep asking, 'How much longer has it got to be?' "

The most sobering statement of the problem appeared in *CA—The Bulletin of Cancer Progress*, in 1959, in a paper by Dr. Edward H. Rynearson of the Mayo Clinic. "You are standing at the bedside of a patient dying of untreatable cancer," Dr. Rynearson told his colleagues. "The patient has already undergone radical surgery, chemotherapy, radiation. Despite all the impressive ministrations science can provide he is still dying and still suffering. There simply is no other treatment now, for there is no treatment for death. . . .

"There are too many instances, in my opinion," Dr. Rynearson went on, "where such patients are kept alive indefinitely by means of tubes inserted into their stomachs, veins, bladders—with the whole sad scene encompassed within the cocoon of oxygen which is the next thing to a shroud." Suppose the physician and his associates agree that these "extraordinary" measures are futile and only prolonging the patient's suffering and the family's distress. "The time certainly has arrived to have a frank discussion with the patient's relatives," says Dr. Rynearson. "Almost never have I met any lack of understanding on their part. Almost never do they wish to have their loved one maintained indefinitely in a tragic interlude of more and more suffering. In most instances, the patient by now has a full understanding of the factors involved and usually is asking for relief of pain, not prolongation of distress."

Who, then, says that "heroic measures" still must be applied to prolong the patient's life? Is it the church? "So far as I know," says Dr. Rynearson, "there have been no voices representative of the Roman Catholic or Greek Orthodox churches or of the Protestant faiths to suggest that physicians should try extraordinary means to keep life going when every process of the body is bent toward extinction. His Holiness Pope Pius XII, within the last year of his life, stated the official position of the Roman Catholic Church as not requiring the physician to use *extraordinary* means when only certain death and suffering lie ahead." However, Rabbi William F. Rosenblum of the Central Conference of American Rabbis, representing the Reform Jewish faith, says, "It is a maxim of Judaism that one must do everything humanly

376

possible to prolong a life." The Union of Orthodox Rabbis of the United States and Canada has taken no official position on the subject.

Some Catholic authorities question whether such medical advances as radiation therapy, oxygen tents, iron lungs, intravenous feeding, etc., are "ordinary" or "extraordinary" measures. They seem to agree that intravenous feeding, for example, should now be classified as ordinary. "But even granted that it is ordinary," writes Father Gerald Kelly, S.J., "one may not immediately conclude that it is obligatory. To me, the mere prolongation of life in the given circumstances seems to be relatively useless, and I see no sound reason for saying that the patient is obliged to submit to it."

Dr. Rynearson concluded that when doctors, family, patient and spiritual adviser agree that the struggle is hopeless "the physician should do all he can to alleviate the patient's suffering and make no effort to prolong his life.

"Some may say: 'You are trying to play God,' " Dr. Rynearson conceded. "I reject that charge. I believe that it is actually the physician who prolongs life by using extraordinary measures who is 'playing God.' " Dr. Rynearson also knew that others would ask: "What would you do if this occurred in your own family?" His answer: "The travail and misfortune I am speaking about did occur to a member of my immediate family. We kept her in her own bed in her own home and made certain she suffered as little as possible until she was released by death."

Following the publication of Dr. Rynearson's paper, which received widespread approval within the profession, I discussed the problem with a number of specialists in geriatrics (the medical treatment of old people). Did Dr. Rynearson's recommendations for the patient dying of incurable cancer apply equally to patients dying of chronic and degenera-tive diseases of old age? "If the case is hopeless, if everything has been tried and has failed, I see no difference," was a typical answer. "But what we need first is wide-open discus-sion of this problem, between physicians and laymen. With general understanding that this is not euthanasia but the very opposite, I think we shall get somewhere."

"We had better get somewhere and soon," added another geriatrician. "This problem is getting more pressing all the time. I have dedicated my life to caring for old people. But when their hour is come I shall devote my energy to keeping them free from pain, not to prolonging a misery called 'life.' "

Then he continued: "Incidentally, we all ought to be grateful to Rynearson for making the Catholic position clear. Too few people, even Catholics, understand it. The late Pope Pius XII was a wise as well as a holy man. He had still more to say on this subject, and I think it's worth quoting. 'Euthanasia, deliberate provocation of death,' His Holiness stated in 1957, 'is obviously condemned by moral law. But, with the consent of the dying person, it is permissible to use narcotics with moderation to alleviate suffering, even if the narcotics hasten his death. In this case, death is not directly desired but is inevitable, and proportionate motives sanction measures which may hasten its advent.' "

→ ◆ ←

### SPECIALIZATION

**D**riving through Texas, I found our Army squadron surgeon practicing in a small town. "With all your training," I said, "how come you aren't up in San Antonio specializing?"

"Why, I do specialize," he said. "I specialize in *people*."

—*John W. Morrison, Jr.*

378

# How Much Can You Stand?

HARRY EMERSON FOSDICK

Every important life story has two aspects: the things a man has energy enough to do and the things a man has stability enough to stand. Many of the worst tragedies that afflict individuals today come from inability to stand life's strain. In our day the virtues most emphasized are those associated with progress. The ancient world did not believe in progress. Marcus Aurelius, Roman emperor, even said that an open-eyed man, forty years of age, had seen everything that ever had been or ever would be. But the modern man stands on tiptoe wondering what new things will happen tomorrow; he expects change and, therefore, values those virtues of adventure, enterprise, inventiveness and strenuous energy which achieve it.

There is, however, another set of qualities which the temper of our time does not encourage: poise, balance, steadiness, stability. In consequence, when one thinks of one's own life, or of the restless civilization of which it is a part, one often feels the topheaviness of it all, as though a tree had specialized in branches and forgotten roots, and now faced the crucial hour when everything depended on whether it could stand.

To be sure, stability is in part temperamental. Our interior gyroscopes are not of one quality, so that some people will always be steadier than others ever can be. I have just been reading again the life of George Washington. He was not a brilliant man. Gates won at Saratoga a more smashing victory, I think, than Washington ever won except at Yorktown, but Gates let ambition enter in and in comparison Washington seemed like a great rock, steadfast. When he won a battle, as at Princeton, he did not lose his head. When he lost one, as at Brandywine, he did not lose his heart. In a desperate, chaotic time, he had amazing stability.

If anyone says that this is partly temperamental, we may agree, and yet we do so desperately need this quality that there must be some way of getting a little of it for ourselves if we seek it aright. The problem touches the lives of all of us, particularly in our handicaps. Reading biography confirms the impression that all human beings are handicapped somewhere, and that in no small degree the quality of any personality depends on the way he is dealing with difficulty and standing up under it.

We thought, perhaps, that a scientist like Pasteur, upon whose titanic work modern medicine rests, must have had lusty health to labor with. We discover that he had a paralytic stroke at forty-six and was handicapped for life. We find Beethoven writing music although deaf and Milton writing poetry although blind. We discover that, in general, the great work of the world has been done by handicapped people. We recall that Wordsworth said of James Watt, "I look upon him, considering both the magnitude and the universality of his genius, as perhaps the most extraordinary man that this country ever produced." But Watt himself we forget—sickly of body, starving on eight shillings a week.

People who stand things handsomely wield a penetrating spiritual influence upon all who know them. Bring on your strong and shining Apollo who never had a handicap, who with integrated personality, fortunate circumstance and physical health has lived untroubled by limitations, and however energetic may be his active service in the world, there are some things he cannot do for us that Helen Keller can. My friend at a Midwestern university tells me that, in all his years there, he never heard such cheering, not even at a football victory, as greeted a hopelessly crippled boy carried in the arms of his companion across the platform to receive his diploma on Commencement Day.

One wonders if this ability to tackle life with courage and steadfastness is going to be distinctive of our new American generation. Many of our children go to school where, as a dean of Columbia College once said, they are asked in the morning what, if anything, they wish to study that day. We are surrounding them in our families with luxuries that we never knew in youth and that our fathers never dreamed of. They are told on every side that personality is a creature of environment, and that the great thing is for everybody to be surrounded by commodious and comfortable circumstances. This is deceiving many of them as to the real secret of living. They are expecting to find life, to pick it up, to get it out of circumstances, and that is a lie. We never *find* life; we create it. Often the best friend a man has is the stimulus and challenge of antagonistic environment to awaken the courageous resistance and endurance of his slumbering soul. All life must be tackled in this spirit. What existence hands us is the raw material out of which something must be made, and it takes steadiness to make it.

This certainly applies to our moral situation. That old moral codes have broken down is obvious. The prevalent idea is that our laxness is modern, but that is nonsense to anyone who knows history. Go back to the seventeenth and early eighteenth centuries and you will find it all there. When was it that Lady Mary Wortley Montagu reported a plan to take the "not" out of the Commandments and put it into the Creed? That sounds ultramodern, but it was in the eighteenth century. When was it that men sneered at a dying Christianity and said that it already was so far gone that it needed only decent obsequies to complete its course? That sounds ultramodern, but it was in the eighteenth century. When was it that the Duchess of Marlborough called at a lawyer's office and the clerk, reporting her call, said he did not know who she was but that she swore so dreadfully he was sure she was a lady of quality? That sounds ultramodern, but it was in the eighteenth century. The fact is we are facing an old fight between orgy and self-control, promiscuous living and decent family life, a fight which has been waged again and again across the centuries, upon the outcome of which depends whether we human beings are really going to be human beings or beasts. In this situation nothing is more needed than poise, balance, level-headedness, good sense and moral stability. There is no place where a real religion operates with more conspicuous success than in this matter. A vital faith in God does contribute to steadiness of character. It does enable a man to stand up under things that otherwise would crush him or bowl him over.

When that kind of faith is lacking, the insecurity of life is terribly increased. We are insecure enough already—economically, domestically, internationally insecure, victims of vicissitude, children of restless change, dreadfully insecure! And now disbelief comes with the profound addition of spiritual insecurity. When Socrates was on trial for his life he said, "Men of Athens, I honor and love you; but I shall obey God rather than you." There was a man who had the capacity to stand his ground, but he had it because there was something deeper than popular judgment on which he could stand.

## Chapter 16/The Tangled Thickets of Sex

*Sex, say the Freudians, is a humming dynamo that
provides much of the power for human achievement.
Sex, say the sociologists, has been greatly overemphasized in our culture. Sex, say the moralists, is
something that should be rigidly controlled—and isn't.
Sex, most observers will agree, is here to stay.
Certainly we live in an age that has achieved
unparalleled frankness. But many perplexing problems
remain for many people. Here seven writers, including
a physician and a minister, discuss some of those
problems and offer some realistic solutions.*

## The Dilemma of Premarital Relations

BETSY MARVIN MC KINNEY

We have heard a great deal
in the past few decades about the dangers of repression and
inhibition. The sexual frustration of unmarried young
women has been made much of, not only by psychologists
but by young men searching for sexual partners. Under the
spell of the current jargon, many young women need little
additional persuasion for activity they have been influenced
to feel is "only normal," or "sophisticated." When romance
enters into this dilemma, the modern young woman can be
made to feel almost more immoral if she withholds her virginity from the man she loves than if she surrenders it.

Many women today are part of a "liberated" generation

for whom sex has become a matter of personal choice, virginity something to be given or withheld on a basis of volition rather than morality. This attitude has led in some cases to an insecurity so great that breakdown has resulted. For the "liberators'" approach contains a fallacy: the supposition that male and female sexual behavior can be evaluated as if they were identical. They are *not* identical. Man's role, sexually, is a single act: the deposition of sperm where it can fertilize an ovum. Woman's role is a more time-taking triple act in which accepting the sperm comes first, pregnancy and childbirth second and lactation (nursing) third. By man's *completing* his sexual activity, a woman's is merely *initiated*.

It seems to be assumed in our society that the woman's own cycle can be repressed and inhibited at will so that she may concentrate exclusively on the part of it that involves impregnation. This is a masculinization of her role. Carried to its conclusion, it would mean the discontinuation of the human race. Yet on this false basis much of our present-day sexual lore is founded. In other places, other moral structures have evolved. A few primitive societies permit indiscriminate intercourse, generally limiting it to a premarital, almost juvenile "testing" period, for the better selection of a mate. When uninhibited sexual intercourse is permitted beyond immaturity, it is invariably in a society which welcomes and cares for all the resulting children, without feelings of "legitimacy" or "illegitimacy." Thus, in these cultures the role of the female is given full recognition.

But in our society premarital experience forces a woman to limit her sexuality to what is, for her, only the introductory phase. At no point does the man suggest that she fulfill her sexual role. If he is thinking of the possibility of a baby at all, he is thinking of how to avoid any such unwanted finale. That he wants the full expression of his own male sexuality is wholly understandable, and there are times when the young woman may feel quite as impelled, emotionally. However, she cannot know in advance just how totally this communion is going to deprive her if she enters it outside of marriage. If she does surrender to his importunings, she is entering a situation of tremendous frustration— socially, spiritually, emotionally and sexually. If she was frustrated before, she is much more frustrated now. For she has set in motion a compelling progression, and she is frustrating the deepest needs of her sexuality by concentrating on this beginning, partial phase. Moreover, it will probably take months of sexual intimacy, if not the complete cycle of pregnancy-childbirth and lactation (now thought to be a final maturing factor in developing woman's full sexual sensitivity), before she can experience anything like the abandoned joy her lover may know almost immediately. This in itself leads to disappointment, for she must pretend to an exaltation she is unlikely to feel.

Despite the fact that nonvirginity is the fairly common status of many unmarried young women nowadays, it is still unsanctioned morally, religiously or socially. Today's young woman may find less disapproval than existed a generation ago, but she is still forced to carry on any premarital affair in secrecy under the ever-present threat of loss of reputation should she be discovered. Instead of being "released" she feels less secure than she has ever been in her life.

Perhaps the most terrible of her moral and spiritual penalties will be the perversion of her sexuality by its frustration. Rather than delighting in her female role and accepting the role, she must disown it, refuse pregnancy, look on it (if it does happen) with dread. Such inhibition makes deeper inroads on personality than is usually recognized. Whether or not she uses contraceptives successfully, she is engaged in denying her own creativity, her very femininity. This is a frustration many men would probably prefer to minimize, for it seriously interferes with what might otherwise be a far less guilt-ridden situation for them. Perhaps they do not realize that "sex" is a considerably less complex act for them than it is for women. It is one of the most thwarting of all situations in which a woman's emotions can entangle her: the situation of the unmarried lover. She is deprived when she most wants to be "liberated." This point is so little recognized by most writers on sex that the frustrated nonvirgin gets far less attention than the far *less* frustrated virgin.

Constituted as we are, the expression of sex via intercourse can do great harm to the unmarried woman. To accept and deal successfully with unavoidable frustration is a mark of both balance and maturity. But to invite avoidable frustration is foolish and immature. Fortunately, continence is not at all harmful, nor is it even impossibly frustrating. And there are two sound ways for a girl to deal with a young man who is insistent: she can marry him or say "No."

⇥ ♦ ⇤

### FEMALE BIOLOGY

*A* woman's first protection against betrayal by her biology is to appreciate that the speedup of her emotions is not only possible but normal during lovemaking. Her best defense is to have no confidence at all in her ability to say nay at the appropriate moment. The belief that any woman can coolly halt lovemaking at some point before she is wholly committed is a trap devised by romantics. Female biology can illuminate or desolate—but it can never be underestimated. *—Marion Hilliard, M.D.*

# Advice for Newlyweds

MARGARET BLAIR JOHNSTONE

As a minister and marriage counselor who has been consulted by hundreds of men and women for advice on marital problems, I know that we moderns can discuss sex facts and functions freely. But in our reaction against puritanism many of us have substituted misinformation for the old-fashioned prudery. Despite present-day frankness, many of those who think they know most about the subject are dangerously misinformed.

To find out how much couples about to be married do know, I test them on a set of eighty questions originated by Dr. Gelolo McHugh of Duke University. The questions are so basic to a wholesome knowledge of sex that the answers can spell the difference between a happy and an unsuccessful marriage. Yet I have never found a premarriage couple who could answer two thirds of the questions correctly. This is in keeping with Dr. McHugh's wider findings gathered from studies conducted among two groups: unmarried men averaging twenty-two years of age and unmarried women averaging twenty. Of more than 2000 tested, the men averaged only 53 correct answers, the women 55.

Quiz yourself on the following samples adapted from the test. Are these statements true or false?

1. Difference in physical size causes sexual incompatibility in marriage. 2. It is dangerous to have sex relations during a woman's menstrual period. 3. There is no sex life for a woman after the menopause. 4. Sex relations should take

place only when the woman wishes it. 5. It is normal for a woman to initiate relations with her husband. 6. Pregnancy can occur even though neither partner reaches a sexual climax. 7. Unresponsiveness in sex relations helps prevent pregnancy. 8. Pleasure from the sexual climax varies greatly from time to time in the same person.

The first four statements are false, five and six are true, seven is false and eight is true. Anyone who has three or more of these facts wrong should seek expert advice.

Many wives and husbands are not enjoying their marriage to the fullest because they never have learned that sex relations can take place healthfully as often as both parties wish and that it is perfectly normal for the woman as well as the man to take the initiative. Every couple should know that pleasure and other emotional reactions do not influence conception, and that intensity and length of reaction vary decidedly from time to time. Few couples I counsel ever consider that there are psychological as well as physical factors to take into account. A satisfying sex relationship depends on more than just knowing about technique. A conditioned emotional frigidity, for example, may occur in women because of a lack of privacy. Overcrowded living quarters restrict the chances for marriage intimacy. Couples should recognize this and make provision for absolute privacy.

Unresponsiveness also can result when there is a mental block caused by poor timing. The average wife feels most relaxed and free of tensions in the evening. A man usually feels most rested and refreshed in the morning just when his wife is concerned with getting up to prepare breakfast and get the youngsters off to school. Compromise is the obvious solution, with each partner trying to cater to the other's preferences. Another common danger facing couples is letting sex become perfunctory. When spontaneity is gone, sexual relations can become as monotonous as washing dishes.

Often couples, in ignorance, secretly and wrongly blame each other for the situations in which they find themselves. Men actually still blame their wives for bearing only daughters. Women without children often inwardly accuse their mates of some premarital excess which, they imagine, has robbed the husbands of the ability to give them children. Both frequently nurse these and other grievances in silence, never dreaming of the damage they are doing to their physical happiness and, of course, to their marriage. When difficulties seem insoluble, husbands and wives together should seek, with the advice of their family physician, the professional help that is available to them. They should not try to establish the blame but to find the answer, and by every means to get over the dangerous impasse which "a little learning" about sex may have brought.

Whenever a couple confess disappointment in marriage and admit that their sexual relationship "is not what we thought it would be," I realize they do not know what full sex experience in love is. One bewildered man told me, "We read all the modern books. We should know the score." Then, as an afterthought, he suggested the key to the puzzle confronting him and his wife: "Sometimes I think the literature itself may be the root of our trouble. If we weren't always reading about what love should be, perhaps we would be a good deal more satisfied with what we have." Sex harmony cannot be achieved by reading. Rather, it is a deep satisfaction, achieved in the give and take of steadily improving experience.

I am constantly asked: "What constitutes full sex experience in love?" One of the best answers I know came from a man who had learned the hard way. He had ruined his marriage through infidelity. "You can buy sex relations," he said. "But you cannot buy the desire to be together after sex needs are satisfied. That's not bought; it's given. And it's not the real thing unless it's shared." Then he added: "Real love is not just physical union. It is spiritual communion."

### LOVE AND MARRIAGE

*T*o know that one is loved, and to love: these are the greatest satisfactions in life and they are not confined to physical relationships. The love of a wife or sweetheart has drawn men back from death has ennobled many lives. A word spoken at the right moment may give more comfort and reassurance than any form of physical contact. The knowledge that another stands by and understands is, in critical moments of life, the ultimate value of love. If it were not for these deeper undercurrents, marriage would long since have ceased to exist as an enduring human relationship.
—*Paul H. Landis*

### FOR A LIFETIME

*W*hat is sex but the *symbol* of the relation of man to woman, woman to man? It consists of infinite different flows between the two beings, different, even apparently contrary. Chastity is part of the flow between man and woman, as is physical passion. And beyond these, an infinite range of subtle communication. At times, sex desire itself departs completely. Yet the great flow of the relationship goes on, undying, and this is the flow of living sex, the relation between man and woman that lasts a lifetime, and of which sex desire is only one vivid manifestation.
—*D. H. Lawrence*

# The Real Cause of Frigidity

HANNAH LEES

When a wife is not happy in her husband's arms, the marriage—however much they enjoy and admire each other—is not likely to be nourishing to either of them. There is no way of knowing how many marriages are haunted by what is commonly called frigidity. It may be a third of them, or half or three quarters. Actually, the number isn't the important thing. What does matter is that the problem always causes unhappiness, and what matters still more is that often the problem need not exist.

Women vary in their sexual responsiveness, and even those who are frequently unresponsive are likely to have far more capacity for passion than they know. Most doctors agree that perhaps 90 percent of so-called frigidity is psychological. Many unresponsive wives could be much freer and happier in their lovemaking with a little more understanding of their feelings. Often what is withering their response is nothing more complicated than suppressed anger or resentment. When they learn to express that anger, and get it over with, they find in themselves an unexpected capacity for response. We all take the fact of marriage so much for granted that we seldom stop to think how close to miraculous it is that two people can spend a lifetime so intimately together without driving each other crazy. Even in the most compatible marriages there are bound to be irritations, conflicts of will and preference.

A New York gynecologist tells of a young wife who came

for a consultation in a panic after only a few months of marriage. Her honeymoon, she said, had been wonderful; she and her husband couldn't have been happier together. They agreed about practically everything. But for the past few weeks she just hadn't felt anything at all when they made love. How could that be? Could she just be falling out of love? She couldn't be that shallow, could she? It *must* be something physical. The gynecologist asked a number of apparently aimless questions. The young wife had a job? How did she manage with the housework? Who did the marketing, the clearing up? Did her husband help her at all?

They did the marketing together, the young woman said. They used to do the dishes together, but—well, she really preferred to do them alone. Her husband had a terribly systematic mother. He always insisted on their doing things the way his mother did. So now she did the dishes alone, her way, but even so she could feel him being critical. Oh, sure, it made her a little mad that he would help only on his own terms. As the young woman talked, she realized that she was much more than a little angry at her husband's criticism, and the resentment had gathered strength because she hadn't dared admit it even to herself. There was nothing wrong with her physically, nothing basically wrong with her love for her husband. Anger—unadmitted anger—had been freezing her response to him.

The anger that froze another wife was far more conscious and far more serious. Her husband was warm and considerate, she told the marriage counselor, and very successful. They had an interesting life, and she really loved him as much as ever except that for the last year or so she hadn't enjoyed his making love to her. He couldn't help knowing, and they both were miserable. The marriage counselor asked many questions. Finally she got around to children. "I want a baby terribly," the woman burst out. "I wanted one right away but my husband said we ought to wait until we were further ahead, and each year there has been some new reason. I don't think he wants me to have a baby, and sometimes I almost hate him for it!"

Hadn't she ever told him? "I used to try, but he brushed me off. I couldn't keep on pushing it." It is easy to see how a woman who felt denied the basic reason for lovemaking would finally resent the lovemaking itself. But it is also easy to see how a man preoccupied with success might not even guess what was going on in his wife's mind if she never really told him.

Understanding anger, acknowledging it and finding a way to express it are the first steps toward freeing oneself of it. These two young women who were helped to recognize their feelings did not experience a return of ardor overnight. But as they were able to unburden themselves, the inhibiting physical effects began to disappear. The cause of the resentment or anger is not usually pinpointed so easily. Many wives today find the role of wife and mother less fulfilling than they had hoped. They want desperately to be good wives and mothers. Yet they are troubled by the feeling that this role is at the same time too much and not enough. Overloaded as their days are with the demands of home and children and husband, they still feel that they should be doing something more useful or, above all, more appreciated. As a young wife once said to me, "The trouble with being a housewife is that you never get promoted like your husband. You never even get gold stars the way the kids do."

Sometimes the resentments caused by everyday life are complicated by more deep-seated attitudes. Some women enter marriage unconsciously suspicious of all men. They may have had brutal fathers or brothers; or they may have been badly treated in some earlier love affair. By the time they fall in love and marry they have forgotten all this—until it wells up in a great dark cloud in the intimacy of the bedroom. It is not uncommon for a woman to feel warmly responsive to her husband and then suddenly—even while she is still longing to love and be loved—have all desire vanish as if someone had turned off a switch.

Women like this, whose responses are rooted in long for-gotten angers, may need psychiatric help or marriage counsel-ing. But the problems may be worked through without pro-fessional help if a wife has the strength and patience to ex-plore her feelings. What am I blaming on my husband that he doesn't deserve? What happened in my life years ago that I still allow to haunt me? If a wife can ask herself these questions, especially if she can make herself talk them over with her husband, her chances of becoming more responsive may be very good.

Another complicated form of anger may spring from what social scientists call "exchanging roles"—the wife assuming leadership of the family. "Go ask your mother," the husband says when the children ask permission to go to the movies. "You decide," he says when his wife wants to discuss whether to send the children to camp. "Here—you budget it," he says, handing over his paycheck. Such a relationship always affects a couple's love for each other. The anger that a woman feels toward a man who has either forced her or allowed her to usurp the leadership of the family is the deepest anger of all and most intimately connected with her feelings toward him as a lover. Most women long for a domi-nant man—not a domineering bully, but someone strong to

lean on in a crisis. If a husband has defaulted on his manhood in the whole fabric of their relationship, how can a
wife respond to it in any one aspect?

Dr. Catherine Bacon, a prominent psychoanalyst, is convinced that the love relationship of many men and women is
crippled by their fear of showing the angry feelings that
arise from the complications and pressures in modern life. It
is natural, of course, to be afraid of anger. We think of it as
destroying love—the love we need to feel for others and the
love we long for. But *repressed* anger is what really destroys
love. The act of love by its very nature is a far from passive
experience. Some of the most satisfying lovemaking is, in
fact, a thinly disguised battle in which, at its best, and miraculously, both can win. All of us can learn to recognize our
resentments and find some direct way of expressing them. If
a woman, instead of stiffening her jaw and taking over, said,
"Look, I'm angry that you are letting me do this," and if the
man instead of retreating said, "Well, I'm not going to let
you; I'm the man in this family," there would never be that
harmful exchange of roles.

It takes practice and sensitivity. But the most amazing fact
about women who have not been able to respond to love
because they were frozen by hidden anger is that it is never
too late to undo it. Husbands and wives who have been
unhappy together for years can, when they face what they
are angry about, begin in their thirties, forties and even
fifties to enjoy each other as lovers.

⇢ ◆ ⇠

Anger is an acid that can do more harm to the vessel in which
it's stored than to anything on which it's poured.
                              —*Glendale, California, News-Press*

# What Sex Means to Women

JOHN KORD LAGEMANN

"How like a woman," a husband may say. The comment, made jokingly or in anger, frequently expresses honest bewilderment. He knows his wife responds differently and acts differently from him in many situations, but why she does often baffles both of them. Many marriages might profit if both partners had a fuller understanding of the special nature of women.

Few men realize how much courage it takes for a woman to accept the feminine role in sex and achieve the complete surrender required for mutual fulfillment. They have never experienced the risks that women have lived with since childhood. Long before a girl is old enough to marry, she has learned from observation and from hearsay of the penalties of ill-advised intimacy with men. From their earliest years, women build up emotional defenses to guard them against premature, harmful or unwelcome intrusion. These defenses, often appearing to be "feminine modesty," are based on fear. And, until a woman is mature enough to manage her own life, these fears serve a useful purpose. It would be wonderful if she could drop these defenses immediately on falling in love and getting married, and proceed at once to find complete expression of her feminine impulses and emotions in marital relations. But marriage cannot transform her sexual attitudes and behavior overnight. Many of her defenses remain.

The conscious ones are the first to go. Fear of pregnancy,

THE TANGLED THICKETS OF SEX

for example, may be replaced by a desire for children; or, for some, it may be relieved by consulting a doctor on a safe means of contraception. The ordinary feelings of shame, shyness and false modesty carried over from girlhood usually yield to experience or to information acquired in talking with a doctor or a marriage counselor.

One of the most important things the young wife learns is that relatively few women achieve climax in the early months of marriage and that at no time is failure a dire emergency. It reflects a way of life and a set of attitudes which have to be modified gradually. They learn, too, that for a woman the climax is an individual matter and that no two women experience it with the same frequency or intensity. Some women are constitutionally more emotional or sensual than others, and are deeply stirred not only by sex but by everything that matters to them. Naturally such women react more passionately than others. The wife whose climax evokes no more than a contented sigh may be just as fulfilled and therefore just as sexually "adequate" as the wife for whom it is an earthshaking experience.

Underlying all of these individual variations is the fact that virtually all women have the potential for sexual arousal and satisfaction. A noted Chicago gynecologist told me how he gets this point of view across to his patients. In a leisurely preexamination chat he draws on his best anecdotes. When his patient laughs, he tells her, "If you can find release in laughter, you can find another kind of release in marital relations." As this doctor points out, a woman's ability to achieve sexual fulfillment has much in common with her sense of humor. Both must be shared to be enjoyed. Neither can be brought about by force, technique or sheer determination. A certain blend of spontaneity and thoughtfulness is essential. Neither is located in any particular part of the body. Both involve a woman's total personality. In most cases, one of the first things young couples learn when they consult a doctor is that a wife's inability to achieve satisfaction is not due to any specific defect or deficiency. The most thorough physical examination seldom reveals any malformation, glandular imbalance or other physical symptom.

But questioning by the doctor may show that the wife has troubles in some other areas of her life besides her relations with her husband. Psychologist Niles Newton, in a book based on her research at the University of Pennsylvania's School of Medicine, indicates where this difficulty commonly lies. Careful study of interviews with several hundred mothers of newborn babies revealed that women who dreaded either menstruation or pregnancy rarely found satisfaction in marital relations. On the other hand, women who accepted menstruation as a matter of course and those who looked on childbirth as a rewarding experience usually reported a good sex adjustment. In other words, the amount of satisfaction a woman gets out of marital relations—and how much satisfaction she gives her husband—are closely bound up with her feelings about all of her body's reproductive functions.

There is one difficulty that may be universal in women with whom failure to achieve satisfaction is a long-continuing problem. They need help in accepting their role as women. When a woman rejects her femininity, it is because she fears being passive and dependent. Instead of looking on marital union as a way of actively *giving* herself to her loved one, she sees it as a challenge to resist the danger of *giving in*. As an eminent gynecologist, the late Dr. Robert L. Dickinson, once pointed out, it takes just as much passion for a woman to fight against her own deepest impulses as to express them fully.

"There is an urge, found in every organism, to express all its capacities," says the psychologist Dr. Paul Rogers. "It exists in everyone and awaits only the proper conditions to be released. These conditions are warmth, understanding, unconditional acceptance by another human being." If anyone can provide these conditions for the full release of a wife's feminine capacities, it is her husband. This may not be easy for him. When his wife fails to respond to him, he is likely to think of it as a challenge to his masculinity. His reaction to the challenge may only make it harder for his wife to respond to him.

No doctor or marriage counselor, of course, will be able to make out a prescription and say, "Follow this and everything will be fine." But at the very beginning he can suggest a way of being together which will get the couple off to a good start in working out their own solution. Dr. Rogers describes it in this way: When hidden fears prevent a wife from achieving sexual completion, her husband's problem is to create a "safety zone" in which she feels free to experience feelings which she usually hides behind a mask. This means that he doesn't judge, criticize, threaten, diagnose or prescribe, or come to her with ready-made notions of the kind of person he expects her to be. Instead, he permits her complete freedom of thought and feeling, and trusts some deep life-urge in her to overcome all obstacles to the expression of all her capacities—sexuality included.

Does this sound familiar? It is Dr. Rogers' way of summing up what he has found most useful in helping his clients untangle their emotional snarls. Most people would say it was also a good definition of love.

# How Men Feel About Sex

DAVID R. MACE, PH.D.

**D**uring the past thirty years I have talked with thousands of husbands about their sexual needs and longings, their fulfillments and frustrations. I have found that although men have individual sexual characteristics, as women do, they also have a number of commonly shared attitudes toward sex. It's highly important that these be understood by women.

The first thing I've noticed is that most men are more self-conscious about sex than women. This may sound surprising, because men talk much more about sex and generally show much more interest in it than women do. But notice *how* they talk about it—almost always impersonally and indirectly, in stories and jokes. They hardly ever talk about their own sexual experience, about their perplexities and disappointments. As a marriage counselor, I nearly always find that wives can discuss their sex lives with more poise and detachment than men can.

Why? There are many reasons. The overwhelming power of sexual desire in a man; the rapidity with which he is aroused by "sexy" pictures or stories that produce hardly any stimulation in a woman; the aggressive drive which sexual needs can develop in him—these explosive forces can produce emotions that bewilder a man and make him fear he will lose control. So he learns, in communicating with other people about sex, to keep it at a safe distance and never let it get too personal. He is on his guard all the time to prevent

an eruption of his emotions that could make him an object of amusement or dismay to others. Partly for this reason, it is usually harder for a man than for a woman to link sex with love and tender emotion. No man really *wants* sex without love. But some have so much difficulty in expressing their affection and their need for love that they make their women feel that the sexual experience is, for them, completely impersonal. And this is, of course, a terrible humiliation to a woman, because she then feels she is being treated as a thing, not as a person.

A woman will understand this better if she will remember that there is a fundamental difference in the roles played by sexual partners. The man's role is to take, the woman's to give. The man has an urge to conquer, the woman to surrender. Sometimes in my counseling I have put it this way: "A man gives love in order to get sex, while a woman gives sex in order to get love." Of course mature love travels a long way from this oversimplified picture, but it is close enough to the truth to have given many couples with whom I have worked a new understanding of themselves.

Another significant fact about a man is that his self-esteem is very deeply rooted in his sexual nature. The way in which he proves his masculinity to himself is by functioning as a man toward the woman he has chosen. At this point his masculine pride is more profoundly involved than in anything else he does. This is why men are so sensitive, and so vulnerable, about their sexuality. Every marriage counselor knows the anguish of the husband who has found himself impotent. Women need to understand this acute sensitivity. For them, there is no counterpart to such an experience. A man's sexual functioning is very complex and, if the involved mechanisms fail, there is only one more terrible expe-

rience he can have—that is when the woman with whom he
has failed treats him with contempt. Men don't *seem* to be
sensitive about their sexuality. But you can be sure that they
are. To make a sexual advance and be refused is deeply
humiliating for a husband. Of course there are times when a
woman may say no; but it needs to be done with great tact.

A man is also sensitive about being able to make his wife
happy in their sexual communion. Many husbands feel dis-
mally inept every time their wives fail to reach a climax. I
remember one husband who spent two hours pouring out his
tale of woe. Then I sent him out and brought in his wife. "I
just don't understand what Bill is so worried about," she
said. "I love him deeply, and I like to have him make love to
me. It doesn't bother me whether I have a climax or not.
Why is he so concerned about it?" The reason was that Bill
felt that his prestige was involved.

These are some of the difficulties a man has in being comfortable about his own sexual nature. But he may have trouble, also, in adjusting his sexual feelings and responses to his
wife's. Often there seems to be a basic incompatibility between men and women in terms of timing. The man gets
sexually aroused far more quickly than his wife. Women get
into the mood for sex only after a slow, gradual process,
which is influenced greatly by romantic atmosphere and
physical contact. This difference between the sexes remains
a control problem for most men for most of their lives, since
it is they who must damp down their desires until their wives
gradually reach the point of being ready to respond.

The same difference in tempo often occurs during intercourse itself, and it can result in discouragement and hurt
feelings on both sides. This is a problem that is often
brought to marriage counselors. Fortunately it can nearly al-

ways be cleared up. But it is the husband who must make the adjustment—by learning to slow down his reactions. The problem reappears in the cooling-off period after sexual communion. The man's sexual feelings die away as rapidly as they arise, while his wife goes through a long, slow process in which she feels happy, contented and romantic. She wants to prolong the sense of physical and spiritual closeness to her husband. Wives often complain to me about this. "Just when I want to hear my husband tell me how much he loves me," said one woman, "he turns over and goes to sleep!"

Men who love their wives are quite ready to make adjustments. But they feel better about it if their wives understand that this takes effort and self-control, that it doesn't come naturally. And an understanding wife will feel, and express, her gratitude to her husband for showing this consideration.

Sex is not everything in marriage, and we must not exaggerate its importance. But neither must we underestimate the great power it has, rightly used, to make all the other aspects of married life and love run smoothly and sweetly.

### TO LOVE

*W*hatever the power of the sexual embrace, it is not for this that we love one another. The act itself may engage us in all sorts of matters ruinous to love, such as deceiving, lying, raping, killing. Love between man and woman, like any other love, is a relationship in spiritual greatness. It is a love generous in offering and generous in receiving; it is full of laughter, mercy and rejoicing. Love nourishes but does not possess; in love we affirm one another but do not dominate. To love is not to win or lose, but to help and be helped. —*Robert Raynolds*

# The Problem of Impotence

WALTER C. ALVAREZ, M.D.

**S**everal women have asked me if anything can be done for the impotence that comes to many men in middle life. One woman who writes feelingly and intelligently—and anonymously—says, "I feel that I am sleeping with a stranger—a good-night kiss seems too much to ask for. If a man is not smart enough to understand a woman's nature, no wonder the divorce courts are full."

Some of the women who are still highly sexed in their forties or fifties miss a sexual life, while others say that although they can easily put up with the lack of sexual life in itself, they cannot easily put up with the lack of any sign of affection on the part of their husband. So often an impotent man fails even to kiss his wife or to caress her in any way. The man retires to his own bed or to his own room. The couple live like brother and sister.

One woman says, "The wife abhors the thought of being just a housekeeper to the man she loves. Impotence is not normal and it is not normal for us to be forced to accept it, no matter how much we love our husbands. A man should be enlightened as to his responsibilities, and to the keeping of his wife's love before he loses it."

So often, in these cases, the wife begs her husband to go to a physician to see if anything can be done. Usually, not only does the man refuse to do this but he refuses even to listen or discuss the subject. In this behavior I think such men are unfair and unwise, although it is true that in most cases a physician cannot help. About all he can do is to discuss the psychological factors. Perhaps he can try the effect of male hormones. Unfortunately, when the impotent man's troubles are psychic in origin and he has all the male hormone he needs, the taking of more cannot help him.

In hundreds of cases I have found that a man who inherited from psychotic ancestors a tendency toward moodiness, a great shyness and great self-centeredness, and such marked hypochondria that he spent a good part of his life worrying about his health and going to doctors, had no energy left for sexual relations.

Perhaps it was impossible for him to love anyone deeply. Many a man of this type will say that even in his youth he didn't care much for girls and seldom took one out. He did not know what to say to them, and he had no spare energy to "waste on them." Often such men have told me that what little interest they had in sex was gone by the time they had reached forty.

In many cases the wife has allowed herself to get stout and unattractive, or perhaps she herself has failed to show much affection. Perhaps she is willing to show some affection only once or twice a month, and this has caused her husband to turn against her. In many cases of this type, the husband's sexual drive also was never strong, and hence perhaps what little drive he had was gone during his forties. Oftentimes, if his wife had remained a good sexual partner, he might have gone on being adequate for a number of years.

*I*t is something to have had, as they used to say, a good man's love. But this is as nothing compared with having loved any man—good, bad or indifferent.                    —*Jessamyn West*

# About Sex: True or Not?

SYLVANUS M. DUVALL

"Jim regards sex as simply a game and me as just another female body. But when I'm with him all my 'proper' feelings are lost in one wish—to make him happy. What shall I do?"

Two generations ago, a clear social code would have required this sixteen-year-old girl to recoil with horror from Jim's "proposition," however great the temptation. Today she has little guidance. How responsible are parents, teachers and clergy for the plight of such young people? Do we provide adequate help in developing standards for our youth to live by? The answer is "No," probably because, as adults, we often are uncertain and confused ourselves.

Our greater scientific knowledge about sex has added to our dilemma. Until that knowledge has been evaluated and digested, uncertainty is inevitable. We have, however, reached a point where much of our confusion about sexual conduct can be cleared up. Here are some of the common fictions about sex, and the facts concerning them:

Fiction: *Sex is essentially beautiful and good.*

Fact: *Sexual experience occurs on different levels.*

To say that sex is beautiful and good is as meaningless as to say that liquids are nourishing and delicious. This nonsense once served a useful purpose: to counteract the opposite fiction that sex is nasty and vulgar. Sex can be beautiful and good, or neurotic and vicious; it can be delightful, or unpleasant, or boring. It is not *essentially* any of these.

Fiction: *A person who is really in love will not be sexually interested in anyone else.*

Fact: *Most men and many women are polyerotic.*

Often a wife will feel that her husband no longer loves her if he shows a normal interest in other women. But no matter how genuine our love for our mates, we will find others of the opposite sex who are physically attractive to us. If we understand this possibility in advance we can usually handle such problems without feeling guilty. People who find each other attractive can work happily together without indulging in sex, just as a treasurer can handle honestly large sums of money that he might be tempted to steal. Those who remain faithful to their marriage partners do so, not because attraction to others is absent, but because of their own moral standards.

Fiction: *Sexual intercourse is a need of all people who are physically potent.*

Fact: *Sexual outlets are a need of all normally developed males, but these do not have to occur through sexual intercourse. The body itself, through nocturnal emission, provides for all the outlet that is physically necessary.*

Sexual intercourse is a normal *desire* of most males and of many females. For some, it can also become an emotional rather than a biological "need." The philanderer is driven by his need to overcome feelings of inferiority, to express hostility toward women or to meet some other neurotic demand. The unwed mother is often love-hungry and emotionally deprived. Promiscuity is common among those who feel inadequate or rejected, who lack strong ties with family or friends, or who lack spiritual roots that give them a sense of personal dignity.

Fiction: *Our traditional sex standards are on the way out.*

Fact: *Our sex code is being violated, but no more so than are our other moral standards.*

Comparison of the Kinsey findings on laxity in sex conduct with reports of corruption in business, government and labor points to a surprising conclusion: Americans observe their sex standards better than they do the moral standards in any other carefully studied area. The crucial question about any code of behavior is not the extent to which it is observed, nor even its future outcome, but its desirability. Morality demands loyalty, not to a practice or even a trend, but to what is good. The basic issue about sex behavior is: What is desirable?

Sexual enjoyment must provide for love and sound family life. No code regarding sex or any other area of life can completely avoid injustices, unhappiness and frustrations. A good sex code is the best compromise between divergent and often conflicting values that we can devise.

Fiction: *The solution to our problem is more "sex education" for our youth.*

Fact: *Men and women of today should concentrate on deeper human values.*

An adequate biological knowledge of sex is part of the education that every well-informed person should have. But something far deeper than textbook information is required. If sex education is to contribute significantly to good living, it must be focused on relationships and standards of behavior. It should teach maturing young people how sex affects their developing emotional life. It should give them guidance in what to expect of others and how to handle difficult situations.

The basic problem of sex today is what it always has been —to integrate it properly into the whole of life. The "case for chastity" is often unconvincing, largely because it is stated in terms of limited personal risks and disadvantages, rather than in terms of the kind of persons we wish to be, the kind of family relationships that will most enrich our lives, the kind of society we want to live in and the permanent values to which we are committed. Certainly, one of the primary reasons for chastity before marriage, and fidelity to the spouse afterward, is the preservation of the best kind of family life.

The task of the educator and the religious leader is to help people, young and old, to fit their sex interests and behavior into a total and constructive concept of self and life, and to develop the moral standards that are required by valid and lasting personal and social goals. We rightly begin by discarding the fictions that continue to delude us; but before us lies the far greater task of developing those deeper insights that will enable us to make sex a happy and a meaningful part of our lives.

⇾ ◆ ⇽

## THE BIG TEASE

*O*ne minor vulgarity of our time is the custom of dressing cocktail waitresses in next to nothing. Is the American man a perpetual adolescent who needs to have his vanity inflated by tipping young women who prance about in ridiculous half-costumes? As a prominent sociologist points out, the abuse of sexual images and enticements is a symptom of decadence in American life. Properly directed, the sexual impulse is a source of power and imagination. But the incessant tantalizing of sexual instincts does great harm to character—not to mention taste. Prudery depresses me. Yet even an era of prudery is preferable to an era of tasteless misdirection of amatory impulses.       *—Russell Kirk*

# Chapter 17/Good Manners—
## The Shock Absorbers of Life

*"Manners," said Ralph Waldo Emerson, that champion nutshell-putter, "are the happy ways of doing things." And he added that people are always watching your manners, and awarding or denying you prizes accordingly. Certainly good manners soften the hard edges of reality. They lie at the heart of that mysterious thing called charm. They can be oil on the troubled sea of matrimony.*

*How to have them? Imagine yourself in the other person's shoes. Then treat him as you would like to be treated—that's all!*

## Manners Are from the Heart
SUZANNE HART STRAIT

One of the pleasantest surprises I've ever had as a parent came one day when a woman stopped me on the street and said with a warm smile, "Your child has the nicest manners." Nice manners? My child? "It was John," she said, answering my unspoken question. "He was at our house the other day. When I went into the room where the boys were, he stood up—and he spoke to me. I'm so pleased when the children recognize me, even in my own house. And when he was leaving, he came to me to say good-bye. It cheered me up for the rest of the day."

I could hardly believe it. Then I remembered a similar

testimonial about Ellen, our oldest child. At a party she had noticed that the mother of the girl giving the party was standing alone. Ellen had crossed the room and said, "This is the most wonderful party I've ever been to, Mrs. Evans. Thank you for inviting me." These cheering little episodes stood out so clearly because at home our children had always seemed so indifferent to mannerly behavior. Tom and I had tried to teach them manners, of course. We felt as Marshal Foch of France did when an unmannerly American once said to him that French politeness was nothing but wind. The marshal replied, "Neither is there anything but wind in a pneumatic tire, yet it eases wonderfully the jolts along life's highway."

In George Bernard Shaw's play *Pygmalion* (from which the musical *My Fair Lady* was adapted), Professor Higgins takes a cockney-talking little flower girl and, by teaching her manners, makes a lady of her. "The great secret, Eliza," Professor Higgins tells her, "is not having bad manners or good manners, or any particular sort of manners, but having the same manner for all human souls."

This *is* the great secret, and even those people who discover it find that it slips away from them sometimes. Possessing the same manner for all people is a rare quality; it is rooted in the ability to see every person as an individual human soul. This is why my son's politeness was so pleasing: not because he had "nice manners," but because he spoke to a friend's mother, saw her as another person. And when Ellen crossed the room to speak to her hostess, she was seeing not a stick figure called HOSTESS but a woman who had worked hard all day on a party and should be thanked.

It is not often that we encounter another person who actually sees us; it is not often that *we* actually look at others. It is hard work to look at someone else and think about him;

most of us are generally too busy, too preoccupied with ourselves to spend the time. Yet isn't this what we are trying to teach our children when we teach them "manners"? We cannot, of course, tell a six-year-old child to try to project himself into the skin of another person and understand how that person feels. But we *can* teach him to say "thank you," and maybe someday when he is saying the words, when he is truly grateful, he will suddenly understand what he is saying and why.

When a child shouts, "Gimme that!" and we ask him to start over by saying "please," we are trying to teach him that shouting orders is not a good way to communicate with others. When we badger a nine-year-old girl to sit down after Christmas and write a letter to Grandmother to thank her for the blouse, the very act of composing the sentences may bring some realization to the self-centered child that her grandmother did spend time and thought on choosing a present. Before true courtesy can be expressed, its techniques must be practiced.

When I see the intense pleasure that courtesy can give, I realize that the pleasure is out of proportion to the effort that produces it. It is more than pleasure in a smoothed path. Courtesy is a reassurance; it is a warm and friendly voice coming to greet us in the dark; it is a hand reaching across the empty space that surrounds every one of us.

⇒ ◆ ⇐

### THE MARK OF A GENTLEMAN

"**M**y boy," a father advised his son, "treat everybody with politeness, even those who are rude to you. For remember that you show courtesy to others not because *they* are gentlemen, but because *you* are one."        —*Alabama Times*

# Love Your Enemies—It'll Drive 'em Crazy

J. P. MC EVOY

**W**ell, maybe it won't drive
'em crazy, but it'll certainly discombobulate 'em. Anyway,
you can waste a lot of energy being nasty to enemies. Wise
old Ed Howe said it years ago: "If you attend to your work
and let your enemy alone, someone else will come along
some day and do him up for you."

But suppose your enemy won't let you alone? What then?
You can do what the man did who was walking the bounds
of his new farm and met his neighbor. "Don't look now,"
said the neighbor, "but when you bought this piece of
ground, you also bought a lawsuit with me. Your fence is
ten feet over on my land." Now this is the classic opening
for a feud that could go on for centuries and make generations of enemies. "Good fences make good neighbors," wrote
poet Robert Frost, but more potent even than good fences
are good boundary lines.

The new owner smiled: "I thought I'd find some friendly
neighbors here, and I'm going to. And you're going to help
me. Move the fence where you want it, and send me the
bill. You'll be satisfied and I'll be happy." The story goes
that the fence was never moved, and the potential enemy
was never the same. He went around talking to himself. He
was in shock; after that he was a slightly mystified but
friendly neighbor.

There is an old saying, "There are no little enemies." Enemies may seem little and unimportant, but be careful. Don't

give them cause to make a career of getting even with you. Be nice to that disagreeable newsboy on the corner. Otherwise he will dedicate himself to working hard and getting rich so he can buy the building you're in and throw you out. Don't "tell off" that snooty, golden receptionist who blocks you from getting to the boss. One day she'll marry the boss, sure as hell, if for no other reason than to get even with you.

There are all kinds of enemies, and one of the arts of living is to learn to tell them apart—so you can either plow around them as a farmer plows around a stump, or get rid of them by making friends of them. A gardener once wrote to the Department of Agriculture in Washington: "I've tried everything I've ever heard about or read, including all your bulletins, on how to get rid of dandelions—and I've still got 'em." He received this reply by return mail: "Dear Sir, If you have tried everything and you still have dandelions, there is one thing left for you to do. Learn to love 'em."

But sometimes you run into a really big enemy—the kind that you can't go under or over or around and who doesn't want to be loved. Crossword-puzzle experts know him by his three-letter name, SOB. One of William Randolph Hearst's favorite editors came to him one day in a towering rage and said, "I can't go on like this. I've tried for years and I just can't get along with that SOB in the accounting department. He goes or I go, and that's final." Hearst had a deceptively mild way of speaking. "You're absolutely right," he said softly to his irate editor. "I'm not surprised that you can't get along with this man. I can't. Nobody can. He is that rare phenomenon, a one hundred percent revolving SOB. But every organization must have at least one SOB. He's ours. You can be replaced. He can't." In this case the editor was the one who went crazy.

Besides the little enemies who can't wait to grow up to get even with you, and the big enemies—the icebergs which show only one seventh of their nasty bulk above the surface of everyday life—there are the most difficult enemies of all, the "In-Betweens." They can be found lurking halfway up the ladder to success, where they can enviously trip you on the way up or gleefully give you a good boot in the pants to help you on your way down. If you ignore the "In-Betweens," they pursue you; if you turn the other cheek, they knock your block off. You can't lick 'em because there are too many of them and you can't join 'em because if you make friendly advances, they think you're afraid and they get twice as ornery. Stand by for an important message: There isn't a thing you can do about them; they're crazy already.

Finally, there is the common garden variety of enemy who never meant to be an enemy at all, and doesn't want to be an enemy, really. He's not mad at *you;* he's mad at the world, and you are wandering witlessly around on his lonely battlefield, stepping on land mines and getting into lines of fire not meant for you at all. Let me tell you about one of them. She was the dark-eyed daughter of our village barber: a small, stormy, economy-size Gina Lollobrigida seen through the wrong end of a telescope. Years ago, I brought my two little girls up from Cuba in the late spring and put them in public school down the road. They talked a very peculiar language neither English nor Spanish—and their first- and second-grade colleagues gave them a hard time, naturally. Especially "Lolla," who was older and the ringleader Terror of the Tiny Tots.

Pat and Peggy came home crying almost every day, so I decided to cheer them up. "Let's have a party," I said. Pat and Peggy's tears dried magically. Right away they got creative: "Ice cream! Cake! Big red balloons!" "And friends?" I said. The tears started again. "We haven't got any friends," Pat blubbered. Peggy wailed. "Nothing but enemies." Then I had an inspiration. "Let's have an enemy party. Let's invite all your enemies—especially the worst ones."

Little Pat and Peggy exchanged knowing looks, and one of them said with an eloquent Spanish gesture, *"Qué pasa al viejo?"* (What goes with the Old One?) Now the angels who have the special job of watching over children's parties must have been pleased to see that the "Enemy Party" was a mad, merry success, and the best time was had by the biggest enemy, little "Lolla," who shrieked with delight.

Pat and Peggy never came crying home from school anymore. Their biggest enemy had turned into their staunchest champion. Nobody dared lift a finger to them—little "Lolla" would have broken it off, pronto. One day "Lolla's" father dropped by to see me. "I come to thank you for asking my little girl to the party," he said. Then he added, mystified, "Why did you do it?"

"Why not?" I told him. "She likes ice cream, cake and big red balloons, just like any other little girl. Yes?"

"Oh, yes," he said, "but do you know something? Nobody ever asked her to a party before. Why?"

A good question. Are the "Lollas" left out because they are enemies, or do they become enemies because they are left out? There are several schools of thought on this, but the Great Teacher settled it long ago. "Love your enemies, pray for them that persecute you, do good to them that hate you . . ." And it'll drive them crazy, because it works!

⇒✦⇐

*W*e cannot always oblige, but we can always speak obligingly.

—*Voltaire*

# The Delightful Game of Conversation

GELETT BURGESS

n San Francisco once I belonged to a small group which met weekly for the purpose of reviving the lost art of conversation. We realized that there is a fundamental principle underlying good talk. This principle—the basis of all good manners—is the avoidance of friction in social contacts, emotional friction caused by irritation, boredom, envy, egotism or ridicule. Here are some of the rules we finally adopted to guide our conversation and make it a delightful game.

*Avoid all purely subjective talk.* Don't dilate on your health, troubles, domestic matters; and never, never discuss your wife or husband. Streams of personal gossip and egotism destroy all objective discussions. Such chatter bores the listener, and the talker, repeating only what he already knows, learns nothing from others.

*Don't monopolize the conversation.* One of my friends was a laughing, attractive person, who told stories well—but too many of them. You roared with laughter, but after a while you grew restless and yearned for more quiet, comfortable talk with plenty of give and take. You couldn't help remembering what John Dryden said about those "who think too little, and who talk too much." Or what Sydney Smith wrote of Macaulay: "He has occasional flashes of silence, that make his conversation perfectly delightful."

*Don't contradict.* You may say, "I don't quite agree with that," but flat contradiction is a conversation-stopper. One should seek to find points of agreement. In that way the subject develops in interest with each one's contribution. "That is the happiest conversation," said Samuel Johnson, "where there is no competition, but a calm, quiet interchange of sentiments."

*Don't interrupt.* Of course when you throw a few grace notes into the talk, such as, "How wonderful!" or, "You mean she didn't know?" it doesn't put the train of conversation off the track. But to interpolate views of your own often leaves the speaker hanging uncomfortably in midsentence. One perfect conversational dinner party is still alive in my memory. It was given in Boston by Mrs. James T. Fields, and there were six present—the ideal number for an intimate dinner; if you have more the conversation is apt to break up into separate side dialogues. Each of us talked and each of us listened. No one interrupted, no one contradicted, no one monologued. The affair had the charm and pleasing restfulness of music.

*Don't abruptly change the subject.* Some people, after patiently—and painfully—waiting for a talker to pause a moment, jump into the conversation with a totally new subject. In our Conversation Club it was an unwritten rule that after a person stopped talking there should be a brief silence in which to reflect, digest and appreciate what had been said. It is the proper tribute to anyone who has offered an idea.

*Show an active interest in what is said.* This brings out the best in a speaker. You need not only your ears to listen well, but your eyes, hands and even posture. I have often tested an article I have written by reading it aloud to friends. What they said about it never helped much, since one often liked what another didn't. But if their eyes went to a picture on the wall, if their fingers fiddled, I knew that the manuscript wasn't holding their interest and I marked the dull spots for revision. There is no surer way to make people like you than to pay them the compliment of interest and sympathy. Prolong their subject, ask more about it, and they expand like flowers in the sun.

*After a diversion, bring back the subject.* Often while a subject is not yet fully considered it is lost in some conversational detour. There is no surer test of being able to converse well than to reintroduce this forgotten topic. This is not only polite and gracious, but it is the best evidence of real interest. Of course, if it is your own story it is futile for you to bring it back to persons who have bypassed it. Let it go, but see that you don't commit their error.

*Don't make dogmatic statements of opinion.* The Japanese tea ceremony is perhaps the most refined social form ever practiced. It is a cult of self-effacement. One of the rules concerns conversation. It is considered vulgar to make any definite, decisive statement. One may speak of anything, but never with an expression of finality. The remark is left up in the air for the next guest to enlarge upon, so that no one is guilty of forcing any personal opinion upon the others. It is a good game, but difficult; try it sometime with your friends. You may state facts as facts; but your application of them should be tentative, with such qualifications as "It seems to me," or "Isn't it possible that—" Those who really know things usually speak thus, "with meekness of wisdom," as St. James says, while the ignoramus is always for cut-and-dried pronouncements.

*Speak distinctly.* While I was a member of the executive committee of the Authors' League I was fascinated by the fact that those who spoke slowly and clearly dominated our meetings. High, hurried voices simply couldn't compete with

Ellis Parker Butler's deliberate words, and his voice maintained his leadership for years. If you observe a group talking you'll find that the one with a low, controlled voice always gets the most respect. The eager, temperamental contenders dash up against it like waves against a rock, and the rock always wins.

*Avoid destructive talk.* We are all likely to make many unnecessary derogatory remarks. Evil, of course, must be condemned. But try to avoid the unnecessary criticism, the desire to raise a laugh through ridicule, the tendency to look on the unpleasant side of life. Cynical comments may sound clever, but they make other people uncomfortable.

So much for the negative side of conversational rules. How can you create an agreeable conversation? The secret is simple. To talk well one must think well. You must think underneath the subject, above it and all around it. This kind of thinking is well illustrated in the conversation of baseball enthusiasts. Are they content with telling the score, the number of hits and runs? Not at all. They discuss a team's potentialities, the characteristics of the different players, the technique of the game. The same principle applies to all conversation. *If you find it hard to talk, learn to think about what you see and hear and read.* As you ponder, associate the subject with your own experience and observation.

To avoid falling into the rut of shoptalk, enlarge your interests by making acquaintances engaged in pursuits other than your own. Develop a curiosity about what has so far been outside your range of knowledge. Read up on subjects that have interested you, that have been outside your field of view. If you enrich your thinking in such ways you need not worry about being able to converse well. Every new experience will make your talk more interesting and more valuable.

# Privacy Is Sacred to Everyone

MORTON M. HUNT

When I was in my teens, I daydreamed of the ideal girl I would some day love. Naturally, she would be beautiful, intelligent and gentle. But the essential thing about her was that she would *understand* me. She would listen to all my innermost thoughts, not only my hopes and fond desires, but my darkest moods and memories, my sorrows and sins. Somehow, though, I never envisioned myself listening to her in return. I would find her dear because she would understand and accept *me;* it did not occur to me to understand and accept *her.* For the desire for self-revelation is both immature and selfish.

Yet, even in adulthood, many people suppose that they have a right, almost an obligation, to express to the people closest to them their doubts and fears, their ugliest or most pessimistic thoughts. I submit that we have no such right. If anything, the obligation is in the other direction: *not* to indulge in total self-revelation to those we love and who love us. Intimacy between any two loving human beings should have limits, for the good of both persons, and when we ignore those limits, we do so selfishly, out of an immature desire to shift our burden onto the other person. But, as a wise rabbi said long ago, "If thy secret oppress thine own heart, how canst thou expect the heart of another to endure it?"

The secret that modern man most often seems to want to confess—to the very person it will hurt worst—concerns sexual infidelity. When a man or woman has an extramarital affair, he or she is likely to be nagged by guilt. Many an adulterer, undetected, almost wishes his wife would find out somehow, so that he might confess and ask forgiveness. Yet when that happens, he frees himself of pain by transferring it to her; he is healed while she suffers.

A marriage counselor told me of a young woman married to a brilliant real-estate developer in his late thirties. Their marriage had been warm and rewarding for some years until one night he told her about a brief, torrid affair he'd had while out of town some months earlier. He said that there had been no emotional significance to it. Having been through it, he felt he'd be able to control such impulses in the future; he said he felt far better for having told her, and believed it would bring them closer than ever before.

He was wrong—as any psychologist could have told him. For since that night their love life, previously sound and happy, has been blighted for her. She finds herself always wondering, "Am I as exciting as that other woman?" She feels suspicious about the women he meets at business, and is in agony whenever he goes out of town. *His* secret has shattered *her* peace of mind.

Why do people make such revelations to those who love them? Was this man's act a genuine effort to become closer to his wife? Her marriage counselor thinks not. The confession was not a mature and loving act. "Let me see how real your love is," he was saying, in effect. "Let's see if you can love me, even if I show you something ugly." Mature love would have made him feel: "This was my wrongdoing. I have no right to free myself of it at her expense."

The same is true of sexual wishes that we never actually carry out. Lewis Terman, a psychologist, made a famous survey some years ago in which he found that a majority of husbands, and a considerable number of wives, sometimes feel longings for extramarital affairs even when their marriages are happy. Total intimacy would call for them to confide such yearnings to their mates; happily, compassion and caution combine to keep most of their mouths shut. I say "happily" because the admission of such desires is tantamount to telling one's mate, "You are not enough for me; you leave me wanting something more." Would the teller like to hear the same?

Like the love between a man and a woman, the affection between two friends may be destroyed by too much intimacy. Friendship involves a blessed freedom to be truthful about ourselves, but, like all freedoms, this one must be exercised with restraint lest it become license. Conscious and unconscious feelings of guilt are aroused when friends know too much about us. These are the beginning of the end. One similarly trespasses beyond the allowable borders of intimacy when he tells a friend the things he dislikes about him if those things are essential parts of his character. To tell a friend you are angry at him because of something he has done may be helpful; to tell him his basic faults, rather than accepting them without comment, is a very different matter.

Consider a woman with whom I had been friendly for years, who once wrote me a long and incredibly revealing letter when I was gathering data for a book on the problems of American women. Writing late at night when she was feeling sorry for herself, she told me that she often bitterly regretted having children. They had brought her far less joy and far more emotional upset than she'd ever expected, and, while she often loved them, quite often she hated them. A day after I received the letter, she sent a telegram asking me to burn it. Though she and her husband were longtime friends of mine, I have not seen or heard from them since. Friendship can be killed by an overdose of intimacy.

Fundamentally, the desire to pour out our thoughts and to confess our misdeeds to the people closest to us originates in a childish conception of love. As one psychiatrist explains it, "To tell everything—one's past or present misdeeds, one's impermissible wishes—is reminiscent of the way an infant tests and demands parental love. A baby makes a mess—and expects Mommy to clean it up with a forgiving smile. A grown person who tells the worst about himself is symbolically making a mess and asking to be loved despite it."

Still, isn't confession good for the soul? Doesn't the whole practice of psychiatry prove that certain private sorrows and fears, if kept bottled up, will sometimes overwhelm us? Of course—but the crucial question is: If you must confide, to whom should you do so?

In the case of secrets such as I have been discussing, the answer is: Not to the persons you are most intimate with, but to someone detached and uninvolved, unlikely to be wounded by what you reveal. Your minister, rabbi or priest is often an excellent choice as confidant and adviser. And family doctor or lawyer, though he may lack the prerogatives of spiritual leadership, is often able to perform much the same function for the person who needs to relate his inner torment. In more severe problems, it may be necessary to seek a social worker, a psychologist or a psychiatrist. Such people can let us say the worst—indeed, can encourage it—without being harmed by it themselves. Moreover, they are trained to help us learn to live with our own feelings.

But self-revelation to an intimate is unwise, if not downright dangerous. We must set limits to intimacy, not only for our own good, but for the good of those we love.

# There Is Magic in a Word of Praise

FULTON OURSLER

A Broadway comedian once had an excruciating nightmare: he dreamed he was telling stories and singing songs in a crowded theater, with thousands of people watching him—but no one laughed or clapped. "Even at $100,000 a week," he says, "that would be hell on earth."

It is not only the actor who needs applause. Without praise and encouragement anyone can lose self-confidence. Thus we all have a double necessity: to be commended and to know *how* to commend. There is a technique in giving a compliment, a right way to go about it. It is no real compliment, for instance, to praise a man for some obvious attainment. Use discernment and originality. "That was a wonderfully convincing speech you made tonight," a gracious woman once said to a businessman. "I could not help thinking what a fine lawyer you would have made." The merchant flushed like a schoolboy at the *unexpected* character of the tribute.

No one, great or obscure, is untouched by genuine appreciation. Yale's renowned English professor, William Lyon Phelps, related: "One hot summer day I went into a crowded railroad dining car for lunch. When the steward handed me the menu, I said, 'The boys in the kitchen certainly must be suffering today!' The steward looked at me in surprise. 'People come in here and complain about the food, kick about the service and growl about the heat. In nineteen years you are the first person who has ever expressed any sympathy for the cooks back there in the kitchen.' What people want," Phelps concluded, "is a little attention as human beings." In that attention, sincerity is essential. The man coming home after a hard day's work who sees the faces of his children pressed against the windowpane, waiting and watching for him, may water his soul with their silent but golden opinion.

The simple principles of the art of praise—to realize the human need for it, to compliment sincerely, and to train ourselves to look for the praiseworthy—help rub off the sharp edges of daily contact. Women seem to have an instinct for such things; they look at life, so to speak, through their hearts. After his marriage, on February 23, a bridegroom remarked, "I will never forget our wedding anniversary. It will always be the day after Washington's birthday." "And I," his bride answered, "will never forget Washington's birthday. It will always be the day before we were married."

Children especially are hungry for reassurance, and the want of kindly appreciation in childhood can endanger the growth of character; it can even be a lifetime calamity. A young mother told the Reverend A. W. Beaven of a heartaching incident: "My little daughter often misbehaves and I have to rebuke her. But one day she had been an especially good girl, hadn't done a single thing that called for reprimand. That night, after I tucked her in bed and started downstairs, I heard her sobbing. Turning back, I found her head buried in the pillow. Between sobs she asked, 'Haven't I been a *pretty* good girl today?'

"That question," said the mother, "went through me like a knife. I had been quick to correct her when she did wrong, but when she had tried to behave I had not noticed it. I had put her to bed without one word of appreciation."

The same principle—using the kind word—is potent in all human relationships. In my boyhood in Baltimore, a new drugstore opened in the neighborhood, and old Pyke Barlow, our skilled and long-established pharmacist, was outraged. He accused his young rival of selling cheap drugs and of inexperience in compounding prescriptions. Finally the injured newcomer, contemplating a suit for slander, went to see a wise lawyer, Thomas G. Hays. "Don't make an issue of it," Hays advised. "Try kindness." Next day, when customers reported his rival's attacks, the new druggist said there must be a mistake somewhere. "Pyke Barlow," he told them, "is one of the finest pharmacists in this town. He'll mix emergency prescriptions any hour, day or night, and the care he takes with them sets an example for all of us. This neighborhood has grown—there's plenty of room for both of us. I'm taking his store as the pattern for mine."

When the older man heard these remarks—because compliments fly on the winds of gossip quite as fast as scandal— he could not wait to meet the young fellow face to face and give him some helpful advice. The feud had been wiped out by sincere and truthful praise.

Wherever human beings gather, thoughtfulness is needed. In a group conversation the kind person will help everyone to feel a part of the discussion. A friend once paid this tribute to Prime Minister Arthur James Balfour as a dinner host: "He would take the hesitating remark of a shy man and discover in it unexpected possibilities, would expand it until its author felt he had really made some contribution to human wisdom. Guests would leave convinced that they were bigger men than they had thought."

Why do most of us leave unuttered some pleasant truths that would make others happy? It would help if we remembered more often that "a rose to the living is more than sumptuous wreaths to the dead." A charming old gentleman used to drop in at an antique shop near Conway, New Hampshire, to sell merchandise. One day after he left, the antique dealer's wife said she wished they had told him how much they enjoyed his visits. The husband replied, "Next time let's tell him."

The following summer a young woman came in and introduced herself as the daughter of the salesman. Her father, she said, had died. "Since that day," says the shopowner, "whenever I think something nice about a person, I tell him. I might never have another chance."

As artists find joy in giving beauty to others, so anyone who masters the art of praising will find it blesses the giver as much as the receiver. It brings warmth and pleasure into commonplaces and turns the noisy rattle of the world into beautiful music.

Something good can be said about everyone. We have only to say it.

### THE TONIC OF PRAISE

*P*raise is not only gratifying—it is the source of fresh energy which can be measured in the laboratory.

Dr. Henry H. Goddard, in his years at the Vineland Training School in New Jersey, used the "ergograph," an instrument devised to measure fatigue. When an assistant said to a tired child at the instrument, "You're doing fine, John," the boy's energy-curve soared. Discouragement and faultfinding were found to have a measurable opposite effect.        —*Gretta Palmer*

428

# Nine Hints for Guests

## The Matter of Arriving

One looks back rather wistfully to the days when one's guests selected a train, notified their hostess of the time of its arrival and then, barring unforeseen calamity, arrived. To-day the notes of prospective guests, traveling by motor, usually read, "We expect to start on Tuesday, but if the day is too stormy we will wait until Wednesday," or "John has some business with a man in Kingston which will delay us for a couple of hours, but if the man should not be there we will come right on." It is easy to think that it does not matter when one arrives. It does matter. Too often have I declined a pleasant invitation because I expected company which did not arrive until long after the designated time. This annoyance is quite unnecessary. The telegraph and telephone are still available to be used in notifying one of any delay incurred. —*Jane A. Non*

## The Wise Gift

Weekend expenses swell enormously. It would be thoughtful if our friends would tuck a large ham or a bottle of wine into the car as they leave home instead of stopping at the corner drugstore and buying a box of stale candy. Or, as Richardson Wright suggests, an Edam cheese makes a delightful gesture. —*Arts and Decoration*

*The Borrowing Guest*

Perhaps the loudest yells come from the hosts who have had the borrowing weekender with them—the man who borrowed his host's golf sticks and warped a favorite putter out of recognition; the woman who took her hostess's new angora coat for a walk in the woods. How many hostesses have begun the summer with the prayer, "I hope our visitors will not forget this year to bring the clothes they need." You'd do well, too, to bring your own tobacco and have a stock of cigarettes.          —*Sophie Kerr and Sir John Foster Fraser*

*Loyalty*

As a houseguest you are temporarily a part of the family. This means that what is said and done in the bosom of the family is sacred to you. I can't tell you what a poor opinion I have of the guest who regales the next hostess with anecdotes of her previous visits. In other words, be loyal in accepting hospitality.          —*Florence Taft Eaton*

*Appreciation*

Any hostess could tell you how much her pleasure depends upon the guest's reactions to the new surroundings. It is not for the guest who takes it all for granted that she has worked to keep her garden neat, that she has arranged her flowers, hurried to get the curtains up or put pillows in their cool summer slips. She has expected some word of praise. Certainly she will not expect you to spend the first half hour telling her what a topping time you have just had at the Thingamys'. And omit lengthy descriptions of the desirability of living under conditions directly opposite to those of your hostess.

## In Sickness and in Health

If you think yourself in for a bout of sickness, postpone your visit. To most people it is an unpardonable offense in a houseguest to be ill. Nearly as bad, however, is the dieting visitor who must have lemon juice at seven each morning, or hot milk at bedtime or is an expert in the relative values of calories and vitamins. —*E. V. Lucas*

## Can I Do Anything to Help?

There is a new code of manners. The guest must offer to help. The hostess must be ready for the offer. If it is firmly refused, the guest must not insist. In a small kitchen, or at some crucial moment, the presence of even a beloved may drive one to fury. On the other hand, the competent hostess has a list of services which can be performed by guests without too much harassing herself. On the whole, it is worse to be known as a guest who would insist on helping than as a guest who wouldn't lift a finger. —*H. Pearl Adams*

## Independence

Discover your hostess's schedule of hours and adopt it so far as it affects her work and her rest. And then have the courage to go about alone. —*Caroline Geddes*

## Take Your Own and Begone

It is a mistake to overstay one's time. If you have been invited for a week, go on the seventh day, rain or shine. Often a hostess will urge you to stay; but many of us have learned that those extra days are likely to be an anticlimax. And, on leaving, consider that your hostess's patience may be overtaxed when guests begin to wire for the things they have left behind. —*Helen Hathaway and Corra Harris*

431

# Make the Most of Your Blunders

EMILY POST

Since even the best-mannered and best-intentioned of us are liable to accidents, a boner may be made by anyone sooner or later. As a philosophical six-year-old once put it, "Everyone spills his milk sometime."

He made this situation-saving remark at a luncheon when he himself happened to be the center of anguished attention. He was seated at his hostess's right, pink-cheeked and serious, in his Sunday blazer, when the roast chicken was brought in. "My favorite!" he cried, and spread his hands wide, knocking over his untouched glass of milk. Commotion followed, and only young Frank showed poise. One saves embarrassment all around if one has the humor and modesty to take one's boner lightly.

I found myself in a similar predicament at, of all places, the International Dinner of the Gourmet Society. It was a brilliant affair, with a menu that featured all sorts of international specialties, including my downfall—Sweden's garnet-red, syrupy lingonberry conserve. As I was raising my hand in a gesture of agreement with the man on my left, I had the misfortune to intercept a waiter who was trying to pass me a large bowl of the conserve. It upset all over the glittering white damask. I heard the waiter whisper, "Gee!" and in the next instant the president of the society was on his feet. "Ladies and gentlemen," he began, with twinkling eyes, "I have an extraordinary announcement to make to you. Our guest, Emily Post, noted authority on etiquette, has spilled the lingonberry conserve on the tablecloth!" Then, bowing in my direction, he led the applause, and my boner was made to contribute to the success of the evening.

To retrieve someone else's boner calls for quick thinking, the ability to put oneself in another's place and sometimes for ingenuity amounting to genius. There is a story of a White House reception for the diplomatic corps where a young naval aide, confronted with an awkward situation, acquitted himself handsomely. As the line moved toward the President, the wife of a Latin-American minister realized with horror that a piece of her underwear was slipping. Before she could think what to do, her feet were entangled in a web of lace-trimmed silk. Instantly the aide was at her side. With grave dignity, he bent, picked up the offending panties and disappeared. Only the couple directly behind saw what had happened. Later, as she left, a footman offered her, on a silver tray, a discreetly wrapped package.

Probably everyone has had the nightmare of going expectantly to a party to which he was not invited. The nightmare became a reality for a young lawyer and his wife the first time they were invited to dinner by the firm's senior partner. They arrived punctually at 7:45, but on Tuesday evening instead of Thursday. Their host was entertaining that evening for a celebrated English judge. The table was set for fourteen. While cocktails were being served, two more places were added. Impressed and somewhat bewildered by finding themselves in such distinguished and elderly company, the young couple did not know until they got home and looked at their invitation that they had turned up at the wrong party.

Probably the most famous boner of our time was made by

Joseph Grew, our ex-ambassador to Japan. It was saved from becoming a disaster by the quick wit of one of the persons concerned. Grew was speaking at a Red Cross luncheon in Washington, and his topic was selflessness. By way of example he pointed to General George C. Marshall, who had just returned from a grueling trip to China and was due to go off almost immediately to Europe. Nevertheless, he had taken time to come to the luncheon, although, said Grew, he had been looking forward to a "weekend in the country with Mrs. Eisenhower." When the dignitaries roared with laughter, Grew realized the slip he had made. To make matters worse, Mrs. Eisenhower was present.

As soon as he could be heard, he turned to her and said, "Please forgive me, Mrs. Eisenhower, and please apologize to the general for me."

Beaming, Mrs. Eisenhower inquired, *"Which* general, Mr. Grew?"

### A MORTIFIED MOTHER

*A* mother I know had spent the whole summer in the company of her children, thinking only of their needs. On her return to New York in the fall she went for the first time in months to an adult dinner party. To her horror she discovered that, to start conversation with the distinguished man next to her, she said automatically: "I bet I can finish my soup sooner than you can."                                          —*John Mason Brown*

*A*uthor-lecturer Emily Kimbrough was introduced by a ladies'-club chairman with: "Miss Kimbrough is our only speaker today. The rest of the program is entertainment."

—*Bennett Cerf*

# IV

"Wisdom," says the dictionary in a hopeful attempt to
define the indefinable, "is the ability to judge soundly and
deal sagaciously with facts, especially as they relate to life
and conduct." But everyone knows that wisdom is more
than that. It is a kind of glow that lights a man's world
when he has experienced much and drawn the best
from what he has experienced. It is the invisible plus sign
that all of us would like to have added to the sum of our lives.
"Common sense in an uncommon degree is what the
world calls wisdom," wrote Samuel Taylor Coleridge.
Whatever you call it, it remains the distant and difficult
goal that most of us seek through all our days.

# HOW
# TO LIVE
# WITH
# WISDOM

## Chapter 18/Insight—the Greatest Legacy

*The greatest men are usually the simplest, the most approachable and the most willing to share the insights that have made them what they are. Sometimes they have discovered these insights for themselves. Sometimes they were given them by a wise teacher or an understanding parent. In any case, fortunate is the person who is privileged to catch a spark from one of the immortals—and pass it on.*

## Mother Was Right

HELEN HAYES

"Mother, will you read this playscript?" asked my son James. "See if you think I should take the part." The script was for his first major television appearance, and the part was that of a young man with a stammer. I was not at all certain the role was right for James. To sustain a "natural" stammer for three acts is not only difficult; it tends to impose monotony on a character. I was about to say this but checked myself, realizing that I would probably have misgivings about any role he might undertake. James was nineteen and should not be protected from a test, so I remained silent and he accepted the part.

The show was to originate in Hollywood. The day I drove him to a New York airport I could not help wondering if I had prepared my son adequately for this challenge. At this last minute I wanted to buttress him. But how? Finally, at the airport gate, I said, "Jamie, just try to achieve something, and forget about success." Then he was gone. As I walked back to my car I wondered where those words had come from. They had a familiar ring. Then, with a rush of memory, I heard my mother's voice speaking them to me when I made *my* theatrical debut fifty-six years ago.

My mother, Catherine Hayes Brown, was a slight, plain woman full of quiet determination that I should become an actress. My childhood was spent in stern and sober preparation for that future. What was remarkable about her was not her insistence that I take dancing and dramatic lessons— ambitions in this direction were shared by countless other mothers—but her resolve that I remain unspoiled by it all. She believed that children should be loved and disciplined, never indulged. I was expected to work very hard at being gay and extroverted during dramatic lessons, and equally hard at being mannerly at home. I had little freedom, but I had what children most need—the feeling of security that comes only from firm guidance and clearly defined rules.

In 1909, when I was nine, Mother learned that Lew Fields, one of the great theatrical figures of the time, was casting six little girls for a musical variety called *Old Dutch*. When Mother and I arrived for a tryout we found the theater clamorous with dozens of child actresses and their mothers. Miraculously, I landed one of the six parts.

When rehearsals began, I witnessed an amazing daily routine. Every morning we children and our mothers sat on a long bench backstage, waiting for Mr. Fields. The moment he arrived, each mother would hiss in her child's ear, "Run kiss Mr. Fields"—then dig a thumb into her daughter's back, like spurs to a colt. And off the little actresses would bound with screams of glad welcome, rope curls flying, to launch themselves at Fields' neck. And each time Fields walked through that stage door I could feel my mother's hand at my back, not to spur me forward but to take hold of my dress and keep me firmly anchored to my seat. "Remember your manners," she'd warn. Even in the fierce competition of the theater she held to her principles.

After Mr. Fields had daily disentangled himself from the kissing children for about a week, he demanded of the stage manager, "Where's the quiet one? I want to talk to her." I was led forward, we had a talk, and that afternoon he rewrote the second-act curtain to include me. He played the part of a man deserted by all his friends save one—me. I came tiptoeing back onstage to climb on his lap and assure him my friendship was steadfast. In comic surprise he threw up his hands, straightened out his legs—and I slid to the floor with a bump. Curtain. Thus was my career launched.

During the run of *Old Dutch* I received considerable critical attention, but mother shielded me from the praise. I remember one evening when an actor burst into our dressing room waving a newspaper column about me and shouting congratulations. Poor fellow, he was taken by the arm and firmly escorted outside. Afterward my mother sat down to have a serious talk with me. "Helen," she said, "the most important thing in life is the knowledge that you have studied and worked hard and done the best that is in you. That's achievement. Success is being praised by others, and that's nice too, but not as important or satisfying. Always aim for achievement and forget about success."

I wish I could say that my mother's advice was immediately heeded and always remembered, but that was not the case. As I grew older I began to see my press notices and I'm afraid I became rather pleased with Helen Hayes. Indeed, achievement and success seemed to me one and the same, so there was nothing to worry about.

Ah, but there was! When I was twenty I became a leading lady in the play *Bab*. The very first time your name is up in lights—well, no thrill can ever quite match that! After the opening night I waited for the plaudits. But the first visitor to my dressing room was the fine actress Ina Claire, and what she brought me was not praise. She shook her head. "Helen, it's not right. You just haven't mastered the part."

And there behind her was my mother, saying, "You must go back to drama school. . . ."

"Back to school!" I wailed. "But I'm a *star!*"

"You won't be one long at this rate," Ina said. "You've a few hard facts to face, my child. You've reached the age where you can no longer get by on just being young and cute. From here on you have to be an *actress*." I was hurt and humiliated, but in my heart I knew she was right. I went back to school and studied for four long years, keeping up my stage roles as well. At the end of that time I had learned my trade. Success might follow or it might not, but I knew that I was an actress and that was precious knowledge.

All this was what I had tried to say to my son that last moment at the airport. I wanted him to know that success without achievement is nothing, but achievement can stand alone. Had he understood? Many opportunities had already come his way because he was the son of Charles MacArthur and Helen Hayes, and it could be so easy for him to spend the vital years drifting along on his name and his charm.

Weeks later I saw his performance on the TV screen. I thought he was outstanding—he had mastered the speech impediment; it had not mastered him. The critics also gave him high praise. His career had begun most auspiciously.

And yet I secretly wondered if it had been all too easy. Perhaps he had acquired only a trick of speech, without learning the importance of work and study. Then one afternoon some weeks later James walked into my room and said casually, "Mother, I forgot to tell you about an adventure I had when I was out in California."

"What adventure?"

"Well, that stammer worried me. I wanted to get it right, make it part of the character—not just look like an actor pretending to stammer, but really do it. So I went to special corrective classes at Stanford University for people with speech defects. It was fascinating."

I closed my eyes and breathed a sigh of thanksgiving, for I knew now that James was safe. His grandmother's advice had come down to guide the second generation.

### THE POSITIVE

*H*ow delightful is the company of generous people, who overlook trifles and keep their minds instinctively fixed on whatever is good and positive in the world about them. They have no vanity, they have no jealousy, they have no reserves, and they feed on the true and the solid wherever they find it. And, what is more, they find it everywhere.　　　*—Van Wyck Brooks*

### DRAW THE LINE

*W*e should be careful to get out of an experience only the wisdom that is in it—and stop there; lest we be like the cat that sits down on the hot stove-lid. She will never sit down on a hot stove-lid again—and that is well; but also she will never sit down on a cold one any more.　　　*—Mark Twain*

# A Lesson from Rodin

STEFAN ZWEIG

I was about twenty-five at
the time, studying and writing in Paris. Many people had
already praised my published literary pieces; some of them I
liked myself. But deep down within me I felt that I could do
better, though I could not determine where lay the fault.
Then a great man taught me a great lesson.

One evening at the home of Verhaeren, famous Belgian
writer, an elderly painter was deploring the decline in the
plastic arts. I, young and pugnacious, vehemently opposed
this view. Was there not living, and in this very town, I said,
a sculptor who took rank with Michelangelo? Would not
Rodin's "Penseur," his "Balzac," endure as long as the mar-
ble out of which he had fashioned them? When my outburst
ended, Verhaeren clapped me good-humoredly on the back.
"I am going to see Rodin tomorrow. Come along. Anyone
who admires a man so much has a right to meet him."

I was filled with delight, but when Verhaeren presented
me to the sculptor next day, I could not utter a word. While
the old friends chatted, I felt as though I were an unwanted
intruder. But the greatest men are the kindest. As we took
our leave, Rodin turned to me. "I imagine you'd like to see
one or two of my sculptures," he said. "I'm afraid I have
hardly anything here. But come and dine with me on Sunday at Meudon."

In Rodin's unpretentious country house, we sat down at a
small table to a homely meal. Soon the encouraging gaze of

his soft eyes, the simplicity of the man himself, cured my embarrassment. In his studio, a primitive structure with great windows, were finished statues, and hundreds of little plastic studies—an arm, a hand, sometimes only a finger or a knuckle; statues he had started and then abandoned. The place spoke of a lifetime of restless seeking and labor.

Rodin put on a linen smock and thereby seemed transformed into a workman. He paused before a pedestal. "This is my latest work," he said, removing wet cloths and revealing a female torso in clay. "It's quite finished, I think."

He took a step backward, this heavily built, broad-shouldered old man with the faded gray beard, to take a good look. "Yes, I think it's finished." But after a moment of scrutiny, he murmured, "Just there on the shoulder, the line is still too hard. *Excusez.* . . ."

He picked up his scalpel. The wood passed lightly over the soft clay and gave the flesh a more delicate sheen. His strong hands awakened to life; his eyes kindled. "And there . . . and there. . . ." Again he changed something. He stepped back. Then he turned the pedestal, muttering strange throaty noises. Now his eyes lighted with pleasure; now his brows knit in vexation. He kneaded bits of clay, added them to the figure, scraped some away.

This went on for half an hour, an hour. . . . He never once addressed a word to me. He was oblivious to everything but the vision of the sublimer form he wished to create. He was alone with his work, like God on the first day of the creation. At last, with a sigh of relief, he threw down his scalpel and wrapped the wet cloths round the torso with the tender solicitude of a man placing a shawl round the shoulders of his beloved. Then he turned to go, once more the heavily built old man.

Just before he reached the door, he caught sight of me. He stared. Only then did he remember, and he was visibly shocked at his discourtesy. "Pardon, Monsieur, I had quite forgotten you. But you know . . ." I took his hand and pressed it gratefully. Perhaps he had an inkling of what I felt, for he smiled and put his arm round my shoulder.

I learned more that afternoon at Meudon than in all my years at school. For ever since then I have known how all human work must be done if it is to be good and worthwhile. Nothing has ever so moved me as this realization that a man could so utterly forget time and place and the world. In that hour I grasped the secret of all art and of all earthly achievement—concentration, the rallying of all one's forces for the accomplishment of one's task, large or small; the capacity to direct one's will upon the *one* thing.

I realized then what it was I had hitherto lacked in my own work—that fervor which enables a man to forget all else but the will to perfection. A man must be capable of losing himself utterly in his task. There is—I knew it now —no other magic formula.

→ ✦ ←

## INNER HARMONY

*W*hat is all wisdom save a collection of platitudes? Take fifty of our current proverbial sayings—they are so trite, so threadbare, that we can hardly bring our lips to utter them. Nonetheless, they embody the concentrated experience of the race, and the man who orders his life according to their teaching cannot go far wrong. How easy that seems! But has anyone ever done so? Never. Has any man ever attained inner harmony by pondering the experience of others? Not since the world began. He must pass through the fire.        —*Norman Douglas*

# "More Than One Way to the Square"

ELSA SCHIAPARELLI

As my father and I were standing at the top of a church tower in a small Italian town not far from our home in Rome, I was wondering why he had brought me there. "Look down, Elsa," he said. I summoned the courage to peer down at the village below, with its central square and the complicated surrounding pattern of twisting, turning streets. "See, *carissima*," Father said gently. "There is more than one way to the square. Life is like that. If you can't reach your destination by one road, try another."

Now I understood why I was there. Earlier that day I had begged my mother to do something about the dreadful lunches my sister and I were served at school, but she had refused to take my complaint seriously. When I appealed to Father for help, he declined to intervene. Instead he brought me to this high tower to give me a vivid lesson in the value of an open, questing mind. By the time we reached home I had hatched a plan.

At school the next day, I secretly poured my luncheon soup into a bottle, brought it home and cajoled the cook into serving it to Mother at dinner. The plan worked perfectly. She swallowed one spoonful, sputtered, "The cook must have gone mad!" My sister and I quickly confessed, and Mother announced firmly that tomorrow she would plead our case at school.

In the years that followed I have often seen how resigned

acceptance of an apparent impasse can lead to failure or defeat, while an imaginative and venturesome search for an alternate route can lead to success. It was such an alternate route that led around a seeming roadblock in the path toward my first small success as a designer. I had come to Paris to storm the world of fashion, but I couldn't interest the *maisons de couture* in my sketches. Then one day I saw a most unusual sweater, worn by an American friend. It was plain in color, but its distinctive stitch, hand-knit by an Armenian woman who had brought her native peasant craft to Paris, gave it an interestingly solid look. Suddenly I envisioned a daring pattern integrated into such a sweater, and with the thought came an even more daring idea: if no *couturier* would buy my designs, why not make and sell a Schiaparelli design on my own?

I drew a bold black-and-white butterfly-bow pattern and took it to the Armenian woman. She knitted it into a sweater. The result, I thought, was sensational. To put it to the test, I wore it to a luncheon where the fashion-conscious set of Paris would be gathered. To my great pleasure, it caused something of a furor. The representative of a large New York store wanted forty, to be ready for delivery in two weeks. I accepted the order and walked out of the restaurant on a cloud.

My cloud evaporated abruptly, however, when I stood before my dark-haired, gentle-eyed source of supply. It had taken her almost a week to knit a single sweater. Forty sweaters in two weeks? Impossible! Having experienced success and failure in a single afternoon, I walked dejectedly away. Suddenly I stopped short. There *must* be another road. This stitch did require special skill, but surely there must be other Armenian women in Paris who had mastered it. I retraced my steps. My talented artisan was dubious when I outlined my plan, but helpful. We became veritable detectives on the trail of Armenians who had come to Paris when the Soviets swallowed up their country. One friend led to another until at last we tracked down twenty women who could manage the intricate stitch. And, by deadline, the first shipment from the newborn house of Schiaparelli was en route to the United States.

From that day a steady stream of clothes, accessories and perfumes flowed from headquarters I established in the famed Place Vendôme. I found the world of fashion gay and exciting, full of challenge and adventure. But overnight that world changed when the Nazis occupied Paris. I left my salon and went to America on a lecture tour which helped raise money for medical supplies for the children of the unoccupied zone of France. Then, two months later, traveling home again—another roadblock.

In the United States, the Quakers, with whom I had worked on this project, had entrusted to my care $60,000 worth of vitamins to be delivered to French children. Now, in Bermuda, the first port of call on our zigzag course to avoid enemy submarines, an overzealous customs official refused to allow the continued passage of supplies to a country half occupied by the enemy. I pointed out that vitamins are perishable, that these were to be distributed by the neutral Quakers—a guarantee that they would not fall into Nazi hands. My plea was met with a stubborn shrug of the shoulders. Unhappily I watched the stevedores unload the wooden boxes onto the pier.

As we put to sea again, I found that my mind wouldn't let go of the problem. *Was* there some other route to the square? I poured out my story of frustration to a newspaperman on board, not realizing he would be moved to cable the situation ahead. By the time we reached Lisbon, my plight had been turned into world news! There the British ambassador asked me for full details—and, in a matter of hours, channels were being cleared for the delivery of my priceless vitamins to those needy children living out the war in unoccupied France.

With war's end I returned to Paris and the house of Schiaparelli. Getting together a collection was not always easy. One summer, when I was preparing my winter showing, my sewing girls were called out on strike. Just thirteen days before the showing, I found myself left with only one tailor and the forewoman of the sewing room! Here, I thought, is the test of all tests for Father's advice. Where is the way out this time?

I pondered and fumed, certain that we would have to call off the event—or present an unfinished collection. Then at last the thought dawned on me: Why *not* present the clothes unfinished?

The tailor, forewoman, mannequins, salesgirls and I worked at fever pitch. And, exactly thirteen days later, right on schedule, the Schiaparelli showing took place. What a presentation it was! Some coats had no sleeves, others only one. Many of our creations were still in the muslin-pattern stage, with sketches and pieces of material pinned to them to show what colors and textures they would eventually have. But, in terms of orders and publicity, that unorthodox showing was a great and gratifying triumph.

Father's wise words—and I could hear his gentle voice speaking them—had guided me successfully once again, as they continue to, every year of my life. There *is* more than one way to the square—always.

# The Secret I Learned from Einstein

JEROME WEIDMAN

**W**hen I was a very young man, just beginning to make my way, I was invited to dine at the home of a distinguished New York philanthropist. After dinner our hostess led us to an enormous drawing room. Other guests were pouring in, and my eyes beheld two unnerving sights: servants were arranging small gilt chairs in long, neat rows; and up front, leaning against the wall, were musical instruments. Apparently I was in for an evening of chamber music.

I use the phrase "in for" because music meant nothing to me. I am almost tone-deaf. Only with great effort can I carry the simplest tune, and serious music was to me no more than an arrangement of noises. So I did what I always did when trapped: I sat down and when the music started I fixed my face in what I hoped was an expression of intelligent appreciation, closed my ears from the inside and submerged myself in my own completely irrelevant thoughts.

After a while, becoming aware that the people around me were applauding, I concluded it was safe to unplug my ears. At once I heard a gentle but surprisingly penetrating voice on my right. "You are fond of Bach?" the voice said.

I knew as much about Bach as I know about nuclear fission. But I did know one of the most famous faces in the world, with the renowned shock of untidy white hair and the ever-present pipe between the teeth. I was sitting next to Albert Einstein.

"Well," I said uncomfortably, and hesitated. I had been asked a casual question. All I had to do was be equally casual in my reply. But I could see from the look in my neighbor's extraordinary eyes that their owner was not merely going through the perfunctory duties of elementary politeness. Regardless of what value I placed on my part in the verbal exchange, to this man his part in it mattered very much. Above all, I could feel that this was a man to whom you did not tell a lie, however small.

"I don't know anything about Bach," I said awkwardly. "I've never heard any of his music."

A look of perplexed astonishment washed across Einstein's mobile face. "You have never heard Bach?" He made it sound as though I had said I'd never taken a bath.

"It isn't that I don't want to like Bach," I replied hastily. "It's just that I'm tone-deaf, or almost tone-deaf, and I've never really heard *anybody's* music." A look of concern came into the old man's face. "Please," he said abruptly. "You will come with me?"

He stood up and took my arm. I stood up. As he led me across that crowded room I kept my embarrassed glance fixed on the carpet. A rising murmur of puzzled speculation followed us out into the hall. Einstein paid no attention to it. Resolutely he led me upstairs. He obviously knew the house well. On the floor above he opened the door into a book-lined study, drew me in and shut the door.

"Now," he said with a small, troubled smile. "You will tell me, please, how long you have felt this way about music?"

"All my life," I said, feeling awful. "I wish you would go back downstairs and listen, Dr. Einstein. The fact that I don't enjoy it doesn't matter." He shook his head and scowled, as though I had introduced an irrelevance. "Tell me, please," he said. "Is there any kind of music that you *do* like?"

"Well," I answered, "I like songs that have words, and the kind of music where I can follow the tune."

He smiled and nodded, obviously pleased. "You can give me an example, perhaps?"

"Well," I ventured, "almost anything by Bing Crosby."

He nodded again, briskly. "Good!" He went to a corner of the room, opened a phonograph and started pulling out records. I watched him uneasily. "Ah!" he said at last.

He put a record on and in a moment the study was filled with the relaxed, lilting strains of Bing Crosby's "When the Blue of the Night Meets the Gold of the Day." Einstein beamed at me and kept time with the stem of his pipe. After three or four phrases he stopped the phonograph. "Now, tell me, please, what you have just heard?"

The simplest answer seemed to be to sing the lines. I did just that, trying desperately to stay on tune and keep my voice from cracking. The expression on Einstein's face was like the sunrise. "You see!" he cried with delight when I finished. "You *do* have an ear!"

I mumbled something about this being one of my favorite songs, something I had heard hundreds of times, so that it didn't really prove anything. "Nonsense!" said Einstein. "It proves everything! Do you remember your first arithmetic lesson in school? Suppose, at your very first contact with numbers, your teacher had ordered you to work out a problem in long division or fractions. Could you have done so?"

"No, of course not."

"Precisely!" Einstein made a triumphant wave with his pipestem. "It would have been impossible and you would have reacted in panic. You would have closed your mind to long division and fractions. As a result, because of that one small mistake by your teacher, it is possible your whole life you would be denied the beauty of long division and fractions." The pipestem went up and out in another wave. "But on your first day no teacher would be so foolish. He would start you with elementary things—then, when you had acquired skill with the simplest problems, he would lead you up to long division and to fractions.

"So it is with music." Einstein picked up the Bing Crosby record. "This simple, charming little song is like simple addition or subtraction. You have mastered it. Now we go on to something more complicated." He found another record and set it going. The golden voice of John McCormack singing "The Trumpeter" filled the room. After a few lines Einstein stopped the record.

"So!" he said. "You will sing that back to me, please?" I did—with a good deal of self-consciousness but with, for me, a surprising degree of accuracy. Einstein stared at me with a look on his face that I had seen only once before in my life: on the face of my father as he listened to me deliver the valedictory address at my high-school graduation.

"Excellent!" Einstein remarked when I finished. "Wonderful! Now this!" "This" proved to be Caruso in what was to me a completely unrecognizable fragment from *Cavalleria Rusticana*. Nevertheless, I managed to reproduce an approximation of the sounds the famous tenor had made. Einstein beamed his approval.

Caruso was followed by at least a dozen others. I could not shake my feeling of awe over the way this great man, into whose company I had been thrown by chance, was completely preoccupied by what we were doing, as though I were his sole concern.

We came at last to recordings of music without words, which I was instructed to reproduce by humming. When I reached for a high note, Einstein's mouth opened and his head went back as if to help me attain what seemed unattainable. Evidently I came close enough, for he suddenly turned off the phonograph. "Now, young man," he said, putting his arm through mine. "We are ready for Bach!"

As we returned to our seats in the drawing room, the players were tuning up for a new selection. Einstein smiled and gave me a reassuring pat on the knee. "Just allow yourself to listen," he whispered. "That is all."

It wasn't really all, of course. Without the effort he had just poured out for a total stranger I would never have heard, as I did that night for the first time in my life, Bach's "Sheep May Safely Graze." I have heard it many times since. I don't think I shall ever tire of it. Because I never listen to it alone. I am sitting beside a small, round man with a shock of untidy white hair, a dead pipe clamped between his teeth, and eyes that contain in their extraordinary warmth all the wonder of the world.

When the concert was finished I added my genuine applause to that of the others. Suddenly our hostess confronted us. "I'm so sorry, Dr. Einstein," she said with an icy glare at me, "that you missed so much of the performance."

Einstein and I came hastily to our feet. "I am sorry, too," he said. "My young friend here and I, however, were engaged in the greatest activity of which man is capable."

She looked puzzled. "Really? And what is that?"

Einstein smiled and put his arm across my shoulders. And he uttered ten words that—for at least one person who is in his endless debt—are his epitaph: "Opening up yet another fragment of the frontier of beauty."

# "Practice the Hard Parts"

JACK BENNY

I didn't really understand my father until almost the day he died. I loved and respected him, but he seemed to me a singularly unimaginative man. Meyer Kubelsky ran a small haberdashery in Waukegan, Illinois, and his life seemed circumscribed by his store, our apartment over a butcher shop and the walk between.

Each night after dinner he and Mother would sit over the cleared dining-room table, lean their elbows on the heavy lace cloth brought over from the old country and discuss the day's events. His conversation was confined to the store's receipts that day, his credit difficulties with an underwear manufacturing company, trade rumors of a radical innovation—a coat-front shirt.

On my sixth birthday something happened that should have made me realize there were hidden depths in Father. That evening he handed me a large package. Excitedly, I unwrapped it. It was a violin. "Benny, you should become a violinist," he said. "I'll hire the best teacher and maybe one day you'll be a great musician."

"Yes, Papa," I said. "Thank you very much." I was pleased with the present, but I would have preferred a bicycle or a baseball mitt. I didn't know then what this instrument represented to him. I began to take lessons and soon discovered that my fingers were strong and flexible, and that I had a good sense of rhythm and pitch. I had one major shortcoming, however: I was lazy.

Each night when Father came home he would say to me, "How is Benny Kubelsky, the violinist?"

"Fine, Papa," I'd answer.

"You practice?"

"Sure."

"That's good boy."

There came a night, however, when my glib answer did not suffice. When he asked, "You practice?" and I said, "Sure," he said, "Show me which piece."

I gestured toward the music stand. "That one."

He looked at the music sheet carefully. Then he snorted, "That's an easy piece," he said. "You learned that one a month ago."

"I practiced," I said stubbornly.

With a sigh he sat down in his chair. "I talked to your teacher, Benny. You have talent, he says, but you cheat on the lessons. All the time you play the easy pieces. You could be a great musician, but you must practice the hard parts." He thought a moment and then said, "Not only in music but in any business, some things are easy and some are hard. To be a success in anything, you must practice the hard parts. You should remember that."

"Yes, Papa," I said.

When I was sixteen years old I got a job playing in the pit orchestra at Waukegan's Barrison Theater, accompanying the vaudeville acts. After the first show Father came backstage, his face puzzled. "That is all?" he asked. "Just that jig-jig music for those *tummlers* up on the stage?"

"That's all."

He shook his head sadly. "I had hoped, maybe, a little Schumann."

"I'm sorry, Papa, but after all it is an orchestra and I'm

learning all the time." His face cleared a bit. "That is right," he acknowledged. "You keep studying. Keep practicing the hard parts."

It was a short step from the pit orchestra into a vaudeville act of my own. I started with a lady pianist named Cora Salisbury, then took the stage name of Jack Benny and teamed up with Lyman Woods for a piano-and-violin musical act. One day, on the spur of the moment, I took the violin from under my chin and told a joke. The audience laughed! The sound intoxicated me, and that laughter ended my days as a serious musician.

Music was hard work for me, even though I hadn't really been applying Father's advice. Now, I reasoned, if I could entertain an audience by just breezing out on the stage and telling a few jokes—that was for me! I became a single, a comedian. Ah, but I soon discovered that telling jokes was *not* a breeze after all. Sometimes you could throw a punch line away, other times you had to ride it hard. A pause could set up a joke—or bury it. Timing was the key. In short, there were skills to be mastered in comedy, just as there had been in music. And there were just as many hard parts to practice. The difference was that I had found a field where I really *wanted* to dig in.

During the next few years I wrote my family frequently, but I never quite had the courage to tell them I wasn't playing Schumann in concert halls. Then, inevitably, I was booked into Waukegan. I went to Father's haberdashery and thrust two passes at him. "These are for you and Mom. Tickets to the show."

"Oh . . . the show," he mumbled, not looking at me. "Your cousin Cliff saw it in Chicago last week. He said you carry the violin out on the stage, but you don't play."

"Well, no. You see, Papa, my act has changed. I tell jokes."

He thought for a moment. "Then why carry the violin?"

"It's a prop. It gets a laugh."

"The violin . . . is funny?" He stared at me incredulously. Then he smiled apologetically. "I'm sorry, Benny, but I couldn't laugh." In the years that followed I began to have success in show business. Always, though, the memory of Father's disappointment dulled it. Always there was the sound of his voice saying, "I couldn't laugh." I drove myself, determined to become a star. For every show I rehearsed and rehearsed, revised and rewrote, often to the annoyance of directors and casts who called me a perfectionist. I labored over entrances, exits, music cues, even the commercials.

Just before World War II, I made a picture with Dorothy Lamour titled *Man About Town*, and I asked the studio to hold the première in Waukegan. Father had refused to come to the vaudeville theater, but he couldn't very well ignore a big parade and dinner in my honor. I informed the grand marshal of the parade that I wanted Meyer Kubelsky to sit in the lead car between Dorothy Lamour and me.

Father was eighty then, and a widower. His frame had become lean and shrunken, but he had a blaze of white hair, and his eyes were bird-quick. He settled down in the seat and off we drove, along streets lined with cheering neighbors. Then came a civic reception, followed by a dinner at which people said nice things about me. Finally it was my turn to say something. I had worked hard over the "impromptu" talk, and it got some good laughs. From time to time I'd sneak a look at Father, but his eyes were never on me. He was watching the audience attentively.

When I delivered him home, he still made no comment. I

said good-night and he took my arm. "There is going to be a war," he announced in his thin, old voice.

"Yes," I said.

"America will crush Hitler." He fell silent, but his hand on my arm held me close. When he spoke again, his eyes were far off, on the past. "There have always been pogroms in Europe. That's why your mother and I came to the United States, so our children would never know them. It always seemed to me we owed a debt to America, and I wanted very hard to pay some of it back. Yet I was only a small haberdasher, a nothing. But when I gave my son a violin, I thought if he could make beautiful music . . ."

He sighed and gave a slight shrug of his bony old shoulders. "That was why I was so sad when you stopped playing, Benny. But now I understand. You found you were better at making people laugh, and it is good for people to laugh in these times."

"You think so?" I asked eagerly.

He nodded. "In the old country we never laughed in bad times, and during the good times we didn't laugh much either because we were thinking about the bad times. It is good to laugh, and I'm glad it's Benny Kubelsky who makes it possible."

He paused, then smiled. "And I've heard how you practice the hard parts. Is that true, Benny?"

"Yes, Papa."

"That's good boy," he said.

❖

*T*he world's foremost cellist, Pablo Casals, is eighty-nine. He was asked one day why he continued to practice four and five hours a day. Casals answered, "Because I think I am making progress."

—*Leonard Lyons*

# Six Hours with Rudyard Kipling

ARTHUR GORDON

**T**he year was 1935, the month was June, the English weather was blue and gold. The world was young, and so was I. But, driving down from Oxford in the old Sunbeam I had borrowed for the occasion, I felt my assurance deserting me.

The great man was almost a recluse now, and it was said that he did not care for Americans. Through a mutual friend I had managed to secure permission to visit him. Now as I neared the little village of Burwash, where he lived, I began to experience something like stage fright. And when I found the somber seventeenth-century house and saw my host walking down to the gate to meet me, I grew so flustered that I hardly knew whether to shake hands or turn and run.

He was so small! The crown of the floppy hat he wore was not much higher than my shoulder, and I doubt if he weighed 120 pounds. His skin was dark for an Englishman's; his mustache was almost white. His eyebrows were as thick and tangled as marsh grass, but behind the gold-rimmed glasses his eyes were as bright as a terrier's. He was sixty-nine.

He saw instantly how ill at ease I was. "Come in, come in," he said companionably, opening the gate. "I was just going to inspect my navy." He led me, speechless, to a pond at the end of the garden, and there was the "navy": a six-foot skiff with hand-cranked paddle wheels. "You can be the engine room," he said. "I'll be the passenger list."

I was so agitated that I cranked too hard. The paddle

wheel broke and there I was, marooned in the middle of a fishpond with Rudyard Kipling. He began to laugh, and so did I, and the ice was broken.

A gardener finally rescued us with a long rake. By then my host had me talking. There was something about him that drove the shyness out of you, a kind of understanding that went deeper than words and set up an instantaneous closeness. It was odd: we couldn't have been more different. He was British; I was American. He was near the end of an illustrious road; I was at the beginning of an obscure one. He had had years of ill health and pain; I was untouched by either. He knew nothing about me—there was nothing to know. I knew all about him, and so to me he was not just a fragile little man in a toy boat. He was Kim and Fuzzy Wuzzy and Gunga Din. He was Danny Deever and the Elephant's Child. He was the dawn coming up like thunder on the road to Mandalay; he was the rough laughter of the barrack room, the chatter of the bazaar and the great organ tones of "Recessional." To me he was, quite simply, a miracle, and no doubt this showed in my dazzled eyes, and he felt it.

I had had an ulterior motive in coming, of course. I wanted to meet him for himself, but I was also a puzzled and unsure young man. I had in my pocket a letter offering me a job as instructor in an American university. I didn't really want to be a teacher; I knew I didn't have the selflessness or the patience. What I wanted to be, ultimately, was a writer. But the teaching job was the only offer I had, and, at home, the dead hand of the Depression still lay heavy on the land. Should I play it safe, and say yes to the offer?

What I wanted desperately was for someone of great wisdom and experience in the field of letters to tell me what to do. But I knew this was a preposterous responsibility to thrust upon a stranger. And so I waited, hoping that some-how the heavens would open and the miracle of certainty would descend upon me.

While I waited, he talked. And, as he talked, I began to forget about my problems. He tossed words into the air, and they flashed like swords. He spoke of his friendship with Cecil Rhodes, through whose generosity I had gone to Oxford. "They say we were both imperialists," said Kipling a little grimly. "Well, maybe we were. The word is out of fashion now, and some Englishmen are weak enough to be ashamed of it. I'm not." He questioned me almost sharply about some poets of prominence: T. S. Eliot, Gertrude Stein, E. E. Cummings. I said I thought they were good. "Do you?" he said guilelessly. "Quote me a few lines."

I sat there, helpless, and he laughed. "You see," he said, "that's the trouble with verse that doesn't rhyme. But let's not be too harsh where poets are concerned. They have to live in no-man's-land, halfway between dreams and reality."

"Like Mowgli," I said impulsively, thinking of the brown-skinned boy torn between village and jungle. He gave me a look with his blue eyes. "Like most of us," he said.

He talked of ambition, of how long it took fully to master any art or craft. And of secondary ambitions: the more you had, he said, the more fully you lived. "I always wanted to build or buy a 400-ton brig," he said reflectively, "and sail her round the world. Never did. Now, I suppose, it's too late." He lit a cigarette and looked at me through the smoke. "Do the things you really want to do if you possibly can. Don't wait for circumstances to be exactly right. You'll find that they never are.

"My other unrealized ambition," he went on, "was to be an archeologist. For sheer, gem-studded romance, no other job can touch it." We returned to his study, a large square room lined with bookcases on two sides. There were his desk, his chair, an enormous wastebasket and his pens—the kind you dip in ink. At right angles to the fireplace was a small sofa. "I lie there," he said with a smile, "and wait for my daemon to tell me what to do."

"Daemon?"

He shrugged. "Intuition. Subconscious. Whatever you want to call it."

"Can you always hear him?"

"No," he said slowly. "Not always. But I learned long ago that it's best to wait until you do. When your daemon says nothing, he usually means no."

Mrs. Kipling called us to lunch, and afterward I felt I should take my leave. But Kipling would not hear of it. "I'm still full of talk," he said. "You've eaten my salt, so now you must be my audience."

So we talked. Or rather, he talked while I made super-human efforts to remember everything. He had a way of thrusting a harsh truth at you and then, in the next breath, beguiling you into a wry acceptance of it. "If you're endowed," he said at one point, "with any significant energies or talent, you may as well resign yourself to the fact that throughout your life you will be carrying coattail riders who will try to exploit you. But instead of fretting about this you'd better thank God for the qualities that attract the parasites, and not waste time trying to shake them off."

We talked of friendship; he thought young ones were best and lasted longest. "When you're young," he said, "you're not afraid to give yourself away. You offer warmth and vitality and sympathy without thinking. Later on, you begin to weigh what you give." I said, diffidently, that he was giving me a lot, and his eyes twinkled. "A fair exchange. You're giving me attention. That's a form of affection, you know."

Looking back, I think he knew that in my innocence I was eager to love everything and please everybody, and he was trying to warn me not to lose my own identity in the process. Time after time he came back to this theme. "The individual has always had to struggle to keep from being overwhelmed by the tribe. To be your own man is a hard business. If you try it, you'll be lonely often, and sometimes frightened. But no price is too high to pay for the privilege of owning yourself."

Suddenly the shadows were long on the grass. When I stood up to go, I remembered the letter in my pocket and the advice I had thought I wanted. But now there was nothing to ask. *Do the things you really want to do. . . . Don't wait for circumstances to be exactly right. . . . When your daemon says nothing, he usually means no. . . . No price is too high to pay for the privilege of owning yourself.* I knew, now, that I would refuse the teaching job and wait for my daemon to speak clearly to me.

We walked to the gate, where my host held out his hand. "Thank you," he said. "You've done me good."

The thought that I could have done anything for him was beyond my grasp. I thanked him and climbed into the old Sunbeam. I looked back once. He was still standing there in his floppy hat, a great little man who forgot his own illness and his own problems and spent a whole day trying to help a troubled and self-conscious boy from across the sea.

He had a gift for young friendships, all right. He gave me much more than advice. He gave me a little bit of himself to carry away. After all these years, I feel the warmth of it still.

## Chapter 19/How to Have a Gentle Heart

*Gentlenesss has always been admired, in man or woman. The word comes from an old French term meaning noble, or highborn (thus Chaucer used it in describing his "verray parfit gentil knight"). But by Shakespeare's time, connotations of quietness, kindness and tenderness had crept in. "Her voice was ever soft, gentle and low," says King Lear, grieving for his daughter, "an excellent thing in woman." And an excellent thing gentleness remains. In the strident and clamorous times in which we live, the person of a peaceful nature stands out among us—one who has found the secret of balancing his affections and his acts. What higher compliment can we pay than to say of a friend, "He has a gentle heart"?*

## We Are Afraid of Sentiment

ARDIS WHITMAN

G. K. Chesterton once said that the meanest fear is the fear of sentimentality. How often it robs life of grace and sweetness! Because we are afraid people will think us "soft" we hide our tenderness under a cloak of sophistication. We say "Thanks" when we mean "God bless you," and "So long" when we mean "I'll be lonely without you." Too many of us condemn true sentiment along with sentimentality; by doing so we live on the surface of things when we really want to speak and act from the heart.

463

Who does not remember moments when warm and loving words struggled for utterance and were caught back and replaced by something meaningless? We think we are sophisticated when we are casual and unsentimental, but trying to get along without sentiment is like trying to live in a world without flowers or music or the warmth of a fire.

Sentiment, says Mr. Webster, is "delicate susceptibility." Stop and think how much of what is lovely in life begins in the graces of that delicate feeling. And it is sentiment which sends us to friends and neighbors with outstretched hands so that we steadily widen the circle of the human beings we know and care about. It is sentiment, too, which makes a marriage and a family. For sentiment is to a marriage what goodwill is to a business—the intangible factor, worth more than every "practical" consideration. No marriage was ever destroyed by it; hundreds have been shattered by the matter-of-factness which is its converse.

Who is there so wise, so strong, that he does not need tenderness? "We are all lonely under the stars," wrote the late Powell Davies, minister of All Souls' Church in Washington, D. C., "all strangers and sojourners here on earth." If then we can each of us make for the other a space of warmth and comfort, is that so little a thing?

There is a story of John Carmichael, the Scottish minister, who came to his first church very young and frightened. He felt that he was doing badly and that his people were looking at him with pity and contempt. And then, when he was preparing a sermon one day, to his terror the stern elders of his Scottish kirk filed solemnly into the vestry. But they had not come to reprove him. They had come to tell him not to be afraid. "Next Sabbath before you begin to speak," they said, "we ask you to say to yourself, 'They're all loving me.'

And it will be true. From the oldest to the youngest, we will all be loving you very much."

A few years ago a group of young medical students were training in the children's ward of a large Western hospital. One particular student seemed to be especially loved by the children. They always greeted him with joy. The others could not understand why. Finally they detailed one of their number to follow him and find out what it was about him that attracted the children. The observer detected nothing until night, when the young medic made his last round. Then the great mystery was solved. He kissed every child good-night.

In the end, civilization may be more grateful to its lovers and poets than to its statesmen, for it is they who keep alive what is truly human. And it is this gentle, human, individual thing which can reach out to bind people together across the wide barriers of race and tongue and ancient resentment.

In the last years of his life, Robert Louis Stevenson lived on the island of Samoa. When his friend Mataafa, the Samoan chieftain, was put in prison by the European authorities, Stevenson, though he was then ill and tired, went again and again to visit him. Always he brought some little gift. Deeply moved by this kindness, the Samoans labored long hours to build a road for Stevenson. And when he died they buried him high on a hilltop and made a rule that no firearms should ever be used on the hill, because they wanted him to sleep in peace.

Back of nearly every humanitarian advance is somebody's sentimental motivation. When Dr. Frederick Banting, discoverer of insulin, was a small boy on a Canadian farm, he had a beloved playmate named Janie, who played hockey and baseball with him, skated and ran races and climbed trees. Then one summer Janie suddenly could do none of these things. She died, of "sugar in the blood." Frederick Banting never forgot. Later, moved to service, he went on into medicine. And today millions of diabetics live because he cared about Janie.

Only little people fear to display true sentiment. The great are at home with it as they are with the beauty and wonder of life. Ralph Waldo Emerson lovingly visited the grave of his young wife every day for two years; and though he was a great intellect, ordinary people felt at home with him. "We are simple folk here," a woman of Lexington, Massachusetts, said, after attending one of his lectures, "but we understand Mr. Emerson because he speaks directly to our hearts."

If great people are not afraid of sentiment, then why are we? I think it is because we have been brought up to live our lives in compartments. Sentiment does not belong in business, we say. It does not belong in science, or it does not belong even in our thinking about ourselves. The trouble is that the habits of mind which deprive us of the grace of sentiment grow more constricting every year. "No child is born with a really cold heart," wrote Lin Yutang. This unpleasant trait is so thoroughly an adult fault that we often confuse coldness with maturity. What a sorry comment on our wisdom that we should deliberately choke down what is warmest and best in us! And the rewards of our sophistication are meager, for lack of sentiment does not so much make us objective and wise as cold of heart, insensitive and fearful of life.

How can we keep sentiment alive, especially as we grow older? How can we restore the grace of sentiment once it

HOW TO HAVE A GENTLE HEART

seems to have fled? Our first project should be one of personal inventory. There are many hidden motivations behind our fear of sentiment. The next time you discard a warm and generous "sentimental impulse," ask yourself: "From what am I protecting myself and why? Was it honesty that impelled me, or the wish to pose as a sophisticate? Or the fear of being misunderstood?"

Once these questions have been honestly answered, we will shed some of our false fears. To be sure, it is important not to "gush," not to say what we do not mean. But it is even more important to reject shrewdness and suspicion and respond to the sweet and moving things of life. Perhaps our greatest obstacle is the lack of leisure. Sentiment cannot live in an atmosphere of clock watching and getting ahead. Nothing indeed can gentle and sweeten our lives more than the deliberate setting aside of time for those things which have no "foreseeable practical value." It is in the little things that sentiment is at its best—gestures like the unexpected letter of appreciation we write to a friend whom we saw only yesterday, the gift given to someone simply because "this reminds me of you."

Just as they have the *heart* for sentiment, great people always somehow have the time as well. Ernie Pyle, the beloved war correspondent, never was too busy or too harried with columns and deadlines to sit down and listen to the woes of a lonely soldier, or to write letters home for wounded boys. Surely the time is *there*. It is how we use it that counts.

Once in one of my father's little country pastorates, a farmer's wife died, a plain good woman who had brought up a fine family of sons and daughters. They had all grown and gone away and after she had struggled on alone for a few years with the silent, gnarled man who was her husband, she simply collapsed over the washtub one day. At the funeral, her husband did not weep; and he made no sign of grief as he plodded to the grave.

But when the ceremony was over, he lingered behind to talk to his pastor. He had a small, shabby book in his hand and now he held it out. "It's poems," he said numbly. "She liked them. Would you read one for her now? She always wanted us to read them together. But I never had time. Every day on a farm they was always things to do. But I got to thinking, nobody's doing them today, and it don't seem to matter. I guess you don't get it into your head what time's for until it's too late."

He was right. It is a matter of priorities—of what we are willing to pay for the gentle ties which we know in our hearts we would not forfeit for any amount of money. In our impersonal world, what fools we are if we do not keep alive the little candles, the lovely light of sentiment!

❖

### A DELICATE OPERATION

*T*he gracious heart is never too busy to reveal itself. I recall hearing of a lonely little boy who was devoted to a battered, one-eyed teddy bear. Hospitalized for a tonsillectomy, he took Teddy along and was holding him close when the surgeon came to his bedside and announced that it was time for the operation. A nurse moved to take the bear, but the doctor said gravely, "Leave Teddy there. He needs some attention, too."

Hours later, when the child regained consciousness, Teddy was snuggled against the pillow—and across his missing eye was the neatest bandage a skillful surgeon could devise.

*—Elizabeth Byrd*

# Forgiveness: The Saving Grace
JOHN KORD LAGEMANN

One of the great prison war-
dens of the West, Kenyon J. Scudder, often told this story
of a modern-day miracle: A friend of his happened to be
sitting in a railroad coach next to a young man who was
obviously depressed. Finally the man revealed that he was a
convict returning from a distant prison. His imprisonment
had brought shame on his family, and they had neither
visited him nor written often. He hoped, however, that this
was only because they were too poor to travel, too unedu-
cated to write. He hoped, despite the evidence, that they had
forgiven him.

To make it easy for them, however, he had written them
to put up a signal for him when the train passed their little
farm on the outskirts of town. If his family had forgiven him
they were to put up a white ribbon in the big apple tree near
the tracks. If they didn't want him back they were to do
nothing, and he would stay on the train, go West, probably
become a hobo. As the train neared his home town, his sus-
pense became so great he couldn't bear to look out the
window.

His companion changed places with him and said he would
watch for the apple tree. In a minute, he put his hand on the
young convict's arm. "There it is," he whispered, his eyes
bright with sudden tears. "It's all right. *The whole tree is
white with ribbons.*"

In that instant all the bitterness that had poisoned a life

was dispelled. "I felt as if I had witnessed a miracle," the other man said. "Perhaps I had."

There is *always* something miraculous about the way forgiveness reconciles the irreconcilable. Forgiveness, my father said, is "the saving grace." Essentially it is a religious concept: "Forgive us our trespasses as we forgive those who trespass against us." Modern psychiatry teaches, as Dr. Earl Loomis of St. Luke's Hospital in New York told me recently, that "the experience of forgiving and accepting forgiveness is a prime characteristic of the happy, creative personality." In the give-and-take of everyday existence, people are bound to rub us the wrong way occasionally, to hurt our pride, to take unfair advantage, to be thoughtless or ungrateful. The minor irritations we can usually take in stride. But the serious hurts—betrayal or rejection by someone close to us—fill us with the blind urge to return hurt for hurt. Without the saving grace of forgiveness, injury begets injury until revenge has run its course in mutual destruction.

It very nearly happened to two businessmen in a town where I once lived. P.J. and Jim were lifelong friends and partners in a manufacturing concern. Jim's daughter was engaged to P.J.'s son. One day P.J. learned that Jim had secretly made a deal to join a competing firm. The betrayal was all the more bitter because P.J. had been approached first and had indignantly refused. Vowing revenge, P.J. risked bankruptcy trying to drive Jim's new firm out of business. Jim retaliated by using political influence to raise P.J.'s property assessment. His daughter broke her engagement to P.J.'s son. At this point P.J.'s wife stepped in and said to her husband, "What did it mean when Jim sold out and you didn't? Simply that you were stronger than he. And what are you proving by taking revenge? Simply that you are weak after all!" At her invitation the two families got together and made their peace. Today the two men are friends once more, despite their keen rivalry as businessmen—and now as grandfathers, too.

Often we think of forgiveness as a form of charity. We forget that the benefits extend both ways: it is as beneficial to forgive as to be forgiven. This is not a formula, but a spirit which can bring out the best in people and illuminate every moment of living. It is one of the happy paradoxes of human behavior that the readier we are to forgive, the less we are called on to forgive. "If I had my way," a wise old lawyer said to me recently, "I'd change the marriage promise to read, 'love, honor and forgive.' It would be a healthy reminder of the power that could save many marriages."

The healing of forgiveness often takes time and effort, as one young couple found out through sad experience. John and Julia had been married two years when Julia discovered from letters in John's suitcase that he had been unfaithful to her. She kept her knowledge secret, but the longer she suppressed her resentment, the more it grew. She began to drink too much and to neglect her appearance. One day, while looking for a safety pin, John found one of his letters hidden in Julia's sewing basket. With no more reason for deception, he confessed what he had done and asked to be forgiven. Julia agreed to let bygones be bygones—but the past kept coming up in bitter quarrels, and husband and wife grew further apart.

A marriage counselor made them see their mistake: "Instead of forgiving, you have tried to pretend there was nothing to forgive." Julia had to experience all over again the hurt John had caused her. John had to relive his shame. And as Julia's resentment, so long suppressed, came pouring out, love flooded back into her life. Forgiveness created a new situation in which she could once more trust the man who had wronged her. For forgiveness does not undo what has already been done; it enables us to accept what has been done and to go on from there.

We must learn when and how to cast off our *own* mistakes and shortcomings, too. Most of us at times blunder into accidentally hurting someone. If it's merely a case of hurt feelings, we can usually straighten out the difficulty. But if a physical hurt is involved, we find it hard to forgive ourselves. For years Tom Anderson's life was blighted by the memory of his part in a fraternity escapade that resulted in the death of one of his classmates. He floundered from one job to another. He and his wife separated after six years of marriage. Then the news about Tom became a different story: his wife returned; he earned a fine position. One day he told me what had changed his life.

"I used to think, 'Nothing can undo what I have done.' The thought of my guilt would stop me in the middle of a smile or a handshake. It put a wall between Betty and me. Then I had an unexpected visit from the person I dreaded most in the world to see—the mother of the college classmate who died.

" 'Years ago,' she said, 'I found it in my heart, through prayer, to forgive you. Betty forgave you. So did your friends and employers.' She paused, and then said sternly, 'You are the one person who hasn't forgiven Tom Anderson. Who do you think you are to stand out against the people of this town and the Lord Almighty?' I looked into her eyes and found there a kind of permission to be the person I might have been if her boy had lived. For the first time in my adult life I felt worthy to love and be loved."

It is only through forgiveness of our mistakes that we gain the freedom to learn from experience. But forgiving our shortcomings doesn't mean denying that they exist. On the contrary, it means facing them honestly, realistically.

Can a person be all-forgiving and still be human? A scientist I know spent four years as a slave laborer in Germany. His parents were killed by Nazi street bullies; his younger sister and older brother were sent to the gas chambers. This is a man who has every reason to hate. Yet he is filled with a love of life that he conveys to everyone who knows him. He explained it to me the other day: "In the beginning I was filled with hatred. Then I realized that in hating I had become my own tormentor. Unless you forgive, you cannot love. And without love, life has no meaning." Forgiveness is truly the saving grace.

⇒ ◆ ⇐

### THE CANCELED NOTE

"*I* can forgive, but I cannot forget," is only another way of saying "I will not forgive." Forgiveness ought to be like a canceled note—torn in two and burned up, so that it never can be shown against one.　　　　　*—Henry Ward Beecher*

### I REMEMBER . . .

*A* friend of Clara Barton, founder of the American Red Cross, once reminded her of an especially cruel thing that had been done to her many years before. But Miss Barton seemed not to recall it.

"Don't you remember it?" her friend asked.

"No," came the reply. "I distinctly remember forgetting that."
*—Think*

# Are You a Grievance Collector?

I. A. R. WYLIE

A cross-looking little girl sat on the doorstep of a London backyard and glowered into space. It was her fourth birthday, but unfortunately her parents—preoccupied with the chronic problem of how to meet the rent—had not remembered it until late in the afternoon. All promises of atonement were coldly rejected. She went to bed, hugging her grief. Not for all the birthday presents in the world would she have admitted that she had been enjoying herself hugely. She had been the heroine of a heartrending tragedy. And she had been getting an emotional stranglehold on her parents that would cover her own transgressions for many a day.

That little girl is still vivid to me. Like far-off but still clear vibrations I can feel her sufferings. She is, I have to admit ruefully, myself. For I can still enjoy a good wrong. I can still persuade myself in self-indulgent moments that I have been snubbed, misunderstood or unappreciated. The only difference is that I am now, to some extent, wise to myself. I am also wise to my friends when, for no apparent reason, they retire to heights of gloomy aloofness.

It takes forthright character to come straight out and say, "Why didn't you ask me to your party? I'm your best friend. And I'm sore." (The answer might be so reasonable that my grievance wouldn't have a leg to stand on and would inevitably fall flat.) The majority of us go about with a lofty, frozen air of hurt which gets loftier and frostier as the offender lamentably fails to recognize and admit his offense. But sooner or later we forget what had so grievously offended us or admit privately that we were just indulging in a first-class emotional spree.

Grievance collectors can be of any age. But I think they all start young. The primary urge may spring from a temperamental inclination toward self-dramatization. In my school days I remember a teen-ager who seemed to hate everyone in her class. She rejected our probably halfhearted overtures of friendship. And at regular intervals she ran away from home. Her classmates were made to feel responsible for this: we had been unkind; we hadn't invited her to share in our games; we had even bullied her.

The victim of these injustices was an idolized only child. Too much indulgence by her parents had made her incapable of adjusting herself to the ordinary rough-and-tumble of school life and given her an unwholesome craving for adulation. She wanted to be the most popular girl in her class, but she would not take the necessary steps toward her goal. She wanted privileges handed her on a silver platter; because they were refused her on her terms, she compensated with grievances against us all.

I don't know what became of this girl, but she may well have grown into the sort of woman who was once my next-door neighbor. A low wall divided our backyards, which, in defiance of poor soil and sooty city air, we were trying to make into gardens. So we occasionally exchanged greetings and advice. I soon found that every comment I made was met with some bitter, nagging complaint. Either there was too much sun or my one tree was throwing too much shade. She had been sold inferior bulbs. Her children trampled her flower beds. One day, in exasperation, I said to her, "If ever you admitted that anything had ever gone right with you, I should fall in a dead faint." She never spoke to me again. I had tried to deprive her of her one great satisfaction—her grievance against life itself.

Sometimes a grievance collector faces up to the truth in time to avert disaster. I knew a woman who, being widowed early, had done a magnificent job of bringing up her only son. She sacrificed and worked desperately hard to give him a good education. Until his graduation she was his best friend, and he adored her. Then he grew up, began to go his own way, fell in love. She couldn't accept the natural change, but complained of her loneliness and his neglect. She criticized his girl. Everything he did to appease her only fanned the flames of her imagined grievances. Torn between his love and gratitude and his legitimate needs and aspirations, he began to dread the unhappy encounters with his mother. He quarreled with his girl. His work deteriorated. In the nick of time a friend took the mother in hand. She was intelligent enough to face the truth and bravely cut the "silver cord" which was emotionally strangling her son and herself. She left him to work out his life, free and unfettered. And she now has her reward: she is a self-sufficient, welcome and happy grandmother.

Even those of us who are not collectors often have a pet grievance which we rarely have the heart to toss out of its niche. My own pet relates to my profession. When a novel of mine comes to publication, I usually discover that my publisher has once more let me down: he hasn't advertised it the way he should. As for the critics, they haven't even read the opus, or they would have given it more respectful attention. The public is either misled by the booksellers or just plain dumb; otherwise my book would be a best seller.

Only by a great emotional effort do I bring myself to admit that the great work which cost me so dearly in time and
thought isn't, after all, so great. Once I've made that acknowledgment, some of the fever goes out of my hurt. Instead of brooding over my grievance, I try to give my mind
to writing a better book.

We all know someone who is convinced that his boss
discriminates against him, that his good work is unrewarded.
He never acknowledges to himself that he is getting just
about what his ability and energy deserve. If he gave his
work the ardent concern that he gives apparent slights and
injustices, the chances are that he wouldn't have any grievances to brood over. If we think we are not appreciated, it is
a good idea to ask ourselves the simple question, "Why?"
Some of us nourish a chronic grievance against what we call
our "luck." It seems to me that people who complain they
are "unlucky" have some defect in themselves which in some
way contributes to their misfortunes. I have come to recognize that my own bad breaks are related to the bad spots in
my capacity and character. That recognition is apt to cramp
the style of any incipient grievance.

Those who seem to have a legitimate complaint against
fate—the blind, the crippled, the apparently disinherited—
are the least likely to complain. Pushed to the wall, as it
were, they often face about and meet their disabilities as a
test of their true, inner worth. They do not unload bitterness
and resentment on innocent friends and neighbors.

There is a cure for the grievance-collecting fever. It is
quite simple and, like so many apparently simple things,
such as loving your neighbor as yourself, it is not easy to
administer. Still, when you feel your temperature rising, give
the cure a fair trial. Take yourself by the scruff of the neck,

set yourself on the witness stand and conduct a ruthless self-examination: "What, Witness, have you put in the pot that you should expect the best bits ladled out to you? What have you done for others that you should expect such tender consideration from them? Are you really as clever and as good as you think? Who and what are you that you, alone of all men, should be spared pain, neglect, injustice?"

Force yourself to look your grievances in the face. People are not normally unkind or unjust. The apparent neglect or snub can almost always be traced to inadvertence, preoccupation or just sheer clumsiness. Evaluate the grievance, then toss it out of court. Do not let it sink unresolved into your subconscious, to breed like poisonous bacteria in your emotional bloodstream.

Even if you have a genuine grievance, don't put it in a glass case and gloat over it. Believe me, you will travel with a lighter heart and surer foot without it.

### EXCUSING

*I*t is curious that our own offenses should seem so much less heinous than the offenses of others. I suppose the reason is that we know all the circumstances that have attended them and so manage to excuse in ourselves what we cannot in others.

—*W. Somerset Maugham*

### STARVATION CURE

*I*f you would cure anger, do not feed it. Say to yourself: "I used to be angry every day; then every other day; now only every third or fourth day." When you reach thirty days, offer a sacrifice of thanksgiving to the gods.          —*Epictetus*

# The Gratitude We Need

A. J. CRONIN

On a fine afternoon in New York, I took a taxi. From the driver's expression and the way he slammed in his gears, I could tell that he was upset. I asked him what was the trouble. "I've got good reason to be sore," he growled. "One of my fares left a wallet in my cab this morning. Nearly three hundred bucks in it. I spent more than an hour trying to trace the guy. Finally I found him at his hotel. He took the wallet without a word, glared at me as though I'd meant to snitch it."

"He didn't give you a reward?" I exclaimed.

"Not a cent, and me out my time and gas. But it wasn't the dough I wanted . . ." he fumbled, then exploded, "If the guy had only said something . . ."

Because his helpful, honest act had not been appreciated, that cabdriver's day was poisoned, and I knew he would think twice before rendering a similar service. The need of gratitude is something we all feel, and denial of it can do much to stifle the spirit of kindness and coöperation.

During World War II a mother in Cincinnati received a letter from her paratrooper son in which he spoke of a woman in a village in Normandy who had taken him into her home when he was wounded and hungry, and hidden him from the Germans. Later on, unhappily, the boy was killed in the Ardennes offensive. Yet the mother was moved by an irresistible intention. She saved up for two years, crossed the Atlantic and located the village referred to by her son. After exhaustive inquiries, she found the woman who had sheltered her son—the wife of an impoverished farmer— and pressed a package into her hand. It was the gold wristwatch her son had received on his graduation, the only object of real value the boy had ever possessed. The mother's act of gratitude so touched people's hearts that it has become something of a legend in and around the village. It has done more than fine speeches to foster good feeling toward Americans.

Gratitude is the art of receiving gracefully, of showing appreciation for every kindness, great and small. Most of us do not fail to show our pleasure when we receive hospitality, gifts and obvious benefits, but even here we can perfect our manner of showing gratitude by making it as personal and sincere as possible. Recently, when touring in southern Italy with my wife, I sent to a friend in Connecticut several bottles of the local vintage which had taken our fancy. It was a trifling gift, yet to our surprise, instead of the conventional letter of thanks, we received a phonograph record. When we played it, we heard our friend's voice speaking after dinner, describing how he and his guests had enjoyed the wine and thanking us for our thoughtfulness. It was pleasant to have this unusual proof that our gift had been appreciated.

Nothing hurts the one who gives so much as an offhand expression of thanks. My old friend Sir James Barrie, whose plays and books reveal such a tender and intimate knowledge of young people, used to relate this story: "One afternoon while I was engaged in a business discussion with a Scottish friend, his young daughter, aged nine, entered with some scones she had specially baked for him. Her father, obviously annoyed by the interruption, made pretense of sampling one scone, murmured a hurried, ungracious word and immediately resumed the conversation. The child, downcast and deeply wounded, went out in mortified silence. Some weeks later, when her mother asked her why she no longer made cookies, the child burst into tears, exclaiming passionately, 'I shall never bake scones again!' And," added Barrie, "throughout her life, she never did."

Gratitude is sometimes more than a personal affair. My son, studying medicine at McGill University, told me of a patient brought into hospital in Montreal whose life was saved by a blood transfusion. When he was well again he asked: "Isn't there any way I can discover the name of the donor and thank him?" He was told that names of donors are never divulged. A few weeks after his discharge he came back to give a pint of his own blood. Since then he has returned again and again for the same purpose. When a surgeon commented on this splendid record of anonymous service, he answered simply: "Someone I never knew did it for me. I'm just saying 'thanks.' "

It is a comforting thought that gratitude can be not merely a passing sentiment but a renewal which can, in some instances, persist for a lifetime. A husband who recalls appreciatively some generous or unselfish act on his wife's part, or a wife who never forgets the gifts her husband has given her, does much to keep the domestic wheels spinning smoothly. W. H. Hudson, British author and naturalist, has written: "One evening I brought home a friend to share our usual evening repast. Afterward he said to me: 'You are fortunate to have a wife who, despite ill health and children to look after, cooks such excellent meals.' That tribute opened my eyes and taught me to show gratitude for my wife's day-to-day herosim, which I had hitherto taken for granted."

It is, above all, in the little things that the grace of gratitude should be most employed. The boy who delivers our paper, the milkman, the mailman, the barber, the waitress at a restaurant, the elevator operator—all oblige us in one way or another. By showing our gratitude we make routine relationships human and render monotonous tasks more agreeable. Some years ago I was staying at the same hotel in Cannes as the English statesman Lord Grey of Fallodon. I noticed that he always warmly thanked the hotel porter who opened the door for him. One day I plucked up courage to ask him why he took the trouble to do it. "Because he is taking the trouble to do something for me," he replied.

A patient of mine in London who worked as a bus conductor once confided to me, "I get fed up with my job sometimes. People grumble, bother you, haven't got the right change for their tickets. But there's one lady on my bus morning and evening, and she always thanks me in a particularly friendly way when I take her ticket. I like to think she's speaking for all the passengers. It helps me to keep smiling."

Sometimes a tip is called for, and then it is well to remember that a smile or a personal word can mean more than the money. A friend of Paul Valéry, the celebrated French man of letters, was in the habit of taking lunch at a certain restaurant in Paris and accepting the service without comment, though he always left a generous tip. One day Valéry accompanied him to lunch. When they had finished their meal and were about to leave, Valéry smilingly thanked the waiter for his efficient service, saying that it had greatly added to the pleasure of his meal. The waiter never forgot those kindly words. Arnold Bennett had a publisher who boasted about the extraordinary efficiency of his secretary. One day Bennett said to her, "Your employer claims that you are extremely efficient. What is your secret?" "It's not my secret," the secretary replied. *"It's his."* Each time she performed a service, no matter how small, he never failed to acknowledge it. Because of that she took infinite pains with her work.

Nothing brightens life—our own and others'—so much as the spirit of thanksgiving. A doctor I knew in South Wales prescribed in certain cases of neuroses what he called his "thank-you cure." When a patient came to him discouraged, pessimistic and full of his own woes, but without any symptoms of a serious ailment, he would give this advice: "For six weeks I want you to say 'Thank you' whenever anyone does you a favor, and to show you mean it emphasize the words with a smile."

"But no one ever does me a favor," the patient might complain. Whereupon, borrowing from Scripture, the wise old doctor would reply: "Seek and you will find." Six weeks later, more often than not, the patient would return, freed of his sense of grievance against life, convinced that people had suddenly become more kind and friendly.

Some persons refrain from expressing their gratitude because they feel it will not be welcome. A patient of mine, a few weeks after his discharge from the hospital, came back to thank his nurse. "I didn't come back sooner," he explained, "because I imagined you must be bored to death with people thanking you."

"On the contrary," she replied, "I am delighted you came. Few realize how much we need encouragement and how much we are helped by those who give it."

Gratitude is something of which none of us can give too much. For on the smiles, the thanks we give, our little gestures of appreciation, our neighbors build up their philosophy of life.

# The Miracle of Sympathy

GELETT BURGESS

When I was in the hospital with a broken hip that might have crippled me for life, a friend came to see me. He was a rough chap, and he scowled as if he were going to strike me. He said, "By God, Gelett, it makes me so mad I could eat tacks."

I laughed, but he didn't. And he went on, swearing my pain and fear away. He bewailed my ill luck and the stupidity of the accident; he deplored eloquently the fate that had made this thing happen to *me*—of all people! Because he so accurately voiced my unhappiness, I forgot for a moment my distress and felt that here at last was a person who really understood my feelings. He could speak the language of pain. He was at home in the climate of sympathy. Other friends came to see me. They probably felt just as sorry for me. But somehow they didn't know, as this fellow did, how much more sympathy is than a friendly gesture or a kindly disposition. It is the miracle of exchanging places, of putting something of yourself and your own real feelings into your relations with other people.

Sympathy requires wit and intelligence and imagination; it can be acquired, as any skill is—touch-typing or playing the piano—by a desire to master it, a definite plan of study and practice. Many of us get the wrong cue from the word itself. Through misuse, sympathy has taken a gloomy sickroom meaning and come to be synonymous in our minds with pity. Instead of sympathizing, we commiserate. The

484

Spanish word *simpático* has far more the connotation we need to follow. *Simpático* suggests a quality that is congenial, winsome, pleasant.

"Sympathy with pain is not the highest form of sympathy," wrote Oscar Wilde. "Anyone can sympathize with the sufferings of a friend, but it requires a very fine nature to sympathize with a friend's success." The kind of sympathy we need to cultivate is the kind which shows a man, in the words of Sir Francis Bacon, "that his heart is no island cut off from other lands, but part of a vast continent."

Out of fear or suspicion or pride, or most often out of sheer laziness, we lock our minds from one another. But for every locked mental door, do believe it, there is a key. And if you spend the time to search, you can find it. In conversation you don't say, "How ridiculous!" You say, "I'm sorry, but I don't understand." You don't say, "It isn't so." You ask, "In just what way?" You don't have a chip on your shoulder; you have an outstretched hand.

All of us think and act on different planes, not only materially but mentally. We have different scruples and different values. How difficult for a hungry bum to apprehend the aims and interests of a millionaire, or for the latter in turn to realize the effect on one's morals of being half starved. To understand the climate of sympathy one must take these different mental planes into account. Often the most diverse characters may meet on the same plane of interest and demonstrate how the miracle of sympathy is accomplished most unexpectedly in daily life. At a ball game you get into enthusiastic conversation with some old codger you'd never think of speaking to outside the park. A mutual interest in postage stamps or model railroads can bring a bank president and a small boy together on the same plane of fellowship. Often even a pet aversion shared may bring you in touch with someone whose plane you could not reach otherwise.

But in practicing the art of sympathy it is not enough to leave these occasions to chance. Turn to the actor for a lesson. The actor re-creates himself temporarily and becomes the character he represents. And what is that but sympathy? Why can't we practice the same understanding sympathy in our contacts with others? If you look closely at us—your fellow men—you will see that we are just as interesting and peculiar and exciting as any character who ever thrilled you on the stage. If you try to understand us as the actor does the characters he plays, as every author has to understand the characters he takes from life, you will go a long way toward Grade-A sympathy.

Many people care profoundly for others yet fail to live in a true climate of sympathy. In their distress they may seem even brutal. But when a wife scolds her husband for falling ill, it is often only her anger that misfortune should overtake him that she voices. Her pity may be heartfelt, but her reproaches appear callous and unkind only because she doesn't know how to express her feeling in any other way. For sympathy is a very fine art. It cannot be practiced with mere words and gestures.

E. V. Lucas has told of a school in England where sympathy is taught. In the course of a term every child has one blind day, one lame day, one deaf day, one day when he cannot speak. The night before the blind day his eyes are bandaged. He awakes blind. He needs help and other children lead him about. Through this method he gets a grasp on what it is really like to be blind. And those who help, having been "blind" themselves, are able to guide and direct the blind with understanding. This method accomplishes what all of us need—daily training in how we can establish a sense of real fellowship with others.

Genuine sympathy is expressed not only by your words but by your eyes, your lighted face. You have to *show* that you care. You must give not a cool sliver of yourself but all. Archibald Rutledge tells of being ferried across a Southern river one day by a poor colored boatman who, on the way over, told Rutledge and his Negro companion, Prince, that his cabin had burned down the night before. "I lost everything," the boatman said. He did not complain, he merely stated a fact.

"Just before we landed," says Rutledge, "I saw Prince searching his ragged clothes, from which he extracted, finally, a nickel, the entire extent of his worldly wealth. He handed it to the boatman.

" 'This will help you start a new house,' Prince said simply." The gift was a royal one, Rutledge concludes, for with it went Prince's heart.

If a friend is telling about his accident, show genuine interest in his experience. How many exclaim immediately, "My brother had an accident just like that," (ever see one puppy snatch a bone from another and run off with it?) and turn the talk into their own channels. We need sympathy often in the common problems of the home—in the discipline of children, for example. It's absurd to hold adult standards for children's conduct. We strive to make them come up to our point of view. It isn't merely that we forget our own childhood: we forget theirs as well. Likewise we need the climate of sympathy in our day-to-day contacts with business associates and casual acquaintances. We remain strange and aloof to those with whom we work. This increases what philosopher William James calls our ancestral blindness to our fellow man.

The gift of sympathy enriches and benefits the life of the person who bestows it quite as much as it does the person who receives it. Do you think the Good Samaritan wasn't in some subtle way repaid for his oil and wine and friendly ministration? Suppose you tire yourself in behalf of a friend. Do you doubt that, although you may be slightly weakened physically, in some higher, subtler way you have gained strength?

Sympathy pays in happiness—in a fuller sense of living and in an increased realization of brotherhood. By participating in the experience of others, our own experience is amplified and we get a higher understanding. By that higher understanding we can give a fuller sympathy, and so achieve a higher understanding still. It is only by this spiritual progress upward, ever sharing, ever learning, that we can hope to learn what life really means.

> It is not wisdom to be only wise,
> And on the inward vision close the eyes,
> But it is wisdom to believe the heart.
> Columbus found a world and had no chart.
> —*George Santayana*

*T*he attributes of a great lady may still be found in the rule of the four S's: Sincerity, Simplicity, Sympathy, Serenity.
—*Emily Post*

*A* good woman inspires a man; a brilliant woman interests him; a beautiful woman fascinates him; and a sympathetic woman gets him. —*Helen Rowland*

# The Art of Understanding Other People

CLARENCE W. HALL

One of the richest hours of my life was spent recently in the company of a woman who had just turned eighty. Though she had been buffeted by what seemed more than her share of ill fortune, Miss Emily had created more happiness for herself and her neighbors than anyone else I've known. For years her humble home was a refuge for the troubled in heart. I asked the secret of her serenity and she replied: "I found it when I overcame the bad habit of judging others."

There is no other quirk of human nature so common or so malicious. All of us at one time or another have been guilty of this cruelty. And many of us have been the butt of it. A prominent minister says, "I have heard people confess to breaking every one of the Ten Commandments except the ninth: 'Thou shalt not bear false witness against thy neighbor.' Yet this is the one we all break most often." What irreparable damage has been done to innocent people by thoughtless indulgence in this vice!

When a neighbor asked Mohammed how he might make amends for falsely accusing a friend, he was told to place a goose feather on each doorstep in the village. The next day Mohammed said, "Now go and collect the feathers."

The man protested, "That's impossible—a wind blew all night, and the feathers are scattered beyond recall."

"Exactly," said Mohammed, "and so it is with the reckless words you spoke against your neighbor."

A minor poet wrote: "Stubbornness we deprecate, but firmness we condone; the former is our neighbor's trait, the latter is our own." Why do we garnish our own traits but tarnish the other fellow's?

The impulse to blame others is a defensive measure so ingrained in our nature that psychologists say if you want to find out a man's weak points, note the failings he has the quickest eye for in others. Hazen Werner tells of a woman who was forever complaining about the untidiness of her neighbor. One day she gleefully drew a friend to her window and said, "Look at those clothes on the line, gray and streaked!" The friend replied gently, "I think it's your windows, not her clothes, that are dirty."

Lack of compassion in judging others arises from not knowing what lies behind a condemned one's actions. We need to hold in our hearts the Chinese proverb: "Be not disturbed at being misunderstood; be disturbed rather at not being understanding." In our everyday relations with others we constantly risk blackening someone's reputation by failing to look beneath the surface with the eye of compassion.

"A lovely widow with three children moved into our village," a friend told me, "and in a few weeks she was the most talked-about woman in town. She was too pretty. . . . Several men had been seen visiting her. . . . She was a poor housekeeper. . . . Her children ran the streets and ate at the neighbors'. . . . She was lazy and spent most of her time lying on the sofa reading.

"One morning our pretty neighbor collapsed in the post office, and the truth soon came out. She was suffering from an incurable disease and couldn't do her housework. She sent the children away when drugs could not control her pain. 'I wanted them to think of me as always happy and gay,' she said. 'I wanted to pass away sometime alone so they would never know.'

"The men visitors were her old family doctor, the lawyer who looked after her estate, and her husband's brother. The town was kind to her for the remaining months of her life, but the gossipers never forgave themselves."

We can halt hasty judgment in its tracks by asking ourselves: Might I not be as bad, or worse, if I'd been faced with that person's troubles and temptations? The habit of judging others tends to reveal about us that unattractive character flaw, self-righteousness. Our very attitude seems to say: I *must* be good; look at all the bad I'm finding in others. Christ's classic rebuke to self-appointed judges was, "Let him who is without sin among you be the first to throw a stone." I heard of a businessman who keeps on his desk a stone with the word "First" lettered on it—a strong reminder.

A recent national poll of American clergymen brought out four simple rules for overcoming the habit of judging others.

First: Be sure you know all the facts, so that your evidence is not merely circumstantial. We share the responsibility of wrong judgments by listening to them. "Whenever I hear a sensational story at someone's expense," says R. V. C. Bodley in his book *In Search of Serenity*, "I try to gauge the mentality and motives of the raconteur, and either discard everything that has been said or try to discover what started the yarn. Do this yourself before hastily judging the subject of gossip."

Second: Remember that, however certain another's guilt may seem, there may be extenuating circumstances. Years ago the Sioux Indians had an impressive ritual. A brave who was about to visit other tribes would raise his hands and pray: "Great Spirit, help me never to judge another man until I have walked two weeks in his moccasins!"

Third: Give your habit of judging others a "reverse twist" by focusing on the graces of people, not their faults. Dr. Walter L. Moore tells of a lecturer who began his addresses by taping a square of white paper on the blackboard. Then he made a tiny black spot in the center. Asked what they saw, all present replied, "A black dot." The speaker said, "Don't any of you see a large square of white?" Develop the habit of seeing the good in people. Comment on it. Practice the art of good gossip. It is amazing how this habit of searching out the best in others enlarges our own souls. Look in your mirror when you are inclined to pronounce harsh judgment on another and see how crabbed you look. Then speak well of someone, and watch kindliness flood your face.

Fourth: Leave all judgments of others' sins to God. Arrogating to ourselves the functions of the Deity is as presumptuous as it is irreverent. "The separation of people into sheep and goats will take place only on the Last Day," Bishop Fulton J. Sheen warns. "Until then we are forbidden to make the classification."

### ALL KNEELING

Shortly after the close of the Civil War, a Negro entered a fashionable church in Richmond, Virginia, one Sunday morning at the beginning of a communion service. When the time came, he walked down the aisle and knelt at the altar. A rustle of shock and anger swept through the congregation. A distinguished layman immediately stood up, stepped forward to the altar and knelt beside his colored brother. Captured by his spirit, the congregation followed. The layman who set the example: Robert E. Lee.
                                                                —*Billy Graham*

# Chapter 20/How to Grow Old—and Not Mind It

*"Grow old along with me! The best is yet to be," sang
Robert Browning in the most famous of all observations
on aging. Perhaps he was being a bit optimistic.
Some of the attributes of youth—vitality, energy,
enthusiasm, good health—are so obviously desirable that
no one could wish to relinquish them.
But growing older does have its compensations
(growing older is much better than simply getting
older), and the wise person will take note of them and
make the most of them. One thing is certain:
Young attitudes will help you defy the years. "To be
seventy years young," said Oliver Wendell Holmes,
"is sometimes far more cheerful and hopeful
than to be forty years old."*

## The Luxury of Aging

DOROTHY THOMPSON

"There are," I remarked at a
party one evening, "distinct advantages to growing old." The
immediate reaction—"How do you know?" . . . "Why do
you even *think* of old age?"—was affectionate and even flattering. But it missed the point. I was not complaining about
growing old. I am looking *forward* to it.

Was I thinking of the often-advertised joys of retirement
in an idyllic cottage, with a modest but certain check coming
in regularly, and nothing to do but "rest"—a life without

further effort? Perish the thought! I know that as long as I live I shall write. If public and publishers cease to be interested I shall write anyhow, for when all effort ceases, one is not old—one is dead. Few people can do as much at sixty-five as they can at fifty. But nearly everybody wants to'have some place in the world of work and usefulness.

The luxury of such late efforts is that they are performed without desire for praise or fear of blame. In old age one loses the ambition for applause, recognition, popularity; the fear of an endangered career; the pain of the slight. Such ambition is a necessary spur to the young. In old age one remembers one's own youth and tries to help the young to realize the ambitions one has, oneself, abandoned. This brings a new, refreshing freedom.

Perhaps one has grandchildren. How different the relationship from that with one's own children! What mother has not known the anguish of her child's wrongdoings? The humiliation of the conference with the teacher about unsatisfactory deportment or inattention to studies? The wakeful night, listening for the return of a sixteen-year-old daughter; the light turned on for a glance at the clock—2 a.m.—3 a.m.? The years with a beloved son, going through a violent adolescence?

Always that identification: What is wrong with *me*? I don't know how to bring up my own children! It's *my* fault. But Sue and Joe grow up and are now worrying about *their* children. You, their grandmother, are not worried a bit. They will turn out all right. It's not *your* job to discipline them anyway. You can just love them. What luxury!

Then—the love of old age. The earlier turbulence is gone—the quarrels, the fears, the bitterness, the secret tears. How dear the very things that once irritated you! The comfort of John's mere presence—the turning toward him in the night and the arm he puts around you, protectively, unconsciously, without waking. The habits and tastes that are as mutual as a shared bed—the foods you both like; the people; the landscapes. The wish of neither to change the other. The being loved for exactly what one is, for better or worse; richer or poorer; in sickness or health. Not to have to explain oneself any more. It takes so *long* to get to be married! But what a luxury is a ripened marriage.

It is said contemptuously that the old enter a "second childhood." I would not say it contemptuously. As one grows older, one becomes aware, like the child, of how little one knows, and with this awareness comes again the child's sense of wonder. As one's sight dims, one seems to recover one's eyes. A beautiful day comes like a lovely gift. One suddenly notices again, as one did in childhood, the form of a leaf, the contour of a tree, the bronze blaze of the Michaelmas daisies, the stars.

As one grows older, one ceases to look for new friends, but all the dearer become the old and tested ones. One eliminates certain activities, things done most of our lives largely because others do them. A different order of priorities has formed. Do I really *want* to go to Mrs. Weaver's cocktail party? Or see the much-talked-of play—and afterward struggle for a taxi? Or would I rather stay home and finish the book I am reading?

As one grows older, mental changes occur. The mind normally reaches maturity at about sixty. Powers of judgment and discrimination increase rather than diminish, as long as the mind is actively used. One is less inclined to accept the popular intellectual idols and slogans of the times, more inclined to contemplation. Once I was eager to reform my fellow men. Now I am more concerned to understand them.

"But" (the young will make the reservation) "you face illnesses." I remember when I was afraid of developing some fell disease. Now I never think about it. I'd *like,* of course, to fall down like an old tree, when my sap has run out. But, as one grows older, one is not striving after the future and therefore not anticipating either its possible achievements or probable pains. One lives more, as children do, in the present. *Today* is precious. Life *now* is happy and fruitful. *Maybe* I will go this spring to Europe or the Middle East. But *today* I'll finish this article. Yes, there are advantages in growing old!

*To every thing there is a season, and a time for every purpose under the heaven:*

*A time to be born, and a time to die; a time to plant, and a time to pluck up that which is planted; . . .*

*He hath made every thing beautiful in his time. . . .*

—Ecclesiastes, Chapter 3

❖ ◆ ❖

"WHAT IS YOUR GLORIOUS AGE?"

*I* have found no differences that are absolute between Eastern and Western life except in the attitude toward age. In China, the first question a person asks the other on an official call is: "What is your glorious age?" If he replies apologetically that he is twenty-three or twenty-eight, the other generally comforts him by saying that he still has a glorious future, and that one day he may become old. Enthusiasm grows in proportion as the gentleman is able to report a higher and higher age, and if he is anywhere over fifty, the inquirer drops his voice in humility and respect. People actually look forward to the celebration of their fifty-first birthday.                                              —*Lin Yutang*

# How to Live Your Bonus Years

MARTIN GUMPERT, M.D.

The chances are good that you will live to a ripe old age, for medical science has added bonus years to average life expectancy. According to current statistics, if you are now 35 you can expect to reach 73; if you are 45 you will probably live to about 74; if 55, to around 76. Individual survival, however, seems to depend upon certain qualities of vitality which are not identical with actual health.

The most vital man I ever met was Edouard Herriot. Suffering from phlebitis and carrying the additional burden of weighing 231 pounds, he nevertheless presided ably over the French National Assembly at the age of eighty-one, vigorously headed his political party, was the tireless mayor of the large city of Lyon. He wrote an autobiography and a book on the sculptor Rodin.

Many elderly persons lead efficient and productive lives who should have been dead long ago—according to medical rules. But disease, by forcing the body to strengthen its defenses, may even contribute to increased vitality. Evidence points to the fact that there is some mysterious force that keeps some people living on, far beyond their normal life expectancy. We all know of people who seem to stay alive simply because they want to—persons in a critical condition who refuse to give up and by willpower alone pull themselves back to life. In a less dramatic way, day by day, each of us determines his life-span.

Do you look forward to pastimes or projects of learning? Do you enjoy simple activities such as eating, talking, playing nonstrenuous games, walking? Then you are probably going to live a long time. But if you suffer from boredom you are being attacked by man's deadliest disease—one that aggravates every ailment and weakens the will to live.

To withstand the assaults of age we need to develop the right emotional attitudes. My case histories abound with instances of people who have taken a spurt toward long life by directing their capabilities into new and constructive channels. Frank answers to the following questions may give an insight into your own situation.

*Are you continually widening your interests?* A sixty-five-year-old retired teacher of Spanish had built up a neurosis over the gnawing fear that her life was nearing its end. Her doctor ordered her to take an inexpensive tour of Mexico "for the climate." She saw places she had talked about all her life, and for the first time chatted with natives in Spanish. The following year she went to Mexico again. Now she conducts tours to Latin America—and is completely happy.

Not all of us can go to a foreign country but, long before old age, everyone can begin to look forward to learning new things, to pursuing pastimes and developing skills. You can expose yourself to new interests in many ways, such as browsing through library shelves, attending lectures, joining in civic or welfare activities. Inquiry into things that are new to you quickens the mind and heart. Luther Burbank wrote in *Harvest of the Years* that he could not pass a strange plant or a carpenter using a new tool without stopping to ask, "What is this? How does it work?" "I'm almost seventy-seven," he once remarked, "but I'm as inquisitive as I was at eight."

*Are you eager to continue your life?* Aging is a process in which most people do more things for the last time, and fewer for the first time. Reverse that and you have an antidote for growing old. I knew a woman to whom a friend said wistfully, "I wish I could grow old gracefully, like you."

"My dear," she answered, smiling, "you don't *grow* old. When you cease to grow, you *are* old."

After retiring at sixty-five as a Stanford University professor, Dr. Lillian J. Martin founded one of the first child guidance clinics in this country and opened an Old Age Center in San Francisco. In her seventies she learned a foreign language and typing. At eighty-nine she managed a profitable 64-acre farm with four sixty-year-old helpers. She lived on because she had interesting things to do.

*Are you affectionate?* Love is one of the most powerful stimulants to a longer, happier life. A utility-company employe was lonely and depressed for months after his wife's death. Finally his children persuaded him to attend his fiftieth class reunion. There he renewed acquaintance with a schoolmate who had been widowed. Not long afterward they were married. At eighty he looked forward to many years in the companionship of a twilight-of-life marriage.

Human warmth is, of course, not limited to romantic love: devotion to your fellow man serves equally well. A retired machinist, puttering in his basement workshop in a crowded section of a big city, looked up one afternoon to see a boy watching through the window. He invited the youngster in and let him try his hand at guiding a piece of wood on the shaping machine. Next afternoon the boy was back with two friends. Today the machinist is a pal to twenty kids to whom he teaches the handling of saw, drill and lathe. The faculty of being genuinely concerned about others enriches anyone's life. The earlier one acquires it, the better fortified he will be for his later years.

*Do you let your emotions rule you?* Giving in to anger is one of our unhealthiest habits. From purely medical considerations, I strongly advise avoiding heated arguments and strong emotional conflicts. Some years ago a medical man I know had a severe coronary thrombosis. Close to death, he discovered real values in contrast to petty ones. Now he is unperturbed at such annoyances as being shouted at while driving, or at not receiving credit for work done on a community project—"Such things are just too trivial." Changing his attitude released emotional tensions and doubtless lengthened his life.

*Do you worry?* Two women patients of mine live in almost identically meager financial circumstances. One adjusted herself to her budget and lives happily within it; the other frets continually, and because she feels her money problem gigantic, it is. Worry is just a bad emotional habit; like any habit it can be broken if you make sufficient effort.

*Do you make friends easily?* As you grow older you must accustom yourself to the loss of lifelong friends and be prepared to make others. To do so, you must have something to offer. You don't need money; offer whatever is pleasant and useful in you. The woman who teaches her young friends to play a better game of bridge or grow a bigger dahlia, or who simply listens well, attracts friends. Chances are that you, too, can offer skills or wisdom, the rewards of age. If you are a specialist in even one small area of knowledge, you are likely to be in demand.

Retirement hung heavily over a former salesman until a friend asked him to give the clerks in his store some tips on how to make more sales. He did it so well that other storeowners asked his help. Winning friends among the young people he instructed gave him new enthusiasm for life.

*Do you have religious faith?* Religious counselors agree that the real comfort of faith comes but faintly to elderly persons who have previously neglected it. How much richer life is for those whose faith helps them constantly during the stresses and trials of everyday living.

Howard Whitman, in *A Reporter in Search of God*, writes that a farm wife once told him, "I don't expect that because I have faith in God no misfortune or tragedies will come my way."

"What *do* you expect?" she was asked.

"I expect that whatever comes, I will be able to accept it," she replied.

The person who has faith in God throughout his life is likely to have faith in others and, most important of all, in himself. Faith in ourselves gives us peace and the assurance that we will overcome disaster and conflict and reach the goals of our life in spite of what may come.

If our day were suddenly increased from twenty-four to thirty-six hours, it is likely that most of us would devote the extra twelve hours to interests and activities for which we formerly had no time. Something like this has happened to our life-span. To utilize our additional years fully, we must develop the attitudes that give life value.

### THE TIME TO LEARN

*W*hen I was young I was amazed at Plutarch's statement that the elder Cato began at eighty to learn Greek. I am amazed no longer. Old age is ready to undertake tasks youth shirked because they would take too long.     —*W. Somerset Maugham*

# A Doctor's View of Advancing Age

MAX JACOBSON, M.D.

**I**f you are under forty, your first impulse will be to put this article down and say, "I'll worry about all that when it catches up with me." The attitude is an impractical self-delusion. A refusal to accept the inevitability of advancing years will only accentuate your personal crisis later. And if you are over forty, you should certainly inform yourself on what to anticipate for the duration of your life-span.

Old age is not a specialized problem but a common one. Now that science can so greatly lengthen our life expectancy, each of us holds within himself a core of fear— a fear of becoming senile, of becoming useless and economically helpless. Yet, despite an avalanche of books, articles and political propaganda, few up-to-date solutions have been proposed. Let us examine some of the ways in which we can proceed to a solution. The first change necessary is to stop emphasizing the words "old age," and to substitute "advancing age." This may sound like quibbling—but actually, when does one begin to be "old"? We are truly old when we begin to suffer the disabilities of old age, and not before. As a life-insurance journal suggested recently, the arterial not the chronologic age is the deciding factor.

The diseases which occur more frequently in advanced years are chiefly degenerative diseases: hardening of the arteries; heart disease; malignant growths such as cancer; strokes; prostate trouble; senility. Degeneration means that the life of the cell actually ebbs out. All division slows down and a dying process begins. Elastic tissue loses snap. Those tissues supplying the higher functions are gradually replaced with less valuable, mostly fatty material.

Let's select one example: sclerosis of the blood vessels—an affliction arising from fatty degeneration of the elastic wall tissues of the blood vessels. Faulty fat digestion is the result of an impaired liver function. The liver digests sugar, fat and protein, building them into body tissue. At the same time it is a storage place for fats, proteins and glycogens. Any impairment of the liver, then, has two bad results: The rebuilding function suffers, and the body is deprived of a valuable storage place.

What has science to offer this temperamental and overworked organ? It has found that amino acids help the liver digest fat and rehabilitate its own cells.

A typical case history from my files will give some idea of this treatment in action. Mr. Bauer was seventy, his wife sixty-seven. During the war they ran a large farm despite lack of help. After the war, the emotional goad removed, farming became an unbearable strain. They considered retiring, and when they came to me they complained of excessive fatigue. I put them on an adequate diet and gave them medication that combined vitamins with amino acids. Within two weeks a gratifying improvement was evident in both of them. First the wife, then the husband, reported their energy had returned. They decided to continue working their farm, a job they had enjoyed for so many years. Instead of retiring to an empty old age, they are still active participants in their community life. I accomplished no miracle in this case. The medications I used are available to every doctor, and are increasingly used.

But tissue breakdowns are not caused by nutritional mistakes alone but by psychological factors as well. The most widely spread misconception on the subject of the aged is the most pernicious: namely, that we are humane and intelligent when we provide them with space in an old-age home, or a pension scaled just above survival level. This puts a potentially valuable social group into an isolated status. The natural fact of growing old has removed the elderly from the mainstream of life and relegated them to social limbo. If they have put something aside during their middle years, the green benches of St. Petersburg, Florida, allow them to decay in style—but the same heartbreaking divorce from life takes place.

Geriatricians (specialists in the diseases of the aged) have been interested in an experiment made at the famous Pavlov Institute. Dogs leading a normal canine family life were placed in solitary confinement, separated by glass windows from other dogs. The isolated dogs not only became maladjusted after a short time but often died prematurely. These deaths were due to changes in their blood vessels which closely resembled arteriosclerosis. We may assume that human beings are even more strongly affected than dogs by such conditioning.

Inevitably, many old people will unconsciously dramatize their dilemma in order to reestablish their fading importance. The outbursts, the childish irresponsibility, the forgetfulness are the results of faulty adjustment and fear. The continued strain of worrying about their future may in some cases actually lead to arteriosclerosis, loss of bowel function and the other tragic symptoms of decay.

The assumption that to be old is to be either senile or incapacitated is basically inaccurate. To alter the current way of thinking, a revolutionary attitude should be adopted. But it should be a revolution of the old instead of the young. And the change should begin as an *interior* revolution. Refusing to be discarded is the first step for the aging to take; actually, an intelligent insistence on their rights will stimulate the elderly rather than exhaust them.

Science makes it possible for aging persons to forestall premature decay. They must use the results of this science to maintain a physical standard that will insure a continuing mental efficiency. For some reason, persons on the seedy side of fifty rarely take the precautions that will insure them a vigorous old age. Roughly 5 percent of my patients come for preventive therapy; 95 percent show up only for repairs, when the body functions are seriously upset. Proper treatment *in advance* might have prevented these crises. Some of the recommendations below will be familiar to the reader; others have been evolved out of personal experience.

1. A respect for advancing age must be restored to our thinking. Such a respect will bring the aged back into the family unit.

2. Automatic age brackets must be eliminated in industrial and civil organizations. No one should be retired at sixty-five unless he so chooses or unless it is medically necessary. Workers should be transferred from strenuous jobs to positions where their experience makes them valuable assets. With the fear of a useless retirement removed, wage earners will feel secure in their work, instead of becoming prey to neuroses and fatigue lags as their age advances.

3. Old-age homes, family-care programs and decentralized villages catering to the senile are necessary institutions. But we must be certain that those relegated to such places have not been committed because of harmless little eccentricities

which could have been avoided by proper medication. Otherwise we become guilty of a social waste which predicates tragic repercussions.

4. The "retirement dream" should be kept realistic. It is a sweet one, but it implies that work is a disagreeable duty. Too many of our citizens attain the dream only to have their decay accelerated by purposeless activity.

If any or all of these propositions are feasible, the contemporary chaos will be considerably reduced. Family units are the keystone to Western civilization. They are undeniably disintegrating. Combined action by industry, government, science and the public can and must remedy the most obvious cause of that disintegration: the old-age problem.

❖ ✦ ❖

## WHAT NEXT?

*O*ne of the unanswered questions of life is: *"When* is old age?" My answer would be: "When we have ceased to wonder." Harold Nicolson, English biographer and historian, says that his grandmother lived in a state of "incandescent amazement." She not only remembered the first steam packet but lived to hear of M. Blériot flying the Channel. The amazement with which this remarkable old lady exulted in the surprises of our astonishing world kept her young. If the young people around her became blasé, she would rap her ebony stick and demand that they greet the surprises of this Jules Verne world with something of the excitement which she felt herself. She lived to be ninety-nine.

Those who wonder are always exultantly asking, "What next?" They have a childlike eagerness. Nor will they be disappointed at death. To them, death itself may seem the most exciting adventure of all.                              —*W. E. Sangster*

# I Am Fifty—and It Doesn't Hurt!

DOROTHY CANFIELD

**D**o you remember the little girl who asked if it didn't feel queer for a few days after you grew up? I think of her when people ask me how I feel about being middle-aged. The answer is, "You don't feel anything sensational. You just go on living."

Actually, being middle-aged is a nice change from being young. Honestly, I mean it. One of the traits of human nature about which there is unanimity of opinion is its love for change. Back at the turn of the century, I was anything but superior to the pleasures of young ladyhood. I "adored" opening the long pasteboard box which meant a bouquet from an admirer. I loved maple-nut sundaes to distraction, and there never was a girl, I am sure, who more heartily delighted in West Point hops. But suppose that by some miracle I should now look young again, and should be invited to dance once a week for the rest of this semester at West Point. I'd rush into it as enthusiastically as I should carry out a sentence to play tag for an hour a day.

I still enjoy playing tennis, riding horseback, skating and mountain climbing. It is true I don't engage in these sports as ferociously as I did at twenty, and for a good reason. I don't need to, or care to. At twenty I was like nearly everybody else of that age, frightfully uncertain and frightfully anxious to prove my worth to myself in the only way youth knows—by beating somebody at something.

Here is one of the pleasures of middle age of which nobody breathes a word to you beforehand: the deliciousness of outgrowing that neuralgia of youthful pain at being surpassed in anything! For moderately successful, healthy-minded older people have found an excuse for existence in some job that the world seems to want done.

My gentle old uncle, when the cat had settled down to sleep in his favorite soft chair, used always to leave her there till she woke up and went away. When we remonstrated with him, he answered, "A cat has so few pleasures compared with those open to me." I have something of the same feeling about the boy who beats me in a race on the ice. He does *so* enjoy beating somebody. And there is so much else I can enjoy of which he doesn't dream. For one thing, I can consciously, disinterestedly, relish the physical delights of the exercise, the miraculous knife-edge poise, the gliding speed, the tingling air, the beauties of the frosty trees. I enjoy these things far more than he does, or than I did at his age, freed as I am now from his single reason for being on the ice: either beating, or learning to beat, somebody else.

Understand me, I do not make the claim that I enjoy my corner of the pond *more* than that magnificent, long-legged kid out there, racing from one end of the hockey field to the other in eagle-like swoops. He is enjoying a wild, physical intoxication which gets considerably dimmed by the years. But as far as that goes, his physical intoxication is not so wild as that of a group of quite little children who, with faces of pure joy, are merely scuffling along on a slide at one end of the pond. The point is that we are all, in different ways suitable to our ages, having a glorious time, and that the young couple who swing dreamily around and around, hands clasped, are not the only ones to enjoy the ice.

I used skating, of course, as a convenient symbol for the

way life is taken at different ages. Now, you will note that of all those age groups on the ice, I, being the oldest, am the only one who has any notion that *everybody* is having a good time. Although the fourteen-year-old kid may be amused by "the kids without even any skates," he is not sorry for them, because he remembers that ages ago he used to enjoy sliding. But it is real pity he feels for the poor fish who's got tied up with a girl and has to steer her around. And probably his pity is even greater for the gray-haired woman who seems to think that cutting circles is skating. The young couple know, of course, that the hockey-playing boys who have not yet found their mates are having a childish good time, but they are convinced that it must be awful to be old, your first love far behind you.

The trouble, you see, is that they don't trust the future. They are afraid to. They are so impressed with the present that what they can't get now, this instant, seems lost forever.

Is it true, as people say, that youth is naturally happier than age because the one lives on hopes, the other on memories, and that while you can change hopes to suit yourself, memories persist in staying more or less the way they actually happened? Stuff and nonsense! Hope's always left, no matter what afflictions have come out of Pandora's box. It's not a question of age. From cradle to grave we say, "I know I used to be a dub, but I've learned my mistakes."

The fear of approaching old age? Having arrived at an age which seemed to me at twenty as forlorn as eighty does to me now, and perceiving that a change of tastes and desire has gone along with a change in age, I cannot help guessing that if I continue to yield myself naturally to the rhythm of the years, I shall find the inner timetable making as close and accurate a connection for me then as now.

## Chapter 21/Toward the Far Country

*Sooner or later, the journey through life ends for each*
*of us. It is easy to see why this must be so. As a wise*
*physician once wrote, "Without the device of death,*
*nature's creative work would have been brought to an*
*end by sheer accumulation of all her past work in her*
*studio. . . . We must accept, therefore,*
*the fact that death is necessary for the Divine*
*Artist's work and . . . be content."*
*With wisdom and grace, we can learn to meet*
*the inevitable. An understanding of grief,*
*a respect for solemn occasions, a fearless knowledge of*
*death can be a part of our lives. Faith in*
*immortality belongs to most of us, whether we are*
*scientists or physicians or laymen.*

## A Bridge for Passing
**Condensed from the Book**
PEARL S. BUCK

I opened my eyes in a Tokyo hotel at five o'clock in the morning, wide awake, totally aware. I had been summoned in some way—not by a voice, or at least I did not hear a voice. I lay motionless in my bed, listening, waiting, convinced that someone was trying to reach me. At quarter to six the telephone rang. I knew immediately what the message would be. "Overseas call, please," a voice said. "From the United States. Pennsylvania."

My daughter's voice came to me over the thousands of miles of land and sea. "Mother?"

"Yes, darling."

"Mother, I have to tell you something." The young voice faltered, then went on resolutely. "Mother, Dad left us this morning in his sleep."

"I thought that was what you had to tell me."

"How did you know?"

"I just—knew."

"Will you come home?"

"Today—on the first jet."

We exchanged the few private words, heart spoke to heart, and I hung up. The day I had dreaded was come. The final loneliness was here.

For a moment there was the longing—oh, that I had never left, oh, that I could have been there when he went. I put it aside. I had discussed this very moment thoroughly with our physician. Some weeks before, I had been invited to go to Japan to work on the filming of my book *The Big Wave*. But could I, should I, leave at such a time? "Go," the doctor said. "It may be many years away, it may be tomorrow. You must continue to live exactly as you have lived. Whenever it comes, you can do nothing to prevent it."

In the seven preceding years, following his first stroke, the man I had known so well, the gentle husband, the wise companion, had become someone else, a trusting child, a helpless infant. Though he continued lovable, patient, as always, slowly there ceased to be communication. Language was lost, eyesight failed, the brain lived only in sleep.

The jet took off from Tokyo at midnight. All day friends had been with me, and their kindness and affection wrapped me around. Now, for the first time since morning, I was alone. Sorrow cannot be assuaged. But years ago I learned the technique of acceptance. The first step is simply to yield oneself to the situation. It is a process of the spirit, but it begins with the body. There, belted into my seat, I consciously yielded my body, muscle by muscle, bone by bone. I ceased to resist; I ceased to struggle. Let come what would, I could do nothing to change what had already happened.

I remembered the day I met Richard Walsh, twenty-five years ago, in Montreal. He was my publisher, and I had just come from China. Although I knew him somewhat through his letters—he wrote the most charming and articulate letters I had ever read—I saw him for the first time there in the Montreal station, sunbrowned and with eyes of a startling blue. I was speechless with shyness, but he was completely at ease as he always was, everywhere and with anyone.

How incredible, I thought now, that for the whole first half of my life I didn't know he existed. We were past our first youth when we met, both resigned, we thought, to unsatisfactory marriages, and both well known in our fields. I firmly refused him in New York, Stockholm, London, Paris and Venice, and then sailed for home in China. But the next spring back in New York was my undoing, and we were married there in June.

I looked at my watch. It was three o'clock in the morning. My mind, unable as yet to face the profound change in my own life, explored the meaning of eternity. If death is only a change, then what is the change? He knew, and I did not. At a moment in his sleep he had died. He was at one instant alive and at the next he was dead. How quickly does the change come?

*Where are you? Do you know I am here high above the earth? Are you here, too? Do you live beyond the barriers of airless space?* I pressed the question into the night, and then withdrew it in a panic. I really do not want to know the truth. If he exists, it will make the waiting alone intolerable. And I cannot bear to know that he does not exist. Let me wait until I find out for myself. If I am right, if we are to be instead of cease to be, my first words to him as I step over will be spoken in love and triumph. "Here I am. Now we know."

The light of dawn that permeates a jet aircraft is wonderfully beautiful. We were flying into the sunrise, into a fountain of light rising over the curved edge of the globe. A spick-and-span hostess was ready with fruit juice. There is a comfort at once superficial and organic in the necessities of eating and drinking, of washing and clothing the body. It seemed to me when I faced the mirror that never again would I care about how I looked, since I would never again hear his words of appreciation and praise. (Of course I did not for a moment believe I was at all what he said I was. As a woman, nevertheless, I liked to hear it.)

As usual, I dressed my long hair. That hair was my bane! When I was small, my mother made yellow curls and then braids. I longed to be grown up and cut it all off. I did cut it off, as soon as I could, but then I let it grow again because he wanted it long. Now I could cut it again, since he would never see it—and then I knew at the same moment that I never would. Everyone in the plane was now awake. Sooner or later we would speak. Yet I knew that no matter how many people surrounded me, within me would be, from now on, a permanent solitude. Traveling had always been a gay business for us. He was a delightful traveling companion. He always knew what there was to see and where we should go, and I went with him in careless happiness.

What fun it had been, how satisfying the years together. In New York we adopted our first two babies and began our life as parents. He had always wanted a big family, and how we enjoyed the gradual accumulation of three sons and six daughters—the youngest the gentle half-American daughter who had come to us from Japan eleven years before. Our dream to live in the country soon became a necessity. We moved to a farmhouse in Pennsylvania, where he taught the children tennis and baseball and golf, swimming and riding. Leaning my head back against the seat, I remembered it all, smiling to myself. A strange peace, warm and live, seemed to flow through me.

The voice on the intercom announced that we would begin the descent for New York. Now friends had to be faced again, and family—and for a moment I dreaded it. It had been easier here in the shelter of those who knew nothing about my journey. In the airport two of my grown daughters waited. I looked into each face, and whatever I had dreaded melted away. It was good to be with those who loved me and whom I loved. On the way to our home in Pennsylvania, I listened as my married daughter talked. He had been the same until two days before. She had come from her house across the brook with her three little children on her morning visit. The children climbed on his bed and kissed him. They went away again, and when she returned a little later he was gone. It was so simple a story that I could bear to hear it told.

The car drove up the familiar driveway at last. The kind people who help me in house and offices and grounds were waiting—and all of our children, gathered from everywhere. He lay on a couch, his eyes closed and his hands loosely at his sides. He wore his tweed suit, the one he liked, a blue-gray, and the dark-blue tie I had given him last Christmas. His hair, only partly white, was brushed back from his forehead. His face was young again, the lines gone, the lips tranquil. I touched his hand that had always been warm and quick to respond. The flesh was cold. The next day in the library, among the books he loved, we had the simple service that the children had planned. Then came the long drive to the cemetery in New York, where his parents are buried.

I pause here, remembering. And what do I remember? This: In the midst of that sorrowful ride, every moment of it such concentrated agony that my very bones ached, I chanced to see from the rear window the long, slow procession of black cars. Yes, but at the very end were two station wagons, and they were fire-engine red. I recognized them immediately. One belonged to my second son, and one to my equally youthful son-in-law. I had winced when they brought them to show me proudly before I went to Japan, and heroically I had admired them. Now here they were, bright and alive in the morning sun. I knew why—and my heart dissolved again in tears and laughter. What a shame, what a pity, that he could not see those two shining red station wagons, doing him honor upon this occasion—and how he would have laughed! *Why do I say "would have"? It is possible that somewhere you were laughing. It is still possible. I maintain my stand, until—*

Our minister spoke the final words of peace and acceptance. My sons and my stepson stood beside me. My daughters walked with me back to the car. Oh, that silent last moment when he must be left behind, and the arrival at the house, now empty! Of these I cannot speak. To other women in like circumstances I can only say that there is no escape from such moments. They must be lived through, not once but many times. "It does not get better," a widowed friend had warned me. "It gets worse." I come back to my home as to a haven whenever I leave it, but it is not the same, and it will never be the same. It is not true that one never walks alone.

After a few weeks I set myself to writing. But it would not do. My mind, lost in thought and memory and question, simply would not busy itself with the creation of other people's lives. I needed work that I had to do, work compelling me to rise early and go to an appointed place. I decided to go back to Japan, to the fishing village, Kitsu, to rejoin the company filming my book.

Our days in Kitsu fell into a pattern. For an hour each morning, while the scenes to be filmed that day were being prepared, there was no need of me. It was then I walked along the beach, past the stone breakwater to the foot of a steep hill. Stone steps led up this hill, and at the top was a little empty stone temple, once a Shinto shrine. A low wall surrounded it, and the view was sea and mountains and sky.

I found my own niche behind the shrine. At the edge of the high cliff was a hollow. There I went every morning and, held in this hollow as though in his arms, I lay at rest. He and I had never been here together. Nor was there communication between us now—I cannot pretend that I heard his voice or even was aware of his presence. What did take place gradually as the days passed was a profound insurge of peace. The warm rock bed in which I lay, the wind rising cool from the sea, the sky intensely blue and the drifting white clouds, the gnarled pine tree bent above my head—of these I became a part. Then I discovered that something of each day's peace was left as residue for the night. Gradually I became stronger. I do not know how this healing came about. I did not pray, if prayer be words or pleading or searching. If the process must be explained, it was simply that I gave myself wholly to a universe which I do not understand but which I know is vast and beautiful beyond my comprehension.

One night when I opened my window I sent a secret message into space, with love. Wherever he is, he heard, or so I dreamed, for a great comfort descended upon my heart.

### THE ONE WHO GOES BEFORE

*A* man is not completely born until he is dead. Why then should we grieve that a new child is born among the immortals? We are spirits. That bodies should be lent us, while they can afford us pleasure, assist us in acquiring knowledge or in doing good to our fellow creatures, is a kind and benevolent act of God. When they become unfit for these purposes and afford us pain instead of pleasure, instead of an aid become an encumbrance, it is equally kind and benevolent that a way is provided by which we may get rid of them. Death is that way.

Our friend and we were invited abroad on a party of pleasure which is to last forever. His chair was ready first and he is gone before us. We could not all conveniently start together; and why should you and I be grieved at this, since we are soon to follow and know where to find him.          —*Benjamin Franklin*

### LOSS OF A FRIEND

*W*ith every friend I love who has been taken into the brown bosom of the earth a part of me has been buried there; but their contribution to my happiness, strength and understanding remains to sustain me in an altered world.          —*Helen Keller*

# Grief's Slow Wisdom
*Condensed from the book: Peace of Mind*

JOSHUA LOTH LIEBMAN

**R**eligion throughout the ages has sought to give men both comfort and courage in the presence of death. It attempts to persuade the mind and the heart to spiritual resignation. Man needs that religious approach but he likewise needs an emotional strategy which will enable him to manage bereavement creatively rather than destructively.

There has been widespread confusion as to the right approach. Should emotion be expressed or repressed? Should sorrow be verbalized or concealed? Should children be exposed to grief or be completely insulated? Answers to these questions are indispensable because unwise attitudes toward grief are the source of many physical and mental ills.

Usually when a person suffers the loss of a beloved one, the immediate result is a terrible inner numbness and a loss of equilibrium, of interest in life. There may be bodily symptoms of pain and distress, continual preoccupation with the image of the deceased, or deep feelings of guilt. The world is a dreary wasteland. Grief, loneliness, despair possess his soul. Almost every person who suffers a severe loss should expect these reactions in greater or less degree, possibly for a period of several weeks or months. If they are understood as temporary manifestations, if the bereaved person is wise enough to accept them rather than to suppress them, the danger of future neuroses may be averted.

Dr. Erich Lindemann, in his work with grief patients at the Massachusetts General Hospital, found many who developed severe depressions and even physical diseases years after the loss of the loved one because they had denied grief at the time. Amazing cures resulted when patients were persuaded to express the pain and sorrow that should have found outlet before.

The discoveries of psychiatry on the importance of expressing rather than repressing grief remind us that the ancient teachers in the Bible had an intuitive wisdom about human nature and its needs which our more sophisticated age has forgotten. Open and unashamed was the expression of sorrow on the part of Abraham and Jacob and David. Our ancestors publicly wept, wore sackcloth, tore their garments and fasted. Modern funerals, on the other hand, are often arranged in such a way as to prevent tears, emotional outbursts and "undignified scenes." But we should remember that we were given tear ducts for just such hours of darkness. Do not be afraid of breaking down under the strain of loss. *Express as much grief as you actually feel.* The pain that you feel now will be the tool and the instrument of your later healing.

Furthermore, the function of friends is to be the sounding board for grief. Trying to distract attention from the loss should come much later in the healing process. At first friends should offer every opportunity to the bereaved to talk about his loss, to dwell upon his sorrow.

A second truth about grief is this: *We must learn how to extricate ourselves from the bondage of the physical existence of the loved one.* When a husband and wife have lived and worked together harmoniously, the death of one leaves an aching void in the fabric of life; the surviving partner yearns for the presence of the comrade and may make the mistake of closing the door to new friends. It is better to seek out new friends who gradually will help us to find the road to life again, who will walk on that road with us.

A mother who loses a young child has suffered one of the most tragic bereavements of all. She feels as though she had lost a part of her very being. When such a tragedy occurs, the love relationship must be reestablished in some way. It would, however, be unwise for this mother to adopt a baby immediately, because unconsciously she might feel disloyal to her own child and make the adopted child the unconscious victim of a deep hostility. A wise solution occurs if the bereaved mother dilutes her affection at first over a wide area by working daily at a nursery school. Then, when the first wound has partially healed, she either adopts a child or has one of her own and bestows upon it her mature and devoted affection.

So, in any bereavement, we must ultimately find some other person or persons in need of our loving care, and that very devotion which we lavish on another life will bring healing to our own spirits.

It must be recognized, of course, that these substitute patterns will not come spontaneously and without effort. The mourner must inevitably live through many lonely hours and empty days. But an unrelenting melancholia which continues for years is often an indication that the love relationship was of a too dependent nature, in fact a counterfeit of love. If a person continues to mourn his dear one without concern for the rest of human life and the tasks waiting to be done, he reveals a kind of inadequacy in his love: He proves that he never really became a mature, self-reliant individual. Difficult as it may be to believe at first, the mourning of certain men and women is really a mourning for themselves, an expression of self-centered pity for their own directionless lives. Nor should we pretend to grieve when we do not feel it, when, for example, an aged parent who has been suffering from an incurable disease is given surcease by death. We must never falsify our emotions.

Life is distorted not merely for adults but for children, when grief is unwisely handled. This is what frequently happens. A father dies, leaving a widow and a young child. At the time of the funeral the little boy is sent to some relative and the widowed mother and all the relatives conspire to conceal from the child the true situation. The father's name is not mentioned or, if mentioned, the conversation is quickly turned to some other channel. The theory behind all this conspiracy of silence about the death of the father is that the little boy should be shielded from grief and pain. This whole process of concealment, while motivated by the highest intentions, can prove to be terribly distorting to the child's emotional development.

In my pastoral work I had occasion to see this truth in action. The bereaved mother sent her seven-year-old girl to a distant relative, believing she was too young "to be around this house with all this sorrow." I urged that the child be brought home immediately, told briefly that her father had died and that her mother needed her to cheer her up. She should be given an important function to perform—to comfort her mother. The little girl returned, persuaded her mother to sit down on the floor and play with her, and the two of them were drawn closer together by the mutuality of their experience.

The supreme illusion is that children cannot stand grief and sadness, that under all circumstances they must be coddled and sheltered against the winds of reality. The truth lies in exactly the opposite direction. The child can stand tears and sorrow, but not deceit. It will not break under honestly presented grief. It may break under the burden of exclusion and exile from the family circle, under the heavy load of adult evasion, half-truths, frozen emotions, hypocritical pretenses.

It is folly to seek too speedy comfort and miraculous cure from grief. The experience of pain somehow has a curative function and any evasive detour around normal sorrow will bring us later to a tragic abyss. We should not demand of ourselves more than nature herself will permit. We should anticipate these stages in our emotional convalescence: poignant grief, empty days, resistance to consolation, disinterestedness in life, gradually giving way under the healing sunlight of love, friendship, social challenge, to the new weaving of a pattern of action and the acceptance of the irresistible challenge of life. Tutored in grief's slow wisdom, we will surmount tragedy and find inner peace.

❖ ✦ ❖

### ANOTHER JOURNEY

*W*hen I am old, I want to live near the railway where I can hear the long whistle of trains trumpeting through the night, hear them pounding the rails, screaming out signals and ringing their bells. By day I'll see them hauling their heavy loads as they sweep across the wide plain. With their force and strength, their minds set upon the far country, they will vitalize me again and fill me with the joy of living. And in my mind I will go with them as far as I can. Then, one night when I am very old and tired I shall not come back, and friends will say, "Wasn't it a nice way to go?"                    —*Nellie L. McClung*

# When You Write a Letter of Condolence . . .

JANET KERN

**I**t happens to someone every day. There in the obituary column of a newspaper is a familiar name, and you must write a letter of condolence. Few duties are more genuinely difficult. Recently, after my mother's death, I was on the receiving end of condolences. What I have learned may help others.

First, you must remember that the proper purpose of a letter of sympathy is not so much to honor the dead as to help the living. Your aim, then, should be to recall past joy, not to heap coals on the fire of sorrow. So write about the life of the departed, not about the death. Write in terms of the momentarily forgotten blessing, not the already overemphasized tragedy. Any bereaved individual could reach at random into a pile of condolence letters and come up with this typical note. "What a great loss this has been to you. I am filled with thoughts of your tragedy." How much wiser was the friend who wrote me: "I will remember your mother's gaiety, friendliness and fine spirit. They don't come like her very often. Both you and your father have been greatly blessed."

Remember that a few comforting words are more welcome than pages of empty prose. And try to start and sustain happy memories. Every recollection of my mother, alive, helped me. It did me immense good to get a letter from a salesclerk who wrote about her "charm and serene quietness. Although I saw her only that one time she came shopping with you, I shall always remember her." What a wonderful, living image of Mother came to mind upon reading that.

For some reason many people consider a letter of condolence an obligation to preach a sermon at the already suffering recipient. It is well to remember that your personal credo may be at variance with what the grief-stricken person himself believes and finds comforting. In the name of compassion, don't subject a bereaved person to high-sounding clichés such as "Time heals." He won't believe it; he will believe simply that you don't realize the depth of his sorrow. "After a while you'll forget" is equally painful. The last thing in the world one wants is to forget. Above all, refrain from indulging in that most arrogant of all clichés, "He would have wanted you to . . ." Advice is not consolation.

If you haven't written within a month, don't write. During the days immediately following the shock of loss, there are solace and therapy in the flood of condolence letters. But there comes a time when the bereaved must take up normal routines, and they don't want to be forced to hark back. They are still in need of consolation—but offer it in person and tacitly, by companionship, rather than in words.

It will not hurt to study models of condolence letters. I recommend one written by Harold J. Laski to Justice Oliver Wendell Holmes on the death of Mrs. Holmes in 1929.

"You know how big a space you both have filled in our hearts," he wrote. "She had, with all her reserve and reticence, a genius for affection. And to see you together was a lesson in the beauty of love. I know that things can never be the same for you again. But I want you to remember that your house was made by her, for me as for others, a place of loving pilgrimage, and that while we live she will be remembered with deep affection."

# In Time of Sorrow: The Gift of Your Presence

SEYMOUR SHUBIN

One morning several years ago my aunt phoned me at my office to ask if I was going to her cousin's funeral that afternoon. "I can't," I told her. "I won't be able to break away."

"Please," she urged. "It won't take more than an hour. You don't have to go to the cemetery, just to the service. You don't know how much the family will appreciate it."

"No one's going to miss me," I said. "It's been at least four years since I've seen those cousins." I felt guilty as I hung up, though. While I did have a heavy schedule that day, I could have rearranged it to fit in the funeral. And I had once been very close to the children of my aunt's cousin. But I reassured myself: Surely, wrapped in their grief, my cousins wouldn't know whether I was there. Why should I disrupt a busy day in order to involve myself in this gloom?

Over the years I had shunned funerals of people not quite at the core of my life: the business acquaintance whose family I had never met, the gentle neighborhood pharmacist with whom I had solved countless problems of the world and whose funeral service would have delayed (by two or three hours) the start of a vacation trip. What good would canceling my appointments do the dead? They were gone; I could not bring them back. Staying away from the funeral did not mean that I mourned them any the less. Like many other people, I was convinced that the bereaved were temporarily beyond any comfort that my presence at the funeral service could bring. I thought of them as walled within their grief, blind and deaf to everything around them. On the rare occasions when I did attend a funeral, I could never bring myself to offer condolences to those who sat in that dread "first row." Of what value were words, a handshake, a kiss?

Then my turn came to sit in that first row. My father, still active though in his seventies, collapsed and died without warning. It was one of those deaths announced to a family in an emergency-ward corridor. Suddenly all you can do is walk back out to your car. Now, on a chill but sun-bright morning, we were being driven by limousine to the funeral, a ride that until that time only other families had taken. Already a fragment of the mystery was being lifted for me; I was aware of *awareness*. For one thing, I found myself grateful that it was a sunny day. But I also felt the aloneness of grief, an apartness from everyone we passed—men going about their work, women shopping. My mother said softly, "They say I should be thankful that I had him this long, but it's only been like a walk around the block." Yes, so it was for her, for my sisters and brother and for myself. No one else could possibly know how brief that walk had been.

Before the service began we entered a room just off the chapel, and soon people began coming in. One of the first was an elderly man I didn't know. He held my hand for a moment as he said, "You wouldn't remember me, but I worked for your Dad when he first started in business. He was a real gentleman." Just that, and he was gone.

But inside, where there had been emptiness, I felt a strange glow. And it grew, this glow, as the line inched by. Here was a cousin only three days out of a hospital; here, business competitors of my father. And between the familiar faces and the strangers were people I was amazed to see: a maid who had worked for my parents long ago, the corner-candy-store owner and his wife, and the television repairman. It was as though, kaleidoscopically, many parts of my father's life were coming together on this day. Then suddenly my wife was saying, "Look who came!" And walking toward us were friends of ours, a couple who hadn't even known my father—yet he had taken time off from work and she had gotten a baby-sitter. I embraced them warmly.

"We wanted to be with you," they said. With *me*, with *us*. Now others were approaching, friends who, though their words might be awkward or mumbled, brought the priceless gift of themselves. How grateful I was for their presence; how infrequently I had given mine.

Afterward there was another revelation. I had long questioned the practice of stopping at the bereaved's home immediately following a funeral—it did not seem right for food and drink to be served as though it were a party. But that day, when we got back to my mother's house, it was good to see the quiet friendliness of neighbors who had spread a table; good to have people coming to reminisce about my father, and now and then to smile. This was not a turning away from mourning; it was a communion of the living.

Recently, the father of a dear friend of mine died, and although I had not known the father well, I made it my business to attend the funeral. Later my friend said to me, "It may sound strange to use the word happy, but there really was a kind of happiness in seeing you. It had nothing to do with being comforted; it was just that I was so glad you were there. I've been to many funerals," he went on, "but I never knew until now how important it was to go." I nodded, remembering the solace of a deep and personal grief shared when I, too, had been in that first row.

# No Final Terror

J. D. RATCLIFF

As he ascended the scaffold
to settle political accounts with King Henry VIII, Sir Thomas
More smiled wryly at the executioner. "See me safe up," he
said, "for coming down I can shift for myself." Few people
face death with such gallantry. The very terms we use for
death express a universal fear: grim reaper, dark angel.

Yet all evidence indicates that death has no terrors. It is
generally welcomed by the aged and infirm. It offers merciful
release to the sick, lifting burdens they can no longer carry. In
sum, the overwhelming majority of people are willing to meet
death when it comes although they have feared it all their
lives. Thousands have "died" by drowning, electric shock,
asphyxiation—only to be revived by prompt medical attention. They have indeed returned from the dead to report
invariably that there was no anguish, no pain, no terror—
merely an all-enveloping peace.

Sir William Osler, the great physician, studied five hundred deaths. Only eleven showed mental apprehension and
only two, signs of terror. Arthur MacDonald, another medical
man, adds his testimony: "The idea that dying is accompanied by severe suffering may arise from misinterpretation of
the physical signs accompanying it. The act is confused with
the symptoms of the disease which preceded death. There
seems to be a pause in nature—the disease has conquered, the
battle is over. The body, fatigued by its efforts to sustain itself,
is ready to die. All is tranquillity."

Dr. John A. Ryle of famed Guy's Hospital, London, noted: "Dying is not so terrible as we have been led to believe. It is often the witnesses who suffer the greater mental pain. Their suffering is usually a matter of untutored sympathy—of *imagining* what the victim must be feeling, and *imagining* what they themselves may be called upon to endure. In their leave-taking from their friends the dying may or may not feel a fleeting wistfulness, but they will know no terror."

Dr. Alfred Worcester, professor emeritus of hygiene at Harvard, has this to say: "Death is almost always preceded by a perfect willingness to die. I have never seen it otherwise. It is always easy at the last. However great the previous suffering, there is always an interval of perfect peace and often ecstasy before death. All competent observers agree that except in imagination there is no such thing as 'death agony.' The contractions of the dying body, it is true, are sometimes distressing sights. They seem to be evidence of suffering but this is only seemingly so—they are merely the contractions of reflex muscles." Similarly, the facial grimaces that often come with death are involuntary and not indicators of pain. Remember, faces are often contorted in sleep—although the sleeper is in no pain.

The most reliable information on what death is like comes from physicians who have faced it. One doctor, carried to the brink by a severe heart attack, described his sensations as those of mild intoxication. Yet he appeared to be in severe pain. Another, nearly carried away by pneumonia, remembered nothing of the critical phase of his disease although he gave signs of being in great distress. He remembered nothing until the crisis was over and he sat up in bed demanding breakfast. Three who drowned but were revived found only peace and pleasantness after the initial struggle was over.

William Hunter, the eighteenth-century anatomist, murmured with his last breath: "If I had strength enough to
hold a pen I would write how easy and pleasant it is to die."

The final flutters of a failing heart pump an ever-diminish-
ing supply of blood. The flame of life burns more and more
dimly. Whatever pain may have attended the final illness
disappears as sensory perceptions fail. There is merciful relief even from such horridly painful diseases as meningitis
and tetanus. After an interval of peace, the oxygen starvation
that goes with failing circulation takes its toll on the brain.
The patient may hear the ringing of nonexistent bells or see
the flashing of nonexistent lights. He may feel a slight restlessness. Gradually he drifts into darkness, without pain,
without sensation. The final blacking out which precedes
death is in no wise different from falling asleep. This is true
of older people who often go to bed and to sleep—and never
wake. It is also true of children.

When a dying person retains his faculties to the very end,
true character is likely to shine out. Those who in life have
been petulant, complaining, use their last breath to express
bitterness about the fate they are meeting. The good and
kindly express good and kindly thoughts. Curiously, the
dying brain sometimes becomes clearer than it has been for
years. Goethe died reciting Greek poetry, although he hadn't
studied the language for fifty years.

Look death in the face. His countenance isn't so terrifying
as we are led to believe. We smile at the small boy fearing
the mysteries of the first grade, at the young girl in an emotional turmoil about her first party. We might save some of
this patronage for man in general and his fear of death. As
sleep is a release from the day's turmoil, death is a relaxing
after the stresses of life. It is usually kindly and welcome.

# Beyond Death There Is Life

*Condensed from the book:* Stay Alive *All Your Life*

NORMAN VINCENT PEALE

**T**he day I received the news that my mother had died I went to my church in New York City and sat in the pulpit. I wanted to feel Mother's presence; she had always told me, "Whenever you are in that pulpit I will be with you."

Then I went into my study. On the table was an old, tattered Bible that I always take with me wherever I go. In an instinctive desire for comfort that day, I placed my hand on it. As I stood looking out toward Fifth Avenue, I suddenly and distinctly felt two cupped hands, soft as eiderdown, resting very gently on my head. It was a feeling of inexpressible joy.

I have always had a questioning mind and even then I tried to deal factually with this experience. I reasoned that it was hallucination due to grief—but I could not make myself believe this. From that moment on I have never doubted my mother's spiritual aliveness. I *know* that she lives and that she will live forever. I have not the slightest doubt concerning the truth and validity of immortality. I believe absolutely and certainly that when you die you will meet your loved ones and know them and be reunited with them, never to be separated again. I believe that identity of personality will continue in that greater sphere of life in which there will be no suffering nor sorrow as we know them here in the physical sense. I hope, too, that there will be struggle, for struggle is essentially good. Certainly there will be ongoing development, for life with no upward effort of the spirit would be incredibly dull.

Many years ago I read a statement by a scientist who said dogmatically, "At death the life of man is snuffed out like a candle flame." He was listened to with some respect because materialistic science was still in fashion. But today he would simply be asked to prove his statement. How does he know? The truth is, he doesn't know, and he cannot prove it. Our belief in immortality is not based upon proof, but we try to find proof because we cannot help *believing* it. Indeed, the instinctive feeling that it is true is one of the deepest proofs that it is so. When God wishes to carry a point with men he plants the idea in their instincts. The longing for immortality is so universal that it can hardly be met with indifference by the universe. What we deeply long for, what we deeply feel, must surely reflect one of the basic facts of human existence.

Such great truths as this are not believed because of proof and demonstration, but by faith and intuition. Intuition is an important factor in the scientific perception of truth. As the philosopher Henri Bergson pointed out, scientists often come to the end of verifiable knowledge, then, by a leap of intuition, arrive at truth. Scientific investigation lends support to our intuition and faith. The old materialistic conception of the universe is fading. Sir James Jeans declared, "All the world is in vibration." Einstein told us, "Matter and energy are interchangeable, one and the same." Scholars, it seems, recognize the deep spiritual something that lies at the core of life.

I talked with Mrs. Thomas A. Edison about her husband's view of the afterlife. The famous inventor believed profoundly that the soul is an actual entity that leaves the body at death. When Edison was close to the moment of death, his physician saw that he was attempting to say something. He bent over and distinctly heard the dying man say, "It is very beautiful over there."

The observed experience of men and women as they pass into the so-called valley of the shadow indicates that on the other side there are both life and beauty. Sometimes, of course, there is pain in sickness, and the path of a human being toward physical death may be difficult. But at the moment of death, as a great physician described it, "A wave of peace seems to come over one." A nurse who has seen many people die told me, "Many patients have given expression, at the moment of death, of having 'seen' something, and often they spoke about wondrous light and music. Some spoke of seeing faces which they recognized. There was often a look of incredulous wonder in their eyes."

I myself was with a friend when his time came to die. As the mist of the valley came over him, suddenly he said, speaking to his son who was sitting beside him, "Jim, I see beautiful buildings. And in one of them is a light, and the light is for me. It is very beautiful." Then he was gone. The son said to me, "My father was a scientist, and in his work he never reported anything that was not a proven fact. The habit of so many years could not change. He was reporting what he saw."

Dr. Leslie D. Weatherhead, of London, declared that once he sat on the bed of a dying man and held his hand. "I must have gripped his hand more tightly than I thought," Dr. Weatherhead said, "for the patient said a strange thing. 'Don't pull me back. It looks so wonderful further on!'"

Not long ago my wife and I visited the little village of

Bethany, near Jerusalem. We stood outside the tomb where once rested the body of Lazarus, at almost the exact spot where Jesus spoke nearly twenty centuries ago to his grieving people: "I am the resurrection, and the life: he that believeth in me, though he were dead, yet shall he live: and whosoever liveth and believeth in me shall never die." It is difficult for me to recall without deep emotion the feeling of absolute certainty I felt as I stood there, for I knew then that those words were absolutely true.

Clearly, God's answer to death is life. In fact, the Bible preaches a faith based on life, not death. It tells us that what appears to be death only seems so, that the real fact is life eternal.

### LET US DARE

*T*oo long our whole concept of immortality has suffered from the peculiar misconception that immortality is a state of being that occurs when we die! But if we are immortal at all, we are immortal now, this very moment. Why postpone our adjustment to a sublime condition? Let us be as fearless in the discipline of our souls as of our bodies. It is amazing how completely tangled nerves relax, how anxieties and fears evaporate if once we incorporate into our daily philosophy of life the slogan, "Use your immortality now."

Let us dare to live as if we are immortal, for then we shall be better prepared for a condition that may be imposed upon us whether or not we choose it. Let us recognize each moment the companionship of a Man who achieved the impossible, let us imitate each moment the daily conduct of the one Man of our climbing race who succeeded in living every day of His mortal life as if He were to live forever.  —*Winifred Kirkland*

# Why I Believe in Immortality

A Symposium compiled by DORON K. ANTRIM

ARTHUR H. COMPTON, *educator, author and Nobel Prize-winning physicist*:

It takes a whole lifetime to build the character of a noble man. The adventures and disciplines of youth, the struggles and failures and successes, the pain and pleasures of maturity, the loneliness and tranquillity of age—these make up the fire through which he must pass to bring out the pure gold of his soul. Having been thus perfected, he will meet what fate from nature? Annihilation? What infinite waste! I prefer to believe he lives on after death, continuing in a larger sphere, in coöperation with his Maker, the work he had here begun.

HELEN KELLER, *author; lecturer; counselor, American Foundation for the Blind*:

Being blind and deaf to the material world has helped me develop an awareness to the invisible, spiritual world. I know my friends not by their physical appearance, but by their spirit. Consequently death does not separate me from my loved ones. At any moment I can bring them around me to cheer my loneliness. Therefore, to me, there is no such thing as death in the sense that life has ceased.

Those with sight so often put their entire trust in what they see. They believe that only material things are real. When a loved one dies and is no longer seen, they lose their contact. Their sense of the unseen is undeveloped, whereas the inner or "mystic" sense, if you will, gives me vision of the unseen. As I wander through the dark, I am aware of encouraging voices that murmur from the spirit realm. I sense the holy passion pouring down from the springs of infinity. Here, in the midst of everyday air, I sense the rush of ethereal rains. I am conscious of the splendor that binds all things of earth to all things of heaven. Immured by silence and darkness, I possess the light which shall give me vision a thousandfold when death sets me free.

HARRY EMERSON FOSDICK, *author; minister emeritus, The Riverside Church, New York City:*

God has put within our lives meanings and possibilities that quite outrun the limits of mortality. William James of Harvard once said that his interest in personal immortality was not of the keenest order; but his belief grew stronger as he grew older and, when asked why, he said, "Because I am just getting fit to live." So, the intellectual and spiritual life of man on earth is not a circle rounded and complete, but a parabola that runs out and out into infinity. This earth furnishes no full draught of the cup of life but a sip of love, beauty, character and truth, and if death end all, the cup is, as it were, ironically withdrawn. A trustworthy God would not behave like that.

DR. WERNHER VON BRAUN, *space physicist:*

Many people seem to feel that science has somehow made "religious ideas" untimely or old-fashioned. But I think science has a real surprise for the skeptics. Science, for instance, tells us that nothing in nature, not even the tiniest particle, can disappear without a trace. Nature does not know extinction. All it knows is transformation. Now, if

God applies this fundamental principle to the most minute and insignificant parts of His universe, doesn't it make sense to assume that He applies it also to the human soul? Everything science has taught me—and continues to teach me—strengthens my belief in the continuity of our spiritual existence after death. Nothing disappears without a trace.

DR. RALPH W. SOCKMAN, *radio preacher and minister emeritus of Christ Church, Methodist, New York City:*

I should hold the hope of immortality had Christ never risen. But as I catch the spirit of Christ's integrity, I feel convinced that I can trust Him when He says about the hope of a life beyond: "If it were not so, would I have told you that I go to prepare a place for you?" The record of Christ did not end on Calvary. The sadhearted women going out in the misty morning to anoint the body of their departed leader; the experience in the garden which sent them rushing back to bring the disciples; the evening walk to Emmaus when a mysterious presence seemed to accompany them and to make their hearts burn within them on the way; the upper room a week later with the disciples gathered about the still doubting Thomas, and then his cry of conviction, "My Lord and my God"—these Easter reports are told with such reserve and artlessness that I cannot believe they were simply inventions.

Something happened which made Jesus more alive in the streets of Jerusalem at Pentecost than He was on Palm Sunday. Was it all a delusion or was it a divine revelation? The conviction that Christ triumphed over death has carried the Christian movement for nineteen centuries. It sustained the hunted Christians hiding in the catacombs. It sends its Easter hopes through the hearts of 600 million followers of Christ.

*Life is a magnificent gift, but it is also an impenetrable mystery. Man alone cannot give himself final answers to the great unanswerables: Who am I? Where did I come from? Where am I going? What am I doing here? This is the role of religion, which proclaims that the answers are to be found only in the mighty realm of the spirit.*

*No human society has ever been known to exist without some sort of religious belief. Beginning only a few short millennia ago with primitive fears and superstitions, such beliefs have progressed and expanded until they encompass such mysteries as faith, prayer, sin, repentance, salvation. Here five writers, representing science, religion and the arts, explore this infinite dimension of finite man.*

## How to Go to Church
RUTH MATTHEWS

Thousands of people are passing up the richest opportunity of their lives every Sunday morning. It isn't that they don't go to church. They do. But once they get there they do not know how to use the limitless power that is within their grasp.

For many church members Sunday morning goes something like this: After a week filled with bustle and tension, and after a late Saturday night, they get up, have breakfast and hustle off to church. They may arrive a little breathless in order to catch the processional hymn. After that they sit back and let God, the minister and the choir take over—and thereby defeat the very purpose for which, presumably, they have come to church. Instead of participating in the worship of God, too many parishioners are mere spectators at a feast that could nourish the soul and refresh the entire being.

A Midwestern friend of mine was troubled when a new minister replaced a beloved pastor who had served her parish for many years. She missed the excellent sermons and warm personality of the older man, and began to feel frustrated and depressed each time she attended the service. "Why should I go," she asked, "since I am getting so little out of it?" It seemed to her that she could use the time better at home, reading and worshiping in her own way. "I don't think you know how to go to church," a good friend told her frankly. "You are getting little out of it because you are giving very little."

She was shocked. She had been a regular church member all her life. She contributed to her church and served on its committees. Wasn't that giving? "The giving I am talking about has nothing to do with money or the time you spend on church work," the friend told her. "I am talking about how much you give *of yourself* in the actual worship of God. Worship isn't merely acquiescence. It is active participation. When you say you don't enjoy going to church, or don't enjoy the minister's sermons, you are missing the point. We can't sit back in the pew and criticize the service as we would a play or a concert. The act of worship is an act in every sense of the word, and each of us must share in it."

By following her friend's suggestions, this woman found what churchgoing could be: a joyous and exhilarating experience. She started coming to church a few minutes early so that she might pray quietly and feel the peace of God's house. Instead of brooding aimlessly over the problems and hurly-burly of the past week, or idly observing the people around her, she tried to clear her mind and think only of God's presence and His nearness to her. If she had pressing problems, sometime during the service she prayed about them, asking for guidance. During prayers and responses, she tried to think every word, every phrase, every sentence, and to say them clearly, to grasp the meaning fully. She applied the same receptive attitude toward the hymns.

And then she came to realize what countless worshipers have known throughout the ages: the worship of God transcends all other human experience. She began to understand that, during those few precious minutes on Sunday, we return to the source of our being. We leave the turbulence and pressures of the world, walk into God's healing presence. We communicate with Him and receive the blessing of peace, and with it the renewal of strength. This peace and strength give our lives a truer perspective of what is and what is not important, and an invulnerability to the world's affronts and outrages upon nerves and minds.

The minister's sermon, the choir music, the fellowship of the other members of the congregation are incidental to the purpose for which we are in this holy place: complete and active communion with God. True, a dynamic minister helps. But no one else can perform the act of worship for us.

Worship means a complete submission of ourselves—our minds, bodies and wills—to a power greater than our finite comprehension. It means a forgetfulness of self, a casting off of everything that binds us to material things. It means an inward searching and an outward humbling of self. We cannot expect to hurry into church at the last minute and be ready for a profound experience. Worship requires an attitude of reverence and expectancy. A member of the Washington Friends' Meeting, a professor of philosophy, reminded me the other day that Quakers in the meetings expectantly wait for God, and that they emphasize the waiting. "We begin our meetings with a period of complete silence, unless someone has 'an experience' and wishes to speak," he said. "We go to church for transformation and we get this by listening—waiting on God."

On this, all religions are in agreement. We need a quiet time and a quiet place in which to see ourselves as part of the great pattern of things, to measure ourselves and our activities in the light of God's presence. The quiet listening gives us time to take our bearings. It quickens our senses and reminds us that we are not alone, that a Higher Intelligence has designed our course. It helps us to see the truth.

In the quiet of worship we find guidance and help in personal problems. The mother of two lively teen-agers told me, "Going to church gives me insight into our family relationships that I would never otherwise have. I believe this comes from making myself receptive to God." A young bus driver put it this way: "I try to shut out of my mind trivial problems and simply open my heart when I am in church. I try to live in tune with my Creator. The closer my communion, the better I can handle my responsibilities. Believe me, you feel responsibilities when you are driving a bus."

Don't be discouraged if there are times in church when the "listening" seems to bring no answer. This has happened to every worshiper who ever prayed. But "wait on the Lord" and you will receive renewed strength and peace, not only for the week to come, but for all your time on earth.

# Why I Know There Is a God

JOHN GLENN

**W**hen I was selected for the space program, one of the first things given me was a booklet containing a lot of information about space. Two paragraphs that concerned the hugeness of the universe impressed me very much. To understand these paragraphs, you have to know what a light-year is. Light travels 186,000 miles per second, equivalent to about seven and one-half times around the earth every second. Now if you start that light ray out straight and let it continue for a year's time, that distance is a light-year—approximately six *trillion* miles!

Let me quote now on the size of our universe: "When we recall that our galaxy is some 100,000 light-years in diameter, the sun being an insignificant star some 30,000 light-years from the galactic center, circling in an orbit of its own every 200 million years as the galaxy rotates, we realize how difficult it is to visualize the tremendous scale of the universe beyond the solar system.

"Nor is the interstellar space of our galaxy the end, for beyond are the millions of other galaxies, all apparently rushing from one another at fantastic speeds. The limits of the telescopically observable universe extend at least two *billion* light-years from us in all directions." This shows how big our universe is. Come back now to what we know of atomic structure, the smallest particles known. Atoms have a great similarity to our solar system and to the universe, for they have electrons rotating about a nucleus in regular patterns.

Now what is the point I am making? It is the *orderliness* of the whole universe about us—from the smallest atomic structure to the galaxies millions of light-years across, all traveling in prescribed orbits in relation to one another.

Could this have just happened? Was it an accident that a bunch of flotsam and jetsam suddenly started making these orbits of its own accord? I can't believe that. This was a Plan. This is one big thing in space that shows me there is a God. Some Power put all this into orbit and keeps it there.

Let's compare our Project Mercury speeds with some of these things we've been talking about. We think sometimes that we're pretty good in this project. We get up to about 18,000 miles an hour in orbit, which is about five miles per second. This is quite fast by our earthly standards, but in terms of what's going on in space, our efforts are puny.

You can't measure God in scientific terms. You can't see, feel, smell or touch religious power; it is intangible.

An airplane may have the most powerful engine in the world, the finest aerodynamic design, but without a certain intangible force it is of limited use. We get direction by reference to our compass.

Now the force that runs the compass defies all our senses: you can't see, hear, touch, taste, smell it. But we know it's there because we see the results. We can look at an instrument in the cockpit, and we can see that our compass is pointing a certain direction. We have faith in the force making that compass work. All of us who fly have staked our lives thousands of times on the fact that this compass will give us the proper reading. The same is true of the Christian principles in our lives. If we will let them guide us, our senses don't have to pick them up. We see the results of their power in our lives and in the lives of others. So we know it's there.

# A Naturalist's Path to Faith

DONALD CULROSS PEATTIE

It was an icy, blustery day when I was sent across the street, at the age of five, with a two-dollar bill to pay my tutor for a week of teaching me to read. In my thick mittens my grip of the bill was muffed; a wild gust blew the money out of my hand. My sister and my aunt, watching from our house, emerged to hunt for the bill. I sat down and shut my eyes. "For goodness' sake, why don't you help find it?" demanded my indignant aunt.

"I'm praying *you* will," I said loftily, from my pious blindness. One way or another, the bill was found. But I did not long preserve the illusion that prayer is a kind of abracadabra producing magical results. Indeed, I soon grew weary of prayer. To ask divinity for favors seemed to me presumptuous. In times of great moment a prayer might rise naturally to my lips. But for fifty years I could not feel empathy with the many humanly small petitions that rise constantly from this troubled earth. Such were not for me to make.

Then, in my fifty-sixth year, I fell desperately ill. The doctors told my wife to be a brave woman and give me up. But hers is a fighting courage and, yes, a praying courage. More, she brought me word that my friend the Neapolitan tailor was praying daily for me, and that the devout waitress in the little restaurant near the hospital included me always in her prayers. I did not question, in my gratitude to them, what weight these petitions could have in the scales that balanced life with death for me. Humbly I discovered a reverence I had lacked. And, lying there in my hospital bed, I decided to trace back over the path of my life by which I had come to it.

I had been baptized and confirmed in a Protestant faith known for its mellow beauty. I had loved that beauty, which to my mind was manifest most superbly in the Gothic cathedrals of England. At seventeen I had made a pilgrimage to these cathedrals, and at each was swept to glory by the soaring gray arches, the celestial rainbows cast by the rose windows, the ancient sculptured detail wrought in such piety so long ago. At York, the choir was in full voice; the organ thundered down the nave in a tide of sound that pulled me to my knees. But even in that moment of rapture I caught hold of the tail of my reason: I recognized that it was the mighty power of architecture (which has been called frozen music) and the oceanic music itself that I was adoring—not God. I was experiencing a passion for manwrought beauty, not a religious exaltation, and I had enough clarity of mind to perceive the difference. Beauty indeed was my guide, until, at the age of twenty, I enrolled in the biological sciences at Harvard, where the professors were great enough to match their subjects. They taught a discipline stern as any religious order's, the discipline of science, and ardently I embraced its tenets.

The first was that no life ever comes from no-life. A culture medium once sterilized and kept sterile would forever produce no growth—plant or animal. Where did life originate? This was a subject for lively discussion with my roommates into late hours. That it might have been formed under unique circumstances here on earth, or that it blew from between the stars as cosmic dust, were ideas equally stirring to my young mind, and I found pleasure in matching this with the words of Genesis: "And the Lord God formed man of the dust of the ground, and breathed into his nostrils the breath of life; and man became a living soul."

A second tenet, equally exciting, was that this planet home of ours had a beginning billions of years ago, and that it must have a predestined end when all life on earth, including man, will cease to be. The sun will shrink and cool and become a dead star; the earth, losing atmosphere and oceans, will drift farther and farther from the sun, until in something less than an eternity of time it will be cold as Pluto, most distant of the planets. This prospect exhilarated rather than depressed me, aware that in theology the end of us all is called the Last Judgment.

Most appealing of all to a young man who loved freedom of thought was a third tenet—namely, that there is no Revealed Authority. I was taught that because you read something in the Koran, or the Rig-Veda, or even the Bible, it isn't necessarily true. Moreover, these professors of mine made clear, science is skeptical of its own authority. Darwin, Mendel, Galton, Sir Isaac Newton, I realized with a thrill, may be scrapped at any time in favor of better explanations.

A fourth tenet of science—and again I marveled at the parallel to the poetry of Genesis—is the fact of evolution. I found that how evolution works is still being argued, but evolution itself is unquestioned—a great and shining fact that makes the world more wonderful.

A fifth tenet was the atomic nature of all matter—not a new idea, but old as the Greek philosophers. I could not guess then that this was a truth that was to reveal more and more terrifying truths.

Out of these tenets was formed for me a creed—the creed of pure science. But was there in it, I would pause to ask myself, any foundation for the faith that brings aid to the soul in travail? I wondered only passingly, having no troubles. I inclined for a time to become a disciple of Aristotle, that Adam of learning who taught that existence had its origin in supreme intelligence, and that everything has an intelligent cause and serves its useful purpose, that purpose being the development of higher planes of existence. Science, thought the great old pre-scientist, had but to put the pieces of the puzzle together to expose for praise the cosmic design, all beautiful.

It is a contenting concept. Many hold to it today. Peace be unto them. But I went on reading of science such as Aristotle did not dream of, and learned that wise men, probing life and its patterns, found nowhere any certainty, in the vast testimony of nature, that the universe was designed for man. Nor yet for any purpose, even the purpose of self-improvement. Aristotle said that life is soul pervading matter. But, I argued to myself, he could not have meant by soul the pure moral spirit revealed by Jesus in such searching truths that the best of Christians must struggle to live by them. No, I saw that Aristotle meant simply life itself. And here, in the morning of my years, I got hold of a form of worship that quarreled neither with science nor cathedral.

It was worship of life, natural life in all its everyday glory. I loved a spider's web with the dew on it. I loved a pine grove, the shade and the scent of it, and its deep sea-song. I loved the call of the white-throated sparrow in the spring rain, silvery and descending like the slant drops themselves. I loved a flower, whose purpose is to make a seed, and the seed itself, tinily secreting its embryo in the palm of my hand, hiding its purpose, which is to make a flower.

This breath, this life, whose very nature is to die, unconquerably proclaims the glory of both variety and order. We are part of that order. We are the stuff of the tree, which like our flesh is protoplasm. We are the stuff of the stars, for at the nuclear core of each molecule of human blood is an atom of that same iron which comes hurtling down in meteoric fragment. More, every atom has a structure like that of the planetary system with its central sun; the very pattern and force of the atom are akin to the revolutions of our solar system. And on this planet of ours, life is the manifestation of some long, slow will to victory that is held up to the sky and the stars.

Armed with this vision, I left college, parting from my roommates, who went their way into the research sciences (where all won scholar's fame). I went outdoors. I went, with vasculum and bird guide, to the Appalachians in late-spring bloom. Summer found me collecting in the whistling, shifting dunes of Indiana, where the grasses inscribe wind-driven circles in the sand. Autumn found me on Mount Washington, exulting that I knew my place in the world at last—that of a naturalist.

Presently I married; and I saw my wife bear a child, and then others. Now truly I was caught up in the web of life. I saw more clearly that man is a part of nature, and whatever he believes must be based upon this fact. A man's blood is seawater, and his tears are salt. The seed of his loins is scarcely different from the same cells in a seaweed. A man who goes in no consciousness of these facts is a drifter and a dreamer, without a home or any contact with reality. I was a believer in divinity, but what I loved was what Thomas Jefferson called "Nature's God." And this adoration of divine nature stood by me; it withstood even the onslaught of tragedy. Our first child and only daughter was suddenly swept from us by disease. But I did not find her wholly gone. In all things little and gay and innocent I could always find again the feet like rain, the laugh like brooks, the eyes like gentians. Life, I thought, is at its old trick of escaping, changing, transmuting into some other lovely shape an imperishable element.

Then, suddenly, after five months in a hospital, I too seemed about to go. A surgeon came to my room. We talked of the meadowlarks he had heard caroling on his early drive from home. Then, with one swift stab of the needle, they put me to sleep. Now I was not there to adore the redwoods as gods rooted in earth, to praise the hermit thrush as heaven's best chorister. Where I was I do not know. No one can say. But it may be that I was not as passive as the body on the operating table.

My wife, as I lay still unconscious and but tenuously holding to breath, spoke to the weary surgeon, who had been working over me for four hours, of my great and grateful love of life. He did not smile; he nodded. "And how that helps!" he told her earnestly. Humbly I take his surgeon's word for it. I do not understand it; I know now how much I do not understand. Through a long convalescence in that top room of the hospital, where an owl came nightly to keep me company in the big pine outside my window, I discovered how healing are the unspoken prayers of gratitude. Besides my friends the tailor and the waitress, I had many others to thank. And my thanks, too, went higher.

Months later, when I was home, the surgeon came to visit me. Perhaps my recovery was some small comfort to him, for he who had given me back my life had just lost one dearer to him than his own, his wife's. The purest prayer, the most skilled science, do not always prevail. Yet in his face was acceptance, trust still in the Great Ally with whose aid we two had won our particular common battle. We did not speak of Him together; there was no need, and He is best talked to alone. We both knew that He is more than life, and more than death. He controverts no scientific law, no natural processes. He will outlast the shrinking sun and chilling stars. In love of Him there is room for all manner of thinking, including that devout wonder with which I am now content.

Over a century ago a young spinster dying of tuberculosis on the Yorkshire moors, a girl named Emily Brontë, dared to define Him:

> Though earth and moon were gone,
> And suns and universes ceased to be,
> And Thou wert left alone,
> Every existence would exist in Thee.

With such assurance, such company, it is easy for a man to travel the last of the road.

### A SCIENTIST KNOWS THERE IS A GOD

*M*an has something more than animal instinct—the power of reason. No other animal has ever left a record of its ability to count ten, or even to understand the meaning of ten. Where instinct is like a single note of a flute, beautiful but limited, the human brain contains all the notes of all the instruments in the orchestra. No need to belabor this point: thanks to human reason we can contemplate the possibility that we are what we are only because we have received a spark of Universal Intelligence.

—*A. Cressy Morrison*

# The Healing Power of Prayer
STANLEY HIGH

At 5:30 seven mornings a week, a Philadelphia businessman goes into the library of his home and takes from his desk what he describes as "the day's most important memorandum." Its mimeographed pages are headed "Prayer Guide of the Prayer Fellowship," and after a Bible reference and brief meditation are listed the names of from fifty to two hundred persons. They may all be total strangers to him, but for half an hour this businessman prays for them, individually or as a group.

He knows his prayers are not the only ones offered that day for these persons. Half hour by half hour around the clock, other people make similar intercession. Among them: housewives, teachers, nurses, a traveling salesman, a bandleader, factory workers—ninety in all. The members of this dedicated group share one tested conviction: the belief, expressed by Alfred, Lord Tennyson, that "More things are wrought by prayer than this world dreams of." Their prayers are definite and practical. Each name in the weekly Prayer Guide is that of a person who has asked for prayer for himself or for whom prayer has been asked by a friend or relative. After each name a problem is listed: alcoholism, broken home, multiple sclerosis, elderly, lonely, financial difficulties. Whatever the trouble, the Prayer Chain seeks "to help open the way for God's answer to that specific person's specified problem." Precedent for such specific prayer can be found in a verse from the Gospel of St. Matthew: "and they brought unto Him all sick people that were taken with divers diseases and torments . . . and He healed them."

"It is not the healing we try to do," said one Fellowship member, "but the bringing." Once a month members of the Fellowship meet for devotions and to exchange experiences. All, as a prerequisite of membership, have had personal experience of answered prayer. Many have, themselves, been listed in the Guide and have joined the Fellowship out of gratitude for help received. And although of different denominations, all members are, in this unusual activity, following the inspiration of an Episcopal clergyman in Philadelphia, the Reverend Alfred W. Price.

Dr. Price is rector of St. Stephen's Protestant Episcopal Church in downtown Philadelphia. When he assumed his post twenty-two years ago, St. Stephen's had lost most of its old constituency to the suburbs, an operating deficit was on the increase, a majority of the vestry favored selling the property and moving to some likelier location. But Dr. Price had already started to introduce himself around the neighborhood, in cheap boardinghouses, tenement attics, even taprooms, offering his services if they were needed. What he found convinced him, and finally the vestrymen, that if ministering to human need is a chief function of the Christian church, then St. Stephen's was exactly where it ought to be.

Soon some of those Dr. Price had visited began to come to his church office. A few wanted money, some a friendly ear for their troubles. But a surprising number wanted his prayers. "Many were near the end of their rope," Dr. Price recalls. "They wanted down-to-earth prayers for down-to-earth needs—and they wanted answers. A little uncertainly at first, I began to pray and to help them to pray as Jesus prescribed we should: positively and all-out, affirming that, even as we prayed, God was already answering.

"At first it amazed me, minister though I am, to find that He actually was. Through this praying together lives were being healed. Alcoholics were being cured, broken homes restored and in some cases illnesses actually overcome."

One evening, after a day in which many from the neighborhood had sought him out, Dr. Price went into the church and sat in the pew once occupied by Dr. S. Weir Mitchell, neurologist and a pioneer in psychosomatic medicine. "I recalled that Dr. Mitchell had often said, 'It is not the body that is ill, but the mind.' I remembered also what another pioneer in the same field, Dr. Richard C. Cabot, had once told our seminary class: 'Ministers, if they really knew how to pray, could probably be doing 75 percent of the healing work of physicians.' Then I opened my New Testament and read—as though it applied to me and to this church—the familiar passage from the Epistle of James: 'Is any sick among you? Let him call for the elders of the church; and let them pray over him, anointing him with oil in the name of the Lord: and the prayer of faith shall save the sick. . . .'"

From this "rediscovery" of the place of healing in the ministry of Jesus, Dr. Price decided to make healing by prayer a part of the public service of St. Stephen's. Every Thursday (except in July and August), for twenty-two years, a sidewalk bulletin board in front of the church has carried this announcement: "Healing Services Today—12:30 p.m. and 5:30 p.m.—All Welcome."

When Dr. Price began his public services, fewer than twenty people attended, most of them passersby who came out of curiosity. Last year nearly 25,000 were reached, and today St. Stephen's is in the forefront of the rapidly spreading movement in the United States which is restoring the ministry of healing to the important place in the church that it once occupied.

A distinguished Philadelphia physician told me: "As doctors we are too often loath to admit the value of spiritual healing. But I have known the work of Dr. Price for a number of years and I can say, without hesitation, that it is of great value both to religion and to medicine." Another doctor, a member himself of the Prayer Fellowship, says, "I have seen too much of the power of prayer in healing to doubt that what are sometimes called 'miracles' do happen. Prayer and the Prayer Fellowship are an indispensable part of my practice."

At the two services I attended about 350 persons were present. They were of all ages, well and shabbily dressed, white and Negro. They represented, I learned later, many faiths and none. A number had come from long distances— from Louisiana, North Carolina, Massachusetts. Some were crippled, a few in wheel chairs. There was no emotional buildup. Dr. Price, a huge man with a voice to match and a matter-of-fact pulpit manner, simply offered prayers of thanksgiving, read the account of Jesus' healing the ten lepers and preached a brief sermon: "If you have come looking for magic, you are in the wrong place. This is a prayer service and your healing is not ours to offer. God has promised that His healing power is available to you. All we can do is to help you appropriate it. . . ."

Those who desired "the laying on of hands" were invited to the altar: "Come in confidence, knowing that the Lord is not on the side of sickness, but of health; that He desires for you, beginning now, a wholeness of soul, mind and body."

The altar rail filled five times until at least three fourths of those present had gone forward. Dr. Price laid his hands on the head of each, saying as though this person alone were present: "May the mercy of God and the love of our Lord Jesus Christ and the power of the Holy Spirit, which are here now, enter your soul, your mind and your body, for healing." When the last had left the altar, he read out the names and prayed for the 150 men and women not present who had requested or for whom requests had been made for prayer.

"Not all who ask are healed," Dr. Price says, "but I have seen the power of prayer accomplish benefits of spirit which may be of even more importance. One theme runs through the thousands of letters we receive: gratitude and thanksgiving. We have yet to receive a letter expressing bitterness and disillusionment."

I have read several hundred of these testimonies. Many include reference to literature which Dr. Price sends to all who ask for prayers, outlining "How you can appropriate God's power." This, he says, is "the indispensable, self-help part of our ministry." Here are quotations from several typical letters he has received:

"This is just a thank-you note from someone who has been greatly benefited by the healing services at St. Stephen's. I am not manifesting, as yet, perfect health, but my spirit lives in a new world. . . ." "We are so grateful for the prayers of St. Stephen's Prayer Fellowship. Our daughter, who had been in a hospital six years for a nervous breakdown, has now been home for over a year and has improved so much she will not need to go back. She is a changed person and our home is so much happier since she has been healed." From California: "There is so much good to report for my wife and myself. In this short span of weeks we have been lifted out of spiritual lethargy and mental anxiety to a new level of thinking. We are deeply grateful. . . ." From North Carolina: "Improvement beyond belief has been effected in my little boy, aged three, ever since our visit to you. I am so thankful for the prayers, joining mine, from your church. . . ."

I heard personal testimonies that were equally heartening. "When I first came to St. Stephen's," a young woman told me, "I was strictly up against it: physically because the doctors had told me I had multiple sclerosis, emotionally because, soon after, I lost my husband. But now when I hear Dr. Price talk about troubled humans becoming 'walking miracles of God's grace,' I know what he is talking about. I have learned to pray, not that God would do something for or to me, but that He could do something through me. And He has. The doctors do not tell me, yet, that I have been healed, although my symptoms have been diminished. But I have found a position in which I can forget myself and be of help to others. The combination of prayer and work has brought such happiness, serenity and purpose that the ills which once looked overwhelming have simply ceased to be an issue. For me, that is healing enough."

Almost incapacitated by Parkinson's disease, an insurance salesman was persuaded by his wife to attend a healing mission conducted by Dr. Price in another city. "When I came to the altar on the first night," he told me, "my hands trembled so they shook the altar rail. But I had an unexplainable conviction that 'this is it.' So I returned the next night and the trembling was less. On the third night it had gone. That was nearly three years ago. I don't boast that the disease has entirely left me. But the fact that I'm back on the job is

proof that something out of the ordinary in the way of healing happened to me. Our doctor calls it nothing short of
miraculous. My wife and I think it is miraculous, too. But
*we call it prayer.*"

Spiritual healing, Dr. Price points out, "is not a substitute
for medical treatment. We believe that all healing is from
God, whether through medicine or prayer or both. Which
gets the credit is unimportant. But this *is* important: just as
doctors work hard at becoming expert in medical treatment,
so more Christians should work harder at becoming expert in
prayer. We would not tolerate a doctor who went about his
work fumbling and uncertain, not knowing what to expect
and not expecting much. But that is the way many of us go
about our praying. Small wonder so much praying is done
with such little result.

"The members of our Prayer Fellowship take time to work
at praying, regularly. They do not pray hesitantly, asking
God to answer. They expect results. As always with that
kind of praying, they get them. When most Christians learn
to pray that way we will see released in the world the power
that Christ came to put within our reach."

### PRAYER FOR DOING

**P**rayer is not a substitute for work; it is a desperate effort to
work further and to be efficient beyond the range of one's powers. It is not the lazy who are most inclined to prayer; those pray
most who care most, and who, having worked hard, find it intolerable to be defeated. —*George Santayana*

**P**rayer changes things? No! Prayer changes people, and people
change things. —*Burton Hillis*

# Quo Vadis?

A. J. CRONIN

**W**e were in Rome with Italian friends whose one desire was to make our stay a festival. Gay excursions to Tivoli and Hadrian's Villa, parties at the Palazzo Doria and on the terrace of the Casino Borghese. The Via Veneto throbbed with color and excitement—sleek cars in slow procession, cafés filled with a fashionable throng, flower stalls riotous with blossoms.

And then one golden afternoon as I drove back alone from a protracted luncheon in a garden near Albano I lost my way. I found myself, to my annoyance, in a poor, dusty and deserted quarter holding nothing of that elegant sophistication to which I had grown accustomed. I drew up. Across the empty street was a small square building of gray stone. At a casual glance it suggested a branch administrative bureau where I could obtain information as to my whereabouts. I left the car, pushed open the door and went inside. Confronted suddenly by the dim and silent interior, I realized that I had stumbled upon an ancient church.

I had seen the famous churches of Rome—St. Peter's and the Lateran, the basilicas of St. Paul and St. Clement. But this small sanctuary was wholly different—bare, simple, empty, yet filled with a strange and reverent recollection of the past. As my gaze became adjusted to the inner twilight it fell upon a plaque set into the worn stone floor. Slowly deciphering the bronze inscription, almost obliterated by the years, I discovered where chance had brought me. This was the chapel of Quo Vadis! Here on this exact spot, according to the legend, the apostle Peter, terrorized by Nero's threats and fleeing from pagan Rome, had been confronted in a vision by his reproachful Lord. And here, opening the mystical interview which sent the fugitive back with courage and faith renewed, were spoken those memorable words: *"Quo vadis? Whither goest thou?"*

Under a queer compulsion I seated myself upon a low wooden bench, all my senses strained and intent. The moments passed; time lost its meaning; the silence echoed in my ears. And then from the cloistered shadows, through the overpowering stillness of that hallowed place, it seemed as though a whisper reached me, faint yet accusing, across the centuries. *"Quo vadis? Whither art thou going?"* Was not this a question which I, or any man, might ask himself today? The thought of those past weeks of pleasure stung me. There came upon me an awareness, sharp as sudden pain, of how fatally I—and others like me—had become absorbed in worldly affairs. We had forgotten, or ignored, the kingdom of the spirit.

In the somber nave, barely illumined by a shaft of light stealing through the transept, I saw this, suddenly, as the blight which lay upon mankind. Throughout the modern world men had become oblivious to the purpose of their being; they sought for temporal honor and material grandeur. The dominant cry was no longer "How much can I do?" but only "How much can I get?" The standards of personal morality had become debased. Current events, reported in the daily press, revealed endless infractions of the moral law which might well chill the heart. Once upon a time, men had ruled their conduct by the Ten Commandments. But how many in their daily round now gave thought to God? What did God matter when we had the best houses, the best automobiles, the best of everything?

How proud were the great democracies to call themselves Christian nations! Yet how few who professed that code of ethics gave more than a passing thought to its heavenly Founder. Many, indeed, had written God off as a pious fable; they never went to church, never spoke a word in prayer. Others temporized smugly in their belief, accepting Christ only as a great man, perhaps a prophet, rationalizing His miracles in terms of popular science, using every convenient device to evade what was most demanded of them. Most pitiful of all were those who, believing in their hearts and drawn to a path of faith, nevertheless through weakness or worldliness failed to follow it.

Yet now, more than ever before, Christendom was in danger, confronted by forces more barbaric than those of the pagan emperors—forces which sought to destroy belief in God, to bury the truth, wrung out of sacrifice and enlightenment, in the darkness of the abyss. How under heaven could we meet this challenge unless we stood firm, sustained by our own faith, twice-armed by our own integrity? Today a global struggle was being waged for the minds, hearts and souls of millions, a deadly struggle between the forces of evil and the forces of good. The enemy, by propaganda, subversion and deceit, was bent on annihilating forever in the rising generation and in generations to come the very concept of man's relationship with his divine source.

Like it or not, America had become the leader of the world, the champion of freedom and of right. Could we win through if we not only failed to show the way by our example but stood, instead, convicted as mere self-seekers, exhibiting our vaunted Christianity as a mockery and a sham?

A shiver passed over me as I sat in this shrine made hallowed by the apostle Peter. I thought of that great saint's martyrdom, and of the dark alcoves of the catacombs where lay the bones of the early Christians who, scorning the ways of ease, had dedicated themselves to their ideal. And I longed with all my soul that we might recover something of that shining faith, constant in life, steadfast in death. Then indeed would mankind, lost in the modern labyrinth, find itself in a spiritual revival, a surging wave of goodwill which would sweep across the world, making that hope forever cherished, the brotherhood of man, a firm reality at last.

This was the gleam upon the dark horizon. Yet such a change in the heart of the world could begin only in the heart of the individual, could succeed only if we would—every one of us—put in practice the fundamental precepts of the great moral laws, fill our churches to overflowing, unite our voices in prayer, mobilize our spiritual resources and loose a fervent new crusade by word and deed to all the corners of the earth. Could we but give effect to the Sermon on the Mount, all the difficulties, apparently insuperable, which confront us would melt like mist before the rising sun.

Was such an idea naïve and unpractical in our modern age? No! To follow this sublime teaching was the supreme goal of our existence. How better could we fulfill the destiny for which we were created than by practicing these eternal precepts, by casting out hatred, pride and greed, by fostering justice, kindness and charity? No matter the creed into which we had been born, this was the essence of true religion. And now religion should be the main concern of our lives, not hidden apologetically in the background as if obsolete, no longer credited by intelligent people. Religion was the only remedy for that sense of futility which haunts so many of us today, a way of life that, apart from its spiritual rewards, worked miracles in human relationships and brought immense dividends in happiness and peace of mind.

Should we not pause, therefore, amid the rush and racket of our daily lives and listen to the inner voice which forever whispers in our ear those two momentous words: *"Quo vadis?"* Then perhaps our eyes would open to the need of these things that are everlasting. Then indeed would we heed where we were going and make our destination, and the destination of all humanity, eternally secure.

As I came slowly out of that little church the setting sun cast a radiance upon the rooftops, upon the domes and pinnacles of the city. And in that glow my spirits lifted. Despite the cruelties which men inflict upon one another, despite the blindness and indifference, the threats of war and the destroyings and dispersings which afflict the nations, I felt there still was hope for the peoples of the earth. The road that we should travel still lay open, if only we would take it.

### CREDO FOR TODAY

*I*n this era of world wars, in this atomic age, values have changed. We have learned that we are the guests of existence, travelers between two stations. We must discover security within ourselves. During our short span of life we must find our own insights into our relationship with the existence in which we participate so briefly. Otherwise, we cannot live! This means, as I see it, a departure from the materialistic view of the nineteenth century. It means a reawakening of the spiritual world, of our inner life, of religion. I don't mean religion as a dogma or as a church, but as a vital feeling. —*Boris Pasternak*

# CONCLUSION

*Does humanity have a future? Is man going to destroy himself? Can he solve the stupendous problems that confront him? Here three hopeful writers tell why they believe that the human race will continue its progress toward the far-off goals of peace and justice and brotherhood for all mankind. Perhaps the final answer lies in two quotations from Pascal. "Man," the great Frenchman wrote, "is only a reed, the weakest in nature, but he is a thinking reed." And it was also Pascal who said, "We know the truth, not only by reason, but by the heart."*

# MAN'S PURPOSE AND DESTINY

# Be Proud You Are Human

ROGER WILLIAM RIIS

I admire the human race. Everybody is running us down, these days, for the mess they say we have made here and there and everywhere. That's short-range stuff. Over the marching and abundant centuries, we haven't made any mess. We have done and are doing a better job than anyone has any right to expect.

From the beginning, we found ourselves alone in a vast universe, and not only alone but the only living thing on this planet which could realize its loneness. We realized it, gave it a good close look, and then turned our attention to making something practical and useful out of an unprecedented situation.

First of all, we found a Light, a God, and we got a sense of direction, a goal to work toward. We proceeded to set up standards for living together. We made the revolutionary discovery that gentleness and kindliness were more practical than brute strength. No other species has ever found that out and used it as a model and practical code of conduct. We observe our ideal standards in remarkable degree. We are honest and trustworthy one with another so that it is the exception, it is news, when we commit a theft. We are decent 99 percent of the time, when we could easily be vile.

With silence and mystery behind us and ahead of us, we make up gay little songs and whistle them, and our feet keep jig time to them. We look life and fate in the eye, and smile. I like that, and I admire the people who do it. Alone among all living things, we have discovered Beauty, and we cherish it, and create it for eye and ear. Alone among living things, we have the power to look at our environment and criticize it and improve it.

Finding it necessary to live together by the millions, we created for ourselves governing systems covering vast geographical spaces. We have conceived the ideal of justice and plan it for all men. Finding that we have to work to stay alive, we work with ability beyond imagining. Out of the earth we take food, and improve that food year by year; we take heat, and light. We enjoy the myriad products of unparalleled ingenuity. Every morning the necessity for the day's work faces us. And we go and do a day's work.

Of a persistence, a daring and ingenuity impossible to surpass, we find ways to move easily under the water and through the air. Now we speculatively eye our neighboring planets. How shall I not admire such a creature?

Whenever he comes to an impassable obstacle, an apparently final barrier, he goes to work at it and, in due time, surpasses it. If he has limits, I do not see where they are. I do not think he has limits. I think he is a child of the universe who inherits eternity. I think he is wonderful, I am his devoted partisan, and I am proud indeed to be one of him.

⇒ ◆ ⇐

### THE PROBLEM OF GOODNESS

*O*ne of the best sermons I have ever heard was delivered by a preacher in a little country church. He said: "People talk to me about the problem of evil, but I will tell you an even greater problem: the problem of goodness. How do you account for the fact that in such a world as this there should be so much self-sacrifice, so much unselfishness, so much love?"    —*Bruce Barton*

# All Men Are My Brothers

JAMES A. MICHENER

I really believe that every man on this earth is my brother. He has a soul like mine, the ability to understand friendship, the capacity to create beauty. All over the world I have met such men. In the most savage jungles of New Guinea I have met my brother and in Tokyo I have seen him clearly walking before me.

In my brother's house I have lived without fear. Once in the wildest part of Guadalcanal I had to spend days with men who still lived and thought in the old Stone Age, but we got along together fine and I was to see those men in a space of only four weeks brought from their jungle hideaways to the airstrips, where some of them learned to drive the ten-ton trucks which carried gasoline to our bombers.

Once in India I lived for several days with villagers who didn't know a word of English. But the fact that I couldn't speak their language was no hindrance. Differences in social custom never kept me from getting to know and like savage Melanesians in the New Hebrides. They ate roast dog and I ate Army Spam and if we had wanted to emphasize differences I am sure each of us could have concluded the other was nuts.

I believe it was only fortunate experience that enabled me to travel among my brothers and to live with them. Therefore I do not believe it is my duty to preach to other people and insist that they also accept all men as their true and immediate brothers. These things come slow.

To my home in rural Pennsylvania come brown men and yellow men and black men from around the world. In *their* countries I lived and ate with them. In *my* country they shall live in my home and eat with me, and it never seems so big a home or so much a place of love as when some man from India or Japan or Tahiti or Fiji shares it with me. I believe that all men are my brothers. I know it when I see them sharing my home.

## THE FUTURE

**M**y faith in the future, though somewhat shaken, is not destroyed. If I sometimes doubt that man *will* achieve his mortal potentialities, I never doubt that he *can*.

All men cannot be masters, but none need be a slave. We cannot cast out pain from the world, but needless suffering we can. Tragedy will be with us in some degree as long as there is life, but misery we can banish. Injustice will raise its head in the best of all possible worlds, but tyranny we can conquer. Evil will invade some men's hearts, intolerance will twist some men's minds, but decency is a far more common human attribute and it can be made to prevail in our daily lives.

I believe all this, because I believe above all else in reason—in the power of the human mind to cope with the problems of life. Because I place my trust in reason, I place it in the individual. There is a madness in crowds from which the wisest, caught up in their ranks, are not immune.

I have known, as who has not, personal disappointments and despair. But always the thought of tomorrow has buoyed me up. I have looked to the future all my life. I still do. I still believe that with courage and intelligence we can make the future bright with fulfillment.                                —*Bernard M. Baruch*

# I Dare You to Be a Pessimist!
*Condensed from the book: Dear Mr. Brown*
HARRY EMERSON FOSDICK

**M**Y DEAR TED: Yes, I saw
that statement by the Federation of American Scientists that
"it appears unlikely that the world will avoid a nuclear holo-
caust if another fifteen years pass without arms-control agree-
ments." We hear warnings from every side of the unique
horror the megaton weapons can bring—the death of countless millions, and the loss of our civilization. Now you want
a letter that will lift from your mind the shadow of discouragement about the world!

My first remark is that it is better to be dismayed than
complacent. Never in all history has mankind faced such
monstrous danger. Today, what man's mind has created—
the techniques of nuclear and bacteriological warfare, for
example—man's character is not controlling. So all of us had
better be disturbed. (No wonder that a physician recently
told one of his patients, "What you need is a few months'
vacation on another planet.") Nevertheless, I am not discouraged and I will try to tell you why. For one thing, the very
fear which we all feel today can have constructive results.
When fear means panic, terror, consternation, it is worse
than useless. But intelligent fear is one of the major secrets
of all human achievement. As Angelo Patri put it, "Education consists in being afraid at the right time." Behind our
schools is the fear of illiteracy and ignorance. Behind our
medical science is the fear of dread diseases. From light-

houses on perilous seacoasts to democracy trying to displace crushing tyranny, man's positive response to danger has been one of the most creative factors in his experience. When the pull of aspiration is backed by the push of intelligent, popular fear, something generally happens. Personally, I am hopeful that fear will have that consequence now in preventing a nuclear war.

For another reason I refuse to surrender to discouragement: The basic causes of our present danger are full of promising good. To be sure, modern science has mounted us on a bigger horse than we yet know how to ride, but only a fool would wish to return to prescientific days. This problem of getting power and then mishandling it is very old. Leonardo da Vinci invented a submarine, then tore up the plans for fear of what men might do with it. And today, scientist J. Robert Oppenheimer, seeing how megaton weapons threaten the world, says, "The physicist has known sin." Our whole society knows the tragic sin of misusing a gift which is inherently promising and good. But my faith is that the time will eventually come when mankind will be endlessly striving for "atoms for peace."

A second basic cause of our present danger is also good: the increasingly intimate interrelationships between all peoples, so that what happens anywhere matters everywhere. This is a fact rich in possibilities of coöperation and mutual understanding. But it is also a fact that is going to keep your generation in turmoil. It inevitably involves vexatious conflicts between diverse groups whose first contacts will take place not in coöperation but in rancor and prejudice. It will mean the violent awakening of underprivileged peoples, demanding almost overnight the standards of living they now see in richer nations. It may well mean a drift toward totalitarianism or collectivism in states whose people are unprepared for democracy. Nevertheless, I refuse to be terrified. This movement toward "one world" is basically hopeful. Granted its dangers! But danger can mean stimulus, not fright.

To sum up this point: We should be encouraged by the fact that our problem is not how to handle debility and feebleness but how to handle power. Science, putting under our control instruments of tremendous efficiency, and breaking down the ancient barriers of isolation with new means of intercommunication, has introduced us to an era of unprecedented power. That is sobering, but I do not find it discouraging. Indeed, it puts a torch to my Christian faith and sets it blazing.

For a further reason I refuse to surrender to discouragement: the changed attitude toward war. A young man like yourself can only with difficulty imagine how radical that change has been. Let me illustrate the appraisal of war that was dominant in my young manhood. "The noblest virtues of man are developed in war. Without war the world would degenerate and disappear in a morass of materialism"—that was Prussian Field Marshal von Moltke. "War is one of the conditions of progress"—that was Ernest Renan, author of a famous life of Christ. "By war alone can we acquire those virile qualities necessary to win the stern strife of actual life" —that was Theodore Roosevelt. Stop a moment and think. Can you imagine anyone outside a mental hospital talking like that today?

War has become the mass murder of civilian populations, plus the unfathomed genetic effects of nuclear fallout for generations to come. Appalling? Yes! But, as John Dewey once said, "Nobody thinks until he has to"; and mankind

now faces a situation which compels thinking hard. I do not
see how anyone can have lived as long as I have, and witnessed the extraordinary about-face in man's thinking about
war, without finding hope rising in him.

I take courage from still another source: the unexpected,
unforeseeable victories of right over wrong in history. Twenty-
five years ago Hitler seemed to be on top of the world. But
did Hitler last? On the contrary, who ever fell more igno-
miniously from the peak of success into the abyss of defeat
and shame? Of course that doesn't prove that Russia will not
push us into war, or that some accidental mistake may not
trigger an explosion of insane nuclear slaughter. But I cannot read history, so constantly echoing Victor Hugo's remark
that Napoleon fell and ended on St. Helena because he
"bothered God," without feeling in my bones that Stalin and
Khrushchev and Mao and all their kind are not history's
final word.

When the fifteenth century was swinging into the six-
teenth here are the big names that filled the ears of men:
Sultan Mohammed II, Pizarro, Cesare Borgia, Charles the
Bold, Baber, Francis I. How much do you know about any
one of them? But here are three other names of that same
era: Columbus, Copernicus, Martin Luther. Any schoolchild
can tell you about them. Is not that a pattern, repeated over
and over again in history—the works of violence perishing,
the achievements of the spirit enduring?

I dare you to be a pessimist. Plunge deep into it. Believe
that all man's ideals are delusions, that any seeming progress
in the past was only a flash in the pan. Agree that the dicta-
torships have the democracies on the run because democracy
is essentially unworkable, that Christian goodwill is all fantasy and fustian and that a nuclear war will soon finish off

civilization and perhaps the human race. If you are going to be a pessimist, be a real one: stop trying to be hopeful.

You can't do it. At once arguments on the other side begin shouting, and will not be silenced. You are going out into a tough and stormy generation, but with hope and trust that a victory *can* be won over the evil forces that threaten the world. Easygoing optimism is silly; thoroughgoing pessimism is fatal; what we need is intelligence, faith, goodwill, courage.

I suspect that you can guess what I am going to say in conclusion. Underneath the reasons I have given for keeping up an undiscouraged fight for a better world lies my religious faith. I don't believe that this universe is, as one materialist put it, "all an affair of chance, the froth and fume of the waves on an ocean of sterile matter." Because I believe that there is Mind behind our lives here, Meaning in them, Purpose running through them, and Destiny ahead of them, all the confidence and hope I have will not down. Such a situation as we face today, far from weakening that faith, calls it out.

I began believing in God for intellectual reasons, and I am confident that they still hold good. But today my faith is militant because the lack of it can paralyze hope and courage, and all confidence in mankind's future. My faith is James Russell Lowell's:

> Truth forever on the scaffold,
>   Wrong forever on the throne,—
> Yet that scaffold sways the future,
>   and, behind the dim unknown,
> Standeth God within the shadow,
>   keeping watch above His own.

# ACKNOWLEDGMENTS

*Part I:* How to Live with People ...... 11
THE HIGH ART OF FLATTERY, by Phyllis Mc-
Ginley, cond. from *The Saturday Evening
Post,* © 1962, The Curtis Pub. Co. LOVE IS
HEALING, by Howard Whitman, cond. from
*This Week Magazine,* © 1950, United News-
papers Magazine Corp. CAN YOU LISTEN?
by Ralph G. Nichols, Ph.D., and Leonard
A. Stevens, based on *"Are You Listening?"*
© 1957 and pub. by McGraw-Hill Book Co.,
Inc. JOY IN DOING GOOD ON THE SLY, by
Gordon Powell, cond. from *The New
South Wales Presbyterian,* © 1961, The
Presbyterian Church of New South Wales.
THE TRUE NATURE OF LOVE, by F. Alexander
Magoun, cond. from *Love and Marriage,* ©
1948 and pub. by Harper & Bros. MATRI-
MONY IS NOT FOR CHILDREN, by Lester
David, cond. from *Good Housekeeping,* ©
1961, The Hearst Corp. THERE ARE NO
SHORTCUTS TO MARRIAGE, by Mary Steichen
Calderone, M.D., cond. from *Redbook,* ©
1964, McCall Corp. WHATEVER BECAME OF
ROMANCE? by Harriet Van Horne, cond.
from *Glamour,* © 1961, The Condé Nast
Publications, Inc. WHY WE CHOOSE THE
MATE WE DO, by Morton M. Hunt, cond.
from *Today's Living,* © 1959, The New
York Herald Tribune, Inc. SENSE AND NON-
SENSE ABOUT HONEYMOONS, by Jerome and
Julia Rainer, cond. from *Modern Bride,* ©
1959, Ziff-Davis Pub. Co. HOW TO GET
ALONG WITH A MAN, by Phyllis McGinley,
cond. from *Vogue,* © 1958, The Condé Nast
Publications, Inc.; this material also appears
in *The Province of the Heart,* © 1958,
Phyllis McGinley, reprinted by permission of
The Viking Press, Inc. WHAT WOMEN WANT
IN THE MEN THEY MARRY, by David R. Mace,
Ph.D., cond. from *Housewife,* © 1961, Long-
acre Press. TOO TIRED TO LOVE, by Marion
Hilliard, M.D., cond. from *Women and Fa-
tigue: A Woman Doctor's Answer,* © 1960
and pub. by Doubleday & Co., Inc. CAN MAR-
RIAGE COUNSELING HELP? by Norman M.
Lobsenz, cond. from *Redbook,* © 1961, Mc-
Call Corp. A MAN DOES THE DARNEDEST
THINGS, by Jean Kerr, cond. from *McCall's,*
© 1959, McCall Corp. HUSBANDS: THE NEW
SERVANT CLASS, by Russell Lynes, cond.
from *Look,* © 1954, Cowles Magazines, Inc.
THE POWER MEN HAVE OVER WOMEN, by
Marya Mannes, cond. from *Vogue,* © 1964,
The Condé Nast Publications, Inc. THE FE-
MALE SHOULD NOT PLAY DUMB, by Hannah
Lees, cond. from *The Saturday Evening Post,*
© 1961, The Curtis Pub. Co. HELP YOUR
CHILD TO WONDER, by Rachel Carson, cond.
from *Woman's Home Companion,* © 1956,
The Crowell-Collier Pub. Co. DO CHILDREN

RUN YOUR HOME? by Sidonie Matsner Gruen-
berg with Llewellyn Miller, cond. from *The
American Weekly,* © 1959, Hearst Pub. Co.
WHAT NOT TO TELL A CHILD ABOUT SEX, by
Ardis Whitman, cond. from *Redbook,* ©
1960, McCall Corp. TEACHING YOUR CHILD
RELIGION, by Harry Emerson Fosdick, cond.
from *World's Work,* 1929. THE DANGEROUS
PRESSURES ON CHILDHOOD, by Norman M.
Lobsenz, cond. from *Redbook,* © 1962, Mc-
Call Corp. PLAIN FACTS ABOUT ADOLES-
CENCE, by Peter Blos, cond. from *Look,* ©
1955, Cowles Magazines, Inc. CONDUCT
CODE FOR TEEN-AGERS, by Jean Libman
Block, cond. from *The American Weekly,* ©
1957, Hearst Pub. Co., with additions by
the author. LET'S ALLOW OUR TEEN-AGERS
TO WORK, by William G. Long, cond. from
*The American Magazine,* © 1955, The
Crowell-Collier Pub. Co. THE PERILS OF
PROMISCUITY, by Marion Hilliard, M.D.,
cond. from *A Woman Doctor Looks at Love
and Life,* © 1956, 1957, Marion Hilliard,
pub. by Doubleday & Co., Inc. WHY DRIVER
EDUCATION IS A MUST, by Paul W. Kearney,
cond. from *Parents' Magazine,* © 1964, Par-
ents' Magazine Enterprises, Inc. THE VALUES
OF YOUNG PEOPLE, by John W. Gardner,
cond. from *Self-Renewal: The Individual
and the Innovative Society,* © 1963, 1964,
John W. Gardner, pub. by Harper & Row,
Publishers, Inc.; this material also appeared
in *Saturday Review,* © 1963, Saturday Re-
view, Inc.
*Part II:* How to Live with Yourself ... 163
STOP, LOOK, AND SEE! by John Kord Lage-
mann, cond. from *Together,* © 1963, The
Methodist Pub. House. ARE YOU LIVING OR
EXISTING? by Stuart Chase, cond. from *The
Nation.* "EVERY, EVERY MINUTE," by Jean
Dalrymple, reprinted from *This Week Mag-
azine,* © 1963, United Newspapers Maga-
zine Corp. BE HONEST WITH YOURSELF! by
T. F. James, cond. from *The American
Weekly,* © 1961, Hearst Pub. Co. NEVER
STOP LEARNING, by James A. Michener,
cond. from an address delivered at Macal-
ester College. SEVEN WAYS TO IMPROVE
MEMORY, by Henry C. Link, Ph.D., and
Robert Norman, cond. from *The American
Magazine,* © 1923, The Crowell Pub. Co.
MAKE YOUR MIND BEHAVE, by Frederick B.
Robinson and M. K. Wisehart, cond. from
*The American Magazine,* © 1929, The
Crowell Pub. Co. UNLOCK YOUR REAL PER-
SONALITY, by Maxwell Maltz, M.D., cond.
from *Psycho-Cybernetics,* © 1960 and pub.
by Prentice-Hall, Inc. THE ART OF PURPOSE-
FUL PAUSING, by Stuart Kinzie, cond. from
*Everywoman's Family Circle,* © 1960, The

Family Circle, Inc. MASTERING TENSIONS, by Walter B. Pitkin, cond. from *Take It Easy,* © 1963, Katherine J. Pitkin, pub. by Simon and Schuster, Inc. BOREDOM AND EXCITEMENT, by Bertrand Russell, cond. from *The Conquest of Happiness,* © 1958, Bertrand Russell, pub. by Horace Liveright, Inc. OF COURSE YOU'RE CREATIVE! by Michael Drury, cond. from *Glamour,* © 1959, The Condé Nast Publications, Inc. YOU ARE TOUGHER THAN YOU THINK, by Norman Vincent Peale, cond. from *The Tough-Minded Optimist,* © 1961 and pub. by Prentice-Hall, Inc. HOW TO INCREASE YOUR ENERGY, by William James, cond. from *The Energies of Men,* reprinted with permission of Paul R. Reynolds, Inc., originally published in *Memories and Studies* in 1911 by Longmans, Green & Co., Inc.; this essay also appears in *Great Essays,* edited by Houston Peterson, pub. by Washington Square Press, Inc. THE IMPORTANCE OF FEELING INFERIOR, by Marie Beynon Ray, cond. from the book, © 1957, Marie Beynon Ray, pub. by Harper & Bros. THE NEED FOR SANCTUARY, by Margaret Blair Johnstone, cond. from *Guideposts,* © 1953, Guideposts Associates, Inc. RETREAT—TO GO FORWARD, by John Kord Lagemann, cond. from *Christian Herald,* © 1961, Christian Herald Assn., Inc. LIVE IN DAY-TIGHT COMPARTMENTS, by Dale Carnegie, cond. from *How to Stop Worrying and Start Living,* © 1946, 1948, Dale Carnegie, pub. by Simon and Schuster, Inc. HOW TO COPE WITH CRITICISM, by Norman Vincent Peale, cond. from *Guideposts,* © 1964, Guideposts Associates, Inc. HUMILITY—BALANCE WHEEL OF LIFE, by Michael Drury, cond. from *Christian Herald,* © 1961, Christian Herald Assn., Inc. THE CHANCE TO GROW, by Ardis Whitman, cond. from *Guideposts,* © 1960, Guideposts Associates, Inc. DON'T BE AFRAID TO BE DIFFERENT, by Stuart Kinzie, cond. from *Guideposts,* © 1957, Guideposts Associates, Inc. DO YOU ACT YOUR PART? by Maud Scheerer, cond. from *The Rotarian,* © 1940, Rotary International. TAKE A HOLIDAY FROM CAUTION, by Elizabeth Byrd, cond. from *Guideposts,* © 1960, Guideposts Associates, Inc. GET INVOLVED! by Morton M. Hunt, cond. from *Today's Living,* © 1961, New York Herald Tribune, Inc. A WHIM A DAY, cond. from "Topics of the Times" in *The New York Times,* © 1955, The New York Times Co.
*Part III:* How to Live with Reality . . . 303
IMAGINATION—THE SECRET OF SUCCESS, by James L. Mursell, excerpt from *Streamline Your Mind,* © 1964, James L. Mursell, pub. by J. B. Lippincott Co. THE INCENTIVE OF FAILURE, by Charles Westrill, cond. from *Future,* © 1961, U.S. Junior Chamber of Commerce. THE RIGHT WAY TO THE RIGHT

JOB, by James Nathan Miller, cond. from *Future,* © 1963, U.S. Junior Chamber of Commerce. HOW TO SELL AN IDEA, by Elmer Wheeler, cond. from *Your Life,* © 1948, The Kingsway Press, Inc. KNOW THE BEST MOMENT, by Stuart Kinzie, cond. from *Together,* © 1963, The Methodist Pub. House. MY ADVENTURES WITH A PAINTBRUSH, cond. with the permission of Charles Scribner's Sons, from *Amid These Storms,* by Winston S. Churchill, © 1932, Charles Scribner's Sons, renewal © 1960, Winston Churchill. EVERYBODY SING! by Mary Martin as told to Charles D. Rice, cond. from *This Week Magazine,* © 1958, United Newspapers Magazine Corp. IT'S FUN TO READ ALOUD, by Charles Laughton, cond. from *This Week Magazine,* © 1950, United Newspapers Magazine Corp. GET IN THERE AND PLAY, by Oscar Schisgall, cond. from *The P.T.A. Magazine,* © 1961, The P.T.A. Magazine. TAKE MUSIC INSTEAD OF A MILTOWN, by George R. Marek, cond. from *Town & Country,* © 1960, The Hearst Corp. WHAT IS A NERVOUS BREAKDOWN? by Robert O'Brien, cond. from *The Rotarian,* © 1960, Rotary International. THE MYSTERIOUS MEDICINE FOR ALCOHOLICS, by Paul de Kruif, cond. from *Today's Health,* © 1960, American Medical Association. DIVORCE IS NO SOLUTION, by Nina Wilcox Putnam, cond. from *Maclean's,* © 1948, Maclean-Hunter Pub. Co., Ltd. THE MODERN HOUSEWIFE—EMANCIPATED OR TRAPPED? by Jhan and June Robbins, cond. from *Redbook,* © 1960, McCall Corp. HOW MUCH CAN YOU STAND? by Harry Emerson Fosdick, cond. from *Physical Culture,* © 1931, Physical Culture Pub. Corp. THE DILEMMA OF PREMARITAL RELATIONS, by Betsy Marvin McKinney, cond. from *Ladies' Home Journal,* © 1961, The Curtis Pub. Co. ADVICE FOR NEWLYWEDS, by Margaret Blair Johnstone, cond. from *Collier's,* © 1952, The Crowell-Collier Pub. Co. THE REAL CAUSE OF FRIGIDITY, by Hannah Lees, cond. from *Redbook,* © 1961, McCall Corp. WHAT SEX MEANS TO WOMEN, by John Kord Lagemann, cond. from *Redbook,* © 1958, McCall Corp. HOW MEN FEEL ABOUT SEX, by David R. Mace, Ph.D., cond. from *Modern Bride,* © 1963, Ziff-Davis Pub. Co. THE PROBLEM OF IMPOTENCE, by Walter C. Alvarez, M.D., cond. from *New York Herald Tribune,* © 1956, Register & Tribune Syndicate. ABOUT SEX: TRUE OR NOT? by Sylvanus M. Duvall, cond. from *Look,* © 1960, Cowles Magazines, Inc. MANNERS ARE FROM THE HEART, by Suzanne Hart Strait, cond. from *Parents' Magazine,* © 1963, Parents' Magazine Enterprises, Inc. THE DELIGHTFUL GAME OF CONVERSATION, by Gelett Burgess, cond. from *Your Life,* © 1947, The Kingsway Press, Inc. PRIVACY IS SACRED TO EVERYONE, by Morton M. Hunt, cond. from *Contemporary*, © 1964, The Denver Post, Inc. NINE HINTS FOR GUESTS: "The Matter of Arriving," by Jane A. Non, in *Harper's*; "The Wise Gift," *Arts and Decoration*; "The Borrowing Guest," by Sophie Kerr, in *The Saturday Evening Post* and *Arts and Decoration*, and by Sir John Foster Fraser, in *The Outlook*; "Loyalty," by Florence Taft Eaton; "Appreciation," by Margaret Emerson Bailey, in *Woman's Home Companion*, Sir John Foster Fraser, in *The Outlook*, Dearing Ward, in *Delineator*, Ethel Shubert, in *American Etiquette*, and Caroline Geddes, in *Woman's Home Companion*; "In Sickness and in Health," by E. V. Lucas, *The Phantom Journal* and *Arts and Decoration*; "Can I Do Anything to Help?" by H. Pearl Adams, in *The Fortnightly Review*; "Independence," by Caroline Geddes, in *Woman's Home Companion*; "Take Your Own and Begone," by Helen Hathaway, in *Manners*, and Corra Harris, in *Ladies' Home Journal*. MAKE THE MOST OF YOUR BLUNDERS, by Emily Post, cond. from *Suburbia Today*, © 1960, Suburbia Pub. Corp.

*Part IV: How to Live with Wisdom* ... 435
A LESSON FROM RODIN, by Stefan Zweig, cond. from *The Catholic World*, © 1940, Missionary Society of St. Paul the Apostle. WE ARE AFRAID OF SENTIMENT, by Ardis Whitman, cond. from *Guideposts*, © 1955, Guideposts Associates, Inc. FORGIVENESS: THE SAVING GRACE, by John Kord Lagemann, cond. from *Christian Herald*, © 1961, Christian Herald Assn., Inc. THE ART OF UNDERSTANDING OTHER PEOPLE, by Clarence W. Hall, cond. from *Christian Herald*, © 1956, Christian Herald Assn., Inc. THE LUXURY OF AGING, by Dorothy Thompson, cond. from *Ladies' Home Journal*, © 1952, The Curtis Pub. Co. HOW TO LIVE YOUR BONUS YEARS, by Martin Gumpert, M.D., cond. from *Christian Herald*, © 1955, Christian Herald Assn., Inc. A DOCTOR'S VIEW OF ADVANCING AGE, by Max Jacobson, M.D., cond. from *Tomorrow*, © 1950, Garrett Publications, Inc. I AM FIFTY—AND IT DOESN'T HURT! by Dorothy Canfield, cond. from *The American Magazine*, © 1929, The Crowell Pub. Co. A BRIDGE FOR PASSING, by Pearl S. Buck, cond. from the book, © 1961, 1962, Pearl S. Buck, pub. by The John Day Co., Inc. GRIEF'S SLOW WISDOM, by Joshua Loth Liebman, cond. from *Peace of Mind*, © 1946, Joshua Loth Liebman, pub. by Simon and Schuster, Inc. WHEN YOU WRITE A LETTER OF CONDOLENCE, by Janet Kern, cond. from *Guideposts*, © 1960, Guideposts Associates, Inc. IN TIME OF SORROW: THE GIFT OF YOUR PRESENCE, by Seymour Shubin, cond. from *Guideposts*, © 1964, Guideposts Associates, Inc. NO FINAL TERROR, by J. D. Ratcliff, cond. from *Liberty*, © 1950, Liberty Magazine, Inc.

BEYOND DEATH THERE IS LIFE, by Norman Vincent Peale, cond. from *Stay Alive All Your Life*, © 1957 and pub. by Prentice-Hall, Inc. WHY I BELIEVE IN IMMORTALITY, excerpt by Wernher von Braun only, cond. from *This Week Magazine*, © 1960, United Newspapers Magazine Corp. HOW TO GO TO CHURCH, by Ruth Matthews, cond. from *Christian Herald*, © 1963, Christian Herald Assn., Inc. WHY I KNOW THERE IS A GOD, by John Glenn, cond. from *Parade*, © 1962, Parade Publications, Inc.
*Conclusion:* ..................... 563
BE PROUD YOU ARE HUMAN, by Roger William Riis, cond. from a Book-of-the-Month Club leaflet, © 1951, Book-of-the-Month Club, Inc. ALL MEN ARE MY BROTHERS, by James A. Michener, cond. from a statement for Edward R. Murrow's series of radio broadcasts, © 1954, Help, Inc. I DARE YOU TO BE A PESSIMIST! by Harry Emerson Fosdick, cond. from *Dear Mr. Brown*, © 1961, Harry Emerson Fosdick, pub. by Harper & Bros.

EXCERPTS: Page 17, *Your Life*, © 1939, The Kingsway Press, Inc. Page 22, *The Arts of Living*, compiled by the editors of *Vogue*, pub. by Simon and Schuster. Page 26 (top), *The High Holy Day Message of The Jewish Theological Seminary of America*. Page 26 (bottom), *The Telescope-Messenger*. Page 31 (top), *Look*, © 1955, Cowles Magazines and Broadcasting, Inc. Page 31 (bottom), *Meyer Berger's New York*, pub. by Random House. Page 39, *Private Lives of the Great Composers, Conductors and Artistes of the World*, pub. by Rider. Page 48, *Life*, © 1961, Time Inc. Page 56, *Esquire*. Page 62, *Boston Evening Transcript*. Page 72, *Together*, © 1959, Lovick Pierce, pub. by The Methodist Pub. House. Page 77 (bottom), quoted in Altoona, Pa., *Mirror*. Page 84 (top), *Collier's*. Page 84 (bottom), *Holiday*. Page 87, *Houdini: His Life-Story*, pub. by Harcourt, Brace. Page 95, *The Saturday Evening Post*. Page 103, *The American Weekly*, © 1961, Hearst Pub. Co. Page 118 (top), quoted in *The American Treasury*, edited by Clifton Fadiman, pub. by Harper & Bros. Page 118 (bottom), *New York Times*. Page 122 (top), *The Golden Book Magazine*, © 1930-1931, The Review of Reviews Corp. Page 122 (bottom), *Physical Culture*. Page 127, *McCall's*. Page 138, quoted by Neill Morgan in *San Diego Tribune*. Page 143 (top), *Memoirs of Childhood and Youth*, pub. by The Macmillan Co. Page 143 (center), *Stillmeadow and Sugarbridge*, pub. by J. B. Lippincott Co. Page 162, *Bread and Wine*, pub. by Harper & Bros. Page 168, quoted in *The Editorial Digest*. Page 173, *House & Garden*, © 1961, The Condé Nast Publica-